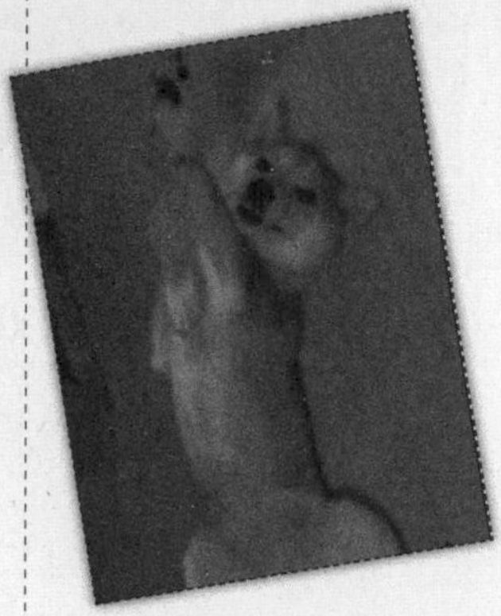

I've said this before, but, even though time goes by very fast in the series and the story takes place in the future, please think of it as all occurring in the present.

—Tsugumi Ohba

I actually get more excited drawing the series within the series rather than the main series.

—Takeshi Obata

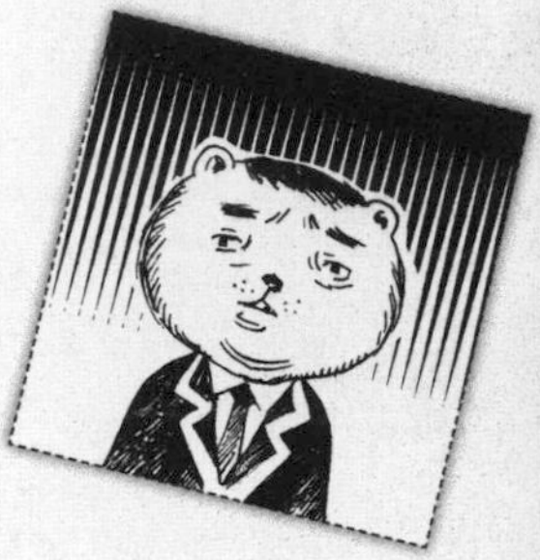

Tsugumi Ohba

Born in Tokyo, Tsugumi Ohba is the author of the hit series *Death Note*. His current series *Bakuman。* is serialized in *Weekly Shonen Jump*.

Takeshi Obata

Takeshi Obata was born in 1969 in Niigata, Japan, and is the artist of the wildly popular SHONEN JUMP title *Hikaru no Go*, which won the 2003 Tezuka Osamu Cultural Prize: Shinsei "New Hope" award and the 2000 Shogakukan Manga award. Obata is also the artist of *Arabian Majin Bokentan Lamp Lamp*, *Ayatsuri Sakon*, *Cyborg Jichan G.*, and the smash hit manga *Death Note*. His current series *Bakuman。* is serialized in *Weekly Shonen Jump*.

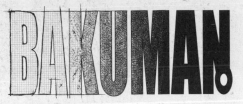

Volume 16

SHONEN JUMP Manga Edition

Story by **TSUGUMI OHBA**
Art by **TAKESHI OBATA**

Translation | **Tetsuichiro Miyaki**
Touch-up Art & Lettering | **James Gaubatz**
Design | **Fawn Lau**
Editor | **Alexis Kirsch**

BAKUMAN。© 2008 by Tsugumi Ohba, Takeshi Obata
All rights reserved.
First published in Japan in 2008 by SHUEISHA Inc., Tokyo.
English translation rights arranged by SHUEISHA Inc.

Printed in the U.S.A.

Published by VIZ Media, LLC
P.O. Box 77010
San Francisco, CA 94107

10 9 8 7 6 5 4 3 2 1
First printing, November 2012

BAKUMAN。

16

ROOKIE and VETERAN

STORY BY
TSUGUMI OHBA

ART BY
TAKESHI OBATA

SHONENJUMP MANGA

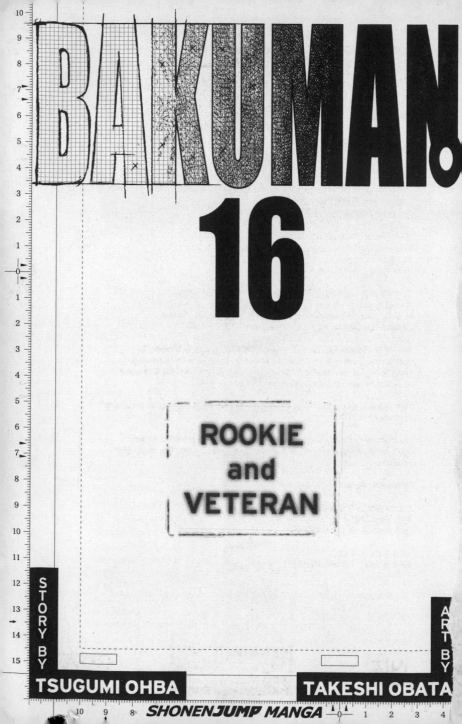

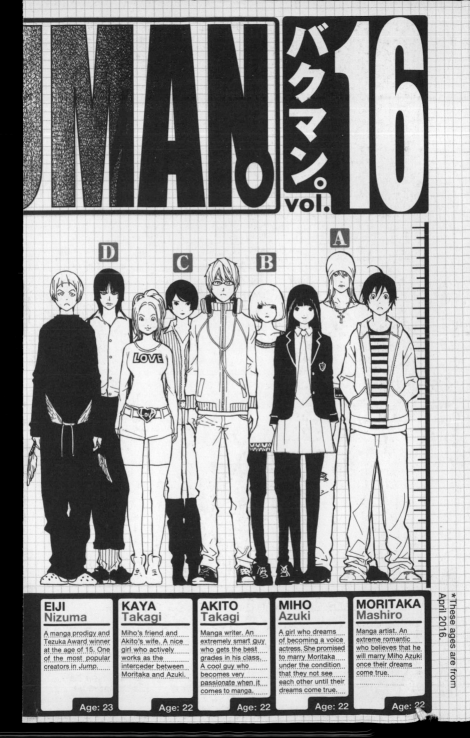

UMAN。 バクマン。 vol.16

D C B A

EIJI
Nizuma

A manga prodigy and Tezuka Award winner at the age of 15. One of the most popular creators in *Jump*.

Age: 23

KAYA
Takagi

Miho's friend and Akito's wife. A nice girl who actively works as the interceder between Moritaka and Azuki.

Age: 22

AKITO
Takagi

Manga writer. An extremely smart guy who gets the best grades in his class. A cool guy who becomes very passionate when it comes to manga.

Age: 22

MIHO
Azuki

A girl who dreams of becoming a voice actress. She promised to marry Moritaka under the condition that they not see each other until their dreams come true.

Age: 22

MORITAKA
Mashiro

Manga artist. An extreme romantic who believes that he will marry Miho Azuki once their dreams come true.

Age: 22

*These ages are from April 2016.

STORY In order to attain the glory that only a handful of people can, two young men decide to walk the rough "path of manga" and become professional manga creators. This is the story of a great artist, Moritaka Mashiro, a talented writer, Akito Takagi, and their quest to become manga legends!

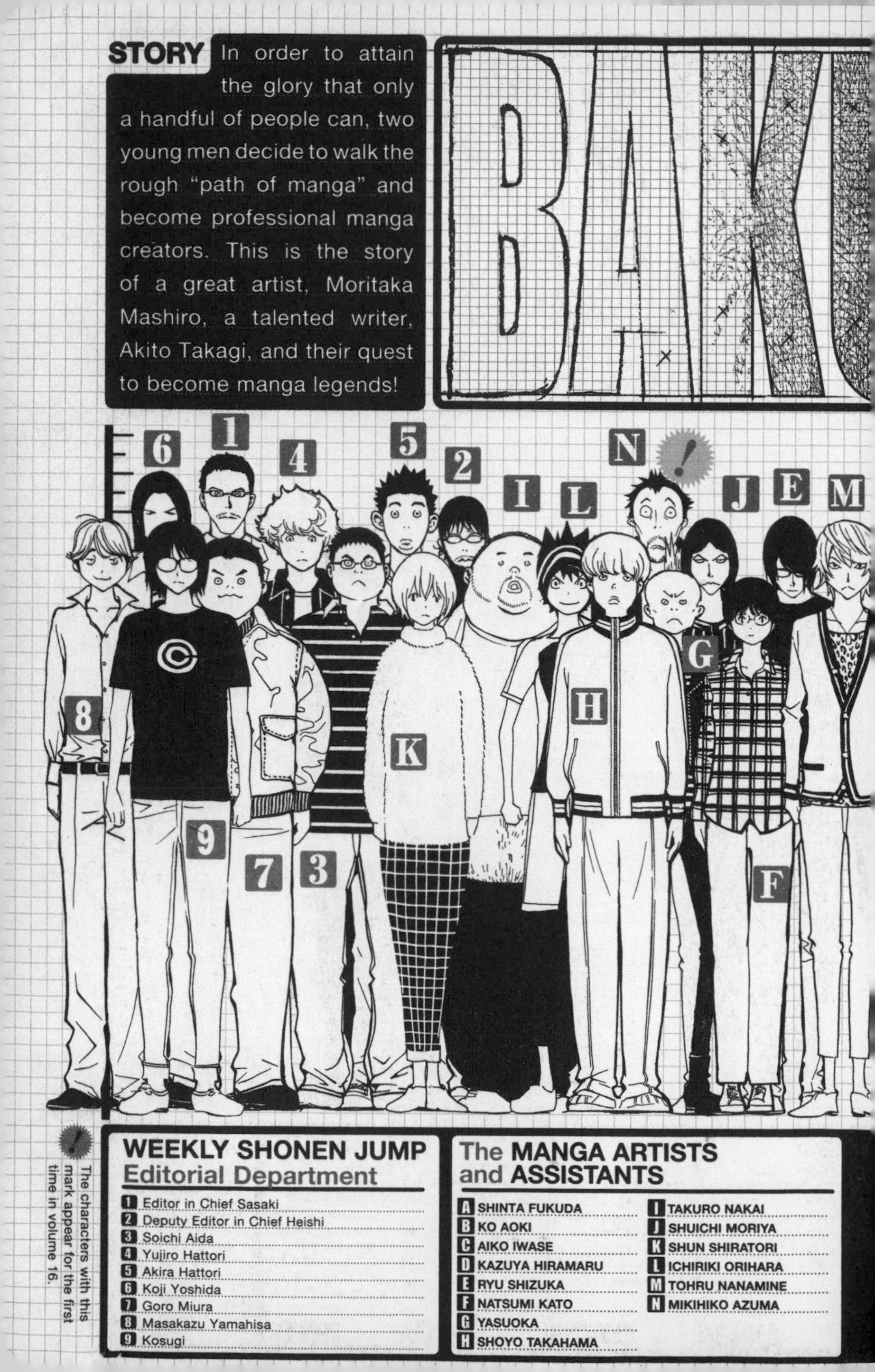
M
E
J
N
L
I
2
5
4
1
6
G
H
K
8
F
3
7
9

! The characters with this mark appear for the first time in volume 16.

WEEKLY SHONEN JUMP Editorial Department

1. Editor in Chief Sasaki
2. Deputy Editor in Chief Heishi
3. Soichi Aida
4. Yujiro Hattori
5. Akira Hattori
6. Koji Yoshida
7. Goro Miura
8. Masakazu Yamahisa
9. Kosugi

The MANGA ARTISTS and ASSISTANTS

- A SHINTA FUKUDA
- B KO AOKI
- C AIKO IWASE
- D KAZUYA HIRAMARU
- E RYU SHIZUKA
- F NATSUMI KATO
- G YASUOKA
- H SHOYO TAKAHAMA
- I TAKURO NAKAI
- J SHUICHI MORIYA
- K SHUN SHIRATORI
- L ICHIRIKI ORIHARA
- M TOHRU NANAMINE
- N MIKIHIKO AZUMA

BAKUMAN。 vol. 16

CONTENTS

(ROOKIE AND VETERAN)

PENCIL ERASER RULER TRIANGLE FRENCH CURVE G-PEN INK MARU-PEN KABURA-PEN

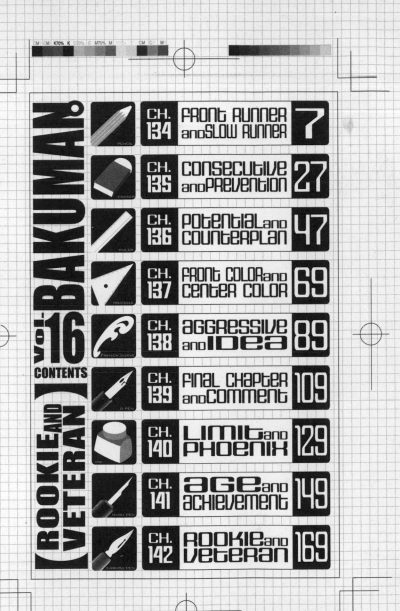

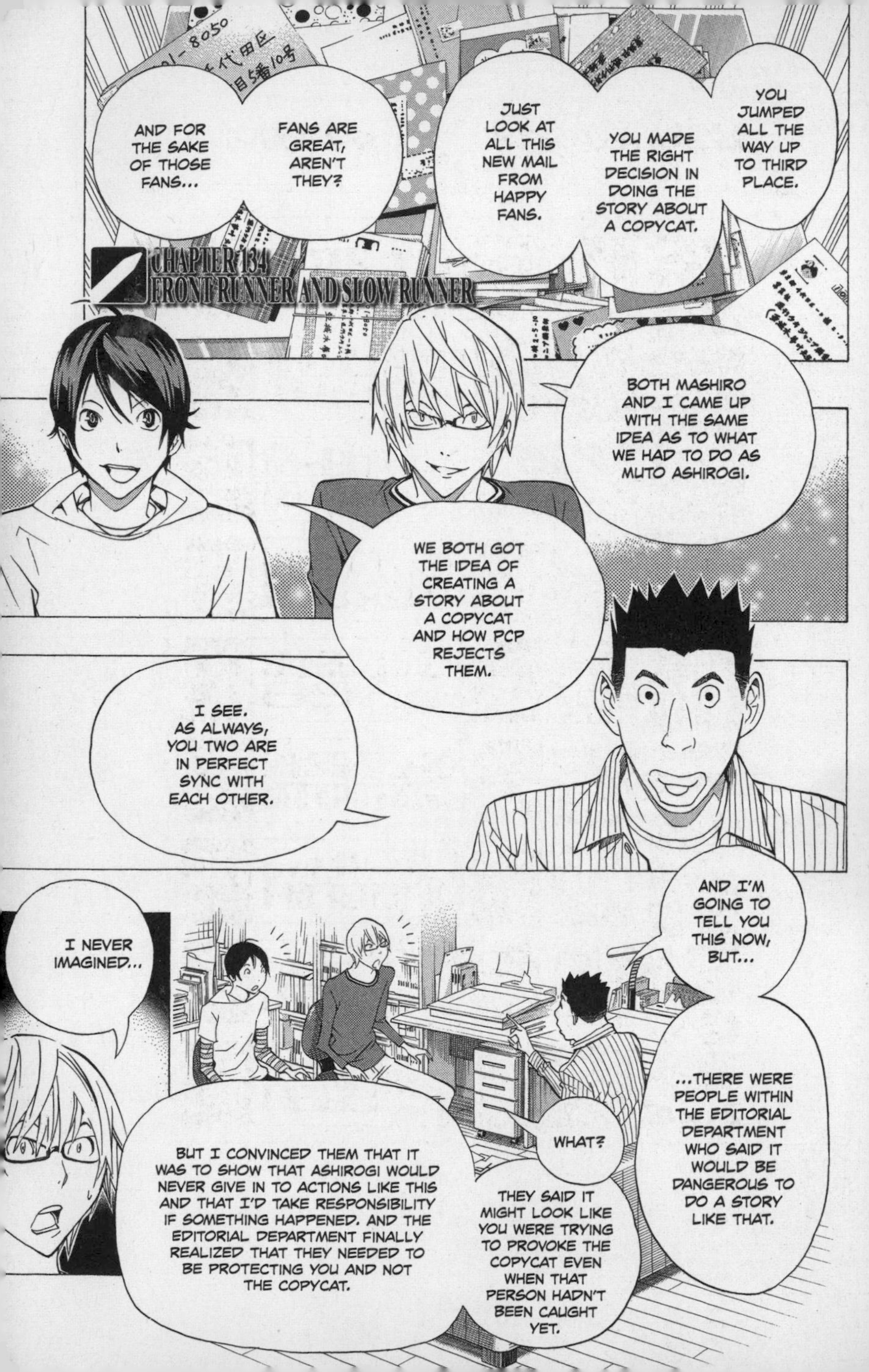
CHAPTER 134
FRONT RUNNER AND SLOW RUNNER
YOU JUMPED ALL THE WAY UP TO THIRD PLACE.
YOU MADE THE RIGHT DECISION IN DOING THE STORY ABOUT A COPYCAT.
JUST LOOK AT ALL THIS NEW MAIL FROM HAPPY FANS.
FANS ARE GREAT, AREN'T THEY?
AND FOR THE SAKE OF THOSE FANS...
BOTH MASHIRO AND I CAME UP WITH THE SAME IDEA AS TO WHAT WE HAD TO DO AS MUTO ASHIROGI.
WE BOTH GOT THE IDEA OF CREATING A STORY ABOUT A COPYCAT AND HOW PCP REJECTS THEM.
I SEE. AS ALWAYS, YOU TWO ARE IN PERFECT SYNC WITH EACH OTHER.
AND I'M GOING TO TELL YOU THIS NOW, BUT...
...THERE WERE PEOPLE WITHIN THE EDITORIAL DEPARTMENT WHO SAID IT WOULD BE DANGEROUS TO DO A STORY LIKE THAT.
WHAT?
THEY SAID IT MIGHT LOOK LIKE YOU WERE TRYING TO PROVOKE THE COPYCAT EVEN WHEN THAT PERSON HADN'T BEEN CAUGHT YET.
BUT I CONVINCED THEM THAT IT WAS TO SHOW THAT ASHIROGI WOULD NEVER GIVE IN TO ACTIONS LIKE THIS AND THAT I'D TAKE RESPONSIBILITY IF SOMETHING HAPPENED. AND THE EDITORIAL DEPARTMENT FINALLY REALIZED THAT THEY NEEDED TO BE PROTECTING YOU AND NOT THE COPYCAT.
I NEVER IMAGINED...

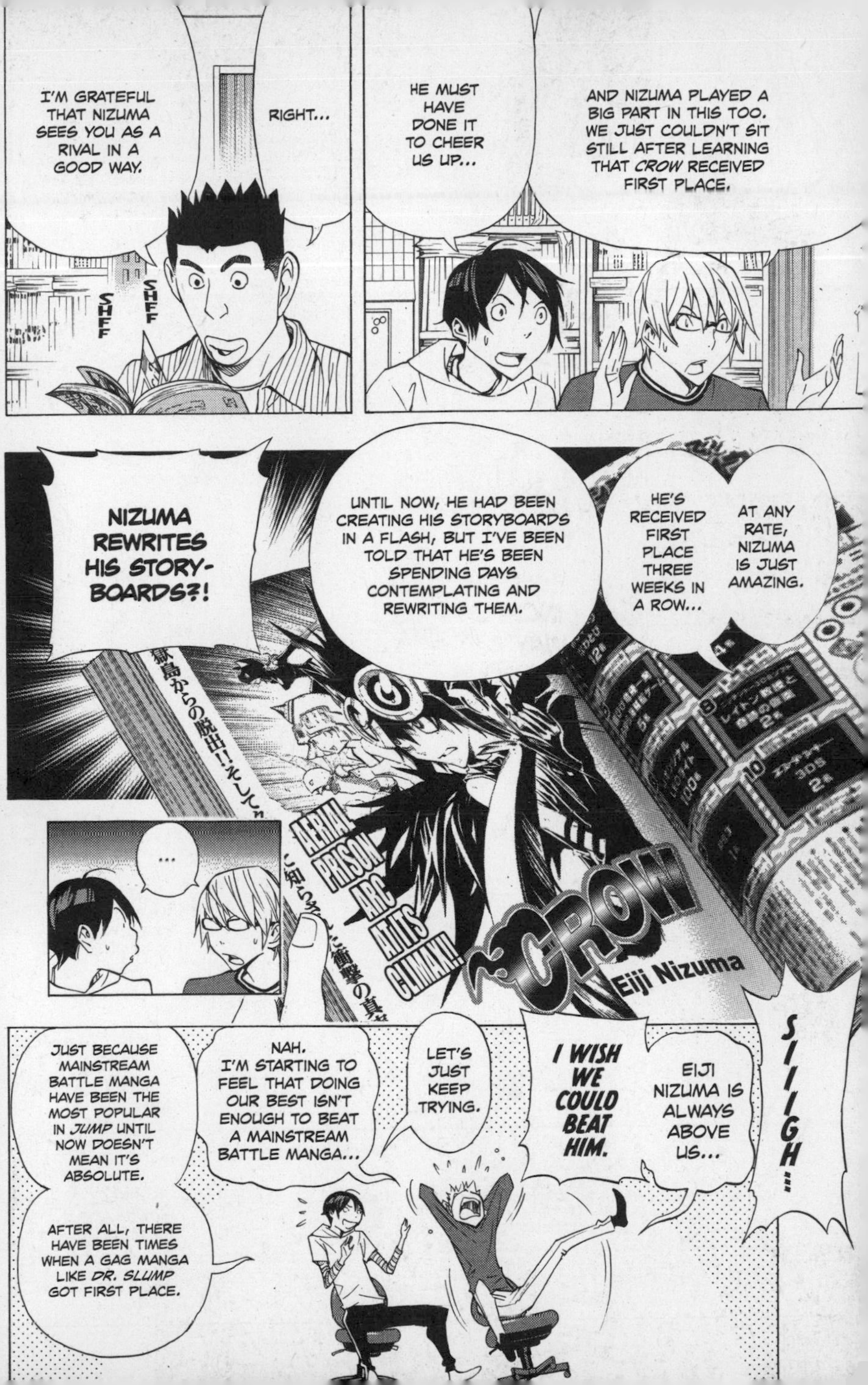
AND NIZUMA PLAYED A BIG PART IN THIS TOO. WE JUST COULDN'T SIT STILL AFTER LEARNING THAT *CROW* RECEIVED FIRST PLACE.
HE MUST HAVE DONE IT TO CHEER US UP...
RIGHT...
I'M GRATEFUL THAT NIZUMA SEES YOU AS A RIVAL IN A GOOD WAY.
SHEFF
SHEFF
AT ANY RATE, NIZUMA IS JUST AMAZING.
HE'S RECEIVED FIRST PLACE THREE WEEKS IN A ROW...
UNTIL NOW, HE HAD BEEN CREATING HIS STORYBOARDS IN A FLASH, BUT I'VE BEEN TOLD THAT HE'S BEEN SPENDING DAYS CONTEMPLATING AND REWRITING THEM.
NIZUMA REWRITES HIS STORY-BOARDS?!
獄島からの脱出!!
CROW
Eiji Nizuma
AERIA PRISON ARC AT ITS CLIMAX!!
...
SIIIGH!!
EIJI NIZUMA IS ALWAYS ABOVE US...
I WISH WE COULD BEAT HIM.
LET'S JUST KEEP TRYING.
NAH. I'M STARTING TO FEEL THAT DOING OUR BEST ISN'T ENOUGH TO BEAT A MAINSTREAM BATTLE MANGA...
JUST BECAUSE MAINSTREAM BATTLE MANGA HAVE BEEN THE MOST POPULAR IN *JUMP* UNTIL NOW DOESN'T MEAN IT'S ABSOLUTE.
AFTER ALL, THERE HAVE BEEN TIMES WHEN A GAG MANGA LIKE *DR. SLUMP* GOT FIRST PLACE.

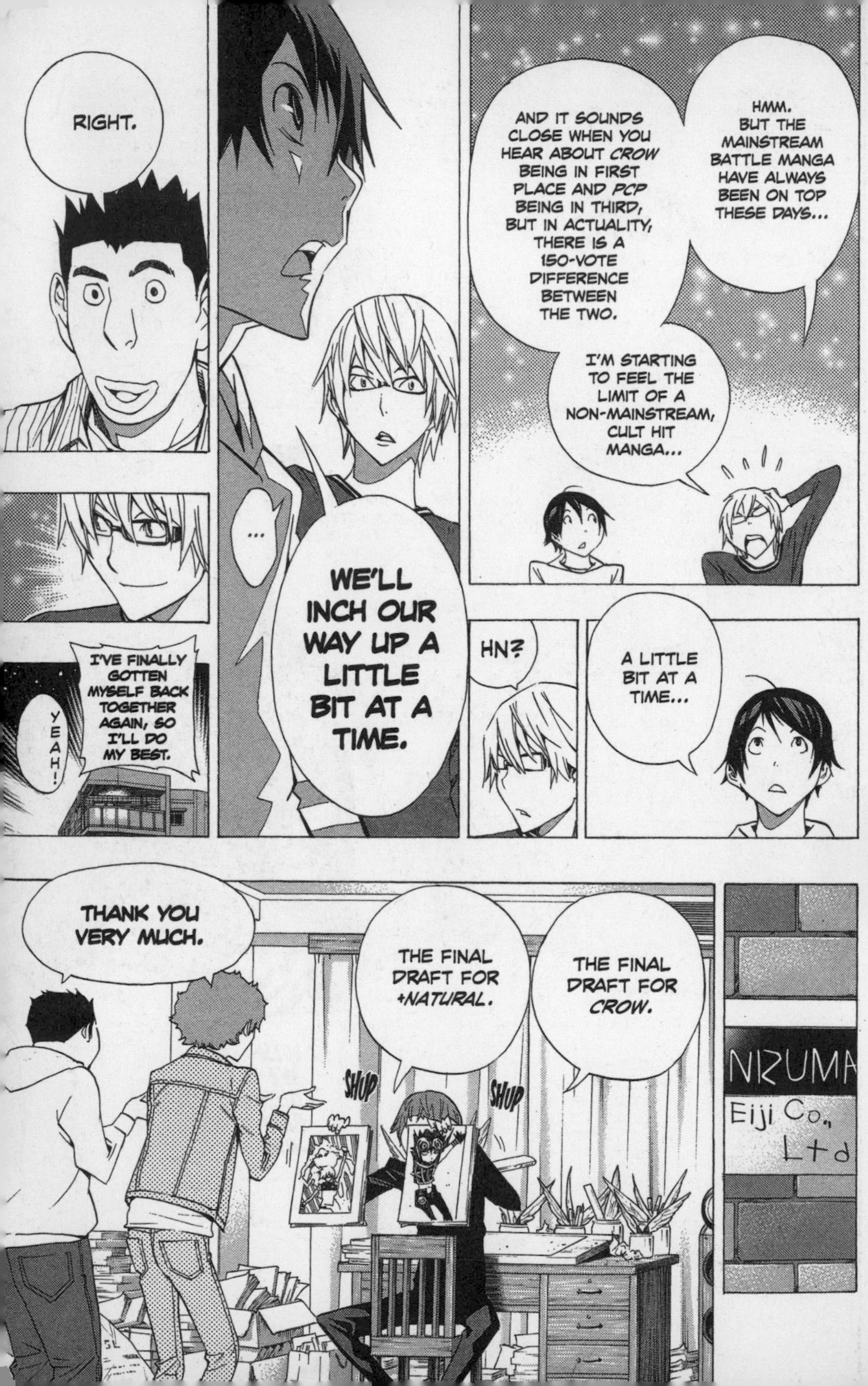

HMM. BUT THE MAINSTREAM BATTLE MANGA HAVE ALWAYS BEEN ON TOP THESE DAYS...
AND IT SOUNDS CLOSE WHEN YOU HEAR ABOUT *CROW* BEING IN FIRST PLACE AND *PCP* BEING IN THIRD, BUT IN ACTUALITY, THERE IS A 150-VOTE DIFFERENCE BETWEEN THE TWO.
I'M STARTING TO FEEL THE LIMIT OF A NON-MAINSTREAM, CULT HIT MANGA...
A LITTLE BIT AT A TIME...
HN?
...
WE'LL INCH OUR WAY UP A LITTLE BIT AT A TIME.
RIGHT.
I'VE FINALLY GOTTEN MYSELF BACK TOGETHER AGAIN, SO I'LL DO MY BEST.
YEAH!
NIZUMA Eiji Co., Ltd
THE FINAL DRAFT FOR *CROW*.
SHUP
THE FINAL DRAFT FOR *+NATURAL*.
SHUP
THANK YOU VERY MUCH.

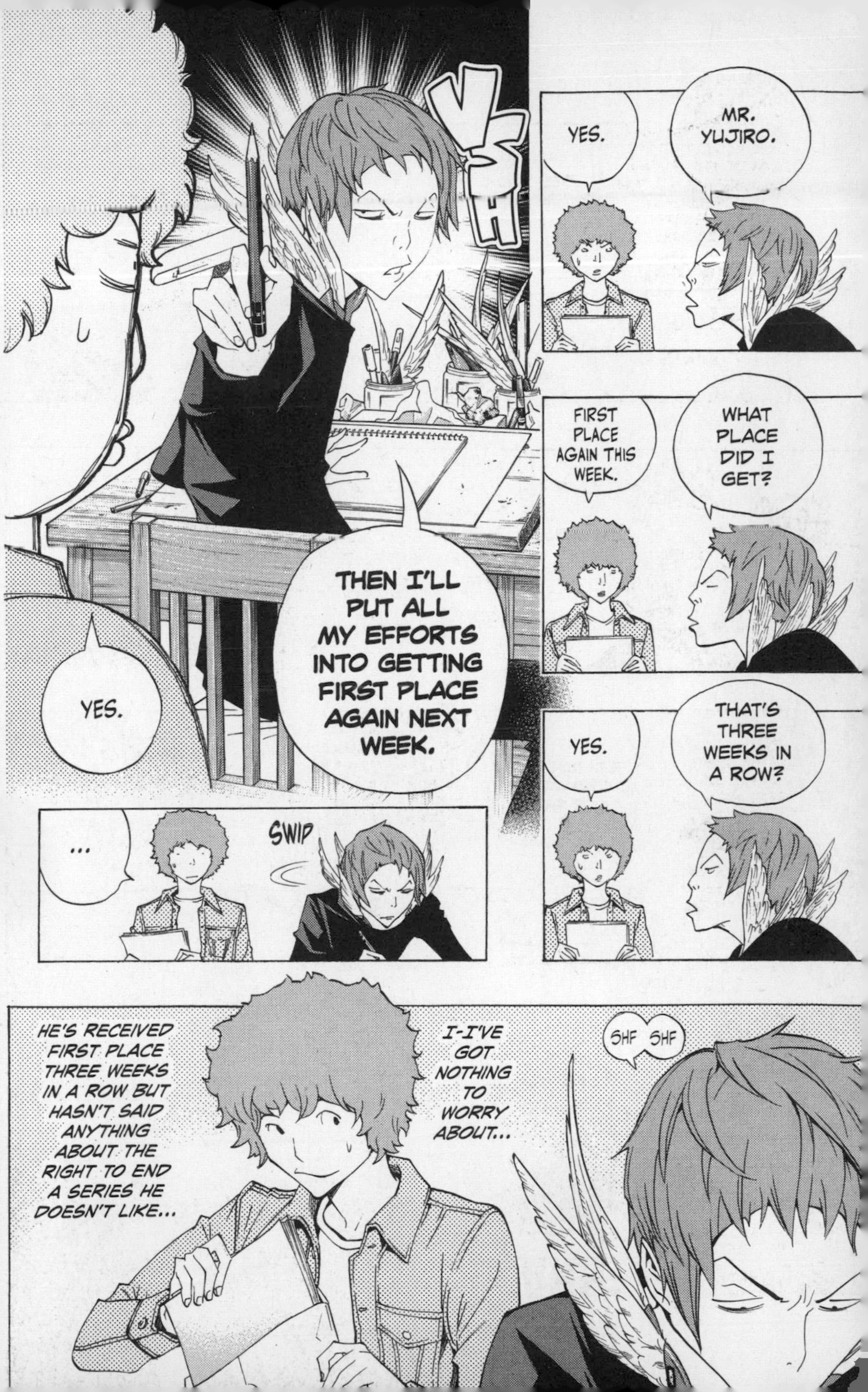
MR. YUJIRO.
YES.
WHAT PLACE DID I GET?
FIRST PLACE AGAIN THIS WEEK.
THAT'S THREE WEEKS IN A ROW?
YES.
VSH
THEN I'LL PUT ALL MY EFFORTS INTO GETTING FIRST PLACE AGAIN NEXT WEEK.
YES.
SWIP
...
SHF SHF
I-I'VE GOT NOTHING TO WORRY ABOUT...
HE'S RECEIVED FIRST PLACE THREE WEEKS IN A ROW BUT HASN'T SAID ANYTHING ABOUT THE RIGHT TO END A SERIES HE DOESN'T LIKE...

READ THIS WAY

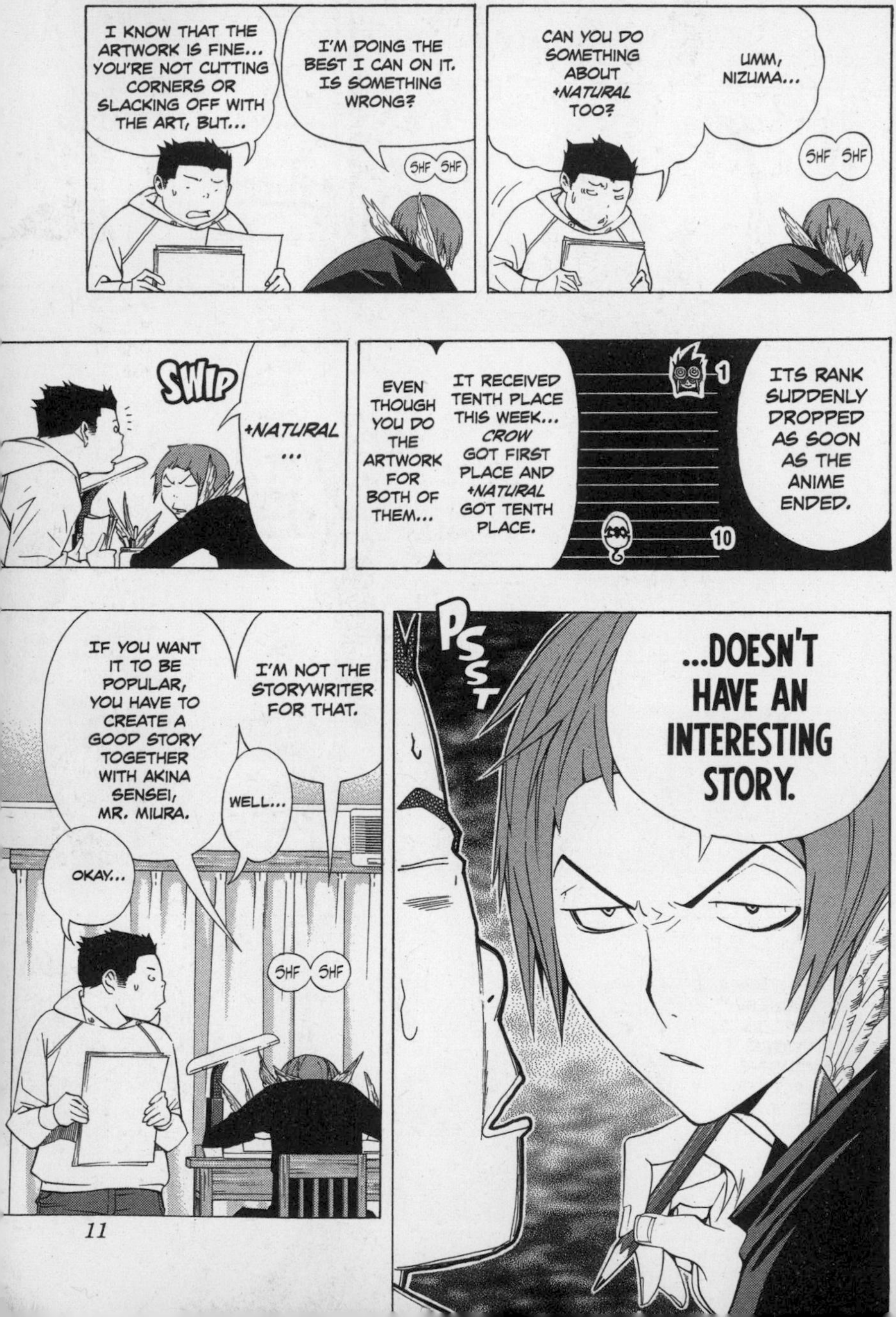
UMM, NIZUMA...
CAN YOU DO SOMETHING ABOUT *+NATURAL* TOO?
SHF SHF
I'M DOING THE BEST I CAN ON IT. IS SOMETHING WRONG?
SHF SHF
I KNOW THAT THE ARTWORK IS FINE... YOU'RE NOT CUTTING CORNERS OR SLACKING OFF WITH THE ART, BUT...
ITS RANK SUDDENLY DROPPED AS SOON AS THE ANIME ENDED.
1
10
IT RECEIVED TENTH PLACE THIS WEEK... *CROW* GOT FIRST PLACE AND *+NATURAL* GOT TENTH PLACE.
EVEN THOUGH YOU DO THE ARTWORK FOR BOTH OF THEM...
+NATURAL ...
SWIP
PSST
...DOESN'T HAVE AN INTERESTING STORY.
I'M NOT THE STORYWRITER FOR THAT.
IF YOU WANT IT TO BE POPULAR, YOU HAVE TO CREATE A GOOD STORY TOGETHER WITH AKINA SENSEI, MR. MIURA.
WELL...
OKAY...
SHF SHF

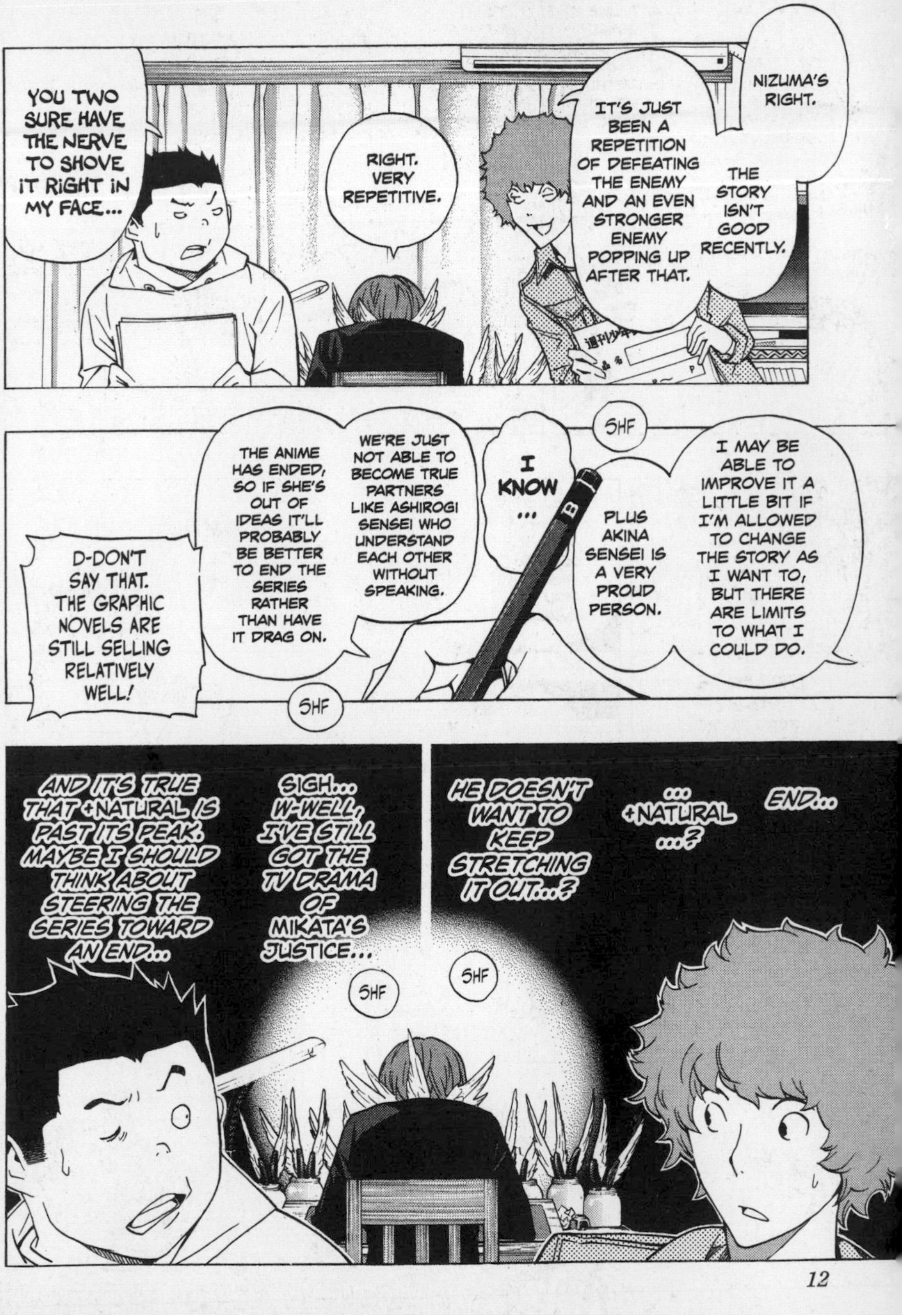
NIZUMA'S RIGHT.
THE STORY ISN'T GOOD RECENTLY.
IT'S JUST BEEN A REPETITION OF DEFEATING THE ENEMY AND AN EVEN STRONGER ENEMY POPPING UP AFTER THAT.
RIGHT. VERY REPETITIVE.
YOU TWO SURE HAVE THE NERVE TO SHOVE IT RIGHT IN MY FACE...
SHF
I MAY BE ABLE TO IMPROVE IT A LITTLE BIT IF I'M ALLOWED TO CHANGE THE STORY AS I WANT TO, BUT THERE ARE LIMITS TO WHAT I COULD DO.
PLUS AKINA SENSEI IS A VERY PROUD PERSON.
I KNOW...
WE'RE JUST NOT ABLE TO BECOME TRUE PARTNERS LIKE ASHIROGI SENSEI WHO UNDERSTAND EACH OTHER WITHOUT SPEAKING.
THE ANIME HAS ENDED, SO IF SHE'S OUT OF IDEAS IT'LL PROBABLY BE BETTER TO END THE SERIES RATHER THAN HAVE IT DRAG ON.
D-DON'T SAY THAT. THE GRAPHIC NOVELS ARE STILL SELLING RELATIVELY WELL!
SHF
END...
...+NATURAL ...?
HE DOESN'T WANT TO KEEP STRETCHING IT OUT...?
SIGH... W-WELL, I'VE STILL GOT THE TV DRAMA OF MIKATA'S JUSTICE...
AND IT'S TRUE THAT +NATURAL IS PAST ITS PEAK. MAYBE I SHOULD THINK ABOUT STEERING THE SERIES TOWARD AN END...
SHF
SHF

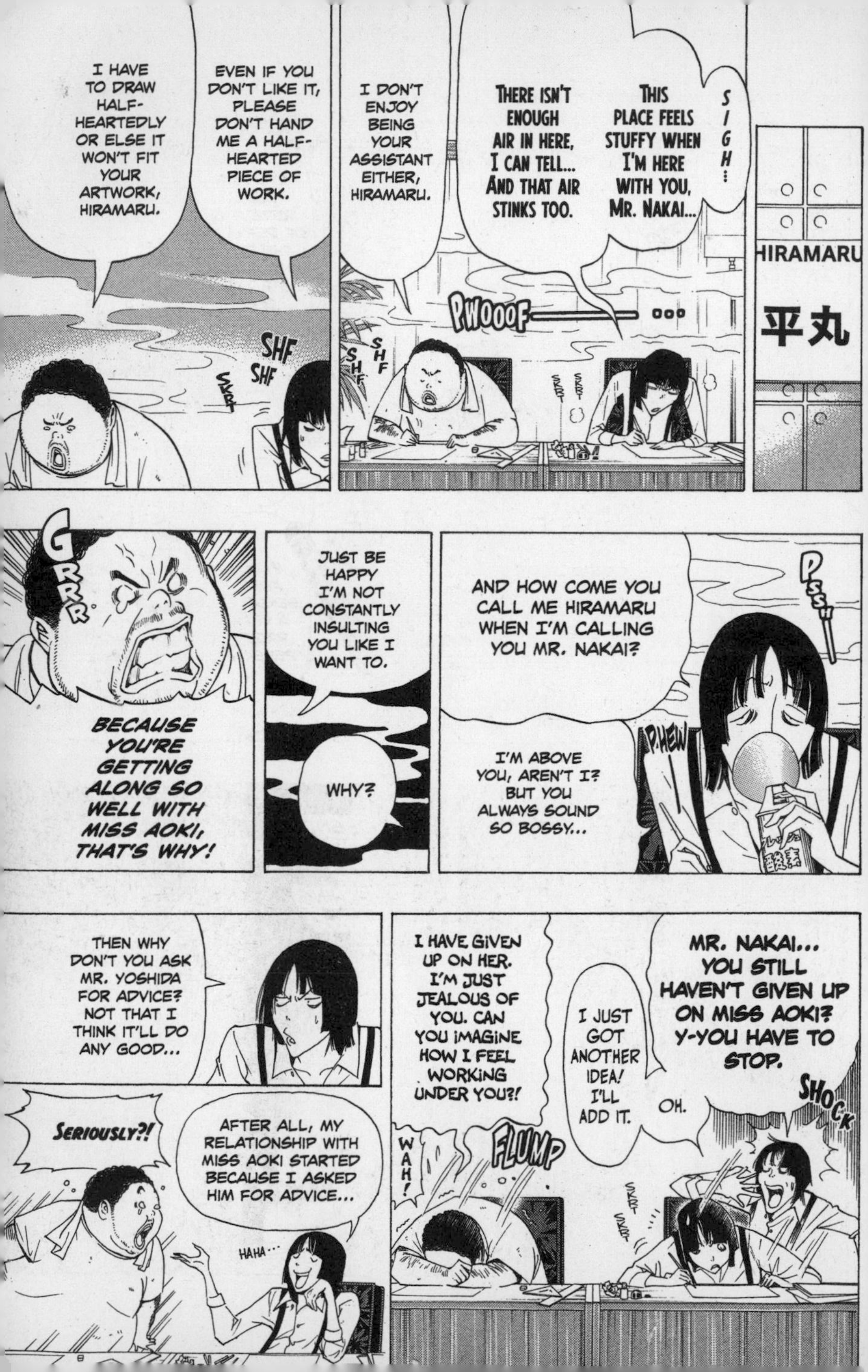
HIRAMARU
平丸
SIGH...
THIS PLACE FEELS STUFFY WHEN I'M HERE WITH YOU, MR. NAKAI...
THERE ISN'T ENOUGH AIR IN HERE, I CAN TELL... AND THAT AIR STINKS TOO.
I DON'T ENJOY BEING YOUR ASSISTANT EITHER, HIRAMARU.
PWOOOF—— ...
SHF SHF
SKRT SKRT
EVEN IF YOU DON'T LIKE IT, PLEASE DON'T HAND ME A HALF-HEARTED PIECE OF WORK.
I HAVE TO DRAW HALF-HEARTEDLY OR ELSE IT WON'T FIT YOUR ARTWORK, HIRAMARU.
SHF SHF
SKRT
PSSH
AND HOW COME YOU CALL ME HIRAMARU WHEN I'M CALLING YOU MR. NAKAI?
P.HEW
I'M ABOVE YOU, AREN'T I? BUT YOU ALWAYS SOUND SO BOSSY...
JUST BE HAPPY I'M NOT CONSTANTLY INSULTING YOU LIKE I WANT TO.
WHY?
GRRR
BECAUSE YOU'RE GETTING ALONG SO WELL WITH MISS AOKI, THAT'S WHY!
MR. NAKAI... YOU STILL HAVEN'T GIVEN UP ON MISS AOKI? Y-YOU HAVE TO STOP.
SHOCK
I HAVE GIVEN UP ON HER. I'M JUST JEALOUS OF YOU. CAN YOU IMAGINE HOW I FEEL WORKING UNDER YOU?!
OH.
I JUST GOT ANOTHER IDEA! I'LL ADD IT.
FLUMP
WAH!
SKRT SKRT
THEN WHY DON'T YOU ASK MR. YOSHIDA FOR ADVICE? NOT THAT I THINK IT'LL DO ANY GOOD...
AFTER ALL, MY RELATIONSHIP WITH MISS AOKI STARTED BECAUSE I ASKED HIM FOR ADVICE...
SERIOUSLY?!
HAHA...

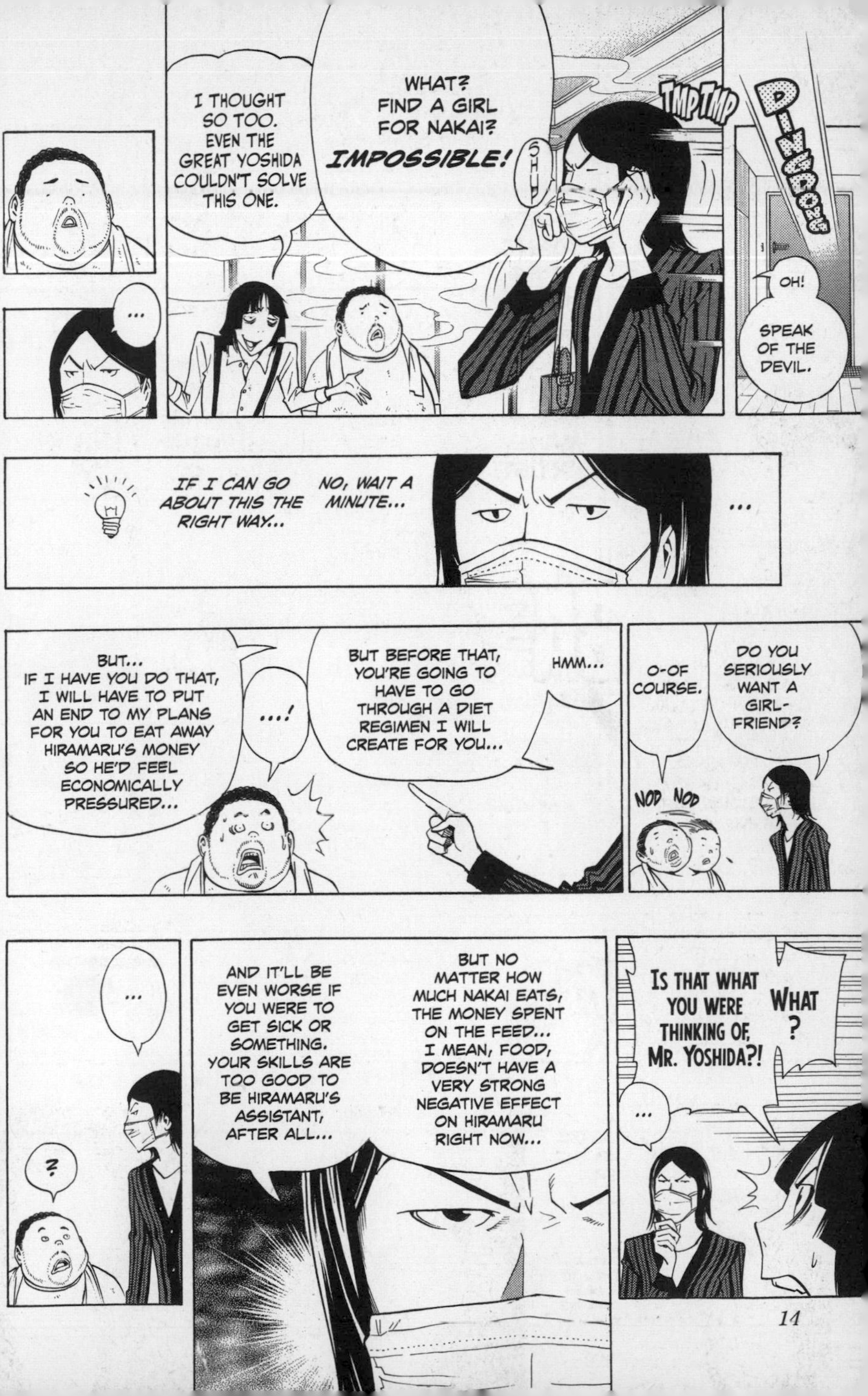
DINGDONG
OH!
SPEAK OF THE DEVIL.
TMP TMP
SHU
WHAT? FIND A GIRL FOR NAKAI? IMPOSSIBLE!
I THOUGHT SO TOO. EVEN THE GREAT YOSHIDA COULDN'T SOLVE THIS ONE.
...
...
NO, WAIT A MINUTE...
IF I CAN GO ABOUT THIS THE RIGHT WAY...
DO YOU SERIOUSLY WANT A GIRL-FRIEND?
O-OF COURSE.
NOD NOD
HMM...
BUT BEFORE THAT, YOU'RE GOING TO HAVE TO GO THROUGH A DIET REGIMEN I WILL CREATE FOR YOU...
...!
BUT... IF I HAVE YOU DO THAT, I WILL HAVE TO PUT AN END TO MY PLANS FOR YOU TO EAT AWAY HIRAMARU'S MONEY SO HE'D FEEL ECONOMICALLY PRESSURED...
WHAT?
IS THAT WHAT YOU WERE THINKING OF, MR. YOSHIDA?!
...
BUT NO MATTER HOW MUCH NAKAI EATS, THE MONEY SPENT ON THE FEED... I MEAN, FOOD, DOESN'T HAVE A VERY STRONG NEGATIVE EFFECT ON HIRAMARU RIGHT NOW...
AND IT'LL BE EVEN WORSE IF YOU WERE TO GET SICK OR SOMETHING. YOUR SKILLS ARE TOO GOOD TO BE HIRAMARU'S ASSISTANT, AFTER ALL...
...
?

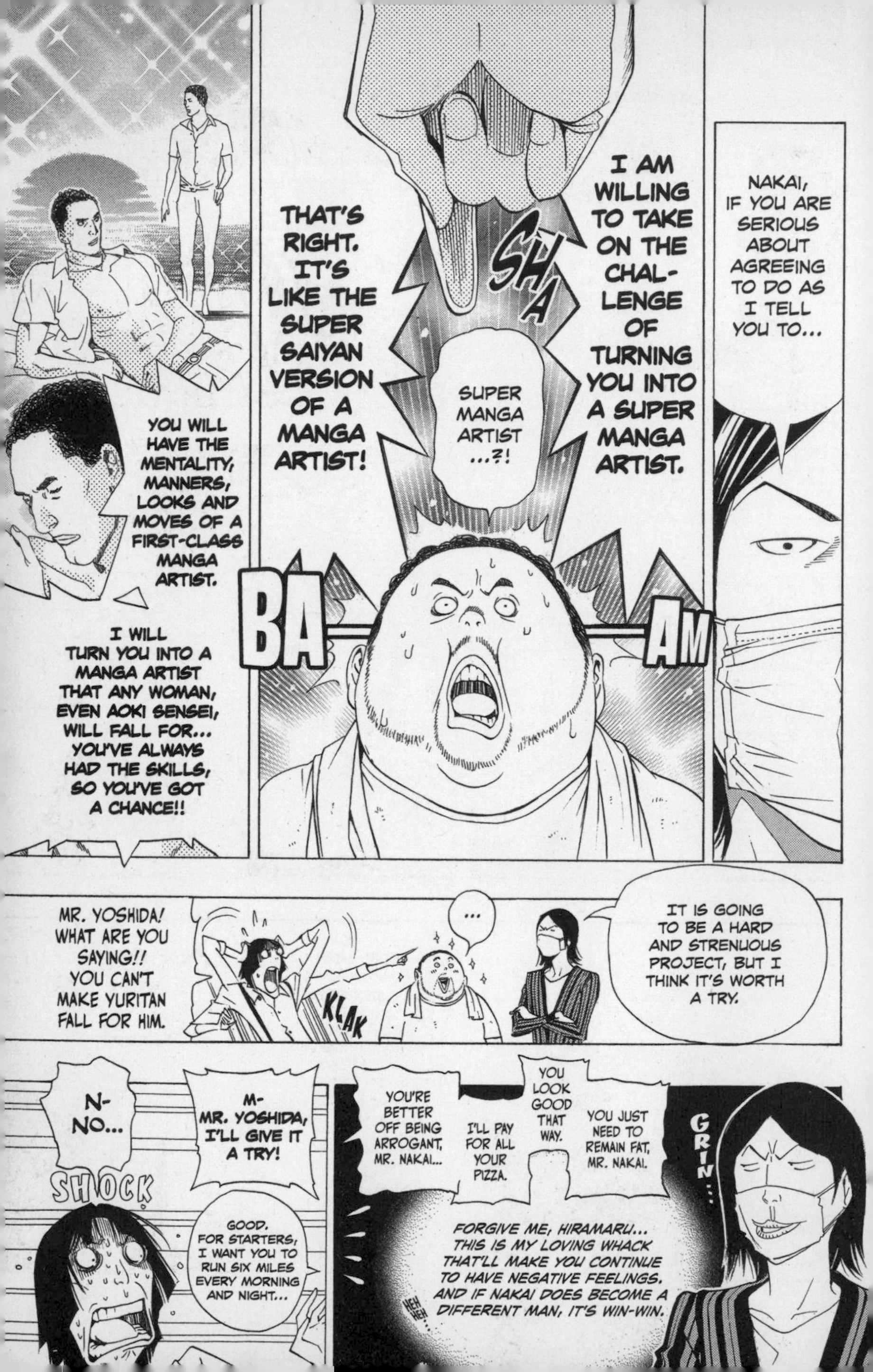
NAKAI, IF YOU ARE SERIOUS ABOUT AGREEING TO DO AS I TELL YOU TO...
I AM WILLING TO TAKE ON THE CHAL-LENGE OF TURNING YOU INTO A SUPER MANGA ARTIST.
SHA
SUPER MANGA ARTIST ...?!
THAT'S RIGHT. IT'S LIKE THE SUPER SAIYAN VERSION OF A MANGA ARTIST!
BA
AM
YOU WILL HAVE THE MENTALITY, MANNERS, LOOKS AND MOVES OF A FIRST-CLASS MANGA ARTIST.
I WILL TURN YOU INTO A MANGA ARTIST THAT ANY WOMAN, EVEN AOKI SENSEI, WILL FALL FOR... YOU'VE ALWAYS HAD THE SKILLS, SO YOU'VE GOT A CHANCE!!
IT IS GOING TO BE A HARD AND STRENUOUS PROJECT, BUT I THINK IT'S WORTH A TRY.
...
KLAK
MR. YOSHIDA! WHAT ARE YOU SAYING!! YOU CAN'T MAKE YURITAN FALL FOR HIM.
GRIN...
YOU JUST NEED TO REMAIN FAT, MR. NAKAI.
YOU LOOK GOOD THAT WAY.
I'LL PAY FOR ALL YOUR PIZZA.
YOU'RE BETTER OFF BEING ARROGANT, MR. NAKAI...
FORGIVE ME, HIRAMARU... THIS IS MY LOVING WHACK THAT'LL MAKE YOU CONTINUE TO HAVE NEGATIVE FEELINGS. AND IF NAKAI DOES BECOME A DIFFERENT MAN, IT'S WIN-WIN.
HEH HEH
M-MR. YOSHIDA, I'LL GIVE IT A TRY!
N-NO...
SHOCK
GOOD. FOR STARTERS, I WANT YOU TO RUN SIX MILES EVERY MORNING AND NIGHT...

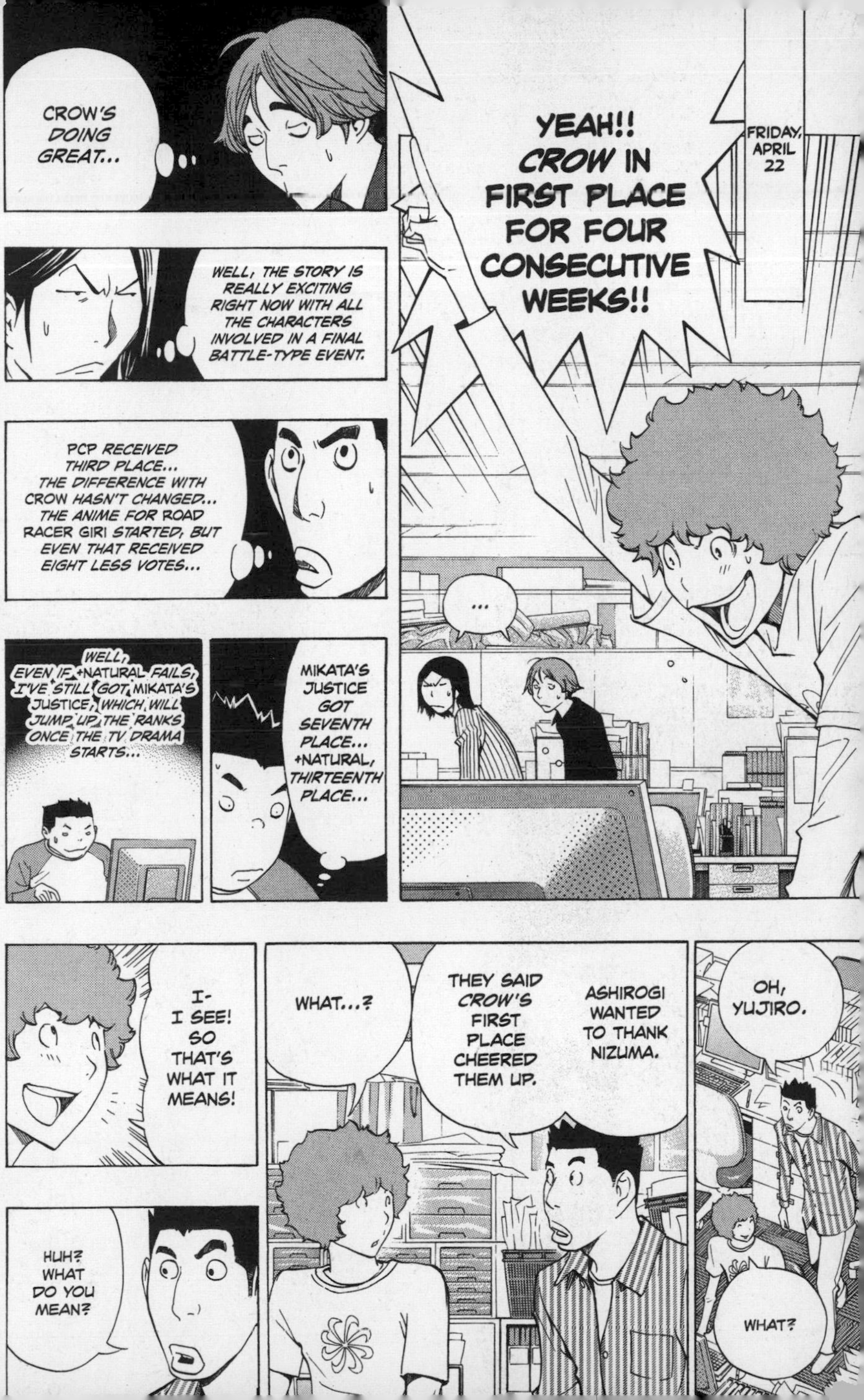
FRIDAY, APRIL 22
YEAH!! CROW IN FIRST PLACE FOR FOUR CONSECUTIVE WEEKS!!
...
CROW'S DOING GREAT...
WELL, THE STORY IS REALLY EXCITING RIGHT NOW WITH ALL THE CHARACTERS INVOLVED IN A FINAL BATTLE-TYPE EVENT.
PCP RECEIVED THIRD PLACE... THE DIFFERENCE WITH CROW HASN'T CHANGED... THE ANIME FOR ROAD RACER GIRI STARTED, BUT EVEN THAT RECEIVED EIGHT LESS VOTES...
MIKATA'S JUSTICE GOT SEVENTH PLACE... +NATURAL, THIRTEENTH PLACE...
WELL, EVEN IF +NATURAL FAILS, I'VE STILL GOT MIKATA'S JUSTICE, WHICH WILL JUMP UP THE RANKS ONCE THE TV DRAMA STARTS...
OH, YUJIRO.
WHAT?
ASHIROGI WANTED TO THANK NIZUMA.
THEY SAID CROW'S FIRST PLACE CHEERED THEM UP.
WHAT...?
I- I SEE! SO THAT'S WHAT IT MEANS!
HUH? WHAT DO YOU MEAN?

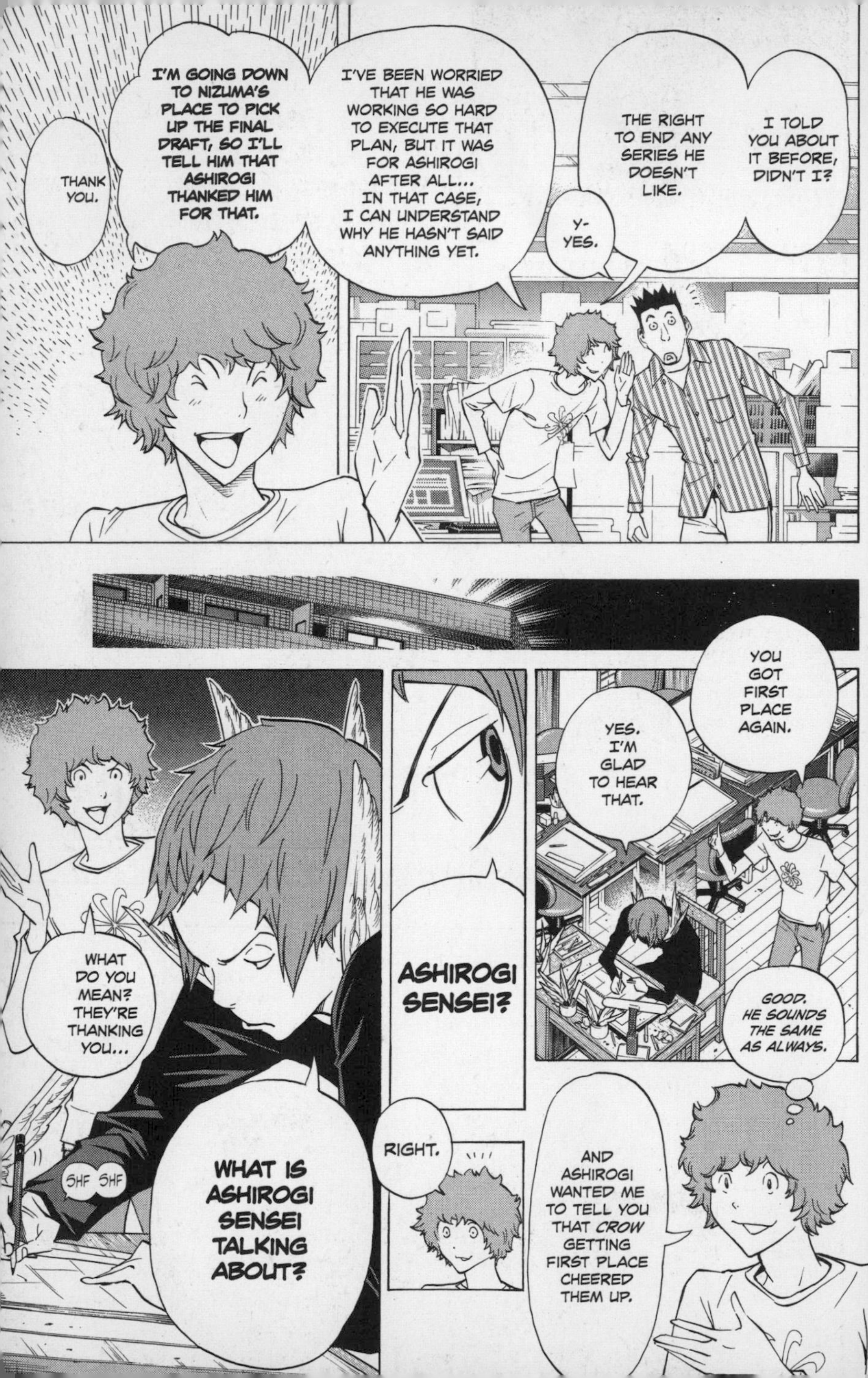
I TOLD YOU ABOUT IT BEFORE, DIDN'T I?
THE RIGHT TO END ANY SERIES HE DOESN'T LIKE.
Y-YES.
I'VE BEEN WORRIED THAT HE WAS WORKING SO HARD TO EXECUTE THAT PLAN, BUT IT WAS FOR ASHIROGI AFTER ALL... IN THAT CASE, I CAN UNDERSTAND WHY HE HASN'T SAID ANYTHING YET.
I'M GOING DOWN TO NIZUMA'S PLACE TO PICK UP THE FINAL DRAFT, SO I'LL TELL HIM THAT ASHIROGI THANKED HIM FOR THAT.
THANK YOU.
YOU GOT FIRST PLACE AGAIN.
YES. I'M GLAD TO HEAR THAT.
GOOD. HE SOUNDS THE SAME AS ALWAYS.
AND ASHIROGI WANTED ME TO TELL YOU THAT *CROW* GETTING FIRST PLACE CHEERED THEM UP.
ASHIROGI SENSEI?
RIGHT.
WHAT IS ASHIROGI SENSEI TALKING ABOUT?
WHAT DO YOU MEAN? THEY'RE THANKING YOU...
SHF SHF

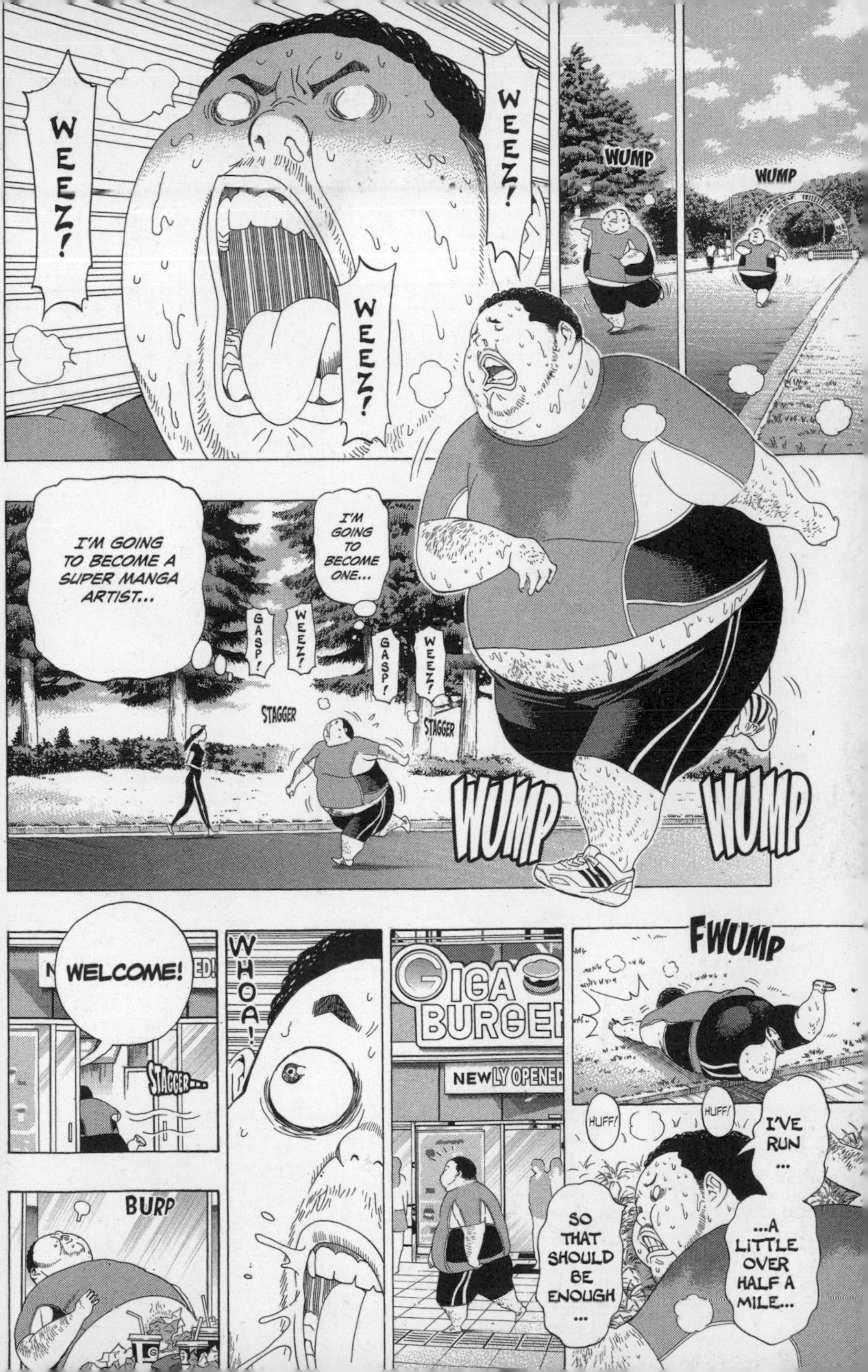
WUMP
WUMP
WEEZ!
WEEZ!
WEEZ!
I'M GOING TO BECOME ONE...
I'M GOING TO BECOME A SUPER MANGA ARTIST...
WEEZ!
GASP!
WEEZ!
GASP!
STAGGER
STAGGER
WUMP
WUMP
FWUMP
HUFF!
HUFF!
I'VE RUN...
...A LITTLE OVER HALF A MILE...
SO THAT SHOULD BE ENOUGH...
GIGA BURGER
NEWLY OPENED
WHOA!
WELCOME!
STAGGER...
BURP

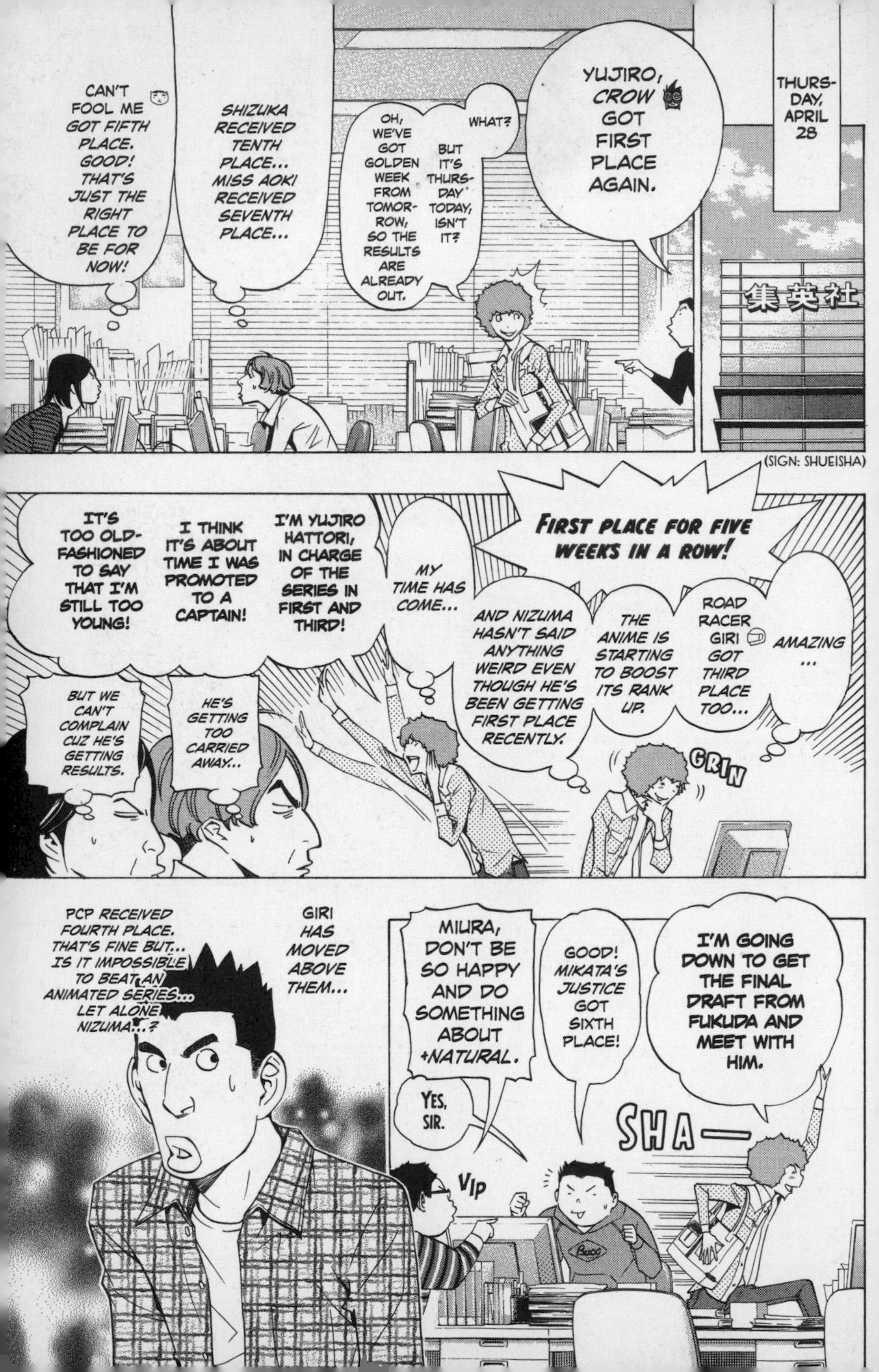
THURSDAY, APRIL 28
集英社
YUJIRO, CROW GOT FIRST PLACE AGAIN.
WHAT?
BUT IT'S THURSDAY TODAY, ISN'T IT?
OH, WE'VE GOT GOLDEN WEEK FROM TOMORROW, SO THE RESULTS ARE ALREADY OUT.
SHIZUKA RECEIVED TENTH PLACE... MISS AOKI RECEIVED SEVENTH PLACE...
CAN'T FOOL ME GOT FIFTH PLACE. GOOD! THAT'S JUST THE RIGHT PLACE TO BE FOR NOW!
FIRST PLACE FOR FIVE WEEKS IN A ROW!
AMAZING...
ROAD RACER GIRI GOT THIRD PLACE TOO...
THE ANIME IS STARTING TO BOOST ITS RANK UP.
AND NIZUMA HASN'T SAID ANYTHING WEIRD EVEN THOUGH HE'S BEEN GETTING FIRST PLACE RECENTLY.
GRIN
MY TIME HAS COME...
I'M YUJIRO HATTORI, IN CHARGE OF THE SERIES IN FIRST AND THIRD!
I THINK IT'S ABOUT TIME I WAS PROMOTED TO A CAPTAIN!
IT'S TOO OLD-FASHIONED TO SAY THAT I'M STILL TOO YOUNG!
HE'S GETTING TOO CARRIED AWAY...
BUT WE CAN'T COMPLAIN CUZ HE'S GETTING RESULTS.
I'M GOING DOWN TO GET THE FINAL DRAFT FROM FUKUDA AND MEET WITH HIM.
SHA—
GOOD! MIKATA'S JUSTICE GOT SIXTH PLACE!
MIURA, DON'T BE SO HAPPY AND DO SOMETHING ABOUT +NATURAL.
YES, SIR.
VIP
GIRI HAS MOVED ABOVE THEM...
PCP RECEIVED FOURTH PLACE. THAT'S FINE BUT... IS IT IMPOSSIBLE TO BEAT AN ANIMATED SERIES... LET ALONE NIZUMA...?
(SIGN: SHUEISHA)

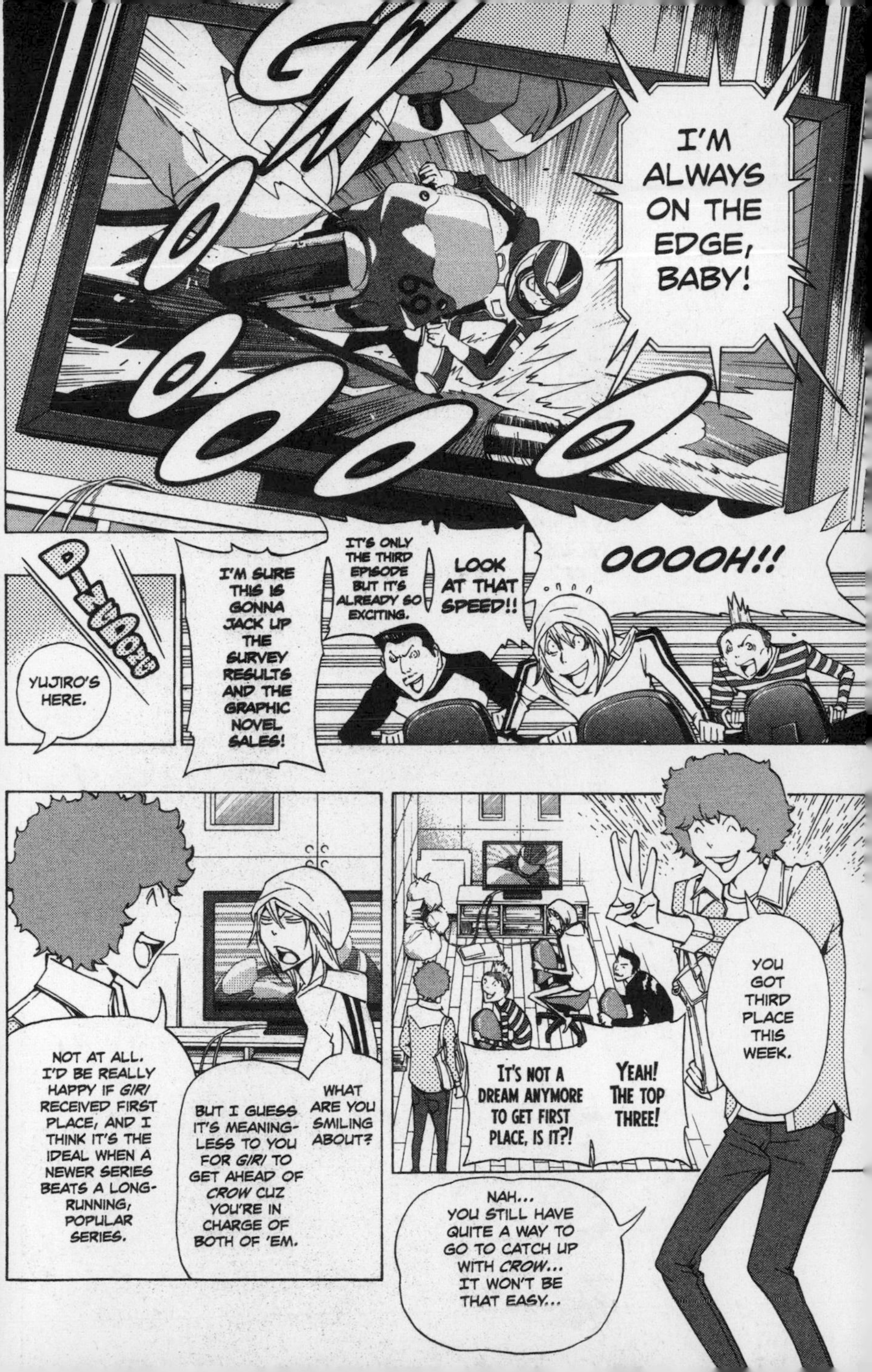
I'M ALWAYS ON THE EDGE, BABY!
OOOOOH!!
LOOK AT THAT SPEED!!
IT'S ONLY THE THIRD EPISODE BUT IT'S ALREADY SO EXCITING.
I'M SURE THIS IS GONNA JACK UP THE SURVEY RESULTS AND THE GRAPHIC NOVEL SALES!
YUJIRO'S HERE.
YOU GOT THIRD PLACE THIS WEEK.
YEAH! THE TOP THREE!
IT'S NOT A DREAM ANYMORE TO GET FIRST PLACE, IS IT?!
WHAT ARE YOU SMILING ABOUT?
NAH... YOU STILL HAVE QUITE A WAY TO GO TO CATCH UP WITH *CROW*... IT WON'T BE THAT EASY...
BUT I GUESS IT'S MEANINGLESS TO YOU FOR *GIRI* TO GET AHEAD OF *CROW* CUZ YOU'RE IN CHARGE OF BOTH OF 'EM.
NOT AT ALL. I'D BE REALLY HAPPY IF *GIRI* RECEIVED FIRST PLACE, AND I THINK IT'S THE IDEAL WHEN A NEWER SERIES BEATS A LONG-RUNNING, POPULAR SERIES.

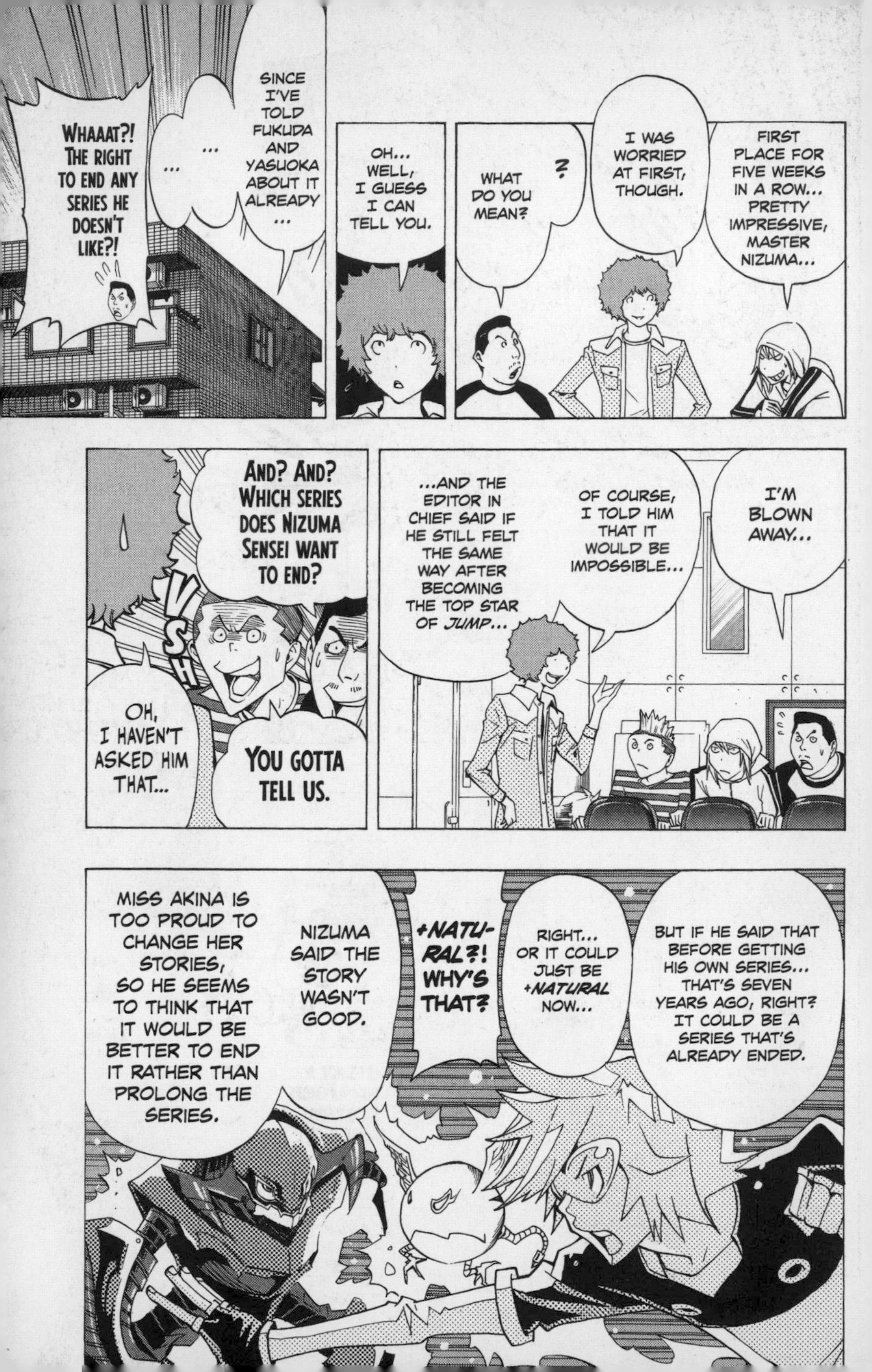
FIRST PLACE FOR FIVE WEEKS IN A ROW... PRETTY IMPRESSIVE, MASTER NIZUMA...
I WAS WORRIED AT FIRST, THOUGH.
?
WHAT DO YOU MEAN?
OH... WELL, I GUESS I CAN TELL YOU.
SINCE I'VE TOLD FUKUDA AND YASUOKA ABOUT IT ALREADY ...
... ...
WHAAAT?! THE RIGHT TO END ANY SERIES HE DOESN'T LIKE?!
I'M BLOWN AWAY...
OF COURSE, I TOLD HIM THAT IT WOULD BE IMPOSSIBLE...
...AND THE EDITOR IN CHIEF SAID IF HE STILL FELT THE SAME WAY AFTER BECOMING THE TOP STAR OF *JUMP*...
AND? AND? WHICH SERIES DOES NIZUMA SENSEI WANT TO END?
VSH
YOU GOTTA TELL US.
OH, I HAVEN'T ASKED HIM THAT...
BUT IF HE SAID THAT BEFORE GETTING HIS OWN SERIES... THAT'S SEVEN YEARS AGO, RIGHT? IT COULD BE A SERIES THAT'S ALREADY ENDED.
RIGHT... OR IT COULD JUST BE *+NATURAL* NOW...
+NATURAL?! WHY'S THAT?
NIZUMA SAID THE STORY WASN'T GOOD.
MISS AKINA IS TOO PROUD TO CHANGE HER STORIES, SO HE SEEMS TO THINK THAT IT WOULD BE BETTER TO END IT RATHER THAN PROLONG THE SERIES.

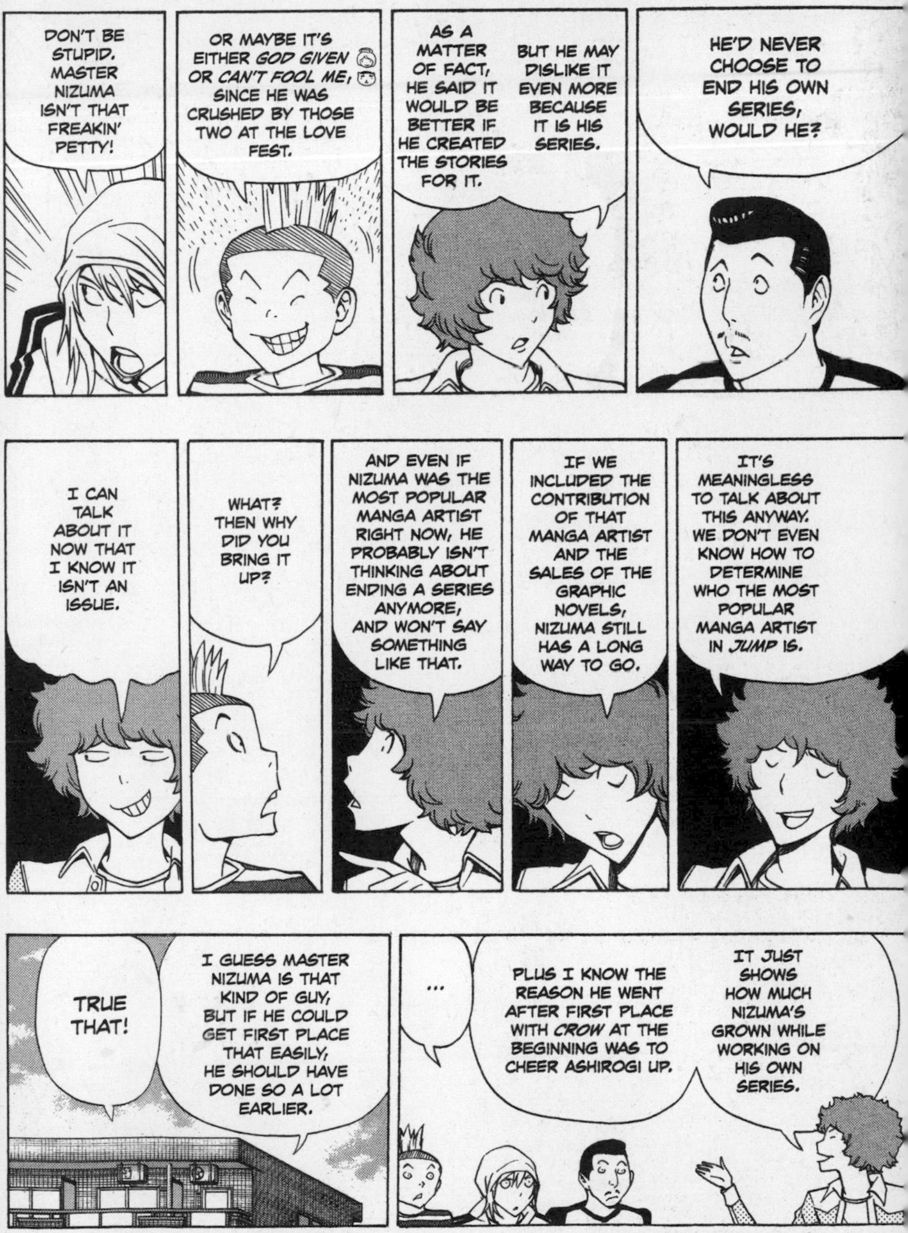
HE'D NEVER CHOOSE TO END HIS OWN SERIES, WOULD HE?
AS A MATTER OF FACT, HE SAID IT WOULD BE BETTER IF HE CREATED THE STORIES FOR IT.
BUT HE MAY DISLIKE IT EVEN MORE BECAUSE IT IS HIS SERIES.
OR MAYBE IT'S EITHER *GOD GIVEN* OR *CAN'T FOOL ME*, SINCE HE WAS CRUSHED BY THOSE TWO AT THE LOVE FEST.
DON'T BE STUPID. MASTER NIZUMA ISN'T THAT FREAKIN' PETTY!
IT'S MEANINGLESS TO TALK ABOUT THIS ANYWAY. WE DON'T EVEN KNOW HOW TO DETERMINE WHO THE MOST POPULAR MANGA ARTIST IN *JUMP* IS.
IF WE INCLUDED THE CONTRIBUTION OF THAT MANGA ARTIST AND THE SALES OF THE GRAPHIC NOVELS, NIZUMA STILL HAS A LONG WAY TO GO.
AND EVEN IF NIZUMA WAS THE MOST POPULAR MANGA ARTIST RIGHT NOW, HE PROBABLY ISN'T THINKING ABOUT ENDING A SERIES ANYMORE, AND WON'T SAY SOMETHING LIKE THAT.
WHAT? THEN WHY DID YOU BRING IT UP?
I CAN TALK ABOUT IT NOW THAT I KNOW IT ISN'T AN ISSUE.
IT JUST SHOWS HOW MUCH NIZUMA'S GROWN WHILE WORKING ON HIS OWN SERIES.
PLUS I KNOW THE REASON HE WENT AFTER FIRST PLACE WITH *CROW* AT THE BEGINNING WAS TO CHEER ASHIROGI UP.
...
I GUESS MASTER NIZUMA IS THAT KIND OF GUY, BUT IF HE COULD GET FIRST PLACE THAT EASILY, HE SHOULD HAVE DONE SO A LOT EARLIER.
TRUE THAT!

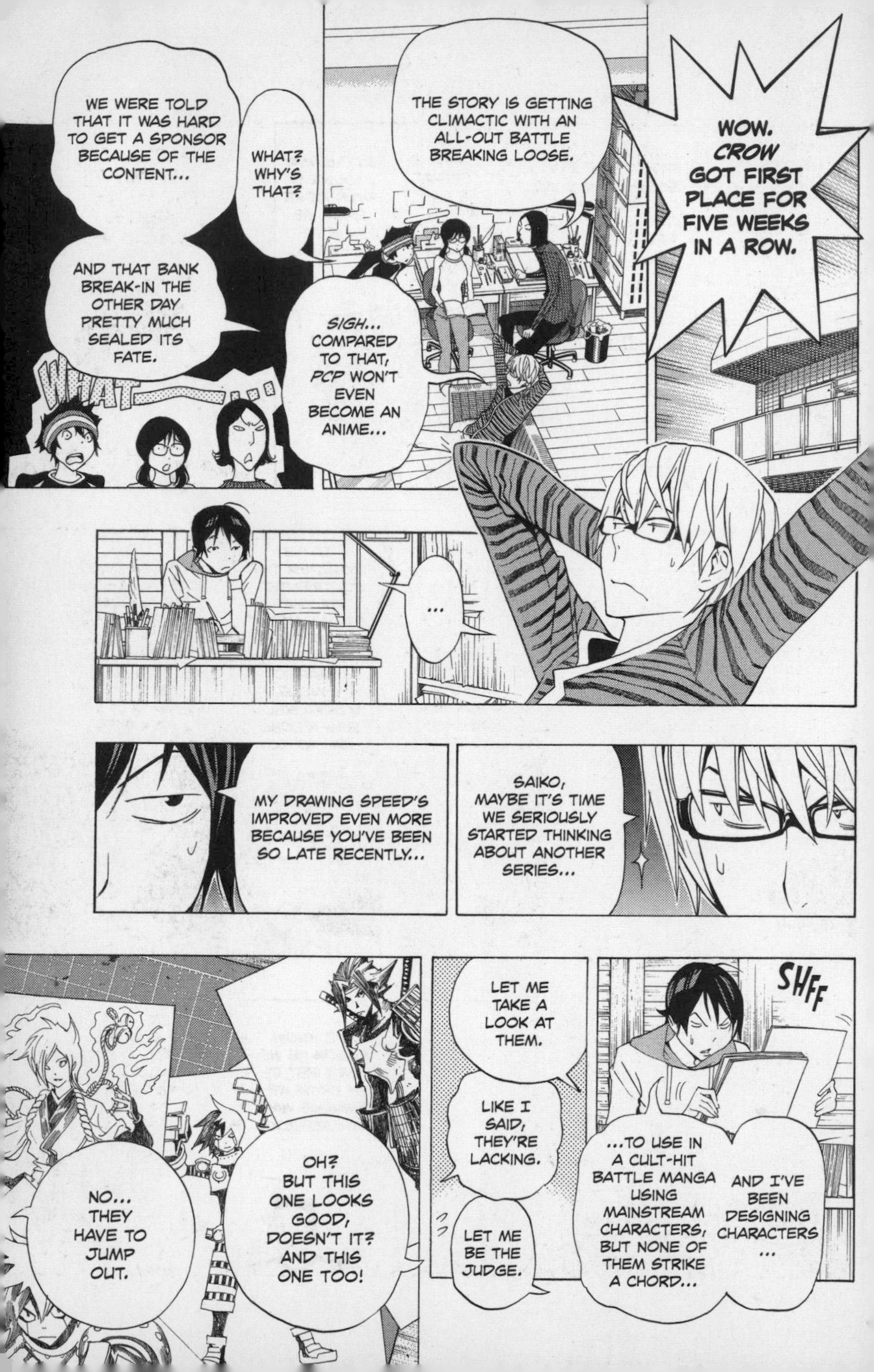
WOW. *CROW* GOT FIRST PLACE FOR FIVE WEEKS IN A ROW.
THE STORY IS GETTING CLIMACTIC WITH AN ALL-OUT BATTLE BREAKING LOOSE.
SIGH... COMPARED TO THAT, *PCP* WON'T EVEN BECOME AN ANIME...
WHAT? WHY'S THAT?
WE WERE TOLD THAT IT WAS HARD TO GET A SPONSOR BECAUSE OF THE CONTENT...
AND THAT BANK BREAK-IN THE OTHER DAY PRETTY MUCH SEALED ITS FATE.
WHAT——...
...
SAIKO, MAYBE IT'S TIME WE SERIOUSLY STARTED THINKING ABOUT ANOTHER SERIES...
MY DRAWING SPEED'S IMPROVED EVEN MORE BECAUSE YOU'VE BEEN SO LATE RECENTLY...
SHFF
AND I'VE BEEN DESIGNING CHARACTERS...
...TO USE IN A CULT-HIT BATTLE MANGA USING MAINSTREAM CHARACTERS, BUT NONE OF THEM STRIKE A CHORD...
LET ME TAKE A LOOK AT THEM.
LIKE I SAID, THEY'RE LACKING.
LET ME BE THE JUDGE.
OH? BUT THIS ONE LOOKS GOOD, DOESN'T IT? AND THIS ONE TOO!
NO... THEY HAVE TO JUMP OUT.

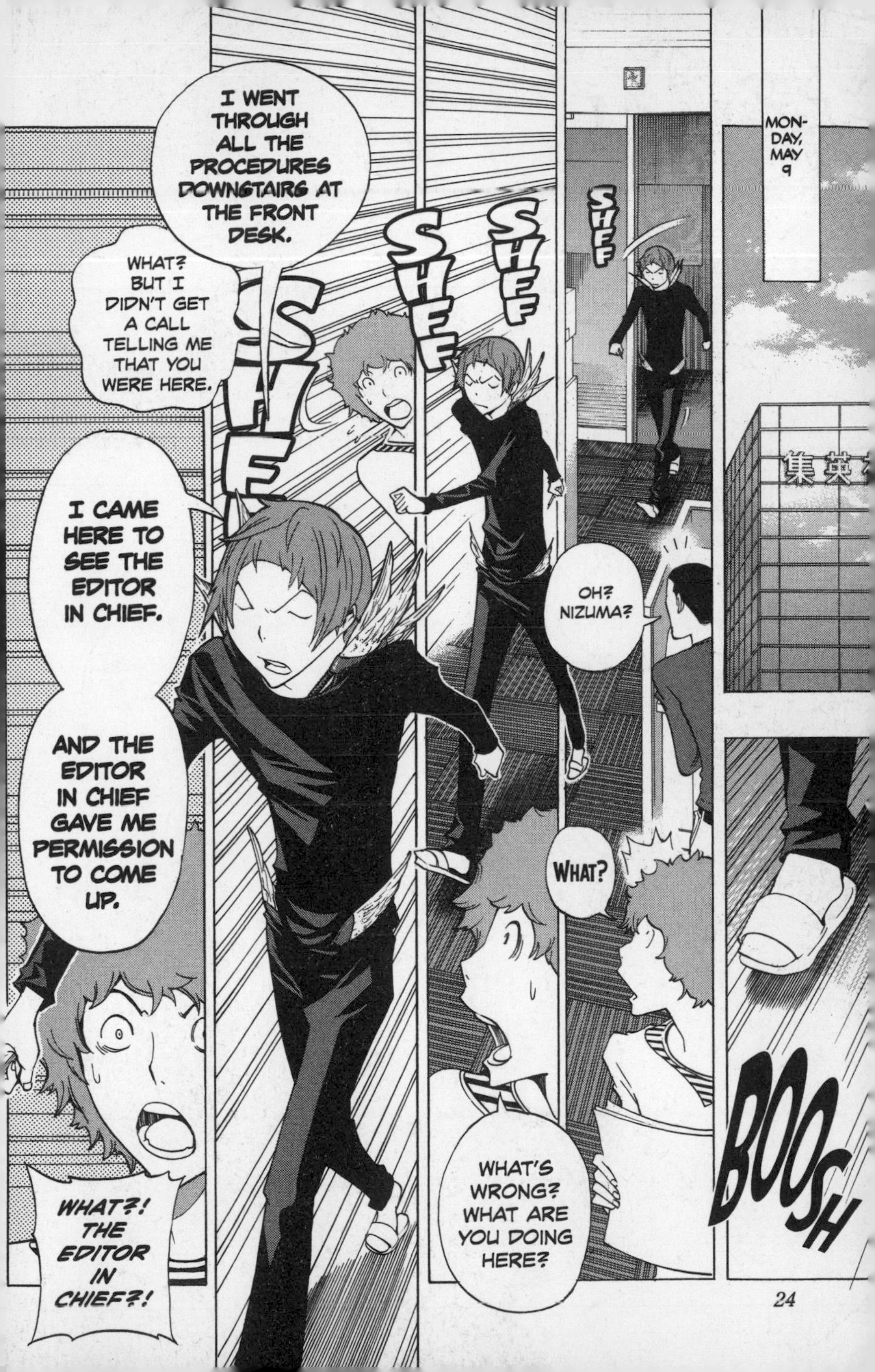

MON-DAY, MAY 9
集英
BOOSH
SHEFF
OH? NIZUMA?
WHAT?
WHAT'S WRONG? WHAT ARE YOU DOING HERE?
SHEFF
SHEFF
SHEFF
I WENT THROUGH ALL THE PROCEDURES DOWNSTAIRS AT THE FRONT DESK.
WHAT? BUT I DIDN'T GET A CALL TELLING ME THAT YOU WERE HERE.
SHEF
I CAME HERE TO SEE THE EDITOR IN CHIEF.
AND THE EDITOR IN CHIEF GAVE ME PERMISSION TO COME UP.
WHAT?! THE EDITOR IN CHIEF?!

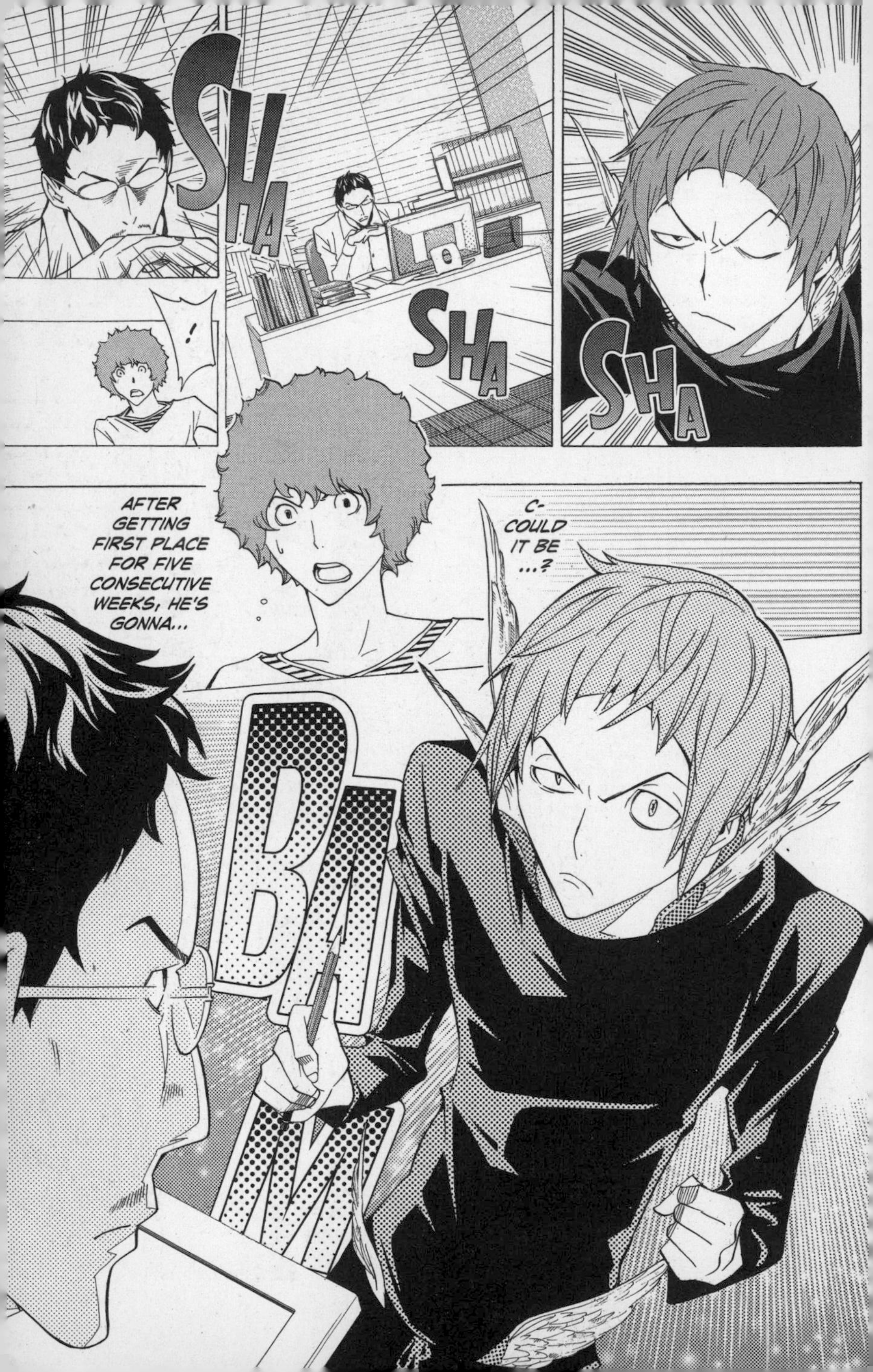
SHA
SHA
SHA
!
C- COULD IT BE ...?
AFTER GETTING FIRST PLACE FOR FIVE CONSECUTIVE WEEKS, HE'S GONNA...
BAM

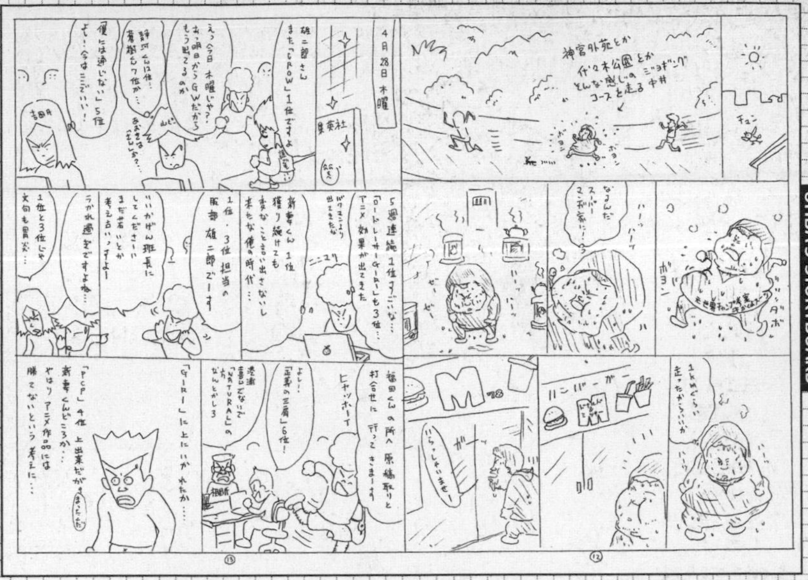

神宮外苑とか 代々木公園とか そんな感じの ジョギングコースを走る 中井
チュン
なるんだ スーパーマンガ家に…!
ハンバーガー
いらっしゃいませー
4月28日 木曜
集英社
雄二郎さん また「CROW」1位ですよ
1位、3位担当の 服部雄二郎でーす
ヒャッホーイ
よし! 「王者の三盾」6位!

OHBA'S STORYBOARD

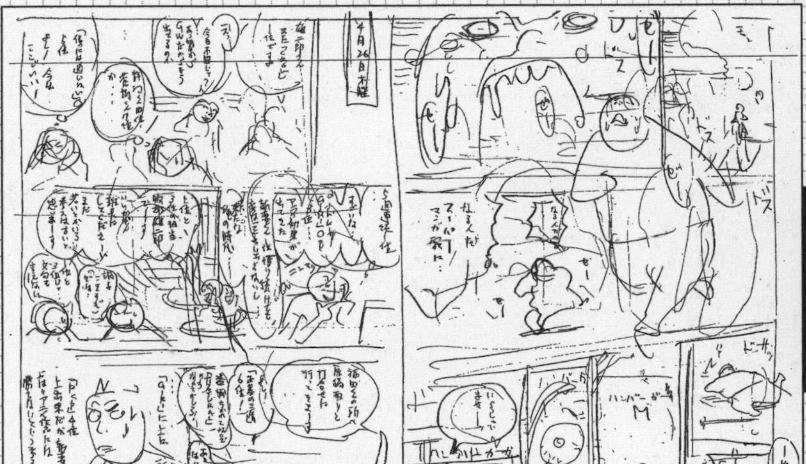

OBATA'S STORYBOARD

COMPLETE!

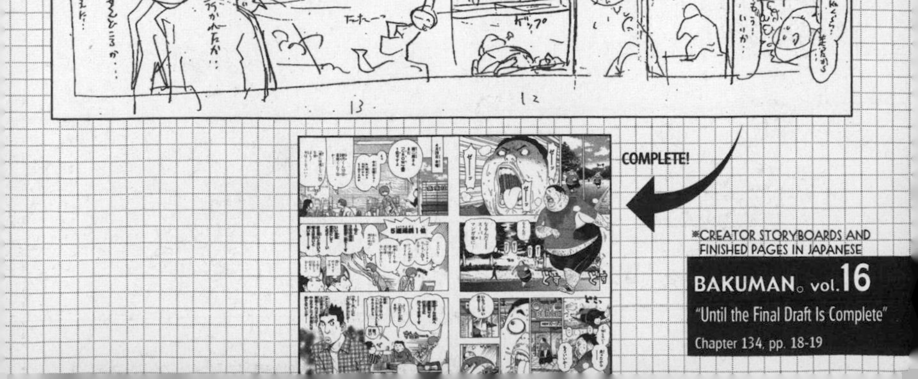

※CREATOR STORYBOARDS AND FINISHED PAGES IN JAPANESE

BAKUMAN。 vol.16

"Until the Final Draft Is Complete"

Chapter 134, pp. 18-19

CHAPTER 135
CONSECUTIVE AND PREVENTION

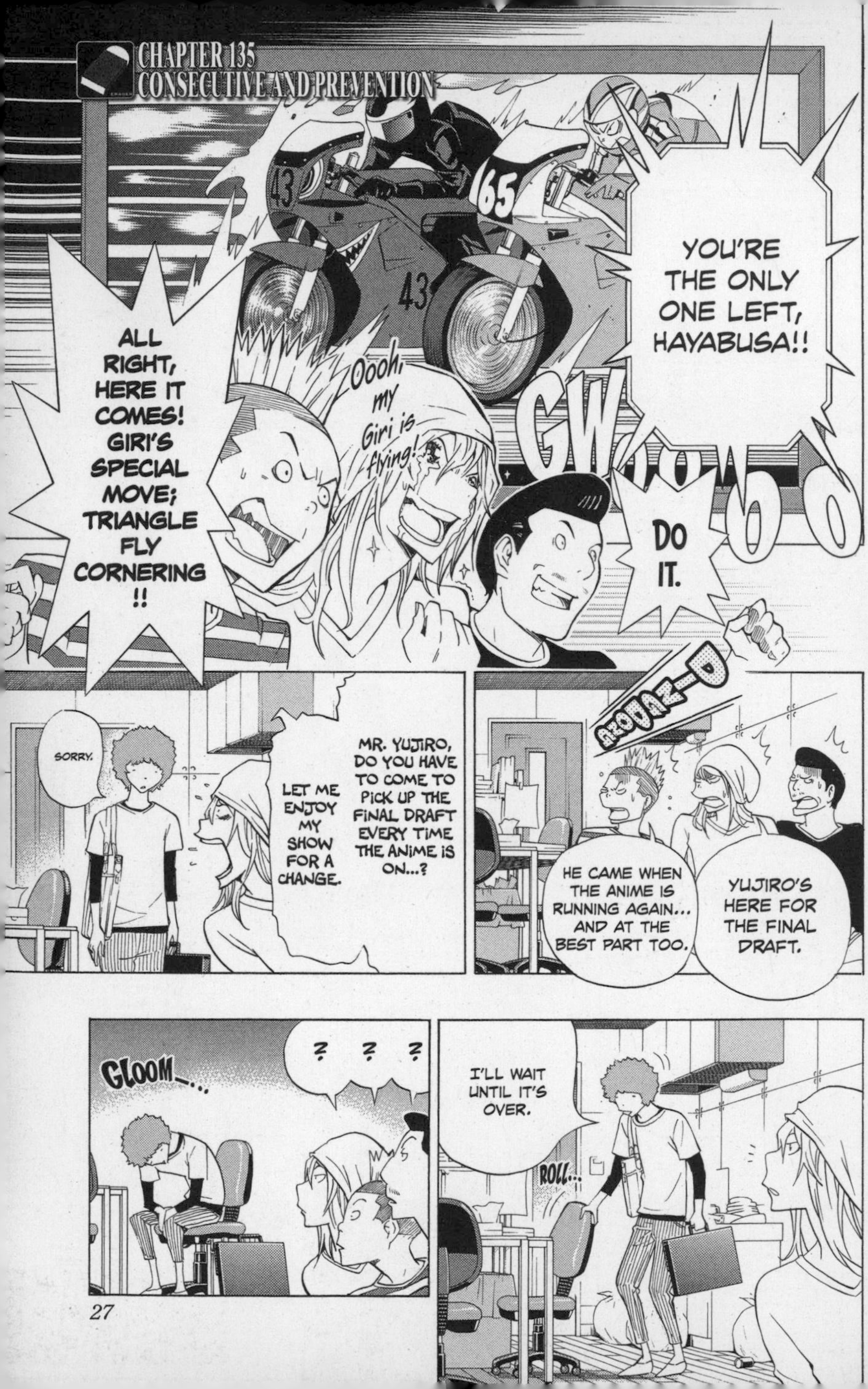
YOU'RE THE ONLY ONE LEFT, HAYABUSA!!
DO IT.
Oooh, my Giri is flying!
ALL RIGHT, HERE IT COMES! GIRI'S SPECIAL MOVE; TRIANGLE FLY CORNERING !!
GROAN-D
YUJIRO'S HERE FOR THE FINAL DRAFT.
HE CAME WHEN THE ANIME IS RUNNING AGAIN... AND AT THE BEST PART TOO.
MR. YUJIRO, DO YOU HAVE TO COME TO PICK UP THE FINAL DRAFT EVERY TIME THE ANIME IS ON...?
LET ME ENJOY MY SHOW FOR A CHANGE.
SORRY.
I'LL WAIT UNTIL IT'S OVER.
ROLL...
? ? ?
GLOOM...

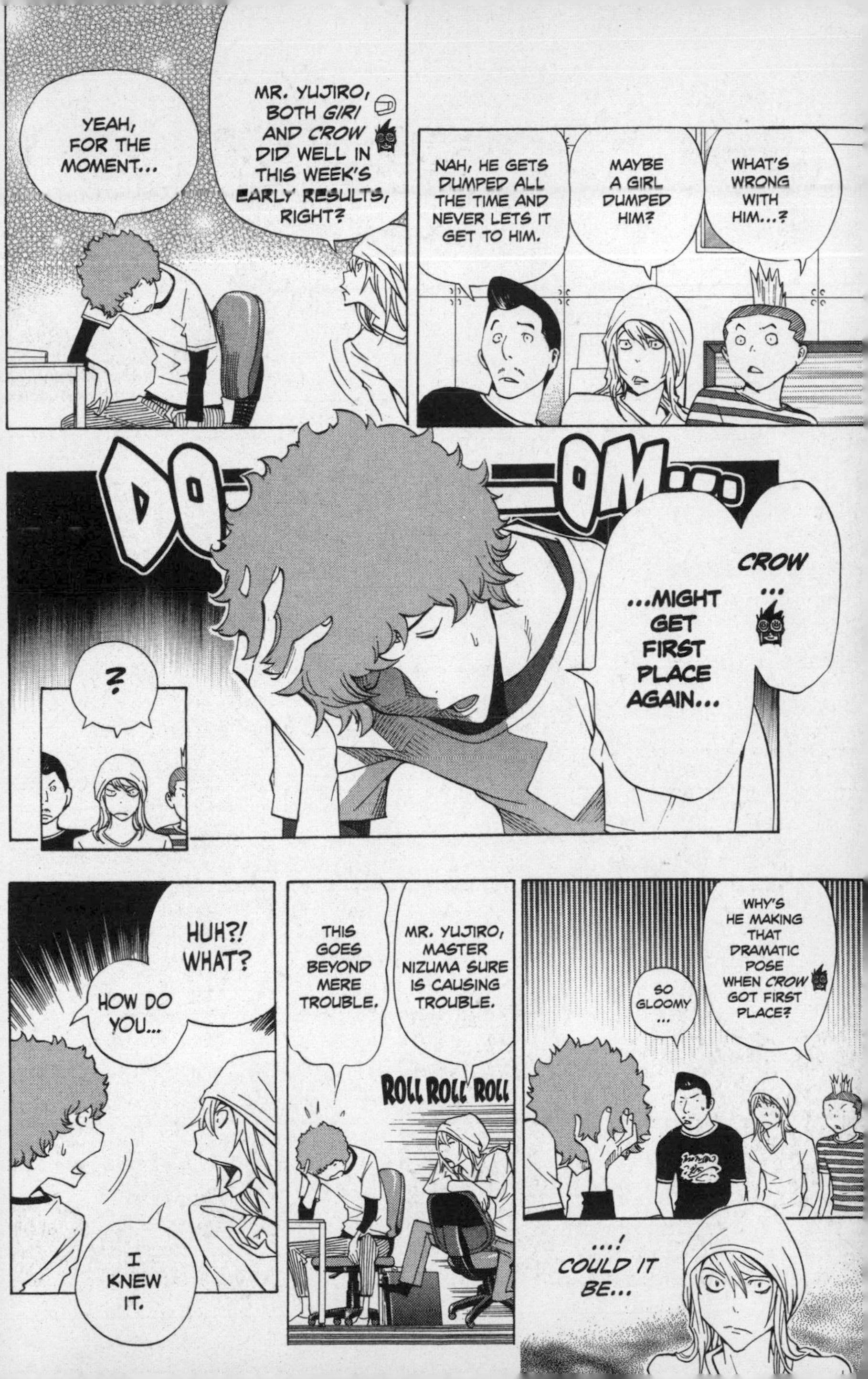
WHAT'S WRONG WITH HIM...?
MAYBE A GIRL DUMPED HIM?
NAH, HE GETS DUMPED ALL THE TIME AND NEVER LETS IT GET TO HIM.
MR. YUJIRO, BOTH GIRI AND CROW DID WELL IN THIS WEEK'S EARLY RESULTS, RIGHT?
YEAH, FOR THE MOMENT...
DO—OM...
CROW ...
...MIGHT GET FIRST PLACE AGAIN...
?
WHY'S HE MAKING THAT DRAMATIC POSE WHEN CROW GOT FIRST PLACE?
SO GLOOMY ...
...! COULD IT BE...
MR. YUJIRO, MASTER NIZUMA SURE IS CAUSING TROUBLE.
THIS GOES BEYOND MERE TROUBLE.
ROLL ROLL ROLL
HUH?! WHAT?
HOW DO YOU...
I KNEW IT.

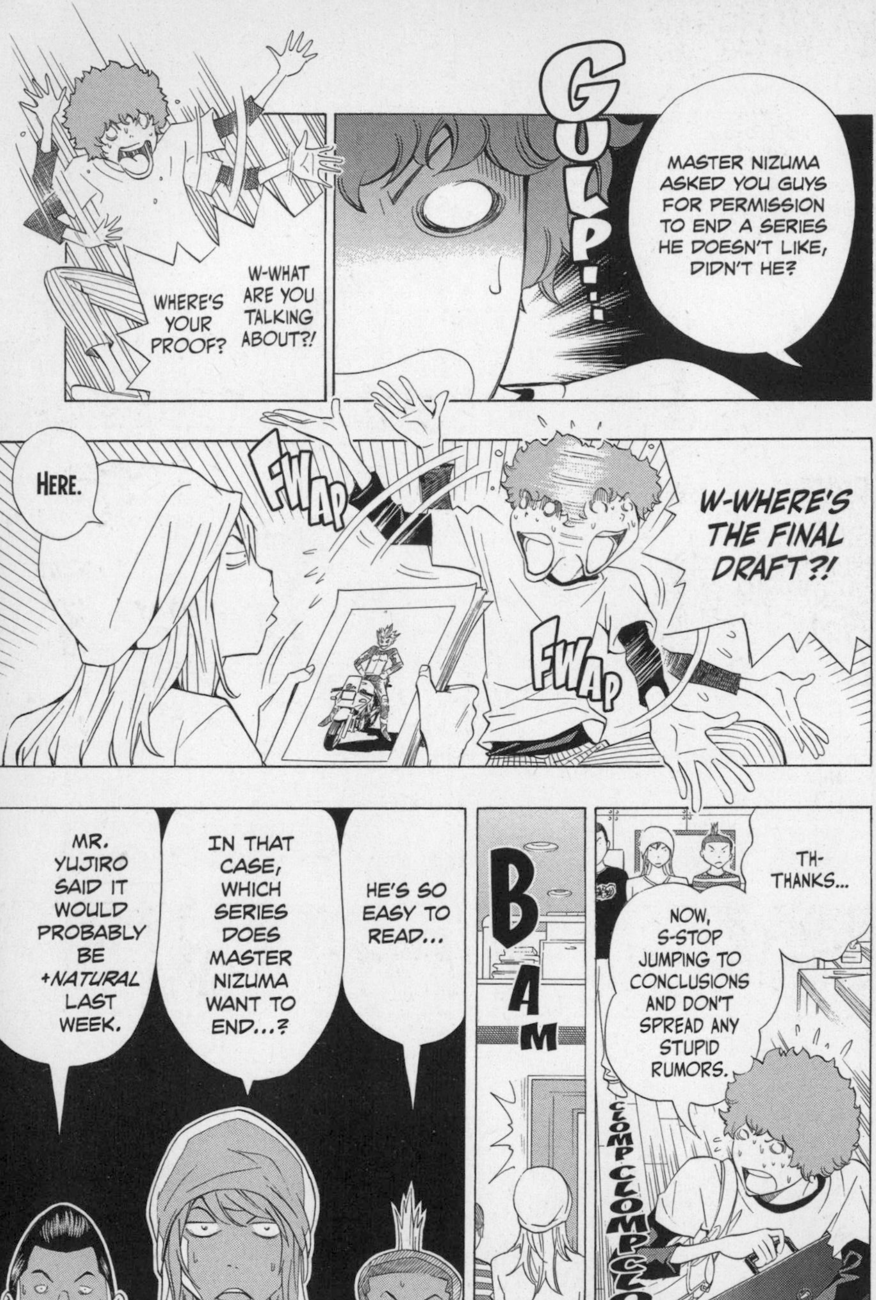
MASTER NIZUMA ASKED YOU GUYS FOR PERMISSION TO END A SERIES HE DOESN'T LIKE, DIDN'T HE?
GULP...
W-WHAT ARE YOU TALKING ABOUT?!
WHERE'S YOUR PROOF?
W-WHERE'S THE FINAL DRAFT?!
FWAP
FWAP
HERE.
TH-THANKS...
NOW, S-STOP JUMPING TO CONCLUSIONS AND DON'T SPREAD ANY STUPID RUMORS.
BAM
CLOMP CLOMP CLOMP CLOMP
HE'S SO EASY TO READ...
IN THAT CASE, WHICH SERIES DOES MASTER NIZUMA WANT TO END...?
MR. YUJIRO SAID IT WOULD PROBABLY BE +NATURAL LAST WEEK.

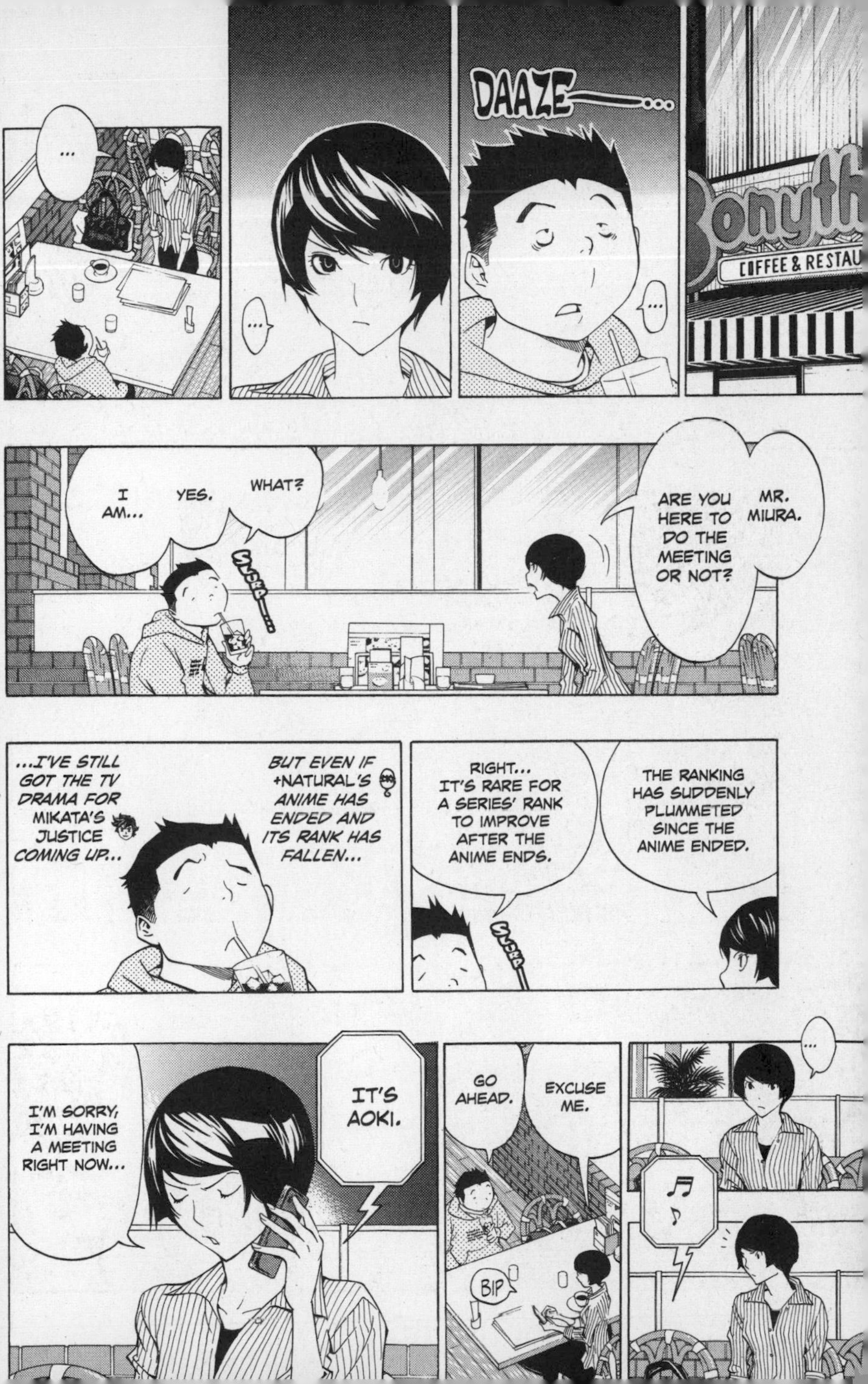
COFFEE & RESTAU
DAAZE———...
...
...
...
MR. MIURA.
ARE YOU HERE TO DO THE MEETING OR NOT?
WHAT?
YES.
I AM...
SLURP...
THE RANKING HAS SUDDENLY PLUMMETED SINCE THE ANIME ENDED.
RIGHT... IT'S RARE FOR A SERIES' RANK TO IMPROVE AFTER THE ANIME ENDS.
SLURP
BUT EVEN IF +NATURAL'S ANIME HAS ENDED AND ITS RANK HAS FALLEN...
...I'VE STILL GOT THE TV DRAMA FOR MIKATA'S JUSTICE COMING UP...
...
EXCUSE ME.
GO AHEAD.
BIP
IT'S AOKI.
I'M SORRY, I'M HAVING A MEETING RIGHT NOW...

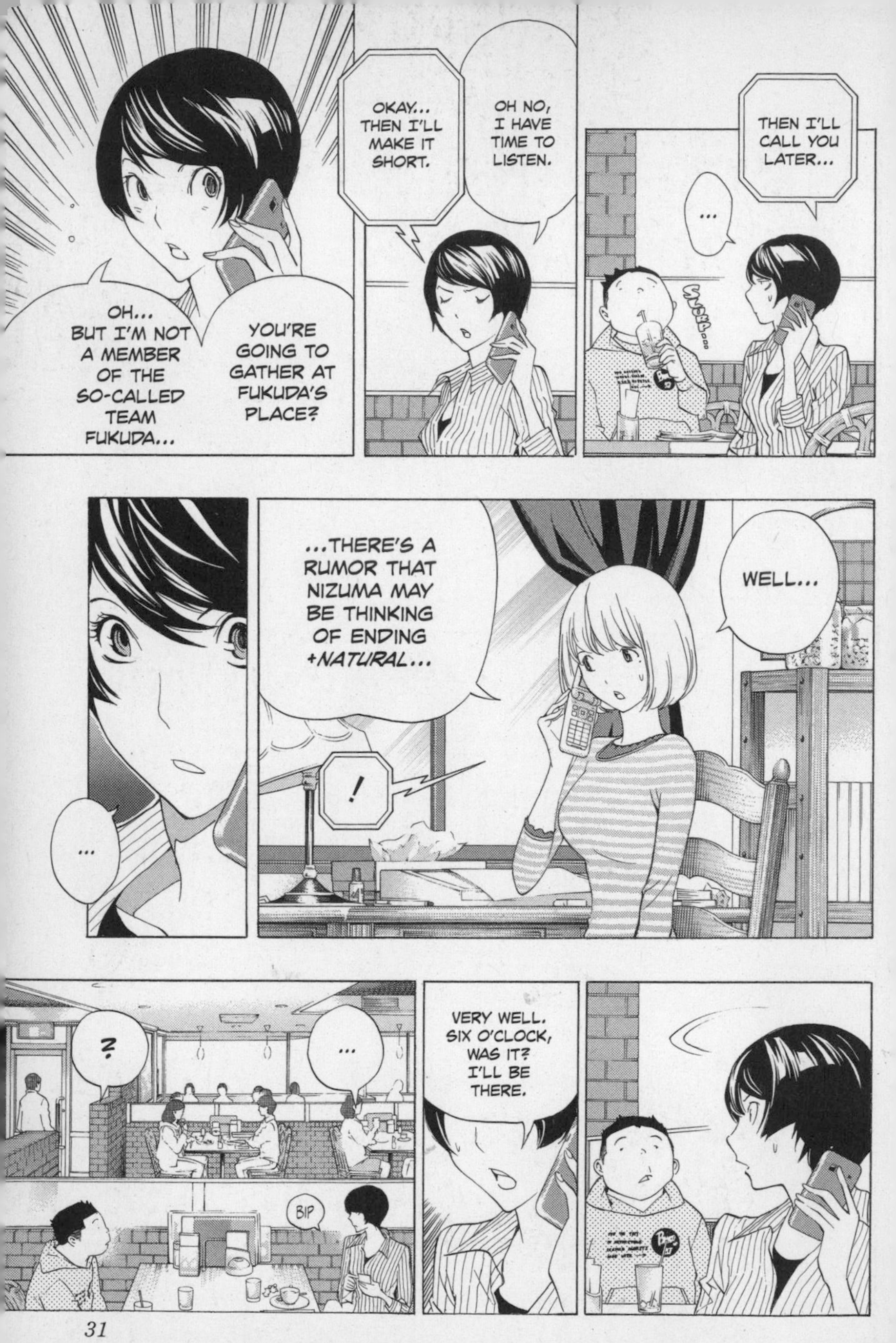
THEN I'LL CALL YOU LATER...
...
OH NO, I HAVE TIME TO LISTEN.
OKAY... THEN I'LL MAKE IT SHORT.
YOU'RE GOING TO GATHER AT FUKUDA'S PLACE?
OH... BUT I'M NOT A MEMBER OF THE SO-CALLED TEAM FUKUDA...
WELL...
...THERE'S A RUMOR THAT NIZUMA MAY BE THINKING OF ENDING +NATURAL...
!
...
VERY WELL. SIX O'CLOCK, WAS IT? I'LL BE THERE.
...
?
BIP

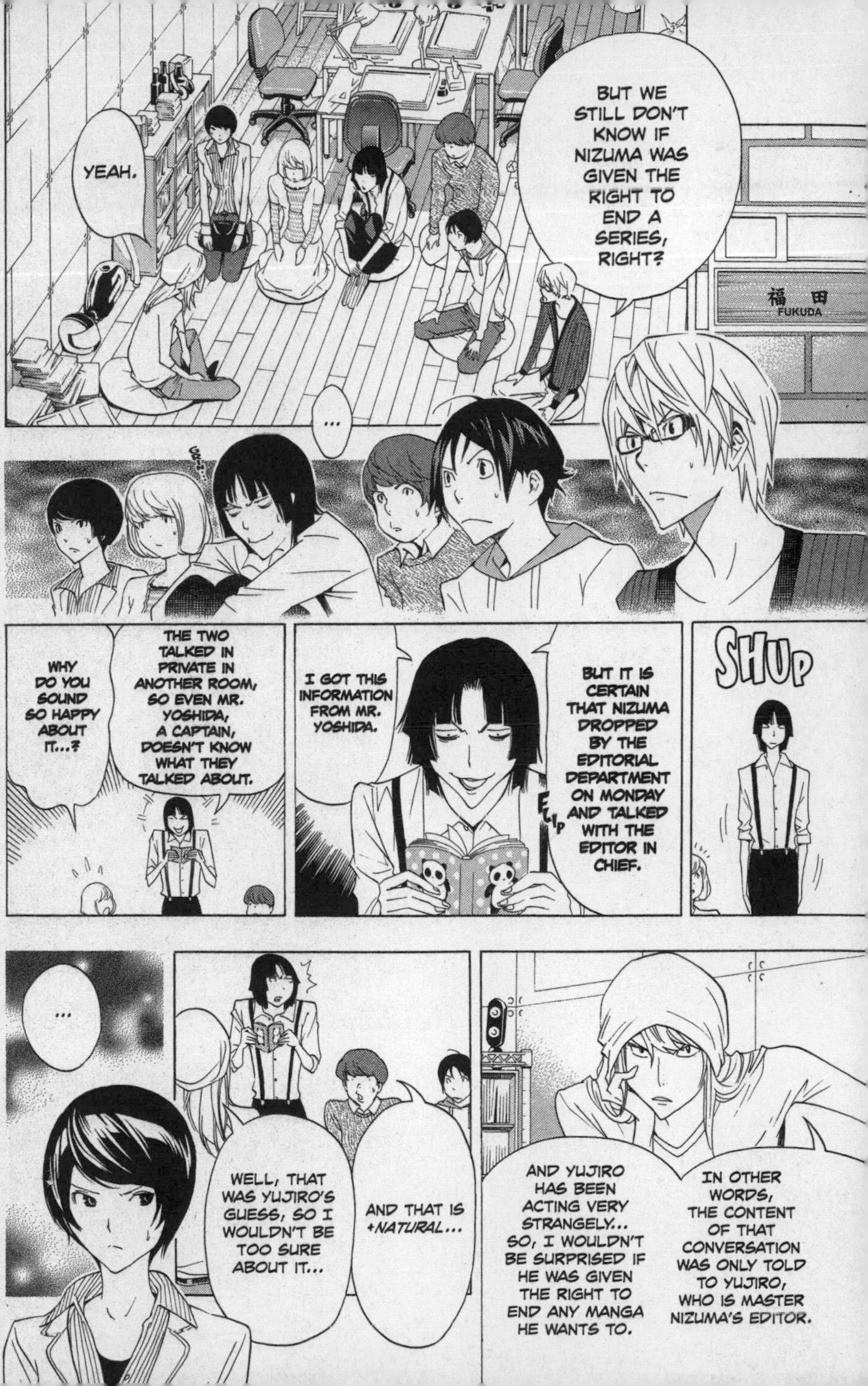
BUT WE STILL DON'T KNOW IF NIZUMA WAS GIVEN THE RIGHT TO END A SERIES, RIGHT?
福田 FUKUDA
YEAH.
...
GRIN...
SHUP
BUT IT IS CERTAIN THAT NIZUMA DROPPED BY THE EDITORIAL DEPARTMENT ON MONDAY AND TALKED WITH THE EDITOR IN CHIEF.
FLIP
I GOT THIS INFORMATION FROM MR. YOSHIDA.
THE TWO TALKED IN PRIVATE IN ANOTHER ROOM, SO EVEN MR. YOSHIDA, A CAPTAIN, DOESN'T KNOW WHAT THEY TALKED ABOUT.
WHY DO YOU SOUND SO HAPPY ABOUT IT...?
IN OTHER WORDS, THE CONTENT OF THAT CONVERSATION WAS ONLY TOLD TO YUJIRO, WHO IS MASTER NIZUMA'S EDITOR.
AND YUJIRO HAS BEEN ACTING VERY STRANGELY... SO, I WOULDN'T BE SURPRISED IF HE WAS GIVEN THE RIGHT TO END ANY MANGA HE WANTS TO.
AND THAT IS *NATURAL...
WELL, THAT WAS YUJIRO'S GUESS, SO I WOULDN'T BE TOO SURE ABOUT IT...
...

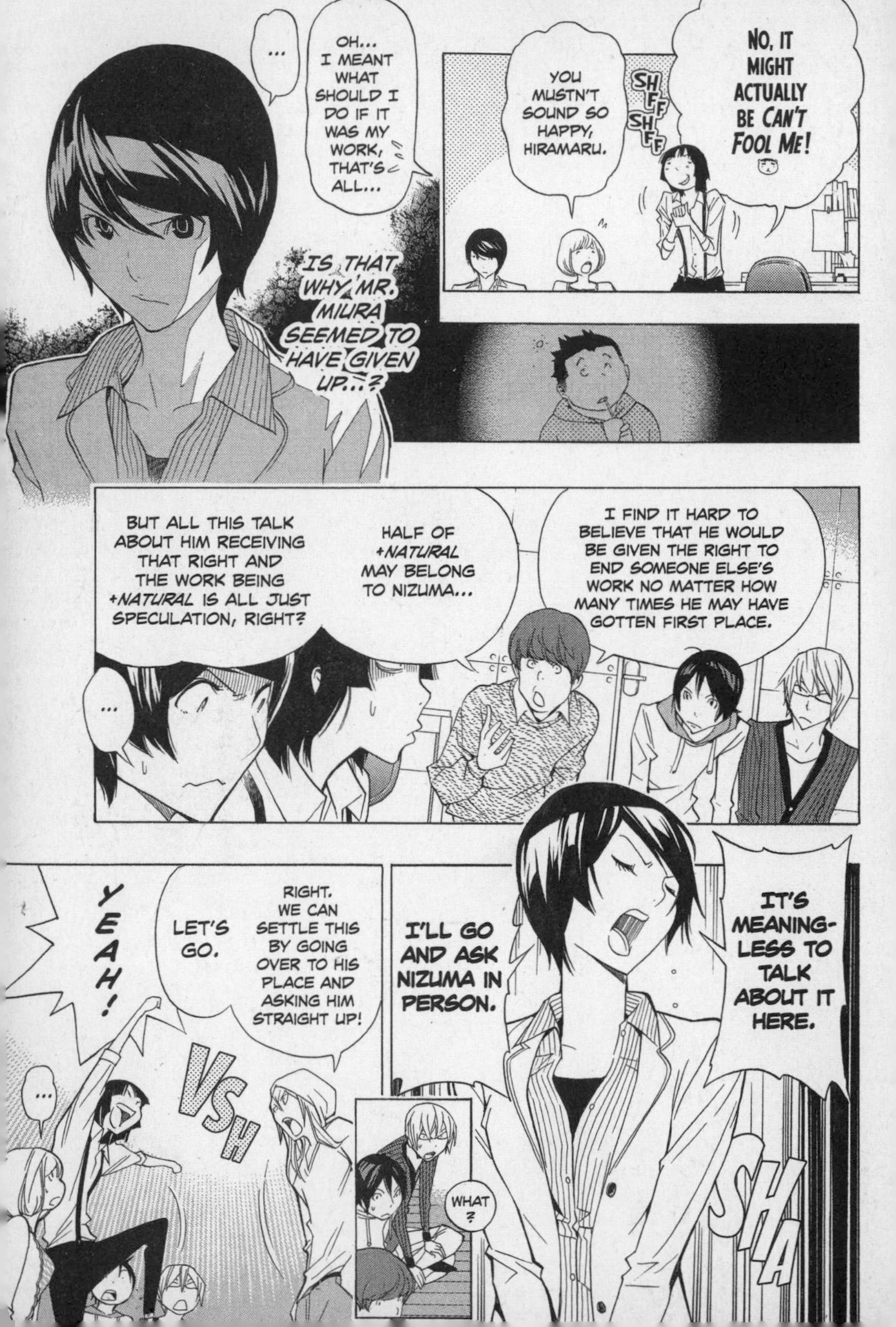
NO, IT MIGHT ACTUALLY BE CAN'T FOOL ME!
SHFF SHFF
YOU MUSTN'T SOUND SO HAPPY, HIRAMARU.
OH... I MEANT WHAT SHOULD I DO IF IT WAS MY WORK, THAT'S ALL...
...
IS THAT WHY MR. MIURA SEEMED TO HAVE GIVEN UP...?
I FIND IT HARD TO BELIEVE THAT HE WOULD BE GIVEN THE RIGHT TO END SOMEONE ELSE'S WORK NO MATTER HOW MANY TIMES HE MAY HAVE GOTTEN FIRST PLACE.
HALF OF +NATURAL MAY BELONG TO NIZUMA...
BUT ALL THIS TALK ABOUT HIM RECEIVING THAT RIGHT AND THE WORK BEING +NATURAL IS ALL JUST SPECULATION, RIGHT?
...
IT'S MEANINGLESS TO TALK ABOUT IT HERE.
I'LL GO AND ASK NIZUMA IN PERSON.
SHA
WHAT?
RIGHT. WE CAN SETTLE THIS BY GOING OVER TO HIS PLACE AND ASKING HIM STRAIGHT UP!
LET'S GO.
YEAH!
VSH
...

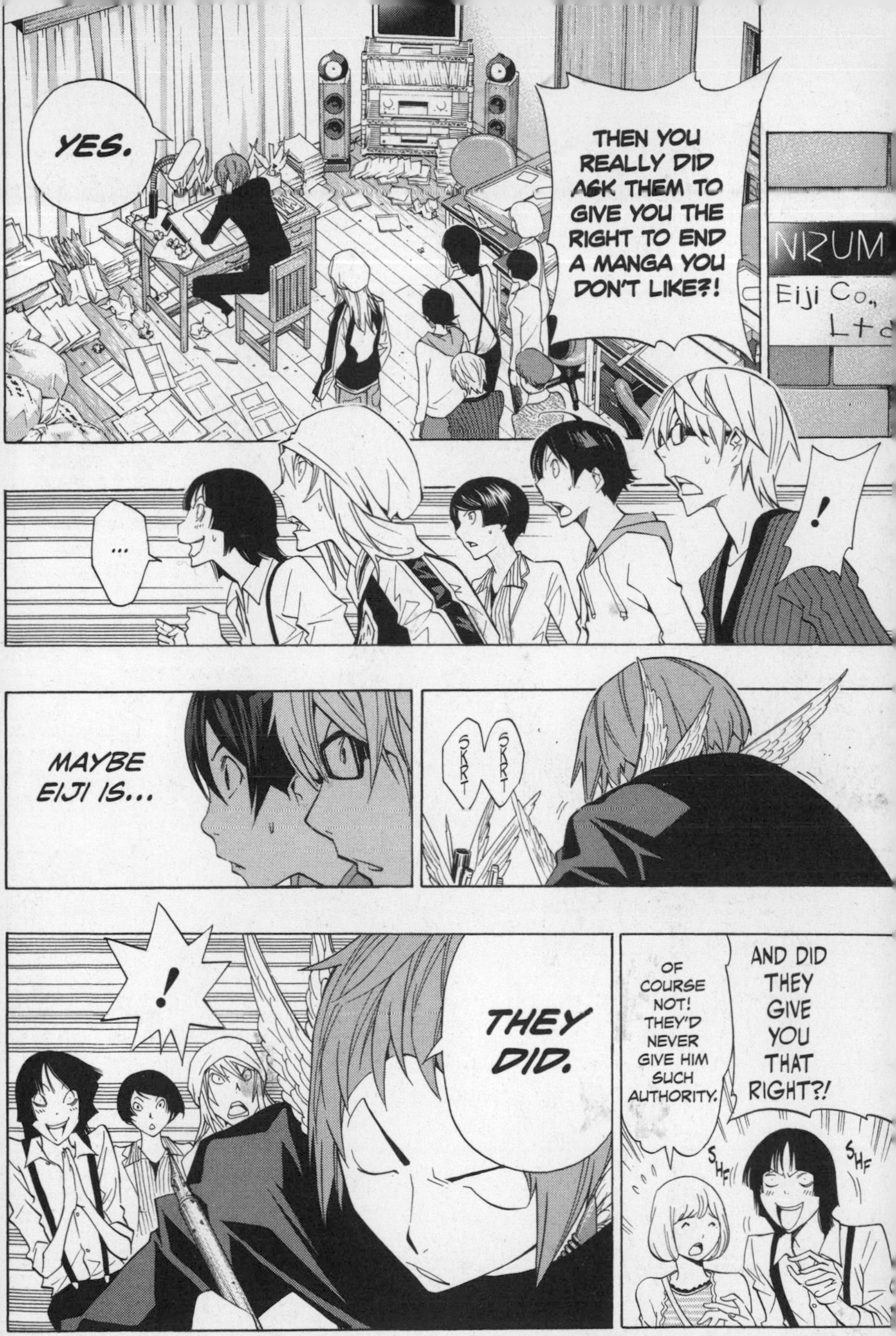
THEN YOU REALLY DID ASK THEM TO GIVE YOU THE RIGHT TO END A MANGA YOU DON'T LIKE?!
Eiji Co.,
YES.
!
...
SKRT
SKRT
MAYBE EIJI IS...
AND DID THEY GIVE YOU THAT RIGHT?!
OF COURSE NOT! THEY'D NEVER GIVE HIM SUCH AUTHORITY.
SHF
SHF
THEY DID.
!

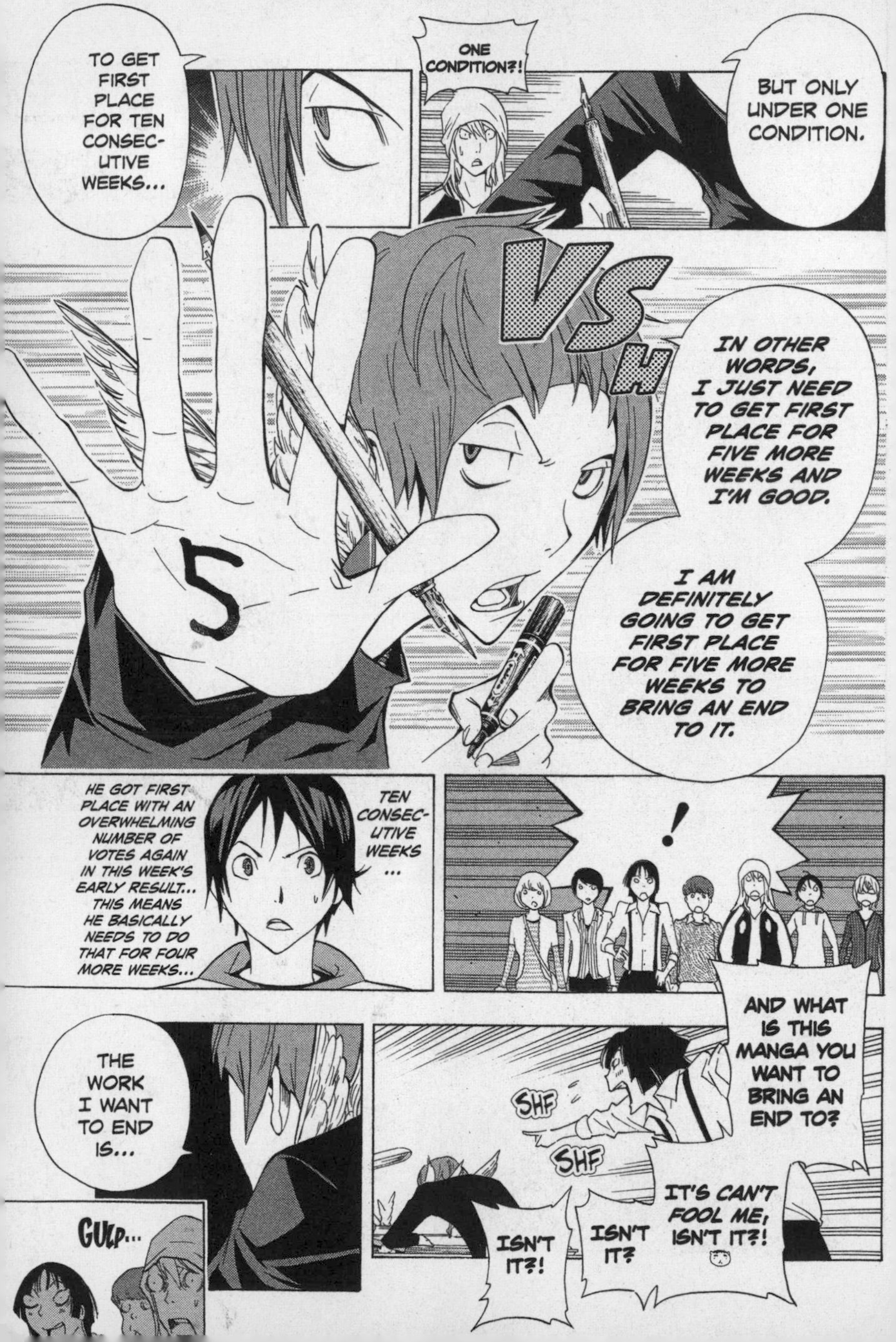

BUT ONLY UNDER ONE CONDITION.
ONE CONDITION?!
TO GET FIRST PLACE FOR TEN CONSECUTIVE WEEKS...
VSH
IN OTHER WORDS, I JUST NEED TO GET FIRST PLACE FOR FIVE MORE WEEKS AND I'M GOOD.
I AM DEFINITELY GOING TO GET FIRST PLACE FOR FIVE MORE WEEKS TO BRING AN END TO IT.
5
!
TEN CONSECUTIVE WEEKS ...
HE GOT FIRST PLACE WITH AN OVERWHELMING NUMBER OF VOTES AGAIN IN THIS WEEK'S EARLY RESULT... THIS MEANS HE BASICALLY NEEDS TO DO THAT FOR FOUR MORE WEEKS...
AND WHAT IS THIS MANGA YOU WANT TO BRING AN END TO?
SHF
SHF
IT'S CAN'T FOOL ME, ISN'T IT?!
ISN'T IT?
ISN'T IT?!
THE WORK I WANT TO END IS...
GULP...

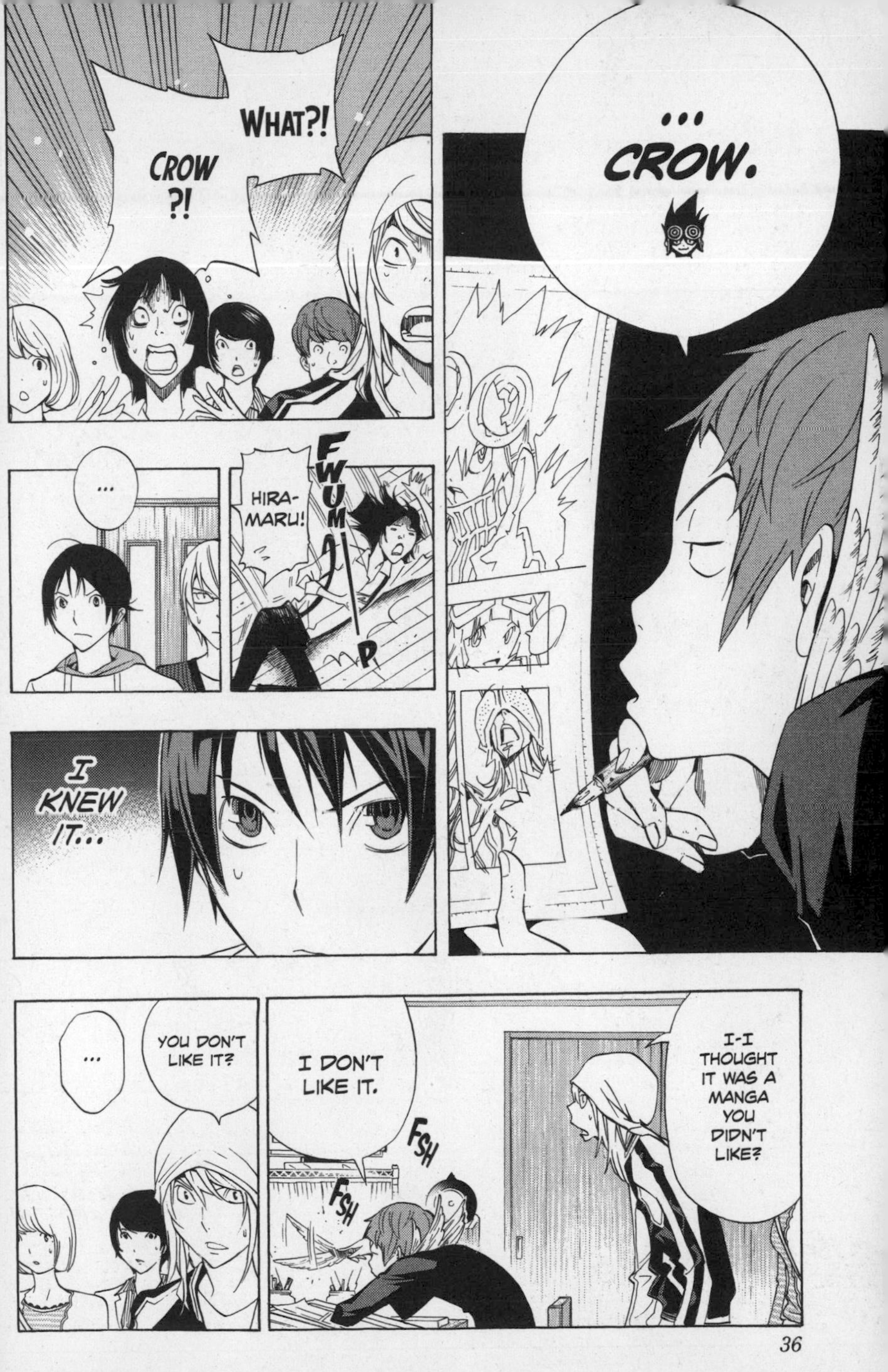
... CROW.
WHAT?!
CROW ?!
HIRA-MARU!
FWUMP
...
I KNEW IT...
I-I THOUGHT IT WAS A MANGA YOU DIDN'T LIKE?
I DON'T LIKE IT.
FSH
FSH
YOU DON'T LIKE IT?
...

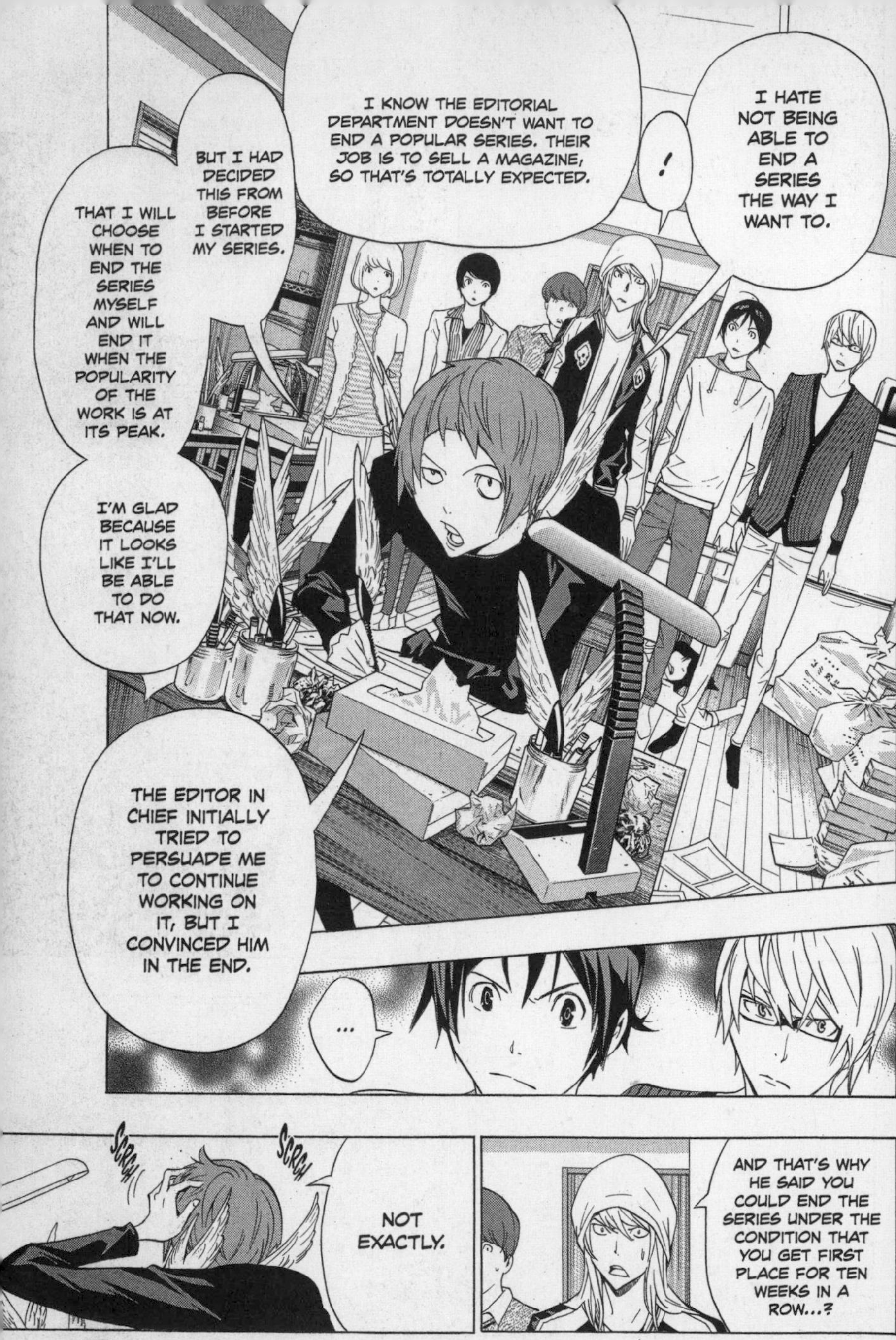
I HATE NOT BEING ABLE TO END A SERIES THE WAY I WANT TO.
!
I KNOW THE EDITORIAL DEPARTMENT DOESN'T WANT TO END A POPULAR SERIES. THEIR JOB IS TO SELL A MAGAZINE, SO THAT'S TOTALLY EXPECTED.
BUT I HAD DECIDED THIS FROM BEFORE I STARTED MY SERIES.
THAT I WILL CHOOSE WHEN TO END THE SERIES MYSELF AND WILL END IT WHEN THE POPULARITY OF THE WORK IS AT ITS PEAK.
I'M GLAD BECAUSE IT LOOKS LIKE I'LL BE ABLE TO DO THAT NOW.
THE EDITOR IN CHIEF INITIALLY TRIED TO PERSUADE ME TO CONTINUE WORKING ON IT, BUT I CONVINCED HIM IN THE END.
...
AND THAT'S WHY HE SAID YOU COULD END THE SERIES UNDER THE CONDITION THAT YOU GET FIRST PLACE FOR TEN WEEKS IN A ROW...?
SCRCH
SCRCH
NOT EXACTLY.

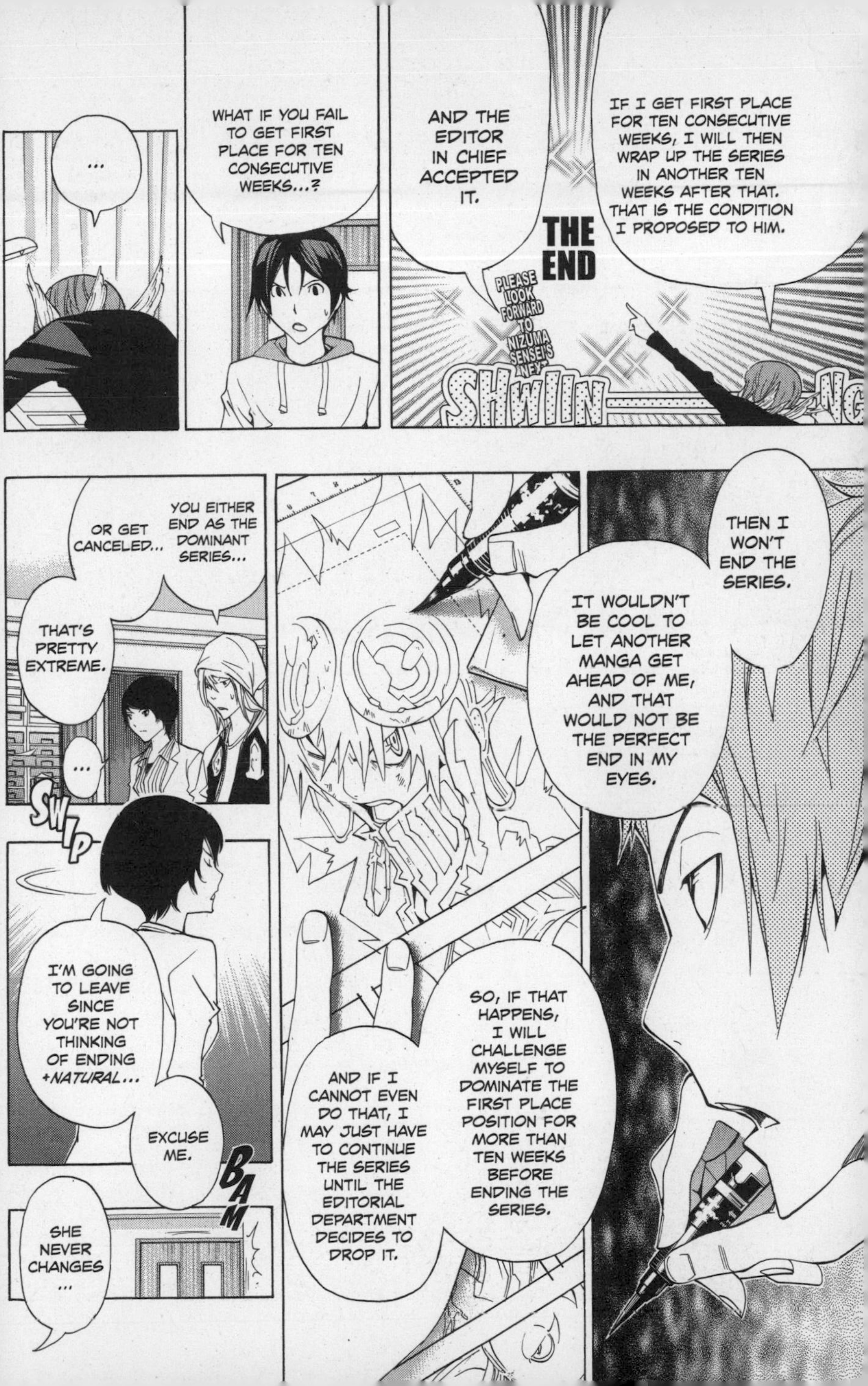
IF I GET FIRST PLACE FOR TEN CONSECUTIVE WEEKS, I WILL THEN WRAP UP THE SERIES IN ANOTHER TEN WEEKS AFTER THAT. THAT IS THE CONDITION I PROPOSED TO HIM.
AND THE EDITOR IN CHIEF ACCEPTED IT.
THE END
PLEASE LOOK FORWARD TO NIZUMA SENSEI'S NEX
SHWIIN-NG
WHAT IF YOU FAIL TO GET FIRST PLACE FOR TEN CONSECUTIVE WEEKS...?
...
THEN I WON'T END THE SERIES.
IT WOULDN'T BE COOL TO LET ANOTHER MANGA GET AHEAD OF ME, AND THAT WOULD NOT BE THE PERFECT END IN MY EYES.
SO, IF THAT HAPPENS, I WILL CHALLENGE MYSELF TO DOMINATE THE FIRST PLACE POSITION FOR MORE THAN TEN WEEKS BEFORE ENDING THE SERIES.
AND IF I CANNOT EVEN DO THAT, I MAY JUST HAVE TO CONTINUE THE SERIES UNTIL THE EDITORIAL DEPARTMENT DECIDES TO DROP IT.
YOU EITHER END AS THE DOMINANT SERIES...
OR GET CANCELED...
THAT'S PRETTY EXTREME.
...
SWIP
I'M GOING TO LEAVE SINCE YOU'RE NOT THINKING OF ENDING +NATURAL...
EXCUSE ME.
BAM
SHE NEVER CHANGES ...

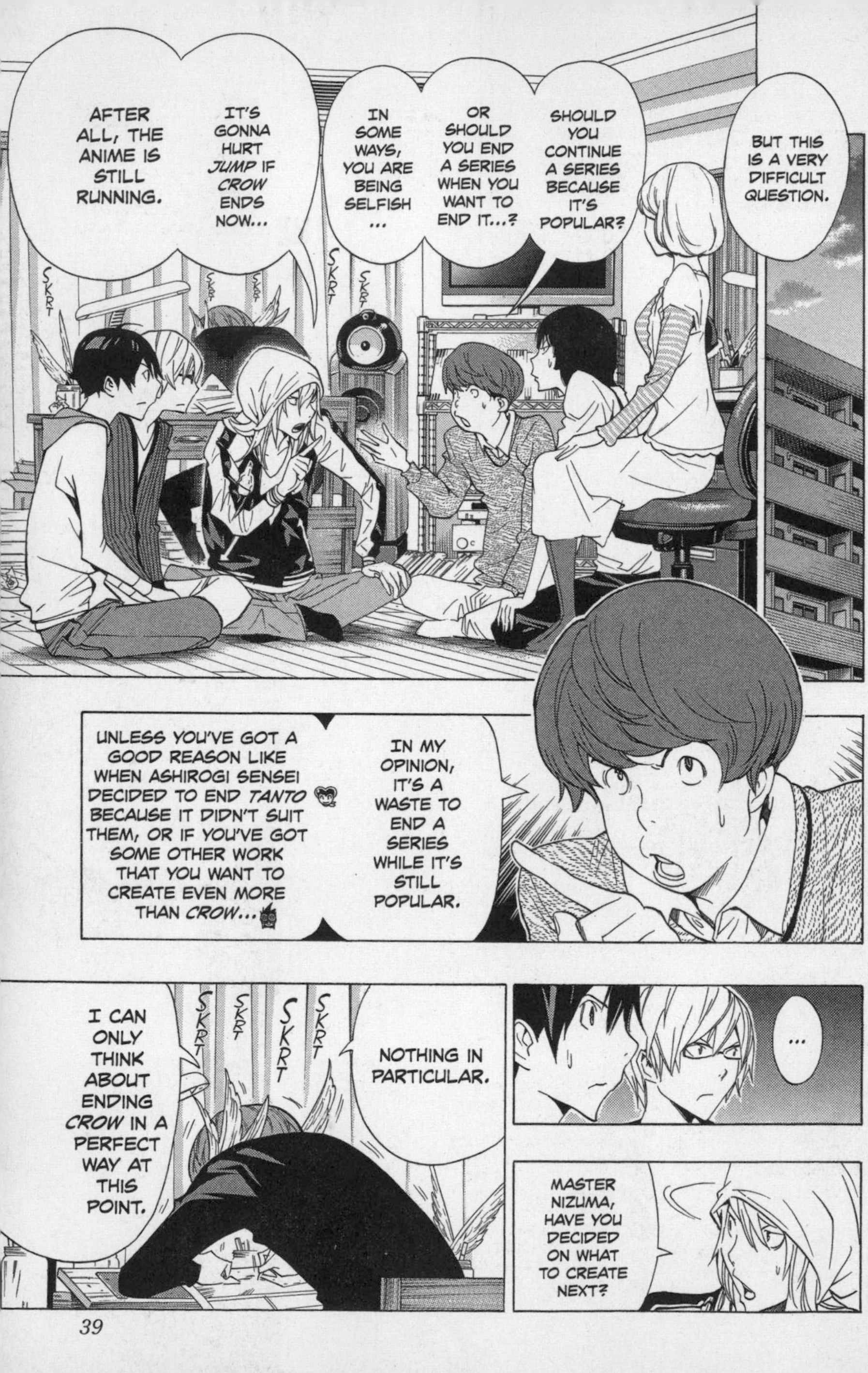
BUT THIS IS A VERY DIFFICULT QUESTION.
SHOULD YOU CONTINUE A SERIES BECAUSE IT'S POPULAR?
OR SHOULD YOU END A SERIES WHEN YOU WANT TO END IT...?
IN SOME WAYS, YOU ARE BEING SELFISH...
IT'S GONNA HURT JUMP IF CROW ENDS NOW...
AFTER ALL, THE ANIME IS STILL RUNNING.
SKRT
SKRT
SKRT
SKRT
SKRT
IN MY OPINION, IT'S A WASTE TO END A SERIES WHILE IT'S STILL POPULAR.
UNLESS YOU'VE GOT A GOOD REASON LIKE WHEN ASHIROGI SENSEI DECIDED TO END TANTO BECAUSE IT DIDN'T SUIT THEM, OR IF YOU'VE GOT SOME OTHER WORK THAT YOU WANT TO CREATE EVEN MORE THAN CROW...
...
MASTER NIZUMA, HAVE YOU DECIDED ON WHAT TO CREATE NEXT?
SKRT
SKRT
SKRT
SKRT
NOTHING IN PARTICULAR.
I CAN ONLY THINK ABOUT ENDING CROW IN A PERFECT WAY AT THIS POINT.

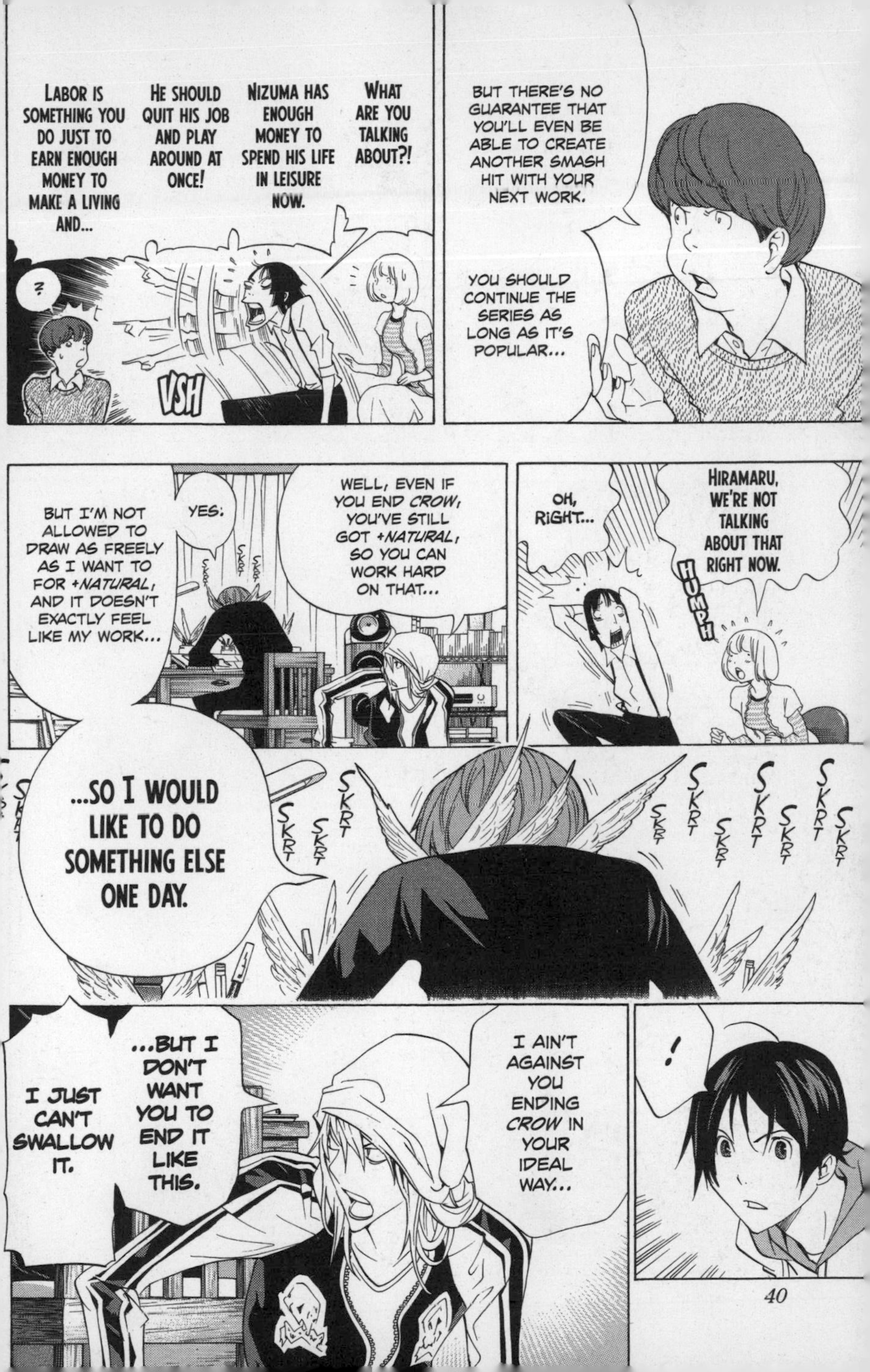
BUT THERE'S NO GUARANTEE THAT YOU'LL EVEN BE ABLE TO CREATE ANOTHER SMASH HIT WITH YOUR NEXT WORK.
YOU SHOULD CONTINUE THE SERIES AS LONG AS IT'S POPULAR...
WHAT ARE YOU TALKING ABOUT?!
NIZUMA HAS ENOUGH MONEY TO SPEND HIS LIFE IN LEISURE NOW.
HE SHOULD QUIT HIS JOB AND PLAY AROUND AT ONCE!
LABOR IS SOMETHING YOU DO JUST TO EARN ENOUGH MONEY TO MAKE A LIVING AND...
?
VSH
HIRAMARU, WE'RE NOT TALKING ABOUT THAT RIGHT NOW.
HUMPH
OH, RIGHT...
WELL, EVEN IF YOU END *CROW*, YOU'VE STILL GOT *+NATURAL*, SO YOU CAN WORK HARD ON THAT...
YES.
SKRT SKRT
BUT I'M NOT ALLOWED TO DRAW AS FREELY AS I WANT TO FOR *+NATURAL*, AND IT DOESN'T EXACTLY FEEL LIKE MY WORK...
SKRT SKRT SKRT SKRT SKRT SKRT SKRT SKRT SKRT SKRT SKRT
...SO I WOULD LIKE TO DO SOMETHING ELSE ONE DAY.
!
I AIN'T AGAINST YOU ENDING *CROW* IN YOUR IDEAL WAY...
...BUT I DON'T WANT YOU TO END IT LIKE THIS.
I JUST CAN'T SWALLOW IT.

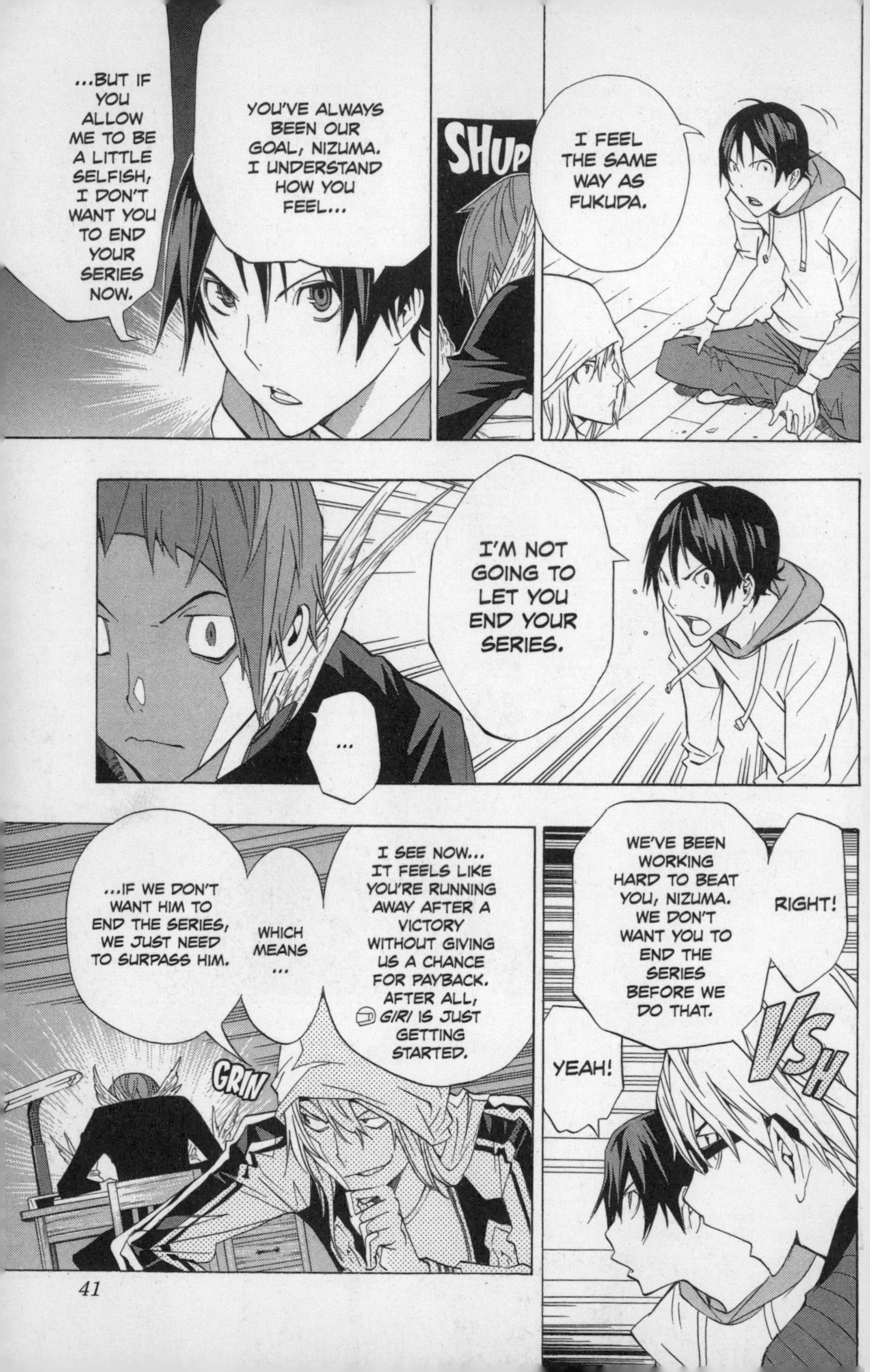
I FEEL THE SAME WAY AS FUKUDA.
SHUP
YOU'VE ALWAYS BEEN OUR GOAL, NIZUMA. I UNDERSTAND HOW YOU FEEL...
...BUT IF YOU ALLOW ME TO BE A LITTLE SELFISH, I DON'T WANT YOU TO END YOUR SERIES NOW.
I'M NOT GOING TO LET YOU END YOUR SERIES.
...
WE'VE BEEN WORKING HARD TO BEAT YOU, NIZUMA. WE DON'T WANT YOU TO END THE SERIES BEFORE WE DO THAT.
RIGHT!
VSH
YEAH!
I SEE NOW... IT FEELS LIKE YOU'RE RUNNING AWAY AFTER A VICTORY WITHOUT GIVING US A CHANCE FOR PAYBACK. AFTER ALL, *GIRI* IS JUST GETTING STARTED.
WHICH MEANS ...
...IF WE DON'T WANT HIM TO END THE SERIES, WE JUST NEED TO SURPASS HIM.
GRIN

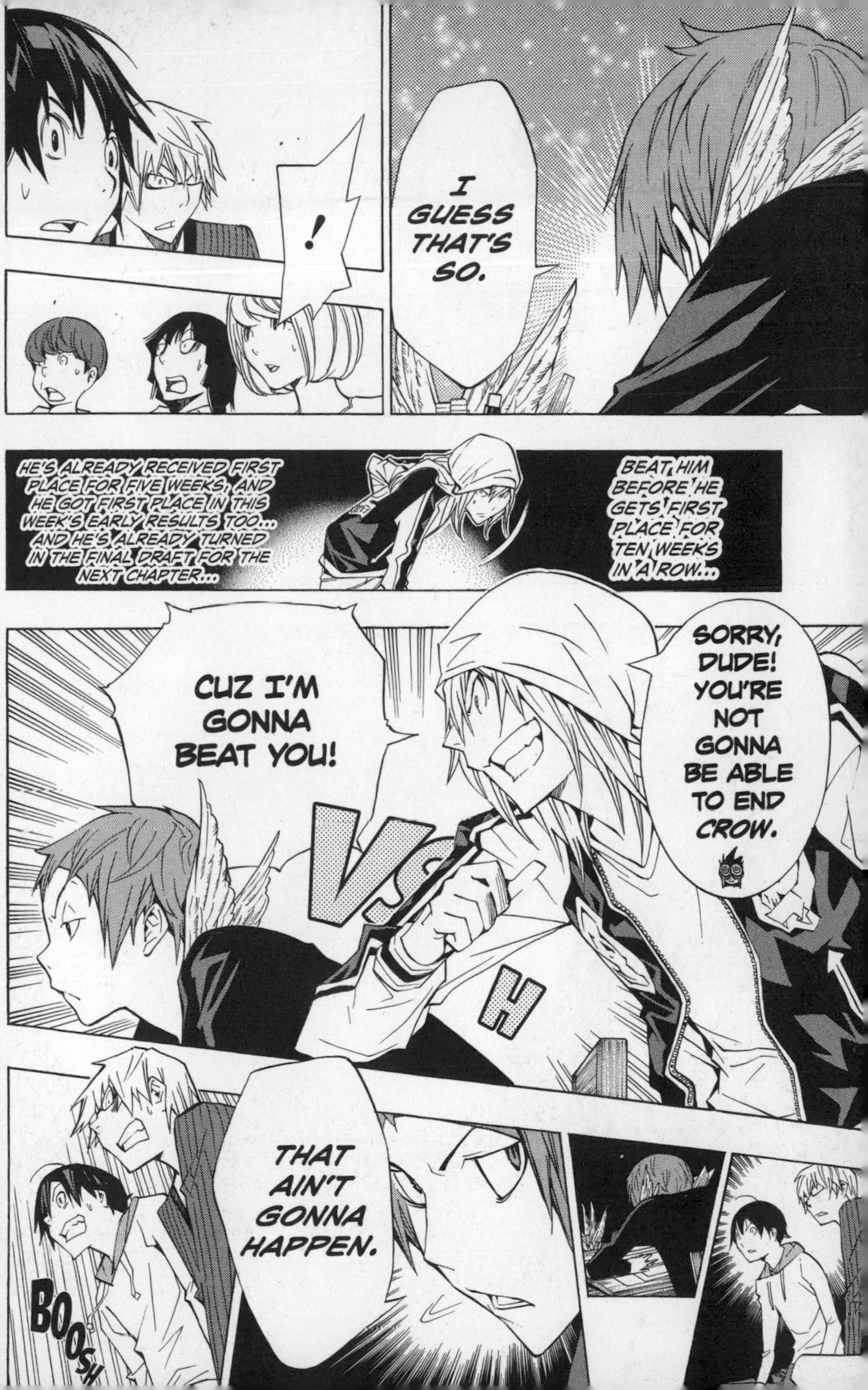

I GUESS THAT'S SO.
!
BEAT HIM BEFORE HE GETS FIRST PLACE FOR TEN WEEKS IN A ROW...
HE'S ALREADY RECEIVED FIRST PLACE FOR FIVE WEEKS, AND HE GOT FIRST PLACE IN THIS WEEK'S EARLY RESULTS TOO... AND HE'S ALREADY TURNED IN THE FINAL DRAFT FOR THE NEXT CHAPTER...
SORRY, DUDE! YOU'RE NOT GONNA BE ABLE TO END CROW.
CUZ I'M GONNA BEAT YOU!
VS
H
THAT AIN'T GONNA HAPPEN.
BOOSH

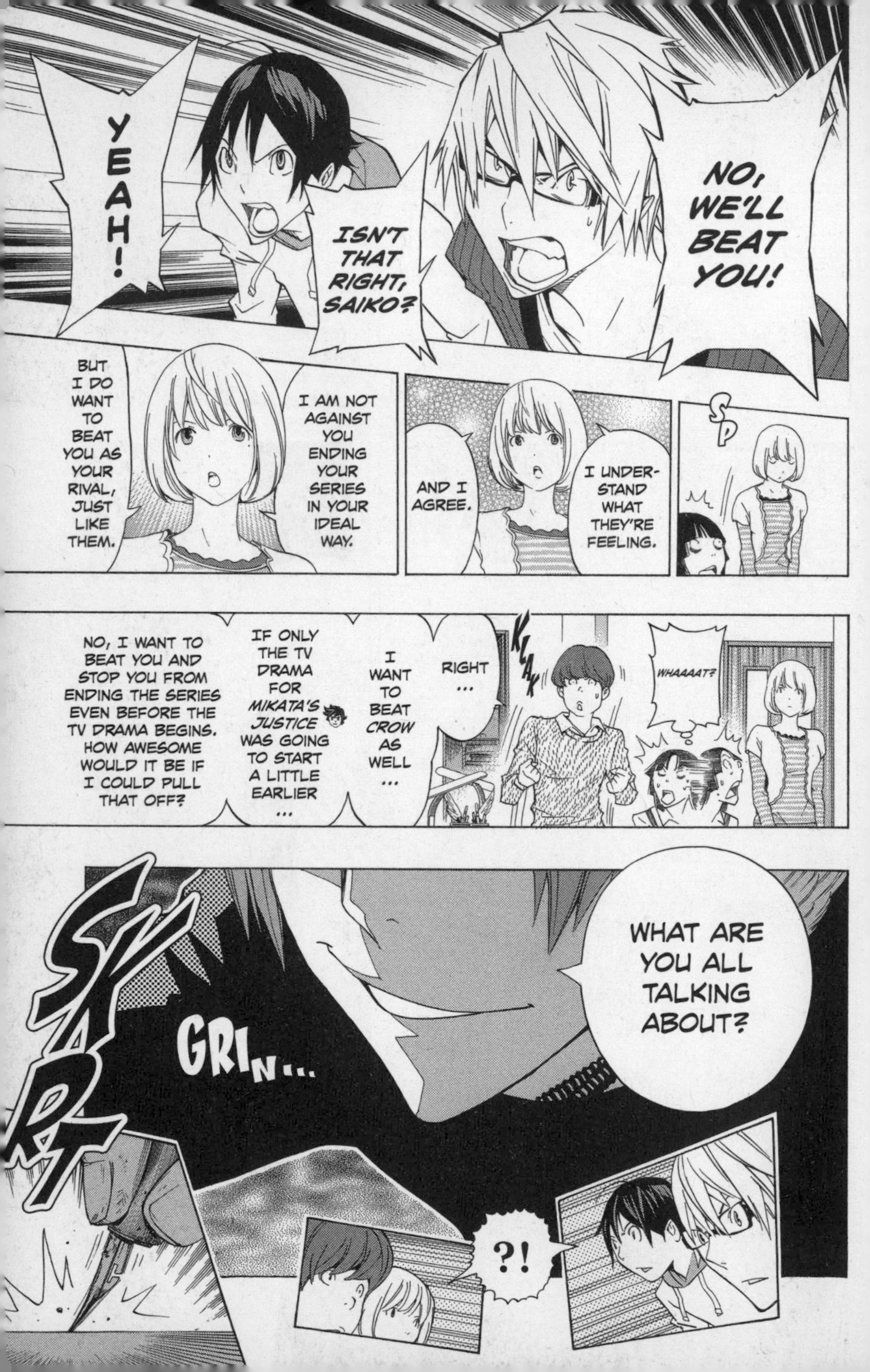
NO, WE'LL BEAT YOU!
ISN'T THAT RIGHT, SAIKO?
YEAH!
SP
I UNDER-STAND WHAT THEY'RE FEELING.
AND I AGREE.
I AM NOT AGAINST YOU ENDING YOUR SERIES IN YOUR IDEAL WAY.
BUT I DO WANT TO BEAT YOU AS YOUR RIVAL, JUST LIKE THEM.
WHAAAAT?
KLAK
RIGHT ...
I WANT TO BEAT CROW AS WELL ...
IF ONLY THE TV DRAMA FOR MIKATA'S JUSTICE WAS GOING TO START A LITTLE EARLIER ...
NO, I WANT TO BEAT YOU AND STOP YOU FROM ENDING THE SERIES EVEN BEFORE THE TV DRAMA BEGINS. HOW AWESOME WOULD IT BE IF I COULD PULL THAT OFF?
WHAT ARE YOU ALL TALKING ABOUT?
GRIN...
?!

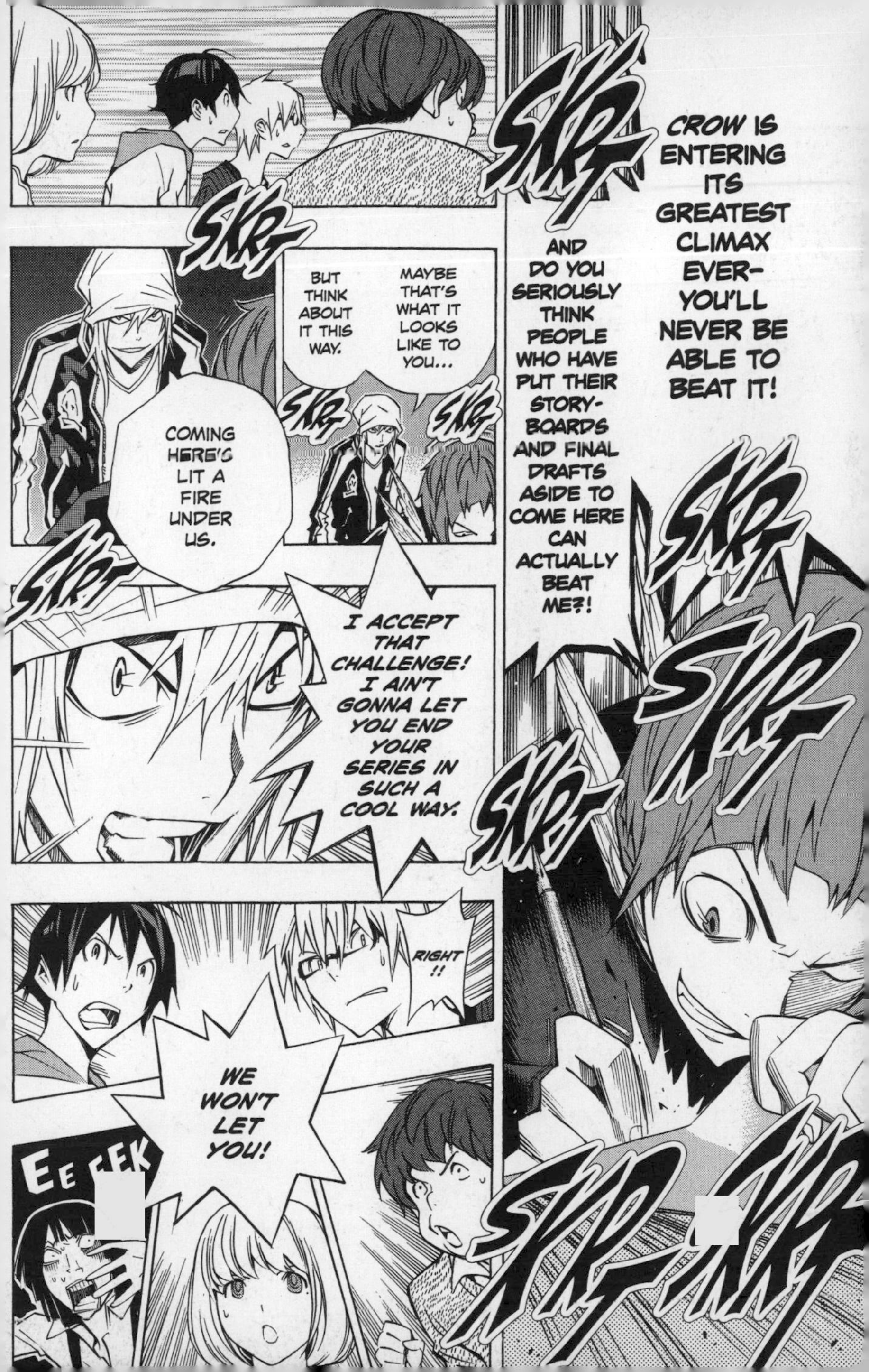
SKRT
CROW IS ENTERING ITS GREATEST CLIMAX EVER–YOU'LL NEVER BE ABLE TO BEAT IT!
AND DO YOU SERIOUSLY THINK PEOPLE WHO HAVE PUT THEIR STORY-BOARDS AND FINAL DRAFTS ASIDE TO COME HERE CAN ACTUALLY BEAT ME?!
SKRT
SKRT
SKRT
SKRT
SKRT
MAYBE THAT'S WHAT IT LOOKS LIKE TO YOU...
BUT THINK ABOUT IT THIS WAY.
SKRT
SKRT
SKRT
COMING HERE'S LIT A FIRE UNDER US.
SKRT
I ACCEPT THAT CHALLENGE! I AIN'T GONNA LET YOU END YOUR SERIES IN SUCH A COOL WAY.
RIGHT!!
WE WON'T LET YOU!
EEEEK

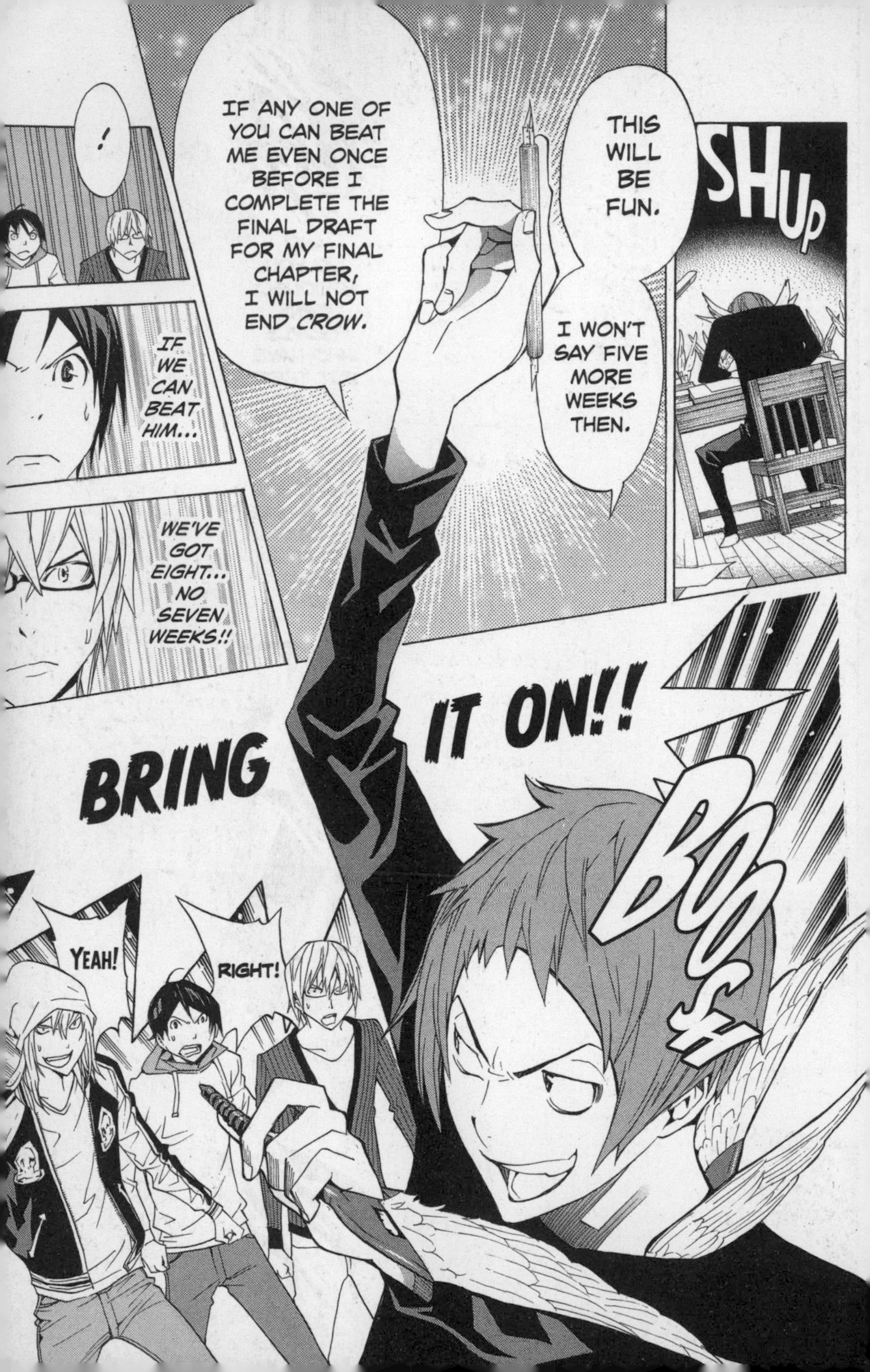
SHUP
THIS WILL BE FUN.
IF ANY ONE OF YOU CAN BEAT ME EVEN ONCE BEFORE I COMPLETE THE FINAL DRAFT FOR MY FINAL CHAPTER, I WILL NOT END *CROW*.
I WON'T SAY FIVE MORE WEEKS THEN.
!
IF WE CAN BEAT HIM...
WE'VE GOT EIGHT... NO SEVEN WEEKS!!
BOOSH
BRING IT ON!!
RIGHT!
YEAH!

OHBA'S STORYBOARD

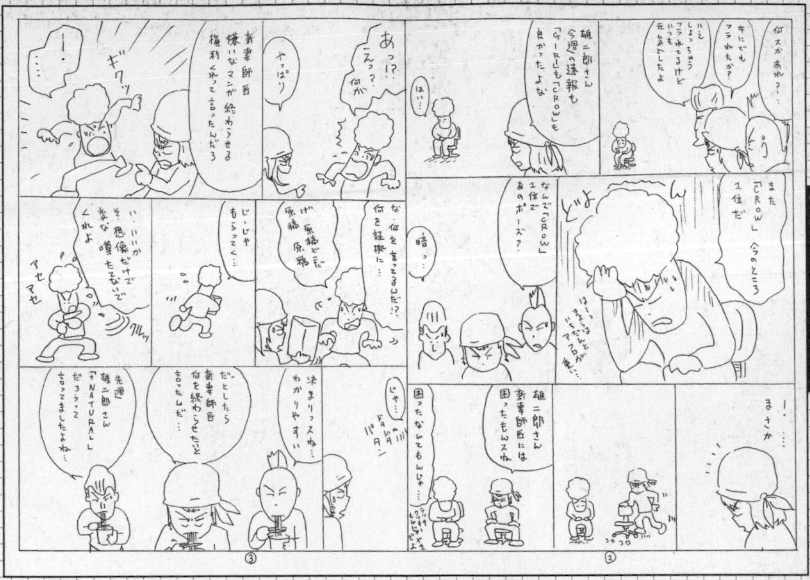

何スかあれ？…
女にでもフラれたか？
いえ しょっちゅうフラれてるけど いつも元気でしたよ
雄二郎さん 今週の速報も「GIRL」も「CROW」も良かったよな
はい…
また「CROW」今のところ1位だ
どよ
なんで「CROW」1位であのポーズ？
暗っ…
まさか
雄二郎さん 新妻師匠には困ったもんスね
困ったなんてもんじゃ…
②
あっ!? えっ？ 何か
やっぱり
新妻師匠 嫌いなマンガが終わらせる権利くれって言ったんだろ
ギクッ
な、何を言ってるんだ!? 何を証拠に…
げ 原稿どこ 原稿 原稿
じ、じゃもらってく…
い、いいか 変な想像だけで噂たてないでくれよ
アセアセ
じゃ…
決まりっスね… わかりやすい
だとしたら 新妻師匠 何を終わらせたいと言ったんだ…
先週 雄二郎さん「NATURAL」だろうって言ってましたよね…
③

OBATA'S STORYBOARD

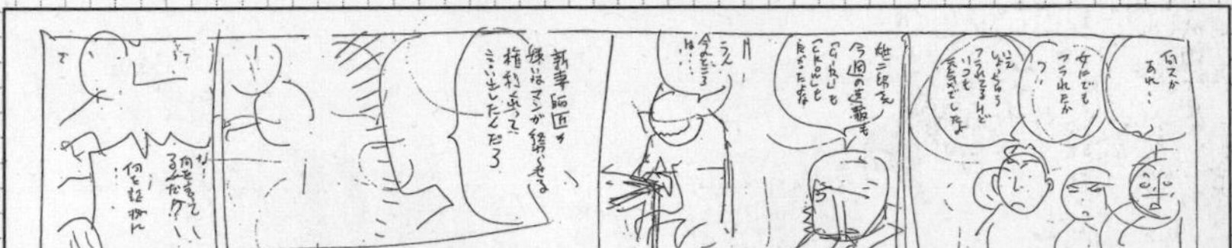

2
3

COMPLETE!

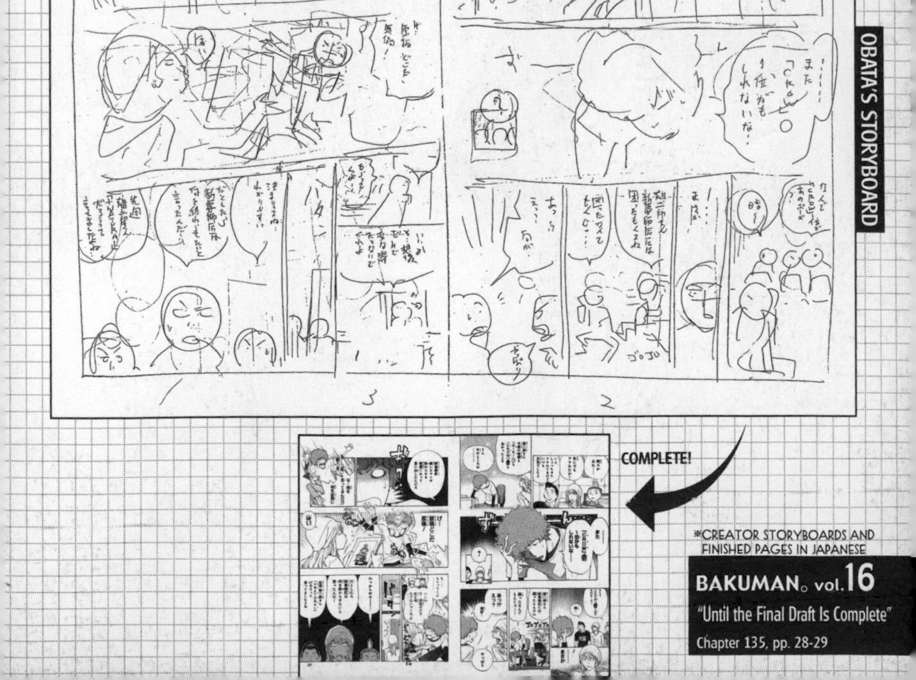

※CREATOR STORYBOARDS AND FINISHED PAGES IN JAPANESE

BAKUMAN。vol.16

"Until the Final Draft Is Complete"

Chapter 135, pp. 28-29

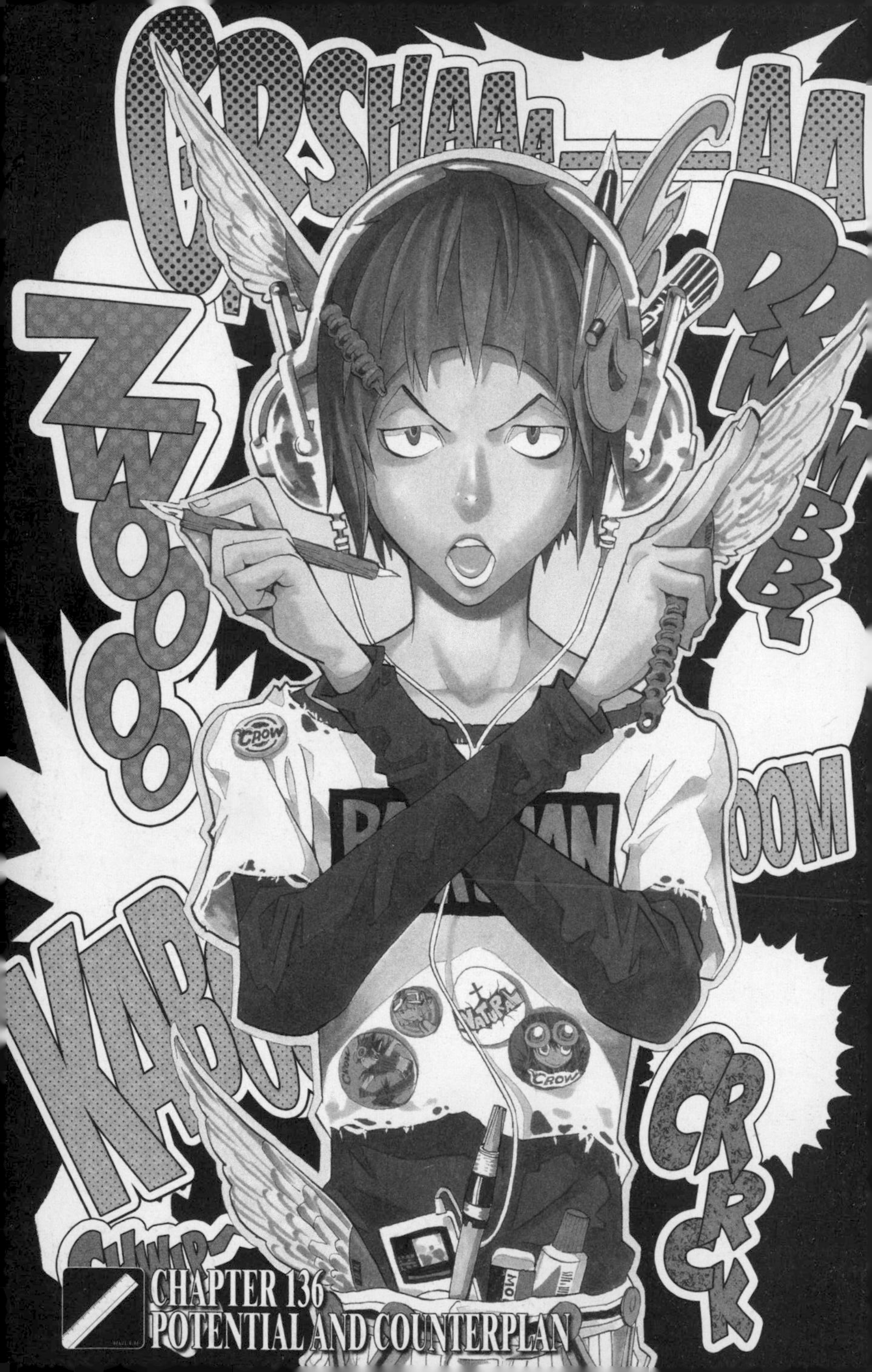
ZWOOOO
OOM
CROW
NATURAL
CROW

CHAPTER 136
POTENTIAL AND COUNTERPLAN

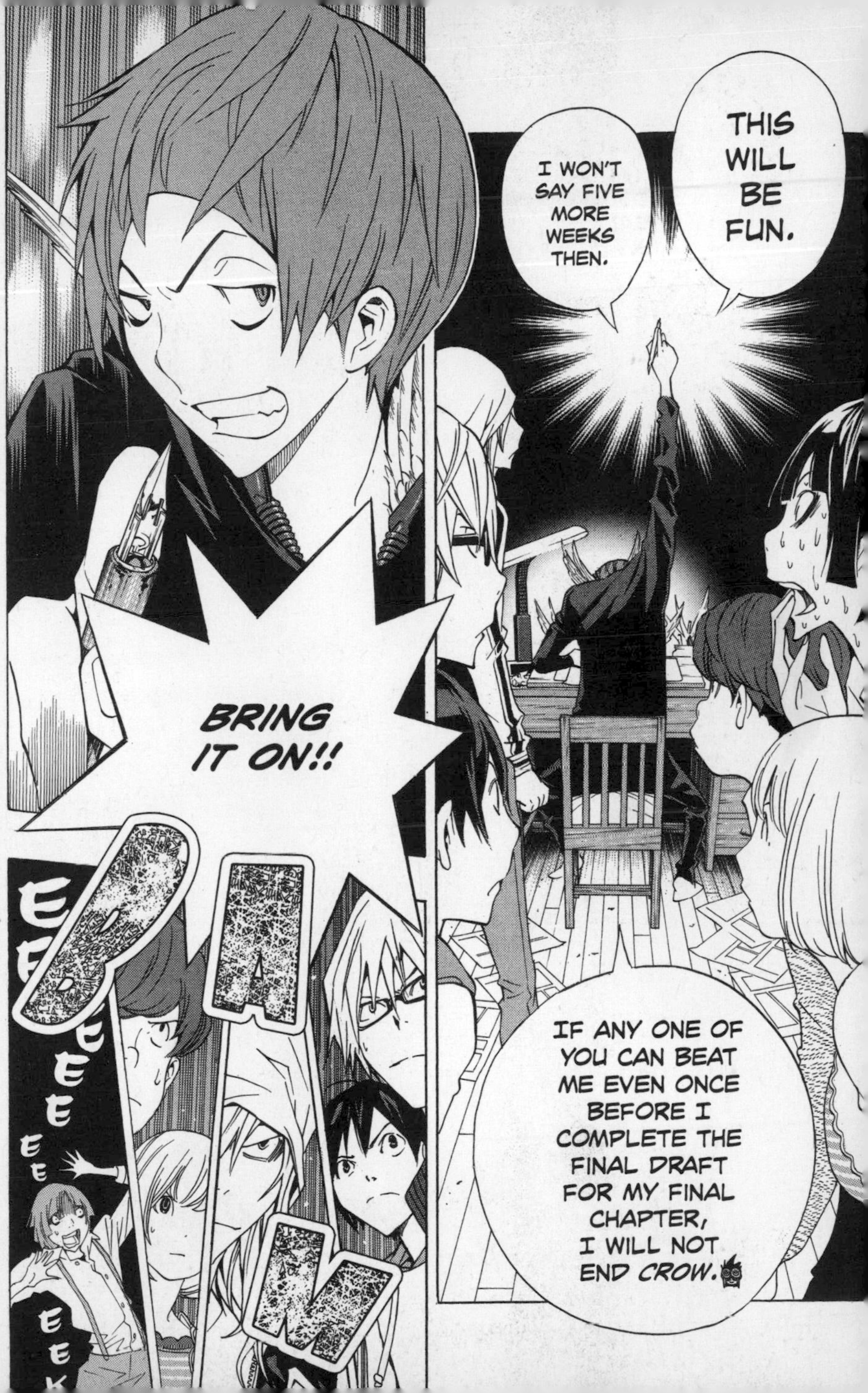
THIS WILL BE FUN.
I WON'T SAY FIVE MORE WEEKS THEN.
IF ANY ONE OF YOU CAN BEAT ME EVEN ONCE BEFORE I COMPLETE THE FINAL DRAFT FOR MY FINAL CHAPTER, I WILL NOT END *CROW.*
BRING IT ON!!
BAM
EEEEEEEEEEEK

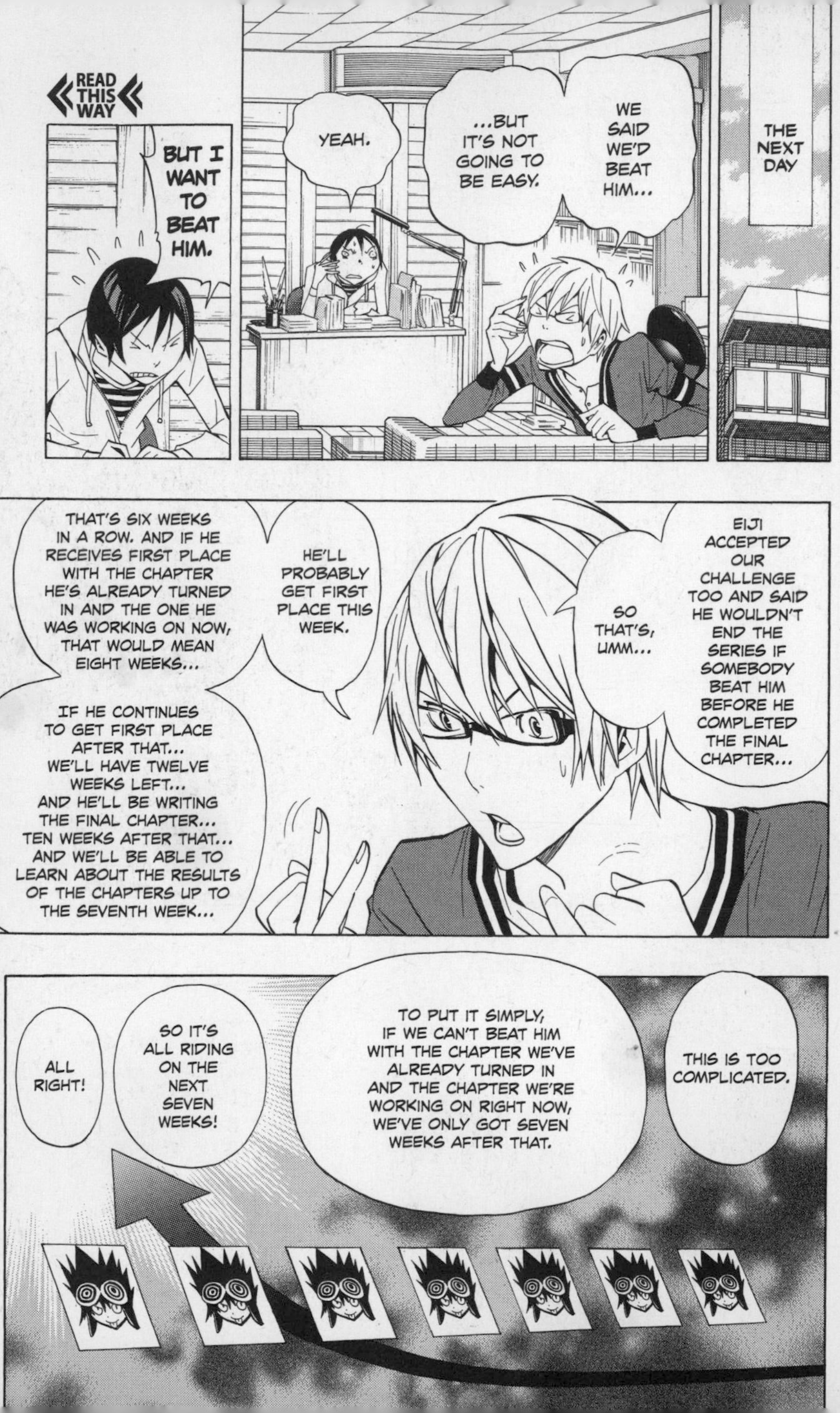
READ THIS WAY
THE NEXT DAY
WE SAID WE'D BEAT HIM...
...BUT IT'S NOT GOING TO BE EASY.
YEAH.
BUT I WANT TO BEAT HIM.
EIJI ACCEPTED OUR CHALLENGE TOO AND SAID HE WOULDN'T END THE SERIES IF SOMEBODY BEAT HIM BEFORE HE COMPLETED THE FINAL CHAPTER...
SO THAT'S, UMM...
HE'LL PROBABLY GET FIRST PLACE THIS WEEK.
THAT'S SIX WEEKS IN A ROW. AND IF HE RECEIVES FIRST PLACE WITH THE CHAPTER HE'S ALREADY TURNED IN AND THE ONE HE WAS WORKING ON NOW, THAT WOULD MEAN EIGHT WEEKS...
IF HE CONTINUES TO GET FIRST PLACE AFTER THAT... WE'LL HAVE TWELVE WEEKS LEFT... AND HE'LL BE WRITING THE FINAL CHAPTER... TEN WEEKS AFTER THAT... AND WE'LL BE ABLE TO LEARN ABOUT THE RESULTS OF THE CHAPTERS UP TO THE SEVENTH WEEK...
THIS IS TOO COMPLICATED.
TO PUT IT SIMPLY, IF WE CAN'T BEAT HIM WITH THE CHAPTER WE'VE ALREADY TURNED IN AND THE CHAPTER WE'RE WORKING ON RIGHT NOW, WE'VE ONLY GOT SEVEN WEEKS AFTER THAT.
SO IT'S ALL RIDING ON THE NEXT SEVEN WEEKS!
ALL RIGHT!

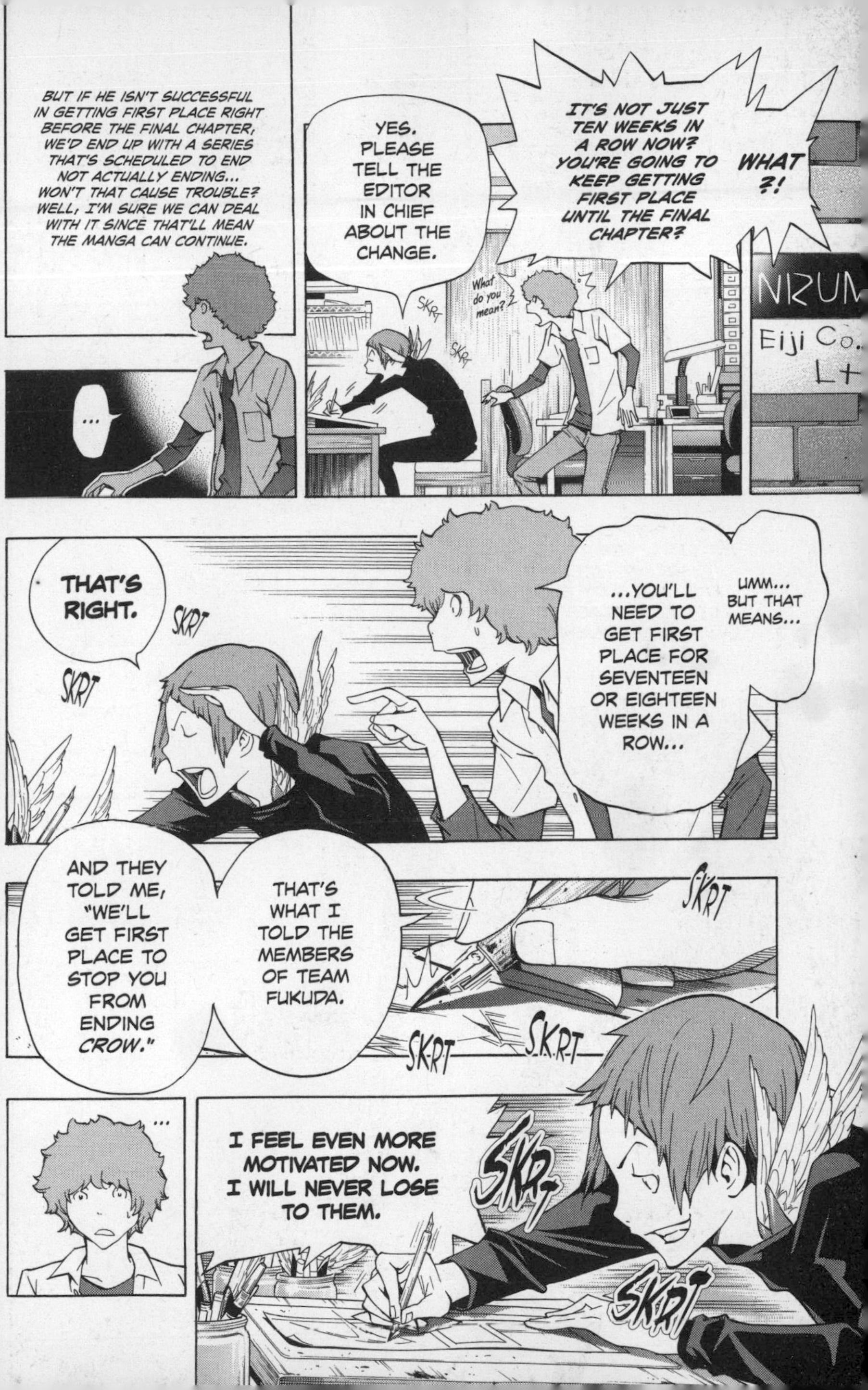
NIZUMA
Eiji Co. Ltd
WHAT ?!
IT'S NOT JUST TEN WEEKS IN A ROW NOW? YOU'RE GOING TO KEEP GETTING FIRST PLACE UNTIL THE FINAL CHAPTER?
What do you mean?
YES. PLEASE TELL THE EDITOR IN CHIEF ABOUT THE CHANGE.
SKRT
SKRT
BUT IF HE ISN'T SUCCESSFUL IN GETTING FIRST PLACE RIGHT BEFORE THE FINAL CHAPTER, WE'D END UP WITH A SERIES THAT'S SCHEDULED TO END NOT ACTUALLY ENDING... WON'T THAT CAUSE TROUBLE? WELL, I'M SURE WE CAN DEAL WITH IT SINCE THAT'LL MEAN THE MANGA CAN CONTINUE.
...
UMM... BUT THAT MEANS...
...YOU'LL NEED TO GET FIRST PLACE FOR SEVENTEEN OR EIGHTEEN WEEKS IN A ROW...
THAT'S RIGHT.
SKRT
SKRT
SKRT
THAT'S WHAT I TOLD THE MEMBERS OF TEAM FUKUDA.
AND THEY TOLD ME, "WE'LL GET FIRST PLACE TO STOP YOU FROM ENDING CROW."
S-K-R-T
S-K-R-T
I FEEL EVEN MORE MOTIVATED NOW. I WILL NEVER LOSE TO THEM.
SKRT
SKRT
...

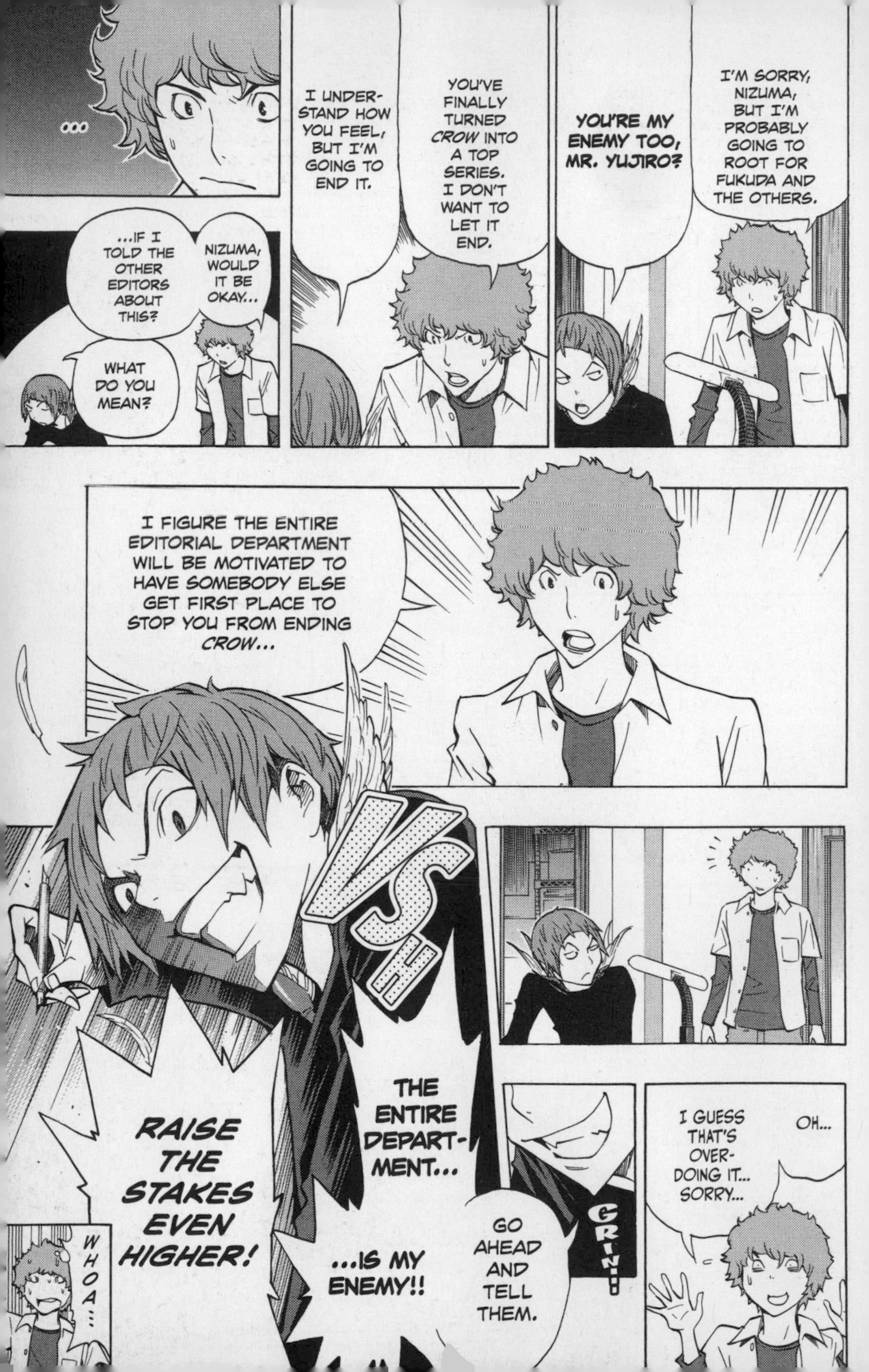
I'M SORRY, NIZUMA, BUT I'M PROBABLY GOING TO ROOT FOR FUKUDA AND THE OTHERS.
YOU'RE MY ENEMY TOO, MR. YUJIRO?
YOU'VE FINALLY TURNED *CROW* INTO A TOP SERIES. I DON'T WANT TO LET IT END.
I UNDER-STAND HOW YOU FEEL, BUT I'M GOING TO END IT.
...
NIZUMA, WOULD IT BE OKAY...
...IF I TOLD THE OTHER EDITORS ABOUT THIS?
WHAT DO YOU MEAN?
I FIGURE THE ENTIRE EDITORIAL DEPARTMENT WILL BE MOTIVATED TO HAVE SOMEBODY ELSE GET FIRST PLACE TO STOP YOU FROM ENDING *CROW*...
OH...
I GUESS THAT'S OVER-DOING IT... SORRY...
GRIN
GO AHEAD AND TELL THEM.
THE ENTIRE DEPART-MENT...
...IS MY ENEMY!!
VS
RAISE THE STAKES EVEN HIGHER!
WHOA...

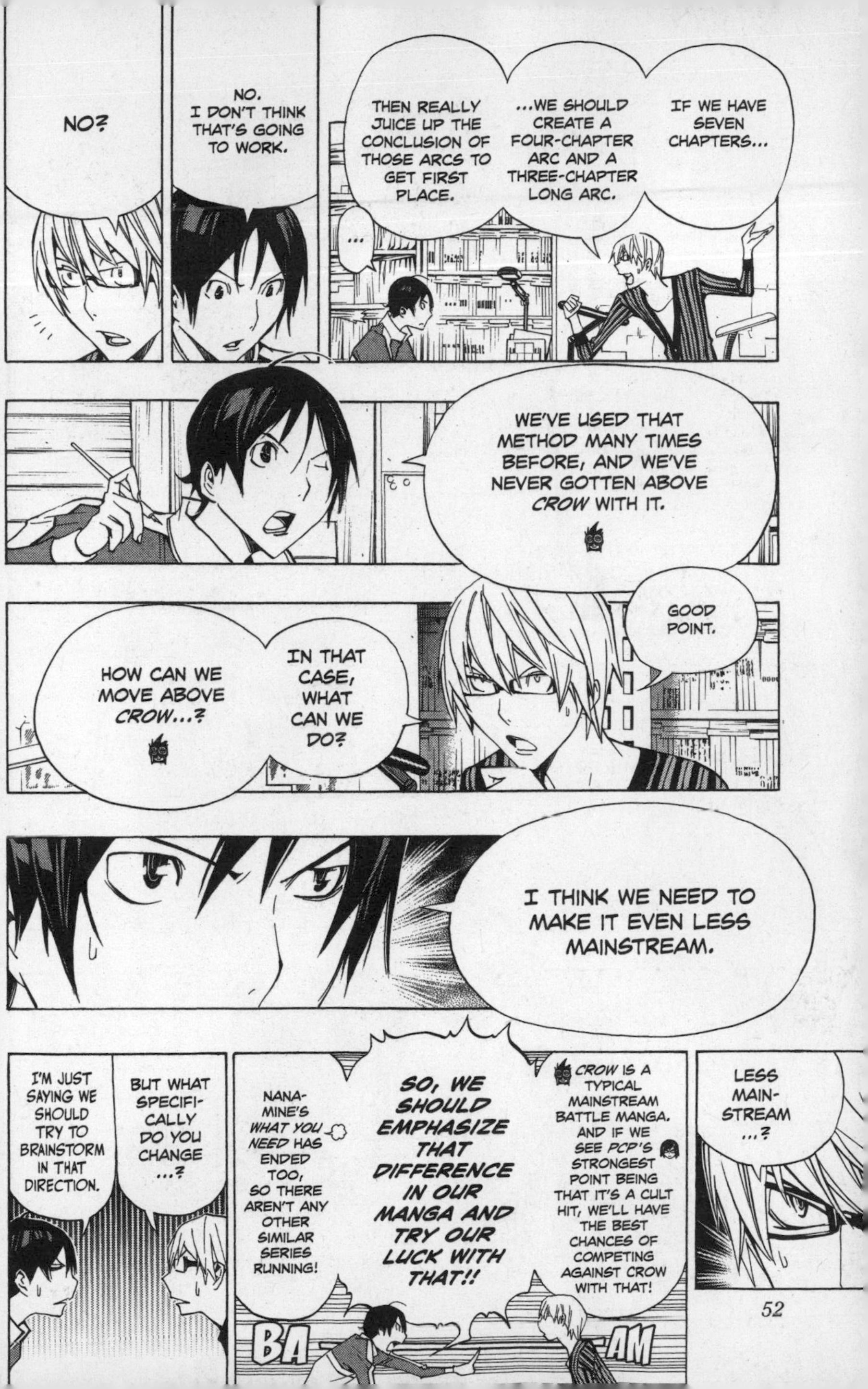
IF WE HAVE SEVEN CHAPTERS...
...WE SHOULD CREATE A FOUR-CHAPTER ARC AND A THREE-CHAPTER LONG ARC.
THEN REALLY JUICE UP THE CONCLUSION OF THOSE ARCS TO GET FIRST PLACE.
...
NO. I DON'T THINK THAT'S GOING TO WORK.
NO?
WE'VE USED THAT METHOD MANY TIMES BEFORE, AND WE'VE NEVER GOTTEN ABOVE *CROW* WITH IT.
GOOD POINT.
IN THAT CASE, WHAT CAN WE DO?
HOW CAN WE MOVE ABOVE *CROW*...?
I THINK WE NEED TO MAKE IT EVEN LESS MAINSTREAM.
LESS MAIN-STREAM...?
CROW IS A TYPICAL MAINSTREAM BATTLE MANGA. AND IF WE SEE *PCP*'S STRONGEST POINT BEING THAT IT'S A CULT HIT, WE'LL HAVE THE BEST CHANCES OF COMPETING AGAINST CROW WITH THAT!
SO, WE SHOULD EMPHASIZE THAT DIFFERENCE IN OUR MANGA AND TRY OUR LUCK WITH THAT!!
NANA-MINE'S *WHAT YOU NEED* HAS ENDED TOO, SO THERE AREN'T ANY OTHER SIMILAR SERIES RUNNING!
BA
AM
BUT WHAT SPECIFI-CALLY DO YOU CHANGE ...?
I'M JUST SAYING WE SHOULD TRY TO BRAINSTORM IN THAT DIRECTION.

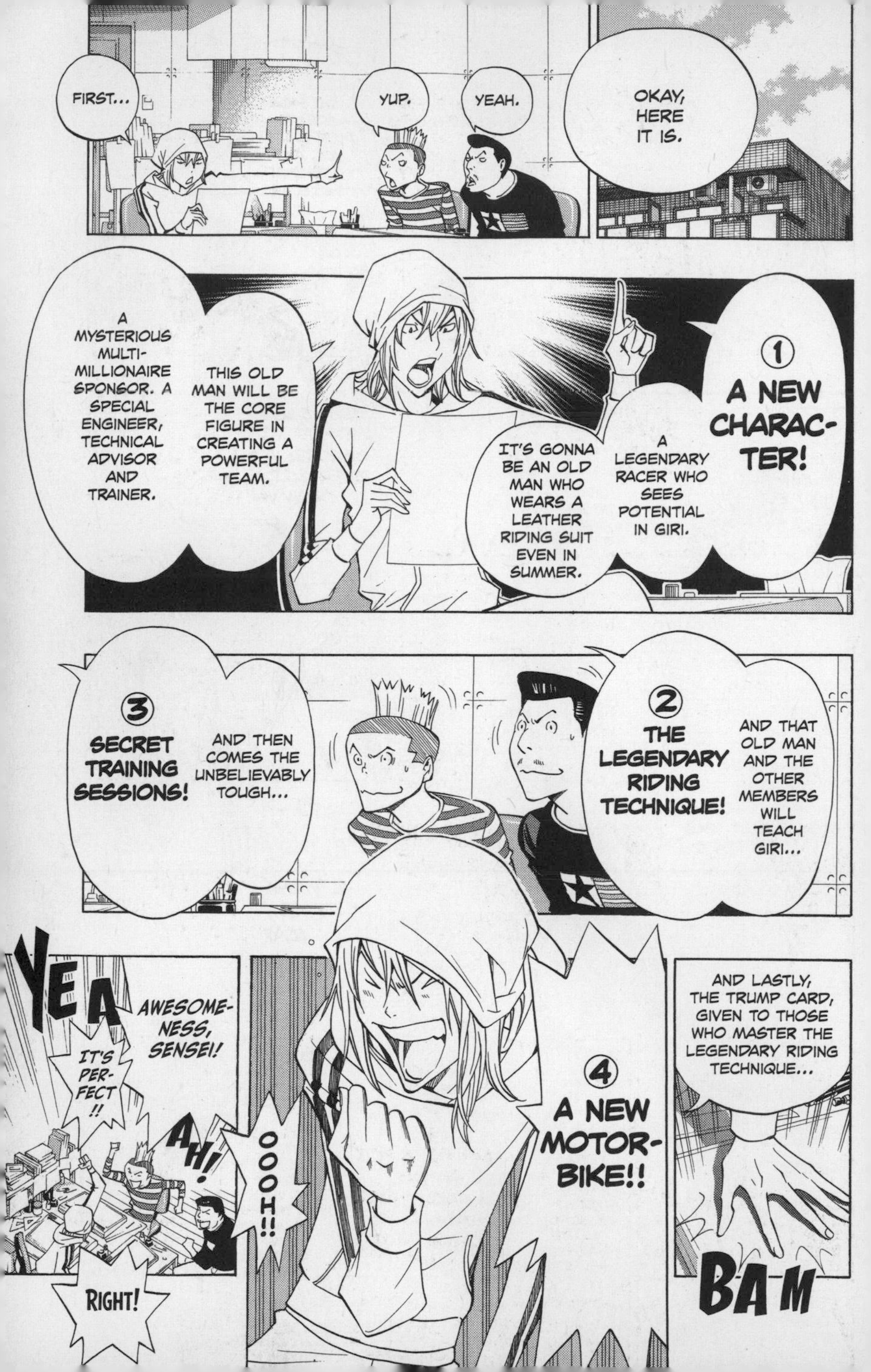
OKAY, HERE IT IS.
YEAH.
YUP.
FIRST...
① A NEW CHARACTER!
A LEGENDARY RACER WHO SEES POTENTIAL IN GIRI.
IT'S GONNA BE AN OLD MAN WHO WEARS A LEATHER RIDING SUIT EVEN IN SUMMER.
THIS OLD MAN WILL BE THE CORE FIGURE IN CREATING A POWERFUL TEAM.
A MYSTERIOUS MULTI-MILLIONAIRE SPONSOR. A SPECIAL ENGINEER, TECHNICAL ADVISOR AND TRAINER.
② THE LEGENDARY RIDING TECHNIQUE!
AND THAT OLD MAN AND THE OTHER MEMBERS WILL TEACH GIRI...
AND THEN COMES THE UNBELIEVABLY TOUGH...
③ SECRET TRAINING SESSIONS!
AND LASTLY, THE TRUMP CARD, GIVEN TO THOSE WHO MASTER THE LEGENDARY RIDING TECHNIQUE...
BAM
④ A NEW MOTOR-BIKE!!
OOOH!!
YEA
AWESOME-NESS, SENSEI!
IT'S PER-FECT!!
AH!
RIGHT!

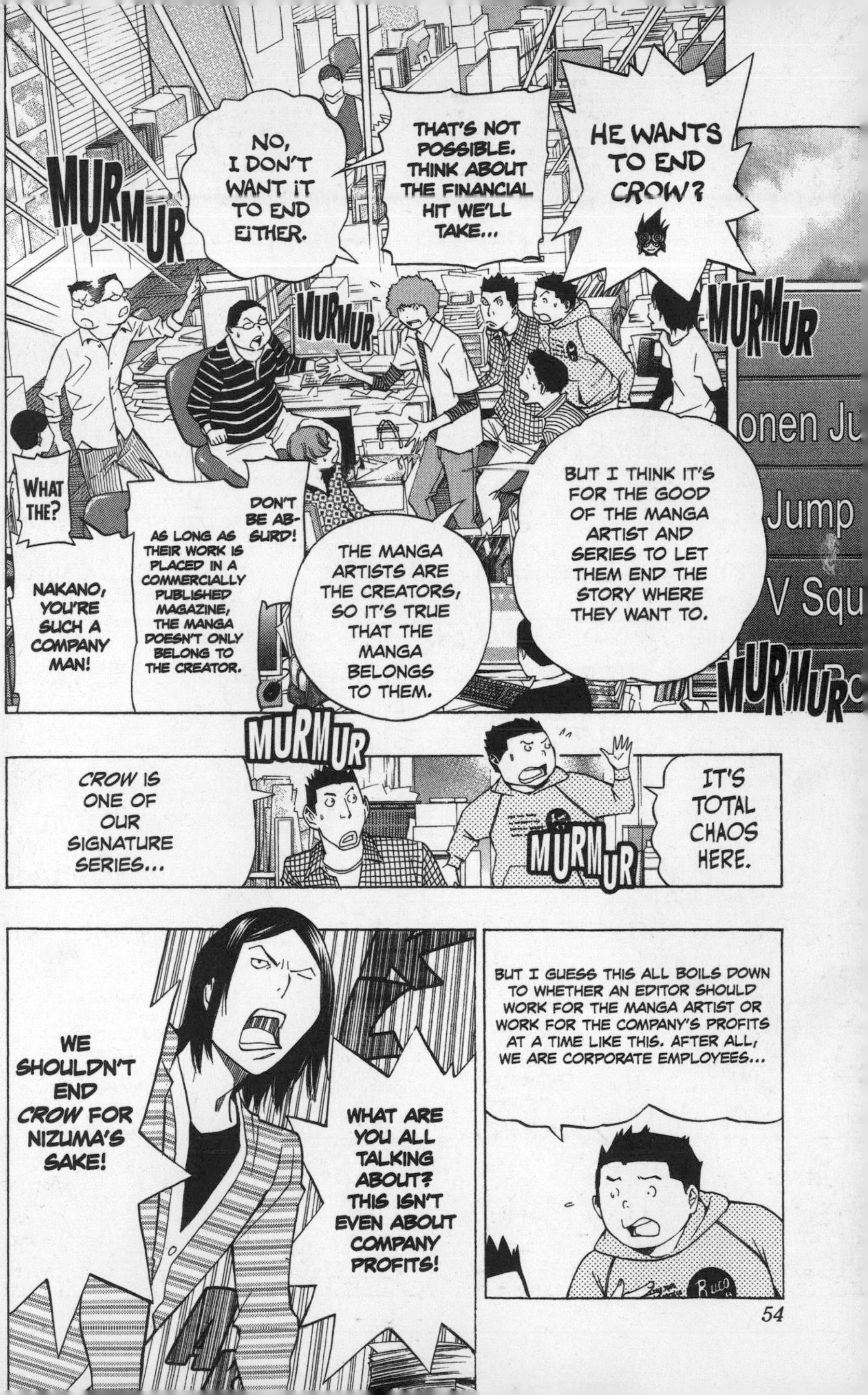
MURMUR
HE WANTS TO END CROW?
THAT'S NOT POSSIBLE. THINK ABOUT THE FINANCIAL HIT WE'LL TAKE...
NO, I DON'T WANT IT TO END EITHER.
MURMUR
MURMUR
MURMUR
BUT I THINK IT'S FOR THE GOOD OF THE MANGA ARTIST AND SERIES TO LET THEM END THE STORY WHERE THEY WANT TO.
MURMUR
THE MANGA ARTISTS ARE THE CREATORS, SO IT'S TRUE THAT THE MANGA BELONGS TO THEM.
DON'T BE AB-SURD!
AS LONG AS THEIR WORK IS PLACED IN A COMMERCIALLY PUBLISHED MAGAZINE, THE MANGA DOESN'T ONLY BELONG TO THE CREATOR.
WHAT THE?
NAKANO, YOU'RE SUCH A COMPANY MAN!
IT'S TOTAL CHAOS HERE.
MURMUR
MURMUR
CROW IS ONE OF OUR SIGNATURE SERIES...
BUT I GUESS THIS ALL BOILS DOWN TO WHETHER AN EDITOR SHOULD WORK FOR THE MANGA ARTIST OR WORK FOR THE COMPANY'S PROFITS AT A TIME LIKE THIS. AFTER ALL, WE ARE CORPORATE EMPLOYEES...
WHAT ARE YOU ALL TALKING ABOUT? THIS ISN'T EVEN ABOUT COMPANY PROFITS!
WE SHOULDN'T END *CROW* FOR NIZUMA'S SAKE!

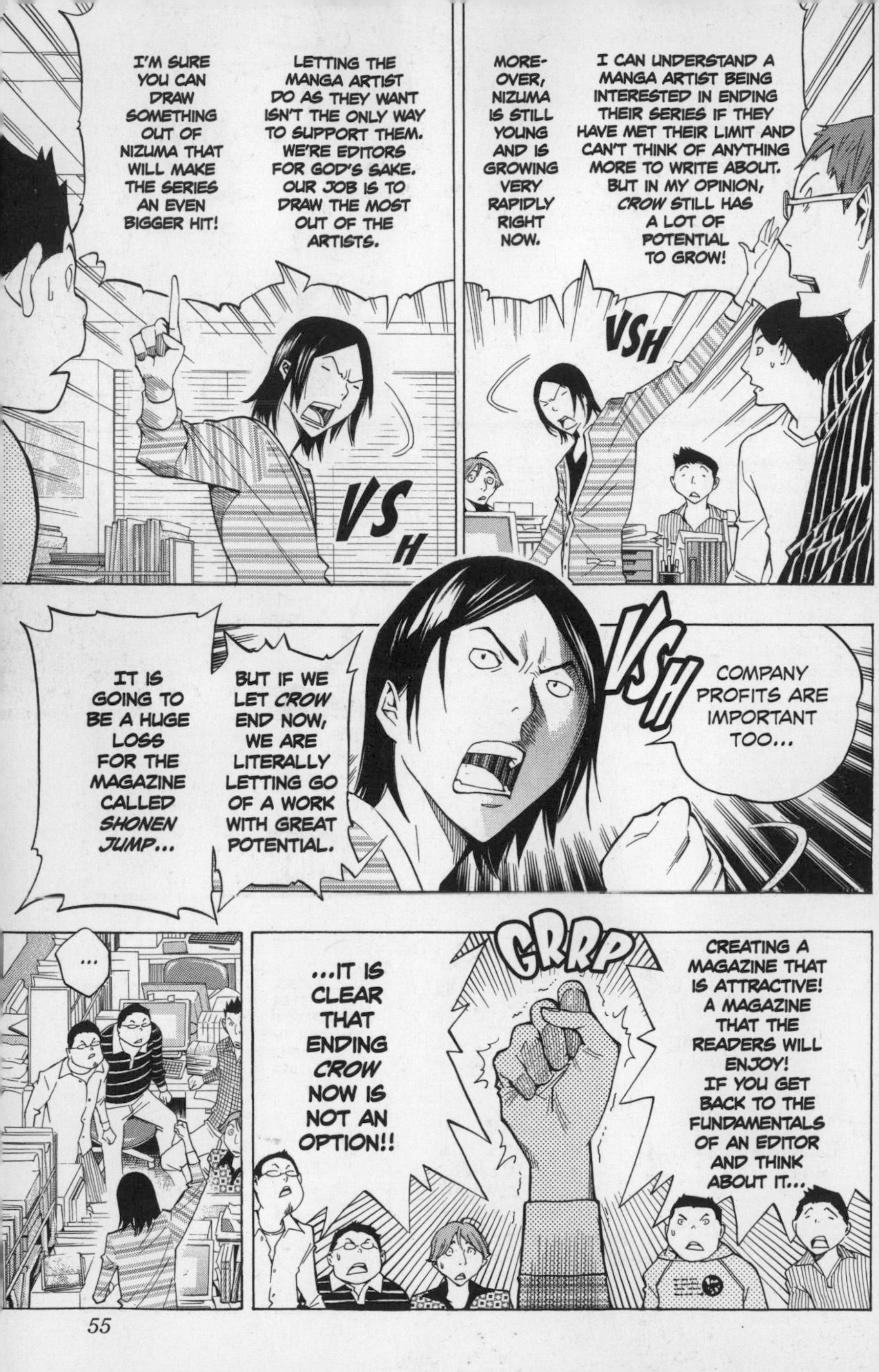
I CAN UNDERSTAND A MANGA ARTIST BEING INTERESTED IN ENDING THEIR SERIES IF THEY HAVE MET THEIR LIMIT AND CAN'T THINK OF ANYTHING MORE TO WRITE ABOUT. BUT IN MY OPINION, *CROW* STILL HAS A LOT OF POTENTIAL TO GROW!
MOREOVER, NIZUMA IS STILL YOUNG AND IS GROWING VERY RAPIDLY RIGHT NOW.
VSH
LETTING THE MANGA ARTIST DO AS THEY WANT ISN'T THE ONLY WAY TO SUPPORT THEM. WE'RE EDITORS FOR GOD'S SAKE. OUR JOB IS TO DRAW THE MOST OUT OF THE ARTISTS.
I'M SURE YOU CAN DRAW SOMETHING OUT OF NIZUMA THAT WILL MAKE THE SERIES AN EVEN BIGGER HIT!
VSH
COMPANY PROFITS ARE IMPORTANT TOO...
VSH
BUT IF WE LET *CROW* END NOW, WE ARE LITERALLY LETTING GO OF A WORK WITH GREAT POTENTIAL.
IT IS GOING TO BE A HUGE LOSS FOR THE MAGAZINE CALLED *SHONEN JUMP*...
CREATING A MAGAZINE THAT IS ATTRACTIVE! A MAGAZINE THAT THE READERS WILL ENJOY! IF YOU GET BACK TO THE FUNDAMENTALS OF AN EDITOR AND THINK ABOUT IT...
GRRP
...IT IS CLEAR THAT ENDING *CROW* NOW IS NOT AN OPTION!!
...

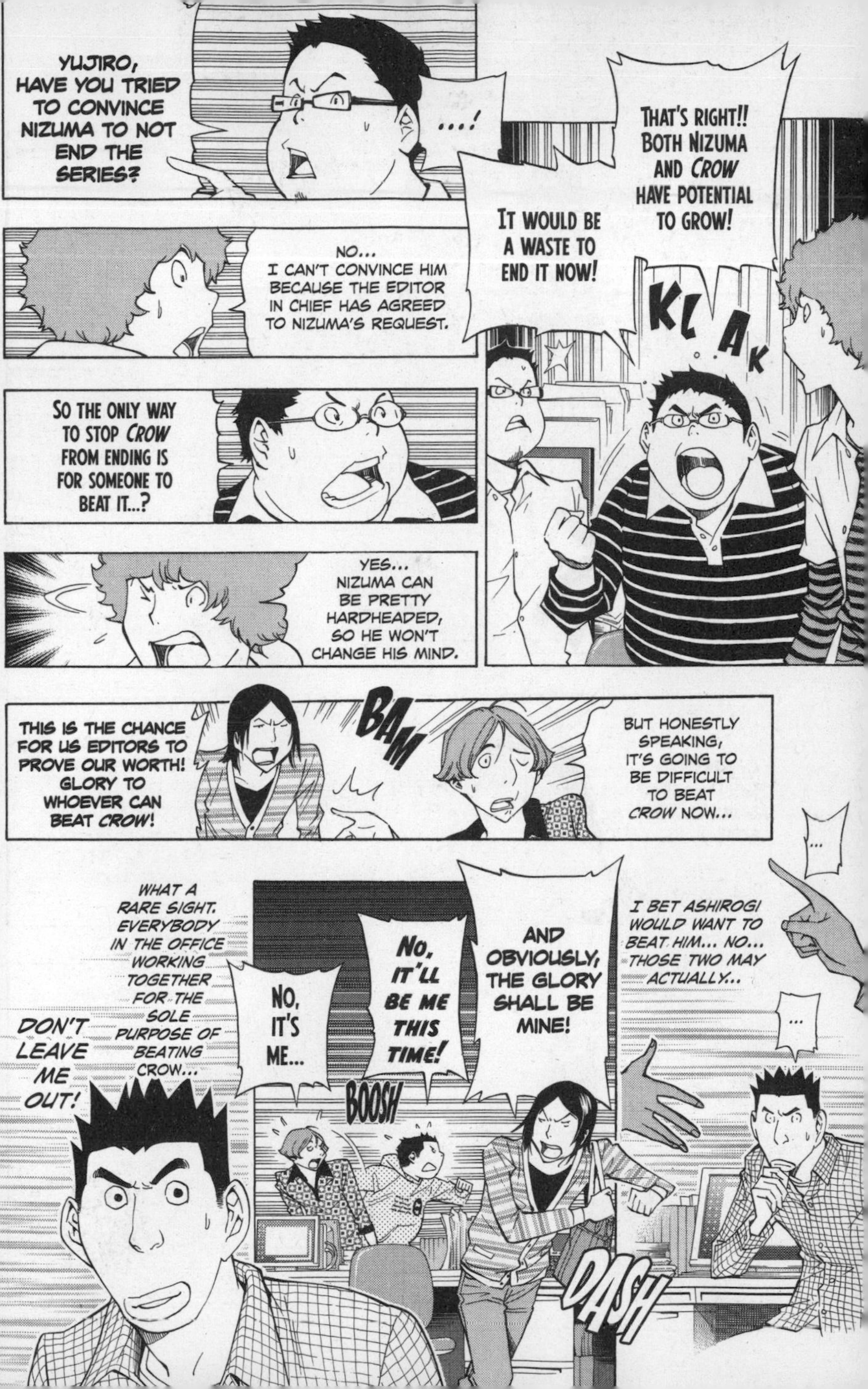
THAT'S RIGHT!! BOTH NIZUMA AND CROW HAVE POTENTIAL TO GROW!
IT WOULD BE A WASTE TO END IT NOW!
KLAK
YUJIRO, HAVE YOU TRIED TO CONVINCE NIZUMA TO NOT END THE SERIES?
...!
NO... I CAN'T CONVINCE HIM BECAUSE THE EDITOR IN CHIEF HAS AGREED TO NIZUMA'S REQUEST.
SO THE ONLY WAY TO STOP CROW FROM ENDING IS FOR SOMEONE TO BEAT IT...?
YES... NIZUMA CAN BE PRETTY HARDHEADED, SO HE WON'T CHANGE HIS MIND.
BUT HONESTLY SPEAKING, IT'S GOING TO BE DIFFICULT TO BEAT CROW NOW...
BAM
THIS IS THE CHANCE FOR US EDITORS TO PROVE OUR WORTH! GLORY TO WHOEVER CAN BEAT CROW!
...
I BET ASHIROGI WOULD WANT TO BEAT HIM... NO... THOSE TWO MAY ACTUALLY...
...
AND OBVIOUSLY, THE GLORY SHALL BE MINE!
NO, IT'LL BE ME THIS TIME!
NO, IT'S ME...
WHAT A RARE SIGHT. EVERYBODY IN THE OFFICE WORKING TOGETHER FOR THE SOLE PURPOSE OF BEATING CROW...
DON'T LEAVE ME OUT!
BOOSH
DASH

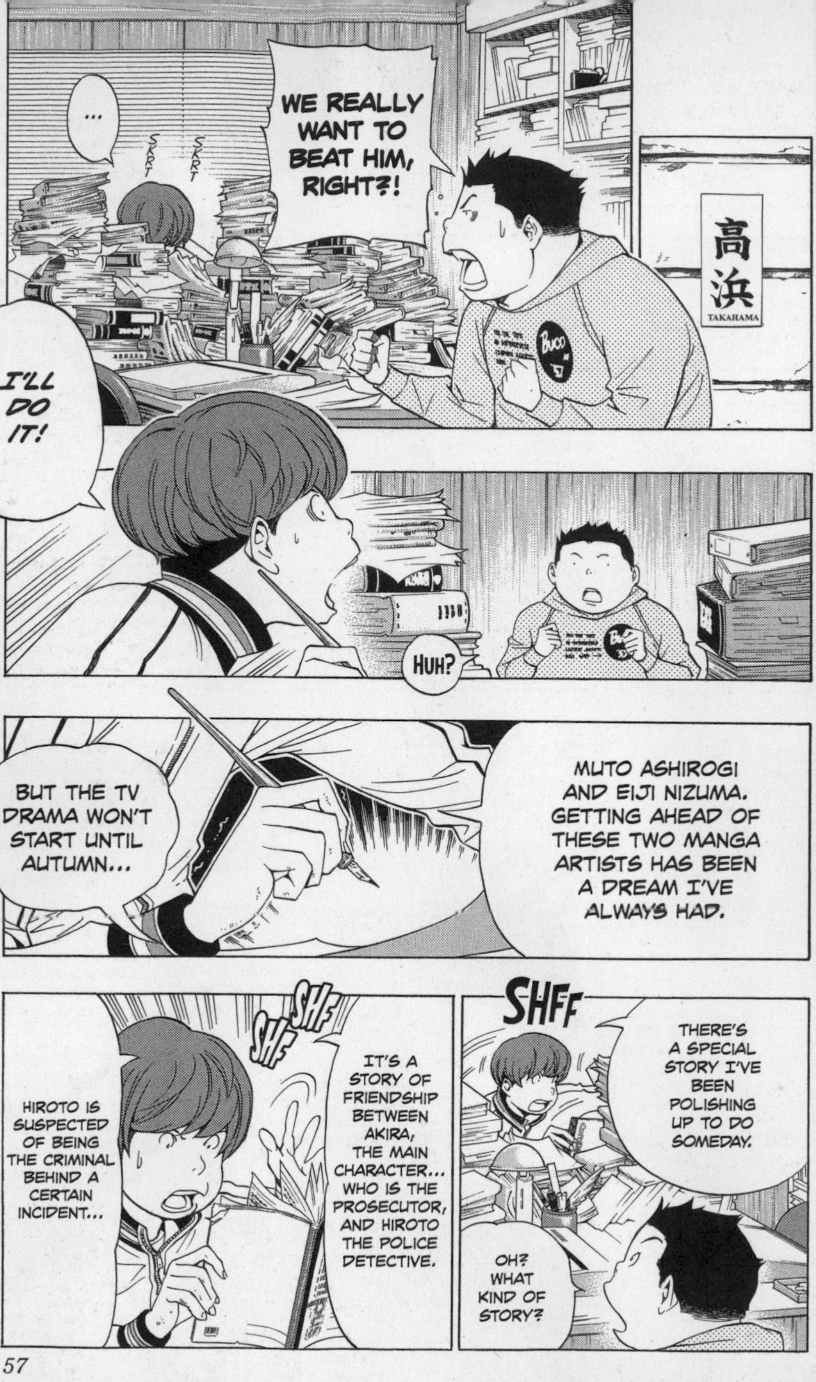
WE REALLY WANT TO BEAT HIM, RIGHT?!
...
SKRT
SKRT
TAKAHAMA
I'LL DO IT!
HUH?
MUTO ASHIROGI AND EIJI NIZUMA. GETTING AHEAD OF THESE TWO MANGA ARTISTS HAS BEEN A DREAM I'VE ALWAYS HAD.
BUT THE TV DRAMA WON'T START UNTIL AUTUMN...
SHFF
THERE'S A SPECIAL STORY I'VE BEEN POLISHING UP TO DO SOMEDAY.
OH? WHAT KIND OF STORY?
SHF
SHF
IT'S A STORY OF FRIENDSHIP BETWEEN AKIRA, THE MAIN CHARACTER... WHO IS THE PROSECUTOR, AND HIROTO THE POLICE DETECTIVE.
HIROTO IS SUSPECTED OF BEING THE CRIMINAL BEHIND A CERTAIN INCIDENT...

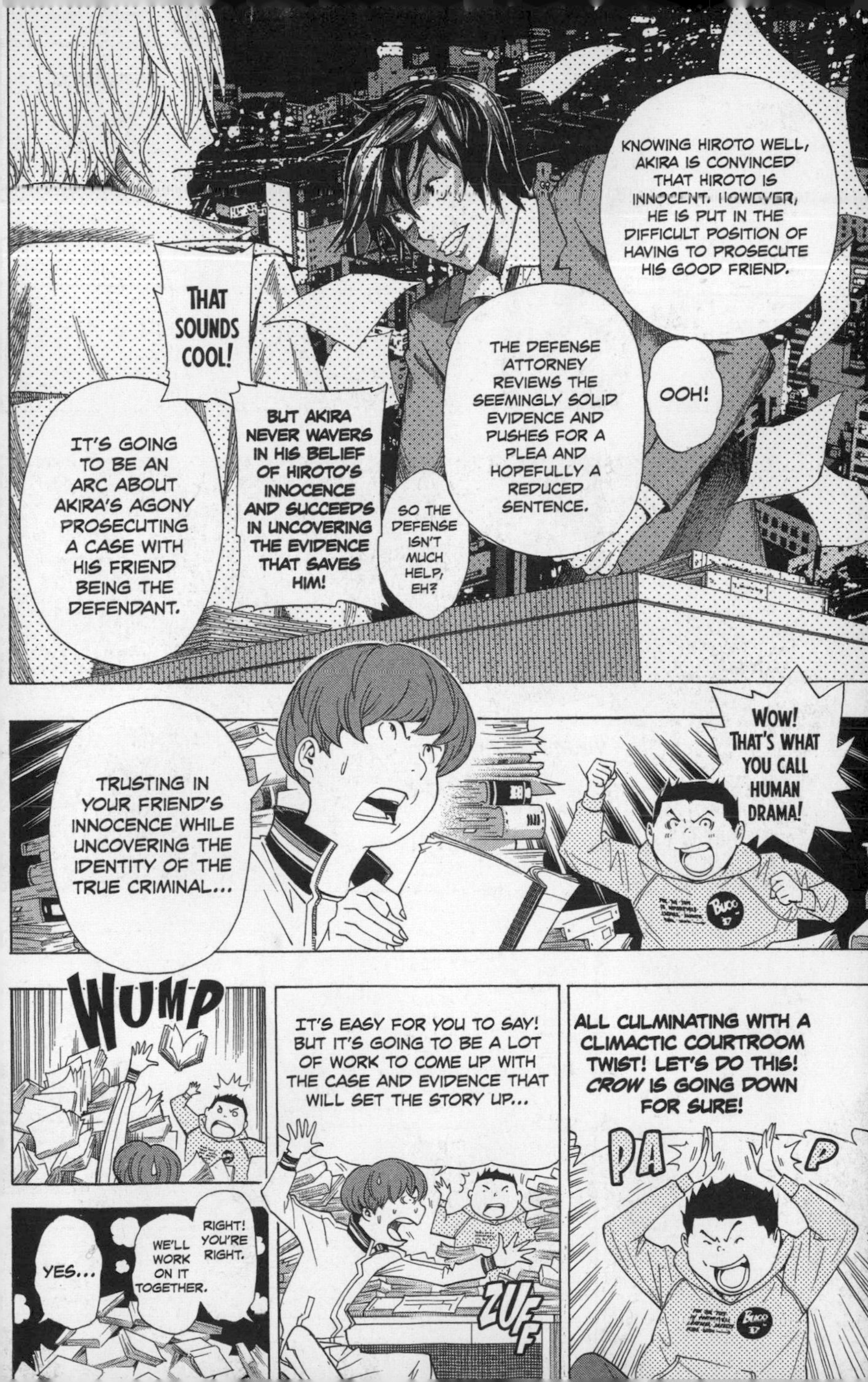
KNOWING HIROTO WELL, AKIRA IS CONVINCED THAT HIROTO IS INNOCENT. HOWEVER, HE IS PUT IN THE DIFFICULT POSITION OF HAVING TO PROSECUTE HIS GOOD FRIEND.
OOH!
THE DEFENSE ATTORNEY REVIEWS THE SEEMINGLY SOLID EVIDENCE AND PUSHES FOR A PLEA AND HOPEFULLY A REDUCED SENTENCE.
SO THE DEFENSE ISN'T MUCH HELP, EH?
BUT AKIRA NEVER WAVERS IN HIS BELIEF OF HIROTO'S INNOCENCE AND SUCCEEDS IN UNCOVERING THE EVIDENCE THAT SAVES HIM!
THAT SOUNDS COOL!
IT'S GOING TO BE AN ARC ABOUT AKIRA'S AGONY PROSECUTING A CASE WITH HIS FRIEND BEING THE DEFENDANT.
WOW! THAT'S WHAT YOU CALL HUMAN DRAMA!
TRUSTING IN YOUR FRIEND'S INNOCENCE WHILE UNCOVERING THE IDENTITY OF THE TRUE CRIMINAL...
ALL CULMINATING WITH A CLIMACTIC COURTROOM TWIST! LET'S DO THIS! *CROW* IS GOING DOWN FOR SURE!
PAP
IT'S EASY FOR YOU TO SAY! BUT IT'S GOING TO BE A LOT OF WORK TO COME UP WITH THE CASE AND EVIDENCE THAT WILL SET THE STORY UP...
ZUFF
WUMP
RIGHT! YOU'RE RIGHT.
WE'LL WORK ON IT TOGETHER.
YES...

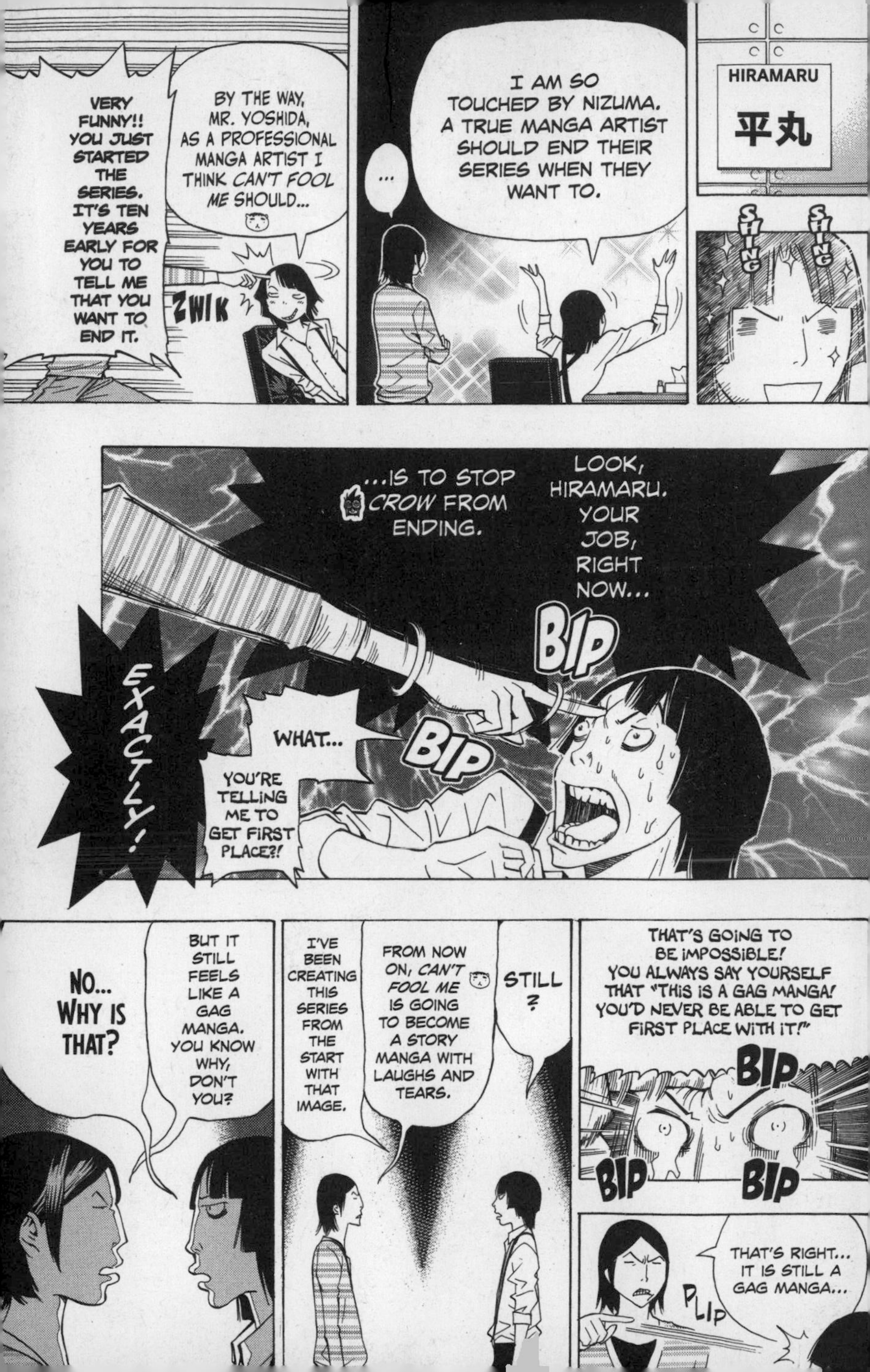
HIRAMARU
平丸
SHING
SHING
I AM SO TOUCHED BY NIZUMA. A TRUE MANGA ARTIST SHOULD END THEIR SERIES WHEN THEY WANT TO.
...
BY THE WAY, MR. YOSHIDA, AS A PROFESSIONAL MANGA ARTIST I THINK CAN'T FOOL ME SHOULD...
ZWIK
VERY FUNNY!! YOU JUST STARTED THE SERIES. IT'S TEN YEARS EARLY FOR YOU TO TELL ME THAT YOU WANT TO END IT.
LOOK, HIRAMARU. YOUR JOB, RIGHT NOW...
...IS TO STOP CROW FROM ENDING.
BIP
BIP
WHAT...
YOU'RE TELLING ME TO GET FIRST PLACE?!
EXACTLY!!
THAT'S GOING TO BE IMPOSSIBLE! YOU ALWAYS SAY YOURSELF THAT "THIS IS A GAG MANGA! YOU'D NEVER BE ABLE TO GET FIRST PLACE WITH IT!"
BIP
BIP
BIP
THAT'S RIGHT... IT IS STILL A GAG MANGA...
PLIP
STILL?
FROM NOW ON, CAN'T FOOL ME IS GOING TO BECOME A STORY MANGA WITH LAUGHS AND TEARS.
I'VE BEEN CREATING THIS SERIES FROM THE START WITH THAT IMAGE.
BUT IT STILL FEELS LIKE A GAG MANGA. YOU KNOW WHY, DON'T YOU?
NO... WHY IS THAT?

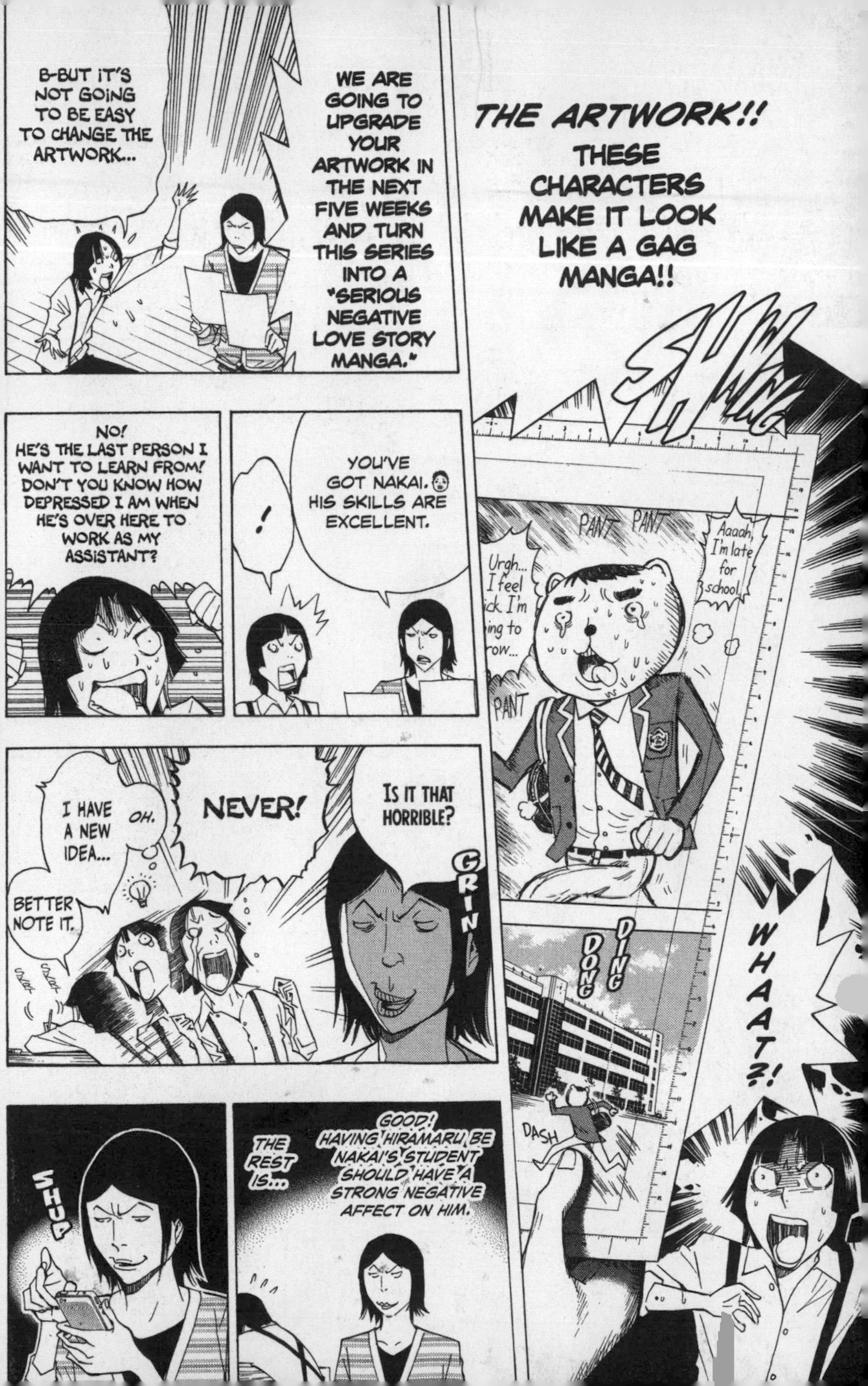
THE ARTWORK!!
THESE CHARACTERS MAKE IT LOOK LIKE A GAG MANGA!!
SHING
PANT PANT
Aaaah, I'm late for school.
Urgh... I feel
PANT
DING DONG
DASH
WHAAT?!
WE ARE GOING TO UPGRADE YOUR ARTWORK IN THE NEXT FIVE WEEKS AND TURN THIS SERIES INTO A "SERIOUS NEGATIVE LOVE STORY MANGA."
B-BUT IT'S NOT GOING TO BE EASY TO CHANGE THE ARTWORK...
YOU'VE GOT NAKAI. HIS SKILLS ARE EXCELLENT.
!
NO! HE'S THE LAST PERSON I WANT TO LEARN FROM! DON'T YOU KNOW HOW DEPRESSED I AM WHEN HE'S OVER HERE TO WORK AS MY ASSISTANT?
IS IT THAT HORRIBLE?
GRIN
NEVER!
OH.
I HAVE A NEW IDEA...
BETTER NOTE IT.
GOOD! HAVING HIRAMARU BE NAKAI'S STUDENT SHOULD HAVE A STRONG NEGATIVE AFFECT ON HIM.
THE REST IS...
SHUP

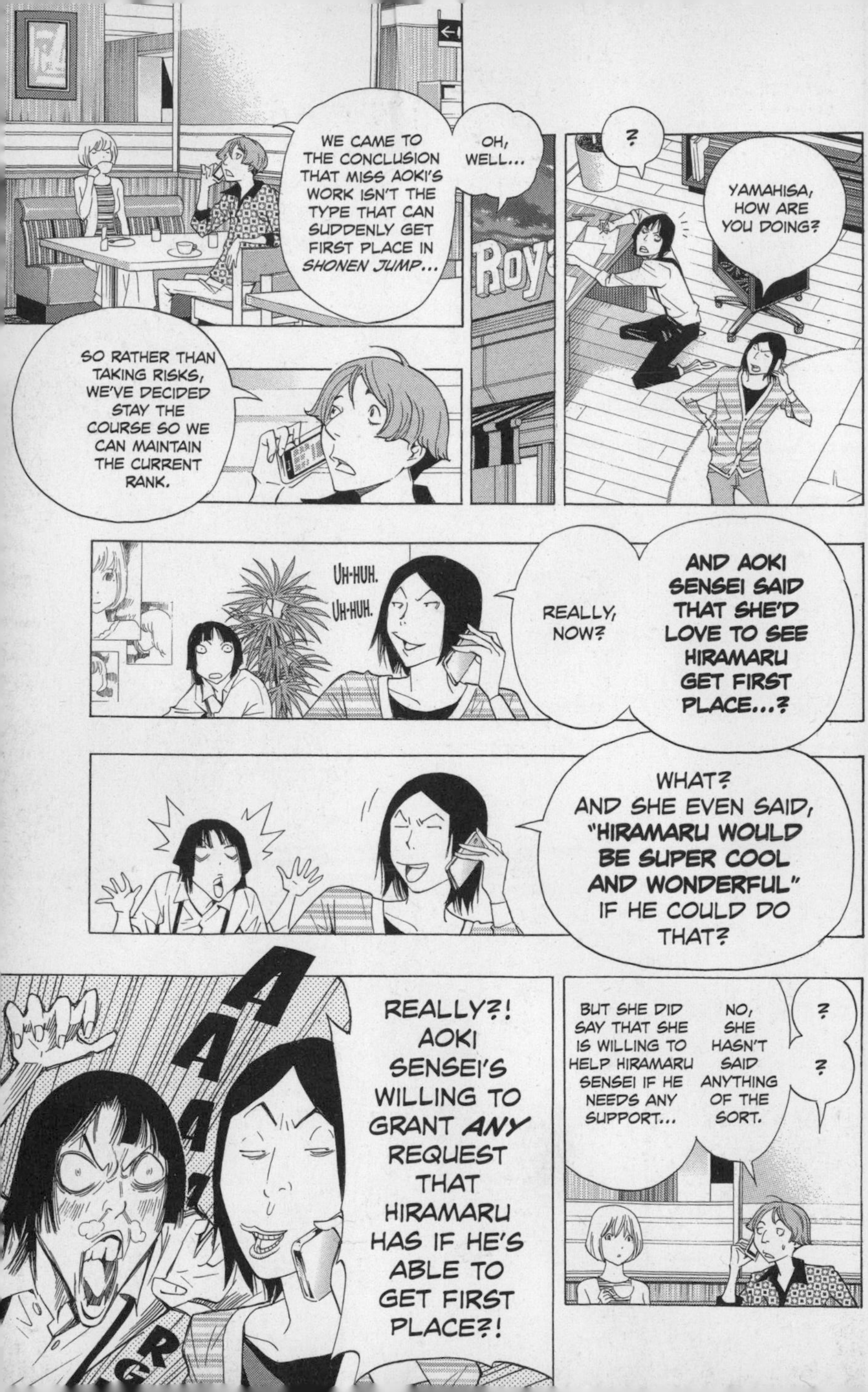
?
YAMAHISA, HOW ARE YOU DOING?
OH, WELL...
WE CAME TO THE CONCLUSION THAT MISS AOKI'S WORK ISN'T THE TYPE THAT CAN SUDDENLY GET FIRST PLACE IN *SHONEN JUMP*...
SO RATHER THAN TAKING RISKS, WE'VE DECIDED STAY THE COURSE SO WE CAN MAINTAIN THE CURRENT RANK.
REALLY, NOW?
AND AOKI SENSEI SAID THAT SHE'D LOVE TO SEE HIRAMARU GET FIRST PLACE...?
UH-HUH.
UH-HUH.
WHAT? AND SHE EVEN SAID, "HIRAMARU WOULD BE SUPER COOL AND WONDERFUL" IF HE COULD DO THAT?
?
?
NO, SHE HASN'T SAID ANYTHING OF THE SORT.
BUT SHE DID SAY THAT SHE IS WILLING TO HELP HIRAMARU SENSEI IF HE NEEDS ANY SUPPORT...
REALLY?! AOKI SENSEI'S WILLING TO GRANT *ANY* REQUEST THAT HIRAMARU HAS IF HE'S ABLE TO GET FIRST PLACE?!
AAAA

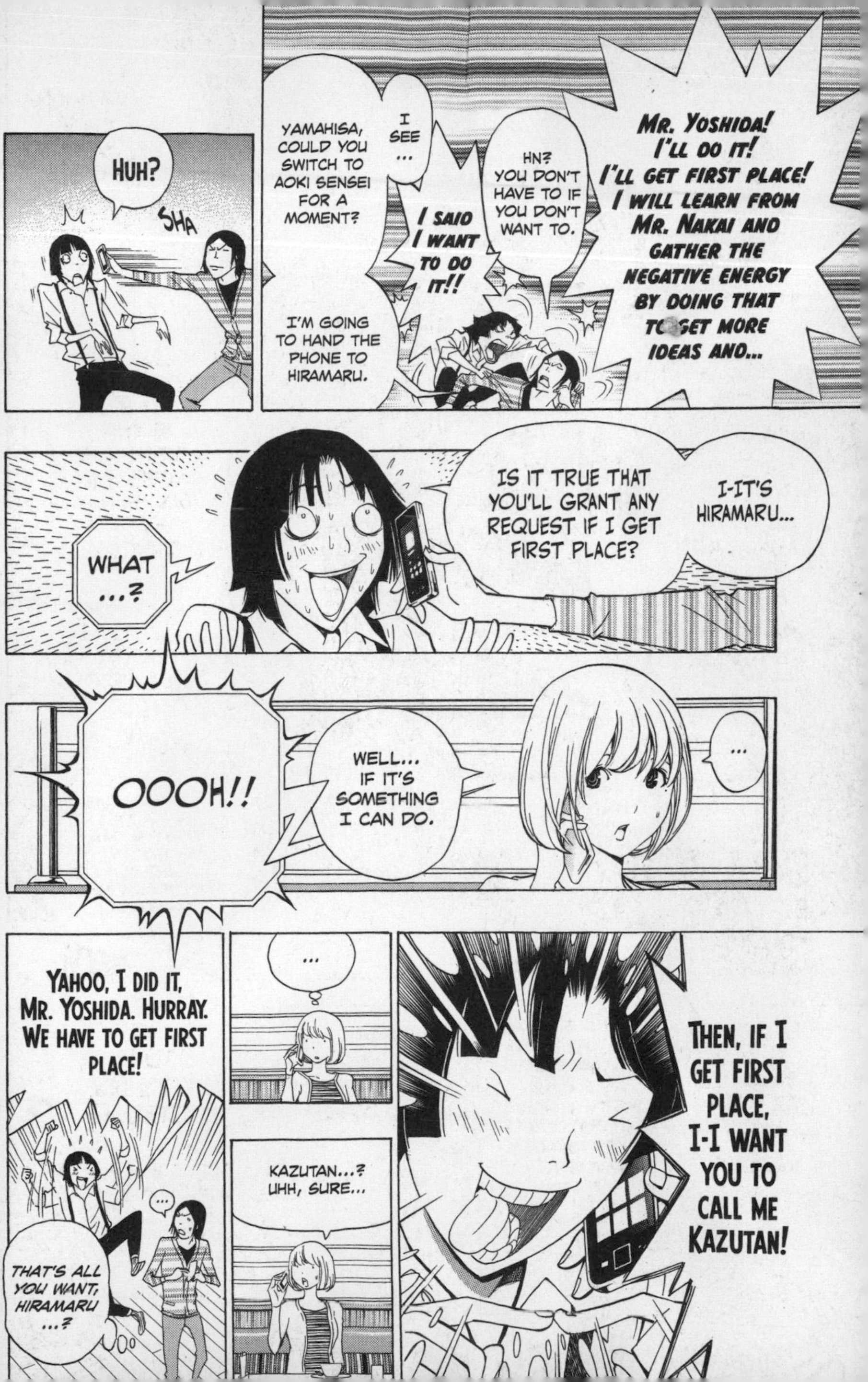
MR. YOSHIDA! I'LL DO IT! I'LL GET FIRST PLACE! I WILL LEARN FROM MR. NAKAI AND GATHER THE NEGATIVE ENERGY BY DOING THAT TO GET MORE IDEAS AND...
HN? YOU DON'T HAVE TO IF YOU DON'T WANT TO.
I SAID I WANT TO DO IT!!
I SEE ...
YAMAHISA, COULD YOU SWITCH TO AOKI SENSEI FOR A MOMENT?
I'M GOING TO HAND THE PHONE TO HIRAMARU.
SHA
HUH?
I-IT'S HIRAMARU...
IS IT TRUE THAT YOU'LL GRANT ANY REQUEST IF I GET FIRST PLACE?
WHAT ...?
...
WELL... IF IT'S SOMETHING I CAN DO.
OOOH!!
THEN, IF I GET FIRST PLACE, I-I WANT YOU TO CALL ME KAZUTAN!
...
KAZUTAN...? UHH, SURE...
YAHOO, I DID IT, MR. YOSHIDA. HURRAY. WE HAVE TO GET FIRST PLACE!
...
THAT'S ALL YOU WANT, HIRAMARU ...?

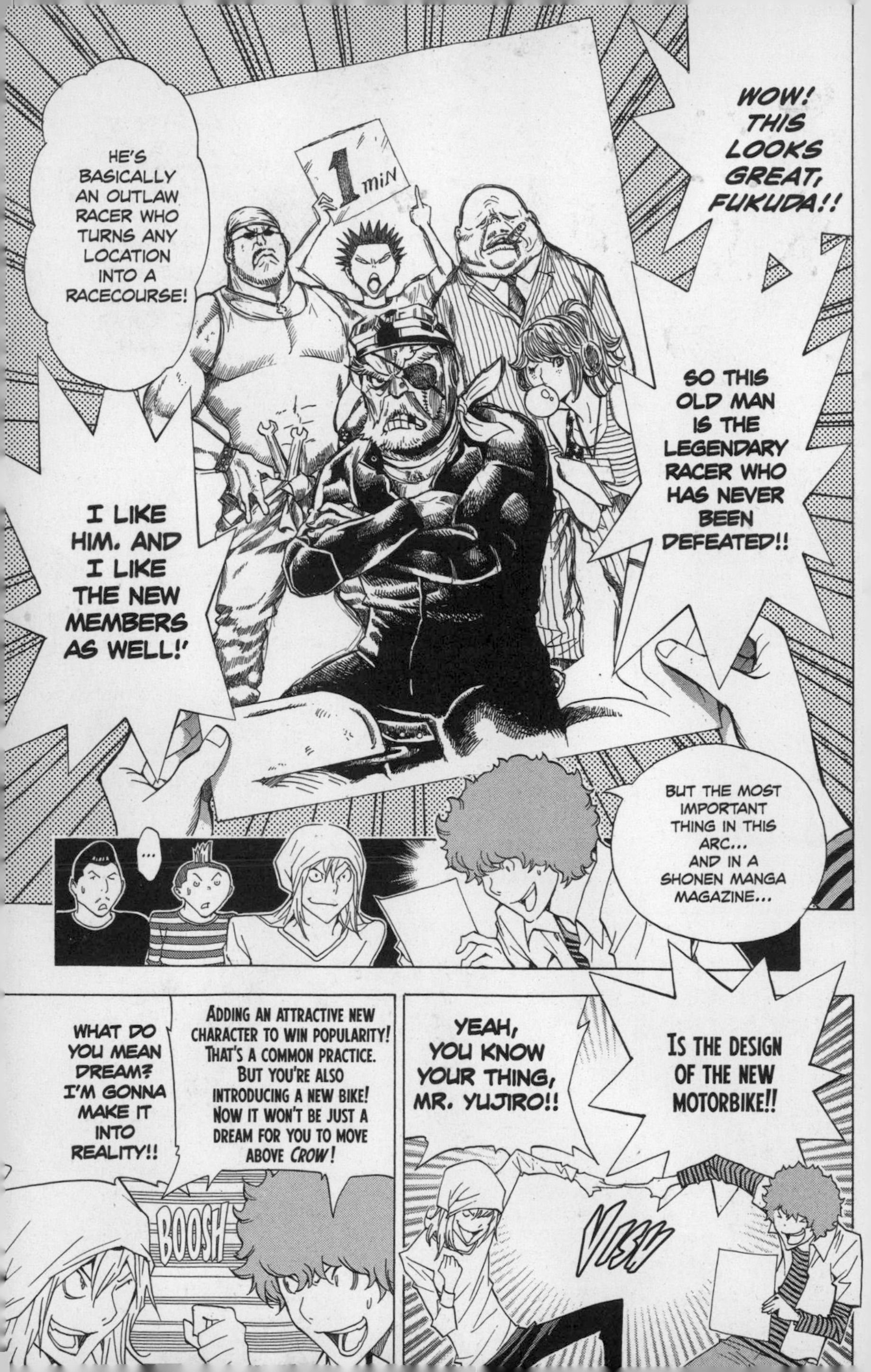
WOW! THIS LOOKS GREAT, FUKUDA!!
HE'S BASICALLY AN OUTLAW RACER WHO TURNS ANY LOCATION INTO A RACECOURSE!
1 min
SO THIS OLD MAN IS THE LEGENDARY RACER WHO HAS NEVER BEEN DEFEATED!!
I LIKE HIM. AND I LIKE THE NEW MEMBERS AS WELL!'
BUT THE MOST IMPORTANT THING IN THIS ARC... AND IN A SHONEN MANGA MAGAZINE...
...
IS THE DESIGN OF THE NEW MOTORBIKE!!
YEAH, YOU KNOW YOUR THING, MR. YUJIRO!!
ADDING AN ATTRACTIVE NEW CHARACTER TO WIN POPULARITY! THAT'S A COMMON PRACTICE. BUT YOU'RE ALSO INTRODUCING A NEW BIKE! NOW IT WON'T BE JUST A DREAM FOR YOU TO MOVE ABOVE *CROW*!
WHAT DO YOU MEAN DREAM? I'M GONNA MAKE IT INTO REALITY!!
BOOSH

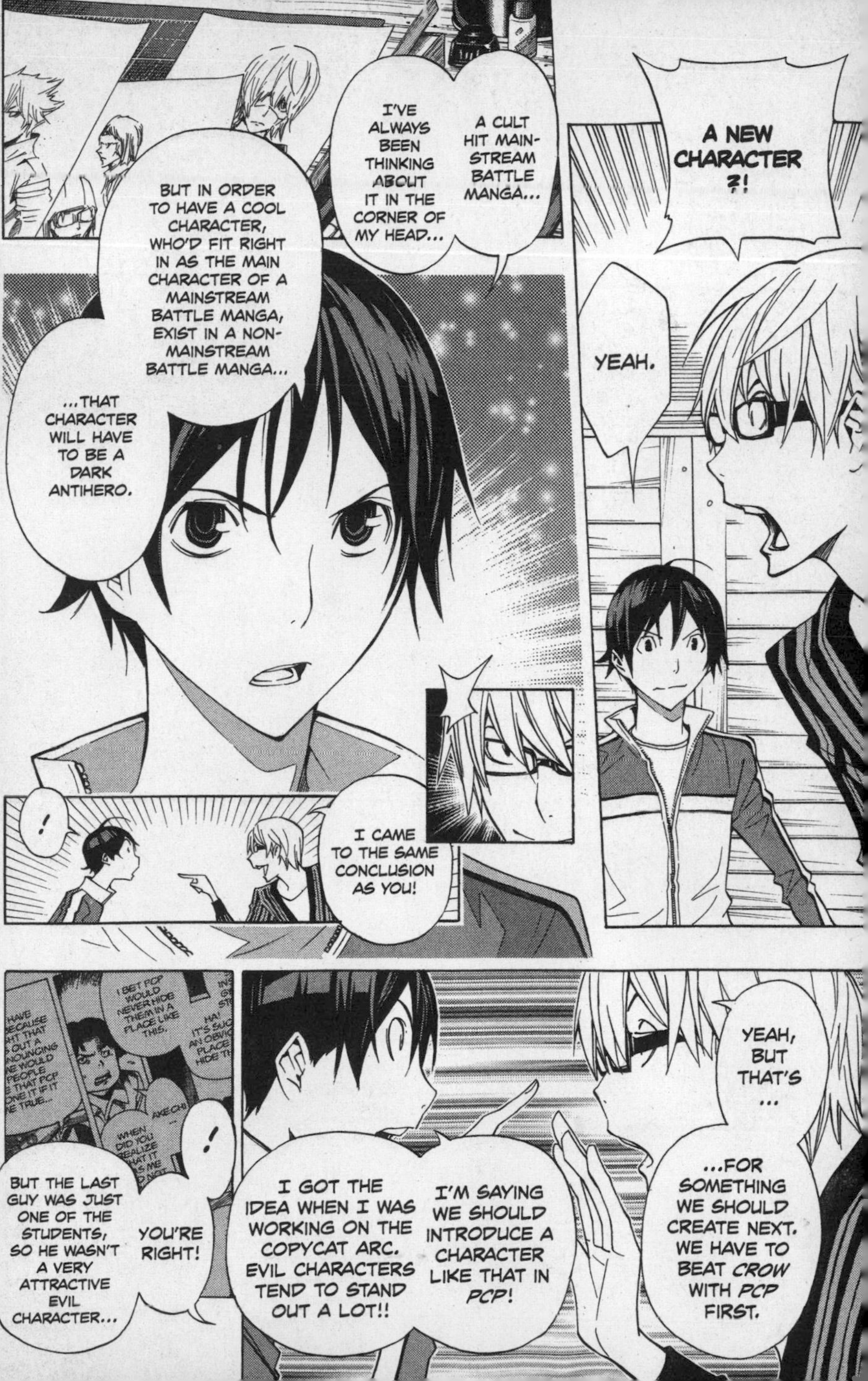
A NEW CHARACTER ?!
YEAH.
A CULT HIT MAIN-STREAM BATTLE MANGA...
I'VE ALWAYS BEEN THINKING ABOUT IT IN THE CORNER OF MY HEAD...
BUT IN ORDER TO HAVE A COOL CHARACTER, WHO'D FIT RIGHT IN AS THE MAIN CHARACTER OF A MAINSTREAM BATTLE MANGA, EXIST IN A NON-MAINSTREAM BATTLE MANGA...
...THAT CHARACTER WILL HAVE TO BE A DARK ANTIHERO.
I CAME TO THE SAME CONCLUSION AS YOU!
!
YEAH, BUT THAT'S ...
...FOR SOMETHING WE SHOULD CREATE NEXT. WE HAVE TO BEAT *CROW* WITH *PCP* FIRST.
I'M SAYING WE SHOULD INTRODUCE A CHARACTER LIKE THAT IN *PCP*!
I GOT THE IDEA WHEN I WAS WORKING ON THE COPYCAT ARC. EVIL CHARACTERS TEND TO STAND OUT A LOT!!
!
YOU'RE RIGHT!
BUT THE LAST GUY WAS JUST ONE OF THE STUDENTS, SO HE WASN'T A VERY ATTRACTIVE EVIL CHARACTER...
I BET PCP WOULD NEVER HIDE THEM IN A PLACE LIKE THIS.

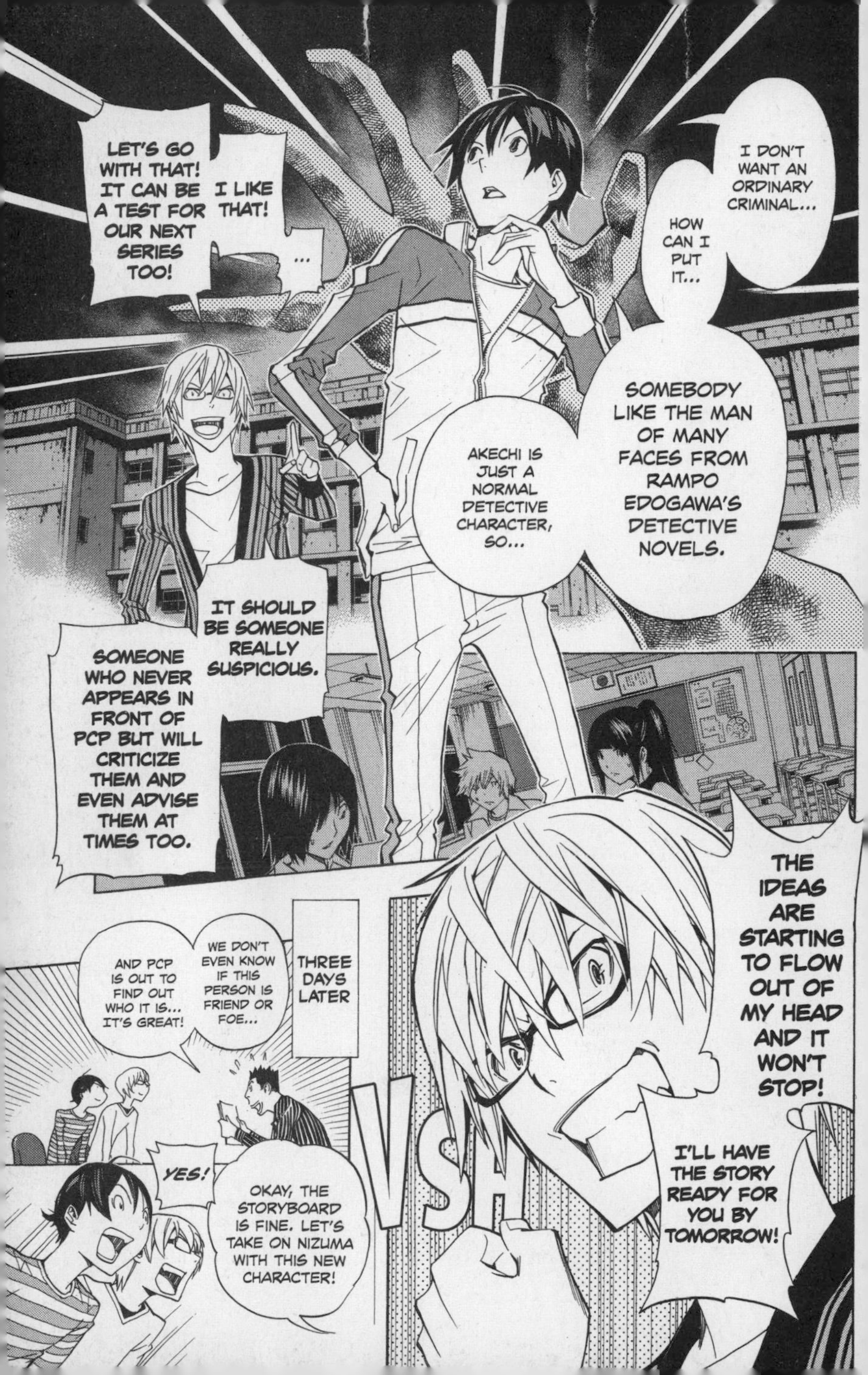
I DON'T WANT AN ORDINARY CRIMINAL...
HOW CAN I PUT IT...
SOMEBODY LIKE THE MAN OF MANY FACES FROM RAMPO EDOGAWA'S DETECTIVE NOVELS.
AKECHI IS JUST A NORMAL DETECTIVE CHARACTER, SO...
...
I LIKE THAT!
LET'S GO WITH THAT! IT CAN BE A TEST FOR OUR NEXT SERIES TOO!
IT SHOULD BE SOMEONE REALLY SUSPICIOUS.
SOMEONE WHO NEVER APPEARS IN FRONT OF PCP BUT WILL CRITICIZE THEM AND EVEN ADVISE THEM AT TIMES TOO.
THE IDEAS ARE STARTING TO FLOW OUT OF MY HEAD AND IT WON'T STOP!
I'LL HAVE THE STORY READY FOR YOU BY TOMORROW!
THREE DAYS LATER
WE DON'T EVEN KNOW IF THIS PERSON IS FRIEND OR FOE...
AND PCP IS OUT TO FIND OUT WHO IT IS... IT'S GREAT!
OKAY, THE STORYBOARD IS FINE. LET'S TAKE ON NIZUMA WITH THIS NEW CHARACTER!
YES!

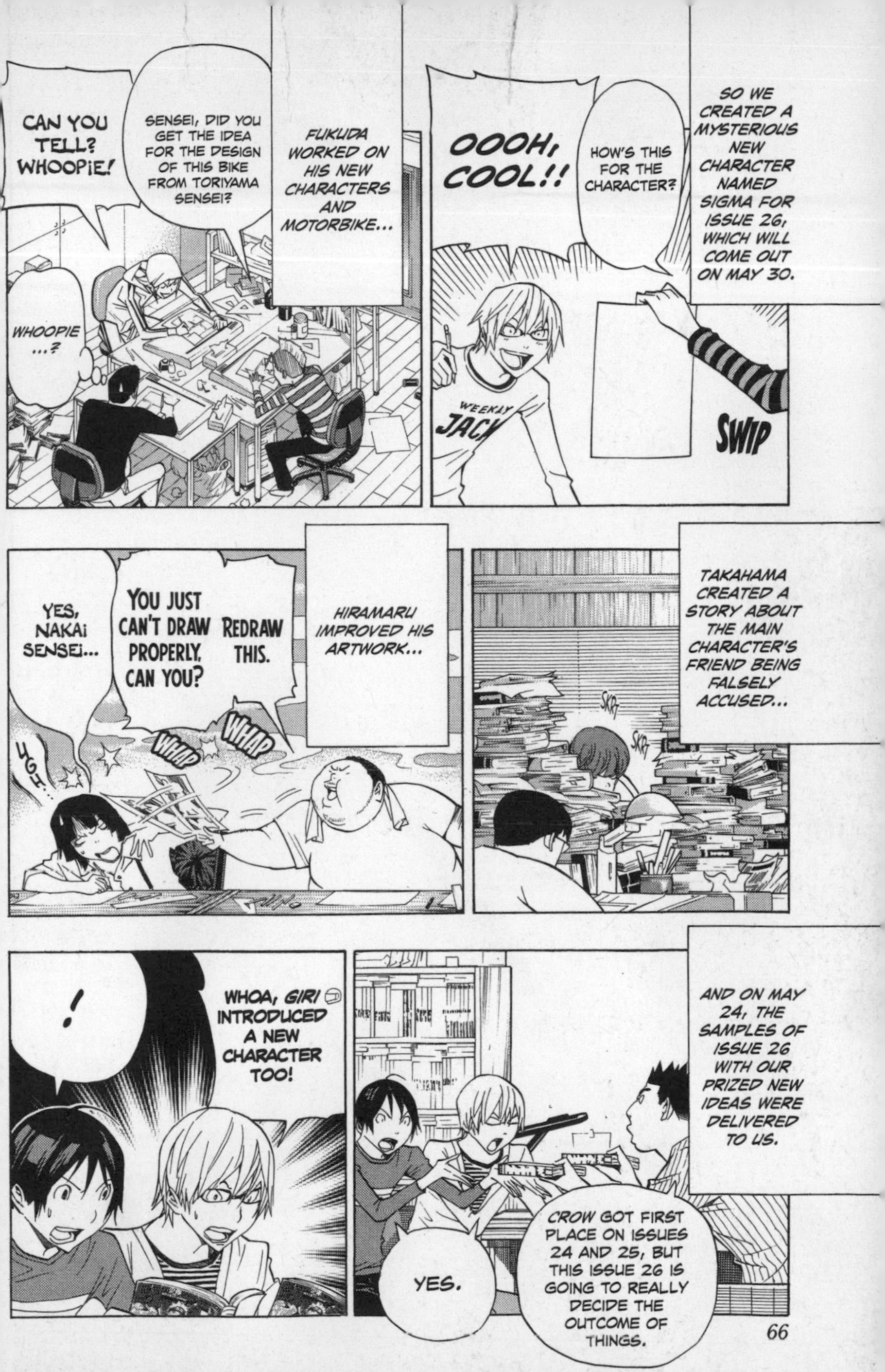
SO WE CREATED A MYSTERIOUS NEW CHARACTER NAMED SIGMA FOR ISSUE 26, WHICH WILL COME OUT ON MAY 30.
HOW'S THIS FOR THE CHARACTER?
OOOH, COOL!!
SWIP
FUKUDA WORKED ON HIS NEW CHARACTERS AND MOTORBIKE...
SENSEI, DID YOU GET THE IDEA FOR THE DESIGN OF THIS BIKE FROM TORIYAMA SENSEI?
CAN YOU TELL? WHOOPIE!
WHOOPIE ...?
TAKAHAMA CREATED A STORY ABOUT THE MAIN CHARACTER'S FRIEND BEING FALSELY ACCUSED...
HIRAMARU IMPROVED HIS ARTWORK...
REDRAW THIS.
YOU JUST CAN'T DRAW PROPERLY, CAN YOU?
YES, NAKAI SENSEI...
WHAP
WHAP
UGH...
AND ON MAY 24, THE SAMPLES OF ISSUE 26 WITH OUR PRIZED NEW IDEAS WERE DELIVERED TO US.
CROW GOT FIRST PLACE ON ISSUES 24 AND 25, BUT THIS ISSUE 26 IS GOING TO REALLY DECIDE THE OUTCOME OF THINGS.
YES.
WHOA, GIRI INTRODUCED A NEW CHARACTER TOO!
!

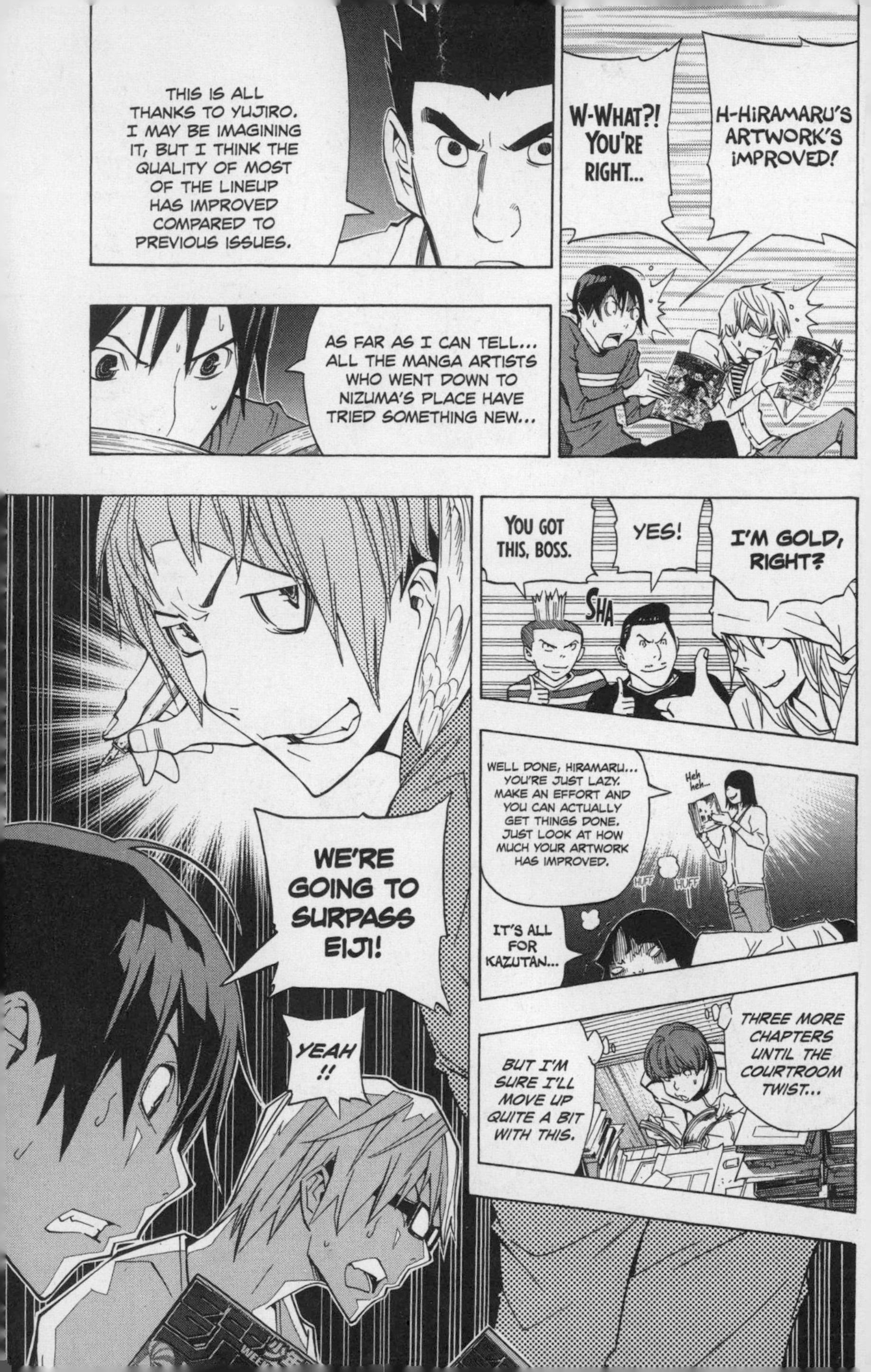
H-HIRAMARU'S ARTWORK'S IMPROVED!
W-WHAT?! YOU'RE RIGHT...
THIS IS ALL THANKS TO YUJIRO. I MAY BE IMAGINING IT, BUT I THINK THE QUALITY OF MOST OF THE LINEUP HAS IMPROVED COMPARED TO PREVIOUS ISSUES.
AS FAR AS I CAN TELL... ALL THE MANGA ARTISTS WHO WENT DOWN TO NIZUMA'S PLACE HAVE TRIED SOMETHING NEW...
I'M GOLD, RIGHT?
YES!
YOU GOT THIS, BOSS.
SHA
WELL DONE, HIRAMARU... YOU'RE JUST LAZY. MAKE AN EFFORT AND YOU CAN ACTUALLY GET THINGS DONE. JUST LOOK AT HOW MUCH YOUR ARTWORK HAS IMPROVED.
Heh heh...
HUFF
HUFF
IT'S ALL FOR KAZUTAN...
THREE MORE CHAPTERS UNTIL THE COURTROOM TWIST...
BUT I'M SURE I'LL MOVE UP QUITE A BIT WITH THIS.
WE'RE GOING TO SURPASS EIJI!
YEAH !!

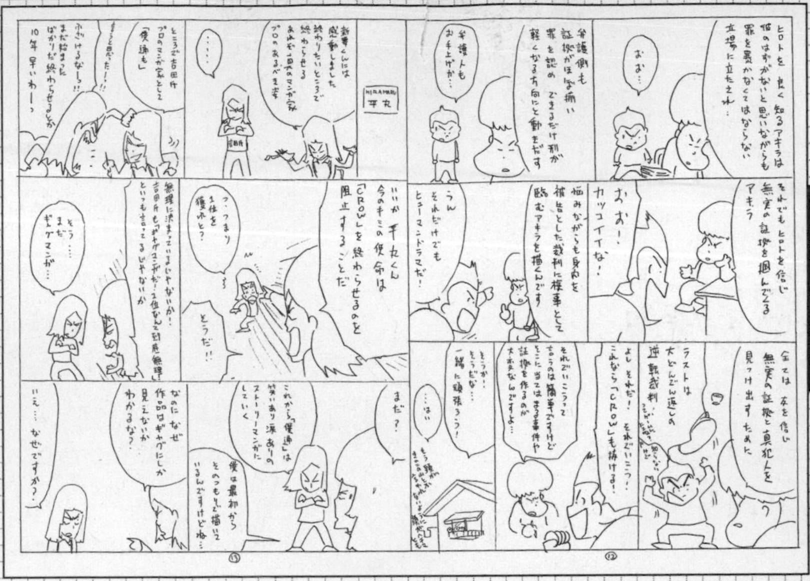
ヒロトを良く知るアキラは
彼のはずがないと思いながらも
罪を責めなくてはならない
立場に立たされ…
おお…
弁護側も
証拠がほぼ揃い
罪を認め
できるだけ刑が
軽くなる方向にと動きだす
弁護人も
お手上げか…
それでもヒロトを信じ
無実の証拠を掴んでくるアキラ
おお!
カッコイイな!
悩みながらも身内を
被告とした裁判に検事として
臨むアキラを描くんです
うん
それだけでも
ヒューマンドラマだ!
全ては友を信じ
無実の証拠と真犯人を
見つけ出すために
ラストは
大どんでん返しの
逆転裁判
よし それだ!
それでいこう!
これなら「CROW」も抜ける!
それでいこうって
そうのは簡単ですけど
そこに当てはまる事件や
証拠を作るのが
大変なんですよ…
そうか…
そうだな…
一緒に頑張ろう!
…はい
新妻くんには
感動しました
終わりにしたいところで
終わらせる
あれぞ真のマンガ家
プロのあるべき姿
HIRAMARU
平丸
……
ところで吉田氏
プロのマンガ家として
「僕通」も
ふざけるなー!!
まだ始まった
ばかりだ 終わらせるとか
10年早いわー
いいか 平丸くん
今のキミの使命は
「CROW」を終わらせるのを
阻止することだ
つ…つまり
1位を
獲れと?
そうだ!!
無理に決まってるじゃないか!
吉田氏も「ギャグマンガだ! 1位なんて到底無理」
といつも言ってるじゃないか
そう…
まだ
ギャグマンガが…
まだ?
これから「僕通」は
笑いあり涙ありの
ストーリーマンガに
していく
僕は最初から
そのつもりで描いて
いるんですけどね…
なのになぜ
作品はギャグにしか
見えないか
わかるな?
いえ… なぜですか?
12
13

OHBA'S STORYBOARD

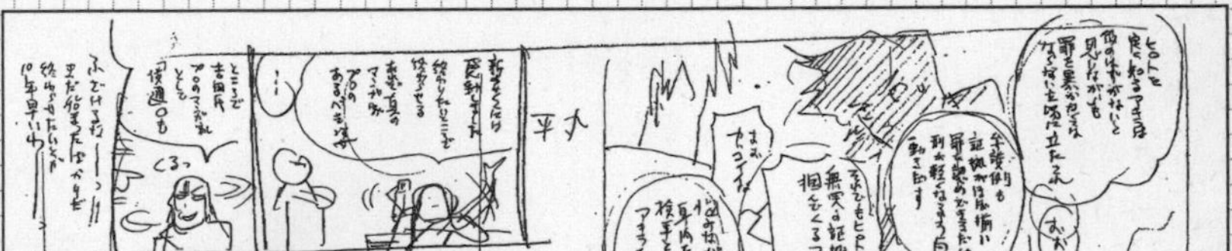

OBATA'S STORYBOARD

COMPLETE!

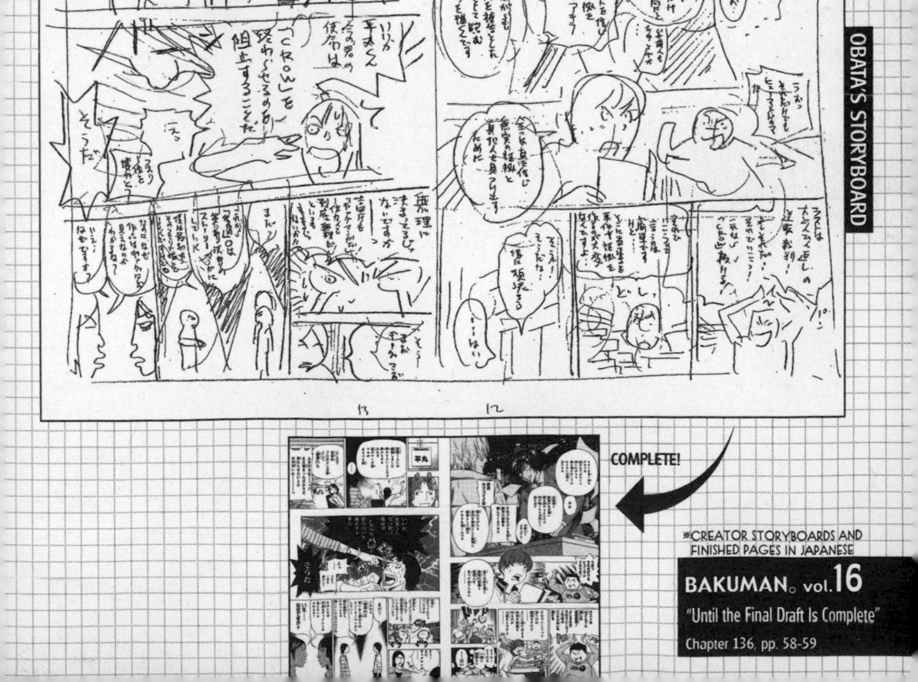

*CREATOR STORYBOARDS AND FINISHED PAGES IN JAPANESE

BAKUMAN。 vol.16

"Until the Final Draft Is Complete"

Chapter 136, pp. 58-59

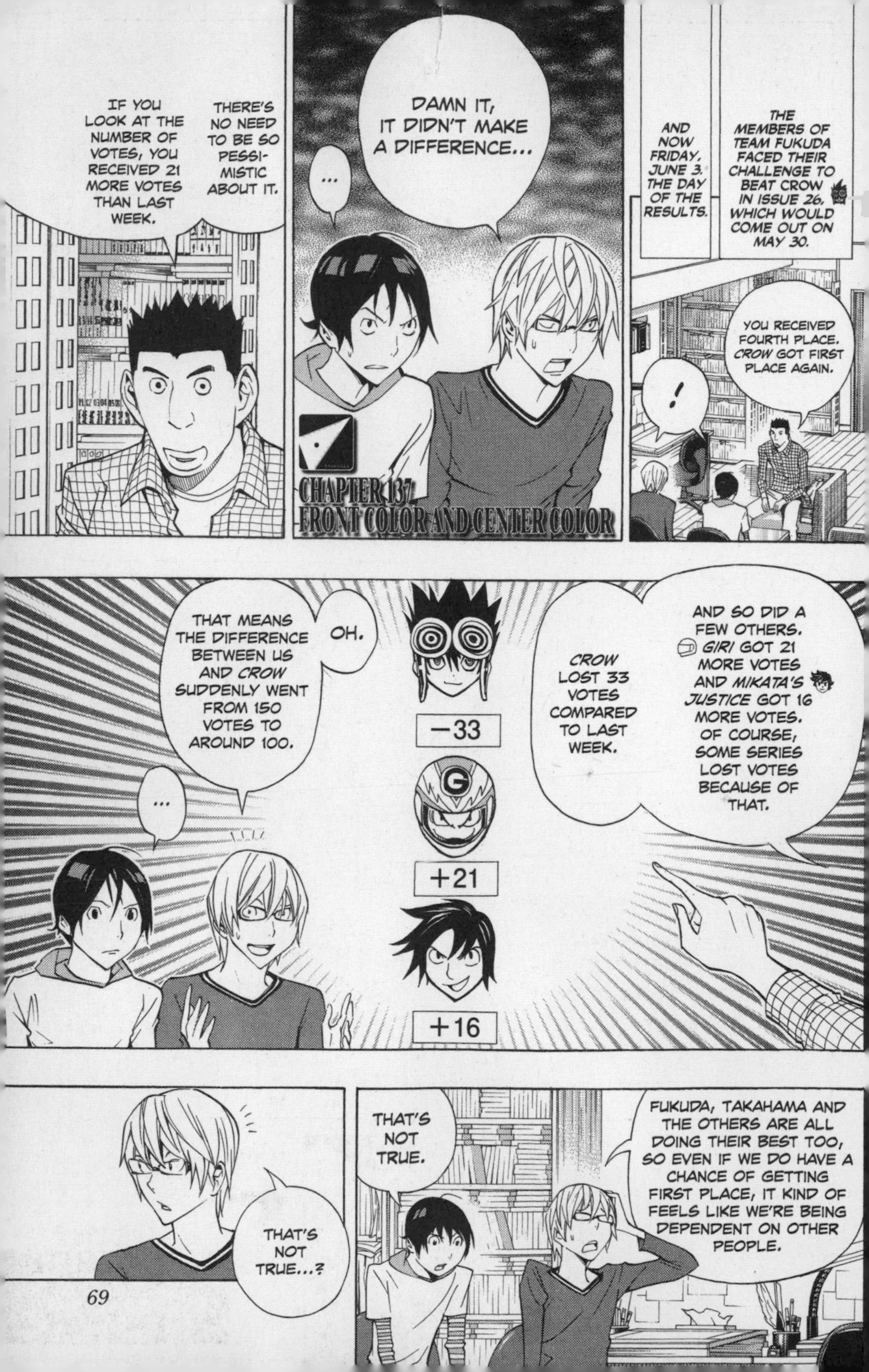
THE MEMBERS OF TEAM FUKUDA FACED THEIR CHALLENGE TO BEAT CROW IN ISSUE 26, WHICH WOULD COME OUT ON MAY 30.
AND NOW FRIDAY, JUNE 3. THE DAY OF THE RESULTS.
YOU RECEIVED FOURTH PLACE. CROW GOT FIRST PLACE AGAIN.
!
DAMN IT, IT DIDN'T MAKE A DIFFERENCE...
...
CHAPTER 137: FRONT COLOR AND CENTER COLOR
THERE'S NO NEED TO BE SO PESSIMISTIC ABOUT IT.
IF YOU LOOK AT THE NUMBER OF VOTES, YOU RECEIVED 21 MORE VOTES THAN LAST WEEK.
AND SO DID A FEW OTHERS. GIRI GOT 21 MORE VOTES AND MIKATA'S JUSTICE GOT 16 MORE VOTES. OF COURSE, SOME SERIES LOST VOTES BECAUSE OF THAT.
CROW LOST 33 VOTES COMPARED TO LAST WEEK.
−33
+21
+16
OH.
THAT MEANS THE DIFFERENCE BETWEEN US AND CROW SUDDENLY WENT FROM 150 VOTES TO AROUND 100.
...
FUKUDA, TAKAHAMA AND THE OTHERS ARE ALL DOING THEIR BEST TOO, SO EVEN IF WE DO HAVE A CHANCE OF GETTING FIRST PLACE, IT KIND OF FEELS LIKE WE'RE BEING DEPENDENT ON OTHER PEOPLE.
THAT'S NOT TRUE.
THAT'S NOT TRUE...?

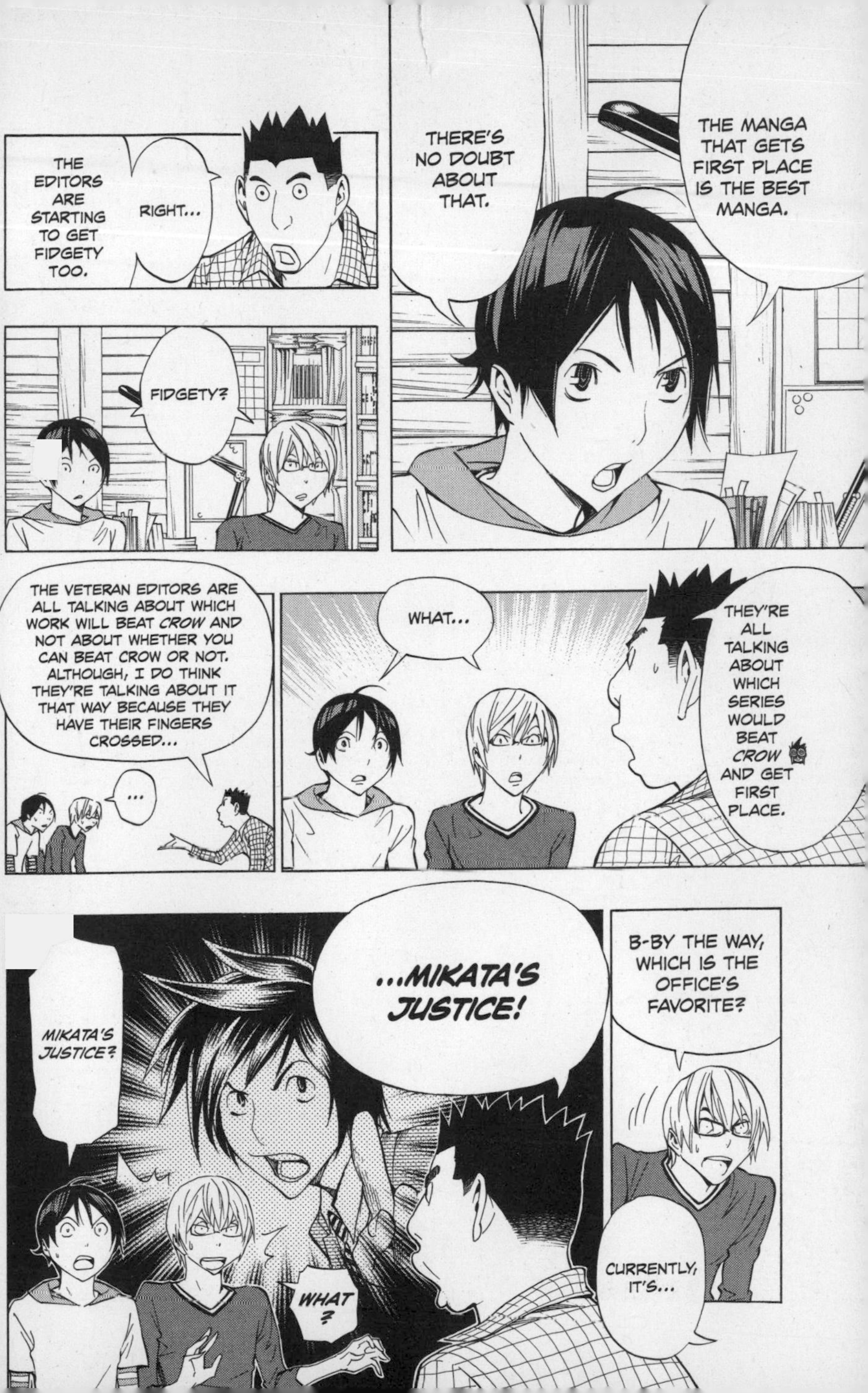
THE MANGA THAT GETS FIRST PLACE IS THE BEST MANGA.
THERE'S NO DOUBT ABOUT THAT.
RIGHT...
THE EDITORS ARE STARTING TO GET FIDGETY TOO.
FIDGETY?
THEY'RE ALL TALKING ABOUT WHICH SERIES WOULD BEAT *CROW* AND GET FIRST PLACE.
WHAT...
THE VETERAN EDITORS ARE ALL TALKING ABOUT WHICH WORK WILL BEAT *CROW* AND NOT ABOUT WHETHER YOU CAN BEAT CROW OR NOT. ALTHOUGH, I DO THINK THEY'RE TALKING ABOUT IT THAT WAY BECAUSE THEY HAVE THEIR FINGERS CROSSED...
...
B-BY THE WAY, WHICH IS THE OFFICE'S FAVORITE?
CURRENTLY, IT'S...
...MIKATA'S JUSTICE!
MIKATA'S JUSTICE?
WHAT?

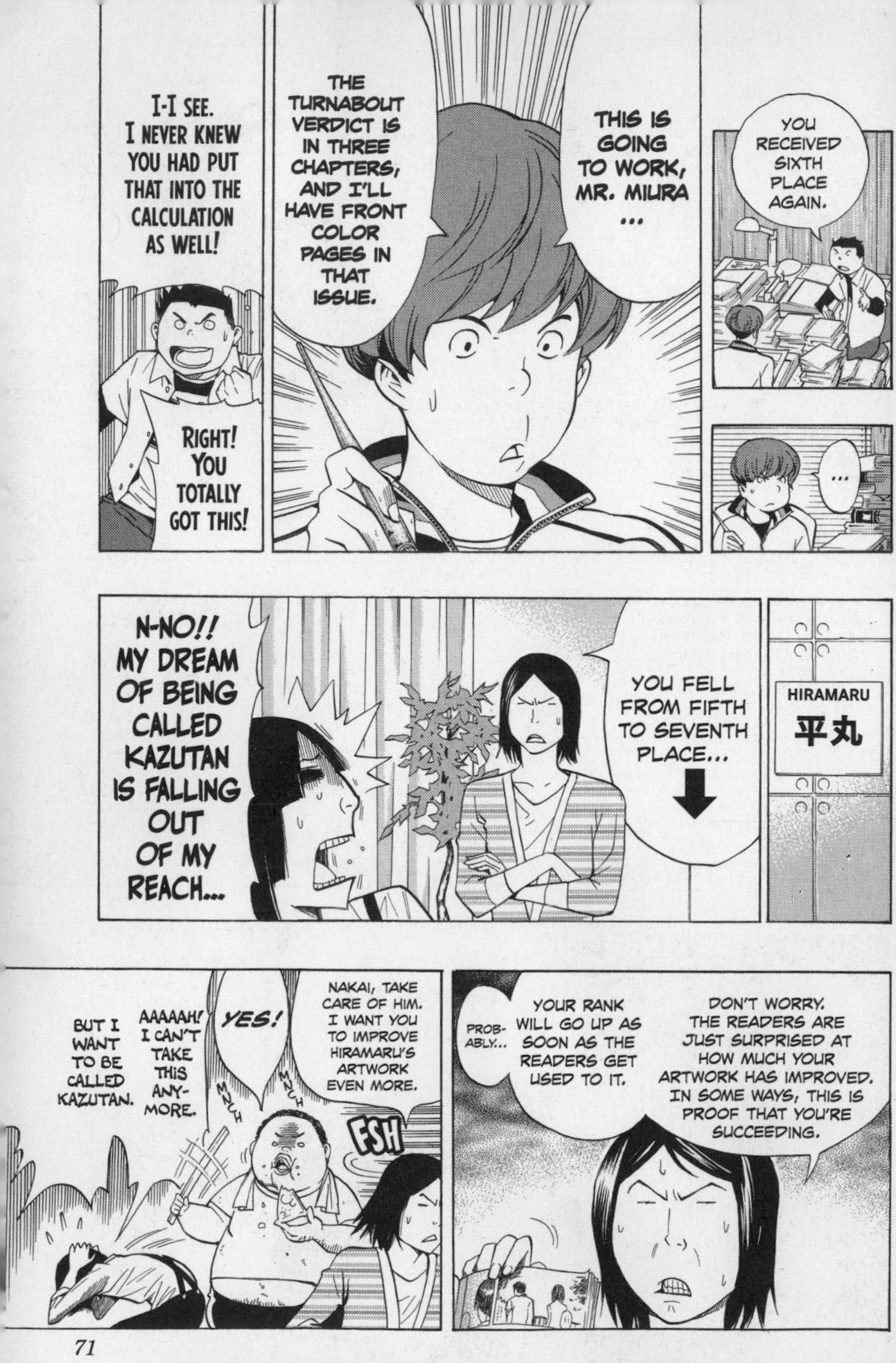
YOU RECEIVED SIXTH PLACE AGAIN.
...
THIS IS GOING TO WORK, MR. MIURA ...
THE TURNABOUT VERDICT IS IN THREE CHAPTERS, AND I'LL HAVE FRONT COLOR PAGES IN THAT ISSUE.
I-I SEE. I NEVER KNEW YOU HAD PUT THAT INTO THE CALCULATION AS WELL!
RIGHT! YOU TOTALLY GOT THIS!
HIRAMARU
平丸
YOU FELL FROM FIFTH TO SEVENTH PLACE...
N-NO!! MY DREAM OF BEING CALLED KAZUTAN IS FALLING OUT OF MY REACH...
DON'T WORRY. THE READERS ARE JUST SURPRISED AT HOW MUCH YOUR ARTWORK HAS IMPROVED. IN SOME WAYS, THIS IS PROOF THAT YOU'RE SUCCEEDING.
YOUR RANK WILL GO UP AS SOON AS THE READERS GET USED TO IT.
PROB-ABLY...
NAKAI, TAKE CARE OF HIM. I WANT YOU TO IMPROVE HIRAMARU'S ARTWORK EVEN MORE.
YES!
MNCH
MNCH
FSH
AAAAAH! I CAN'T TAKE THIS ANY-MORE.
BUT I WANT TO BE CALLED KAZUTAN.

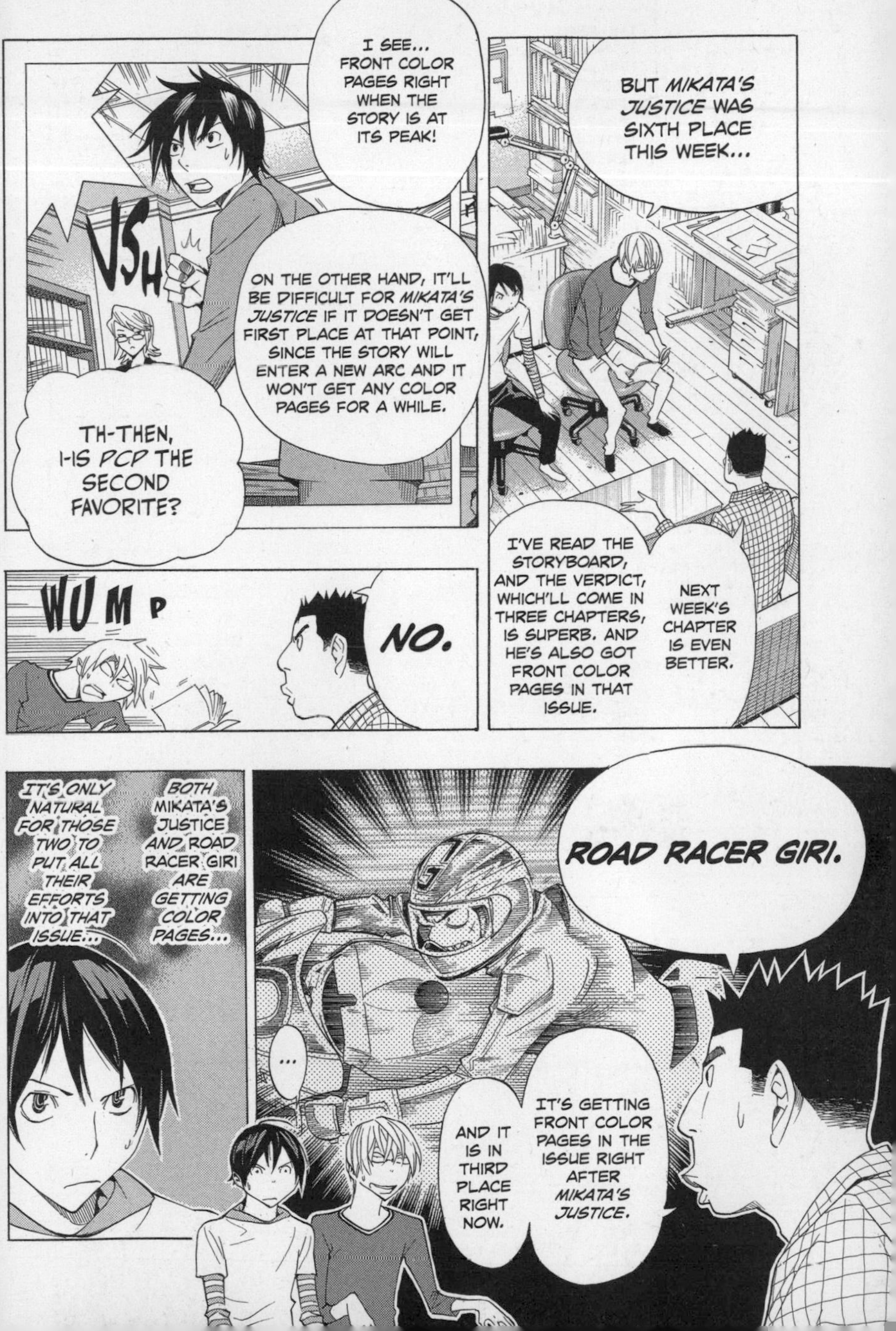
BUT *MIKATA'S JUSTICE* WAS SIXTH PLACE THIS WEEK...
NEXT WEEK'S CHAPTER IS EVEN BETTER.
I'VE READ THE STORYBOARD, AND THE VERDICT, WHICH'LL COME IN THREE CHAPTERS, IS SUPERB. AND HE'S ALSO GOT FRONT COLOR PAGES IN THAT ISSUE.
I SEE... FRONT COLOR PAGES RIGHT WHEN THE STORY IS AT ITS PEAK!
ON THE OTHER HAND, IT'LL BE DIFFICULT FOR *MIKATA'S JUSTICE* IF IT DOESN'T GET FIRST PLACE AT THAT POINT, SINCE THE STORY WILL ENTER A NEW ARC AND IT WON'T GET ANY COLOR PAGES FOR A WHILE.
VSH
TH-THEN, I-IS *PCP* THE SECOND FAVORITE?
NO.
WUMP
ROAD RACER GIRI.
IT'S GETTING FRONT COLOR PAGES IN THE ISSUE RIGHT AFTER *MIKATA'S JUSTICE*.
AND IT IS IN THIRD PLACE RIGHT NOW.
...
BOTH MIKATA'S JUSTICE AND ROAD RACER GIRI ARE GETTING COLOR PAGES...
IT'S ONLY NATURAL FOR THOSE TWO TO PUT ALL THEIR EFFORTS INTO THAT ISSUE...

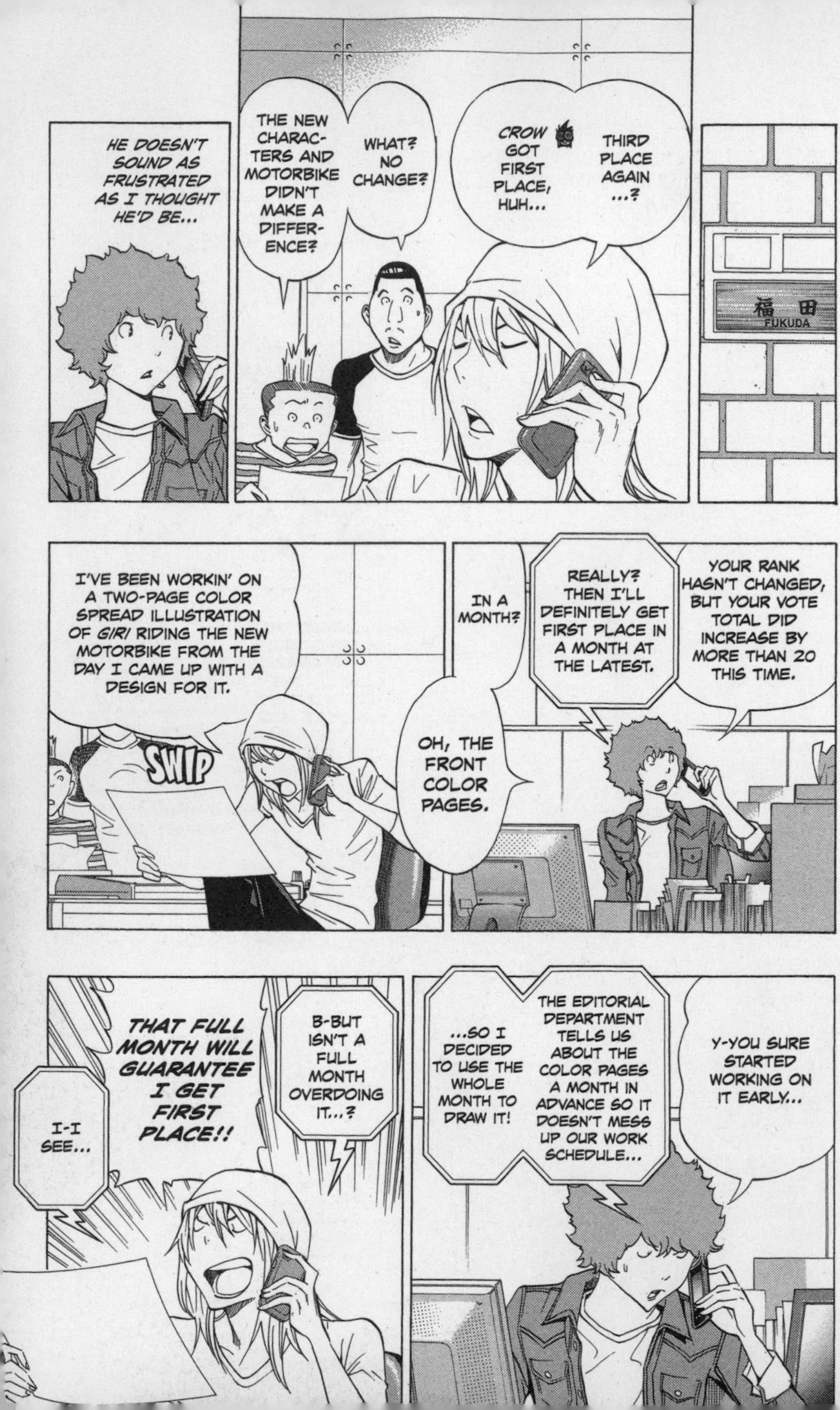

福田
FUKUDA
CROW GOT FIRST PLACE, HUH... THIRD PLACE AGAIN...?
WHAT? NO CHANGE?
THE NEW CHARACTERS AND MOTORBIKE DIDN'T MAKE A DIFFERENCE?
HE DOESN'T SOUND AS FRUSTRATED AS I THOUGHT HE'D BE...
YOUR RANK HASN'T CHANGED, BUT YOUR VOTE TOTAL DID INCREASE BY MORE THAN 20 THIS TIME.
REALLY? THEN I'LL DEFINITELY GET FIRST PLACE IN A MONTH AT THE LATEST.
IN A MONTH?
OH, THE FRONT COLOR PAGES.
I'VE BEEN WORKIN' ON A TWO-PAGE COLOR SPREAD ILLUSTRATION OF GIRI RIDING THE NEW MOTORBIKE FROM THE DAY I CAME UP WITH A DESIGN FOR IT.
SWIP
Y-YOU SURE STARTED WORKING ON IT EARLY...
THE EDITORIAL DEPARTMENT TELLS US ABOUT THE COLOR PAGES A MONTH IN ADVANCE SO IT DOESN'T MESS UP OUR WORK SCHEDULE...
...SO I DECIDED TO USE THE WHOLE MONTH TO DRAW IT!
B-BUT ISN'T A FULL MONTH OVERDOING IT...?
THAT FULL MONTH WILL GUARANTEE I GET FIRST PLACE!!
I-I SEE...

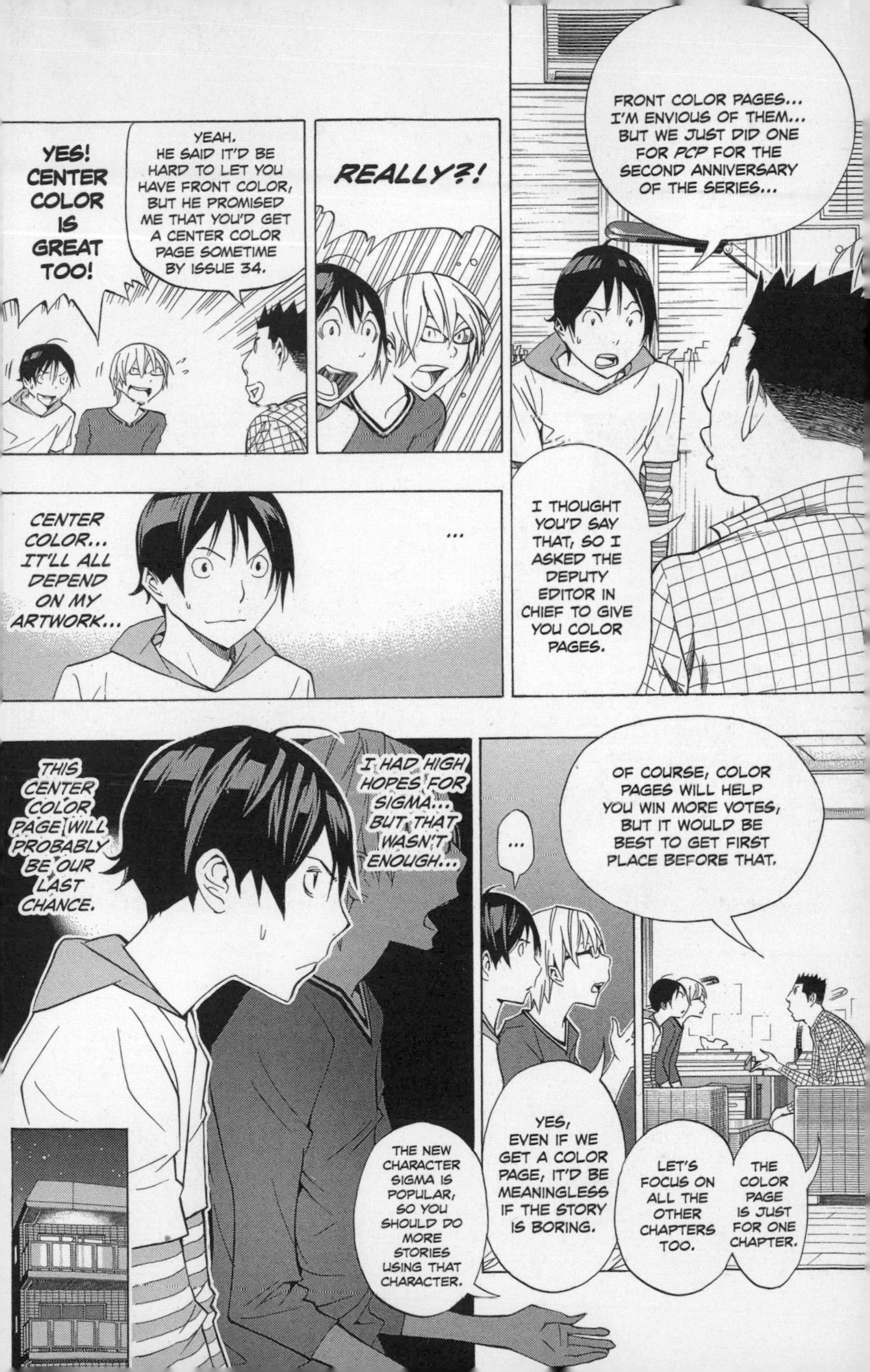
FRONT COLOR PAGES... I'M ENVIOUS OF THEM... BUT WE JUST DID ONE FOR *PCP* FOR THE SECOND ANNIVERSARY OF THE SERIES...
I THOUGHT YOU'D SAY THAT, SO I ASKED THE DEPUTY EDITOR IN CHIEF TO GIVE YOU COLOR PAGES.
REALLY?!
YEAH. HE SAID IT'D BE HARD TO LET YOU HAVE FRONT COLOR, BUT HE PROMISED ME THAT YOU'D GET A CENTER COLOR PAGE SOMETIME BY ISSUE 34.
YES! CENTER COLOR IS GREAT TOO!
...
CENTER COLOR... IT'LL ALL DEPEND ON MY ARTWORK...
OF COURSE, COLOR PAGES WILL HELP YOU WIN MORE VOTES, BUT IT WOULD BE BEST TO GET FIRST PLACE BEFORE THAT.
...
THE COLOR PAGE IS JUST FOR ONE CHAPTER.
LET'S FOCUS ON ALL THE OTHER CHAPTERS TOO.
YES, EVEN IF WE GET A COLOR PAGE, IT'D BE MEANINGLESS IF THE STORY IS BORING.
THE NEW CHARACTER SIGMA IS POPULAR, SO YOU SHOULD DO MORE STORIES USING THAT CHARACTER.
I HAD HIGH HOPES FOR SIGMA... BUT THAT WASN'T ENOUGH...
THIS CENTER COLOR PAGE WILL PROBABLY BE OUR LAST CHANCE.

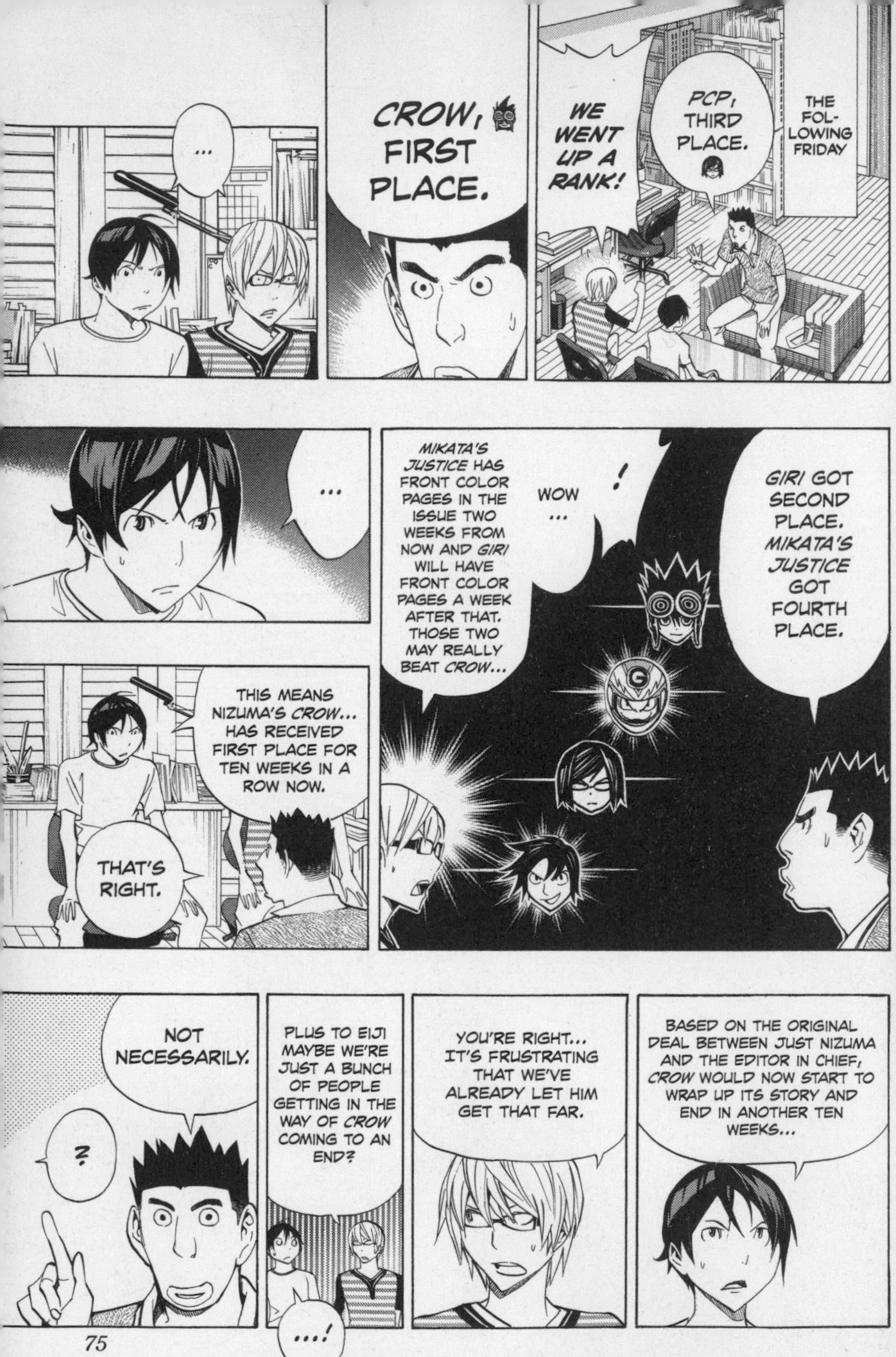
THE FOL-LOWING FRIDAY
PCP, THIRD PLACE.
WE WENT UP A RANK!
CROW, FIRST PLACE.
...
GIRI GOT SECOND PLACE. MIKATA'S JUSTICE GOT FOURTH PLACE.
!
WOW ...
MIKATA'S JUSTICE HAS FRONT COLOR PAGES IN THE ISSUE TWO WEEKS FROM NOW AND GIRI WILL HAVE FRONT COLOR PAGES A WEEK AFTER THAT. THOSE TWO MAY REALLY BEAT CROW...
...
THIS MEANS NIZUMA'S CROW... HAS RECEIVED FIRST PLACE FOR TEN WEEKS IN A ROW NOW.
THAT'S RIGHT.
BASED ON THE ORIGINAL DEAL BETWEEN JUST NIZUMA AND THE EDITOR IN CHIEF, CROW WOULD NOW START TO WRAP UP ITS STORY AND END IN ANOTHER TEN WEEKS...
YOU'RE RIGHT... IT'S FRUSTRATING THAT WE'VE ALREADY LET HIM GET THAT FAR.
PLUS TO EIJI MAYBE WE'RE JUST A BUNCH OF PEOPLE GETTING IN THE WAY OF CROW COMING TO AN END?
...!
NOT NECESSARILY.
?

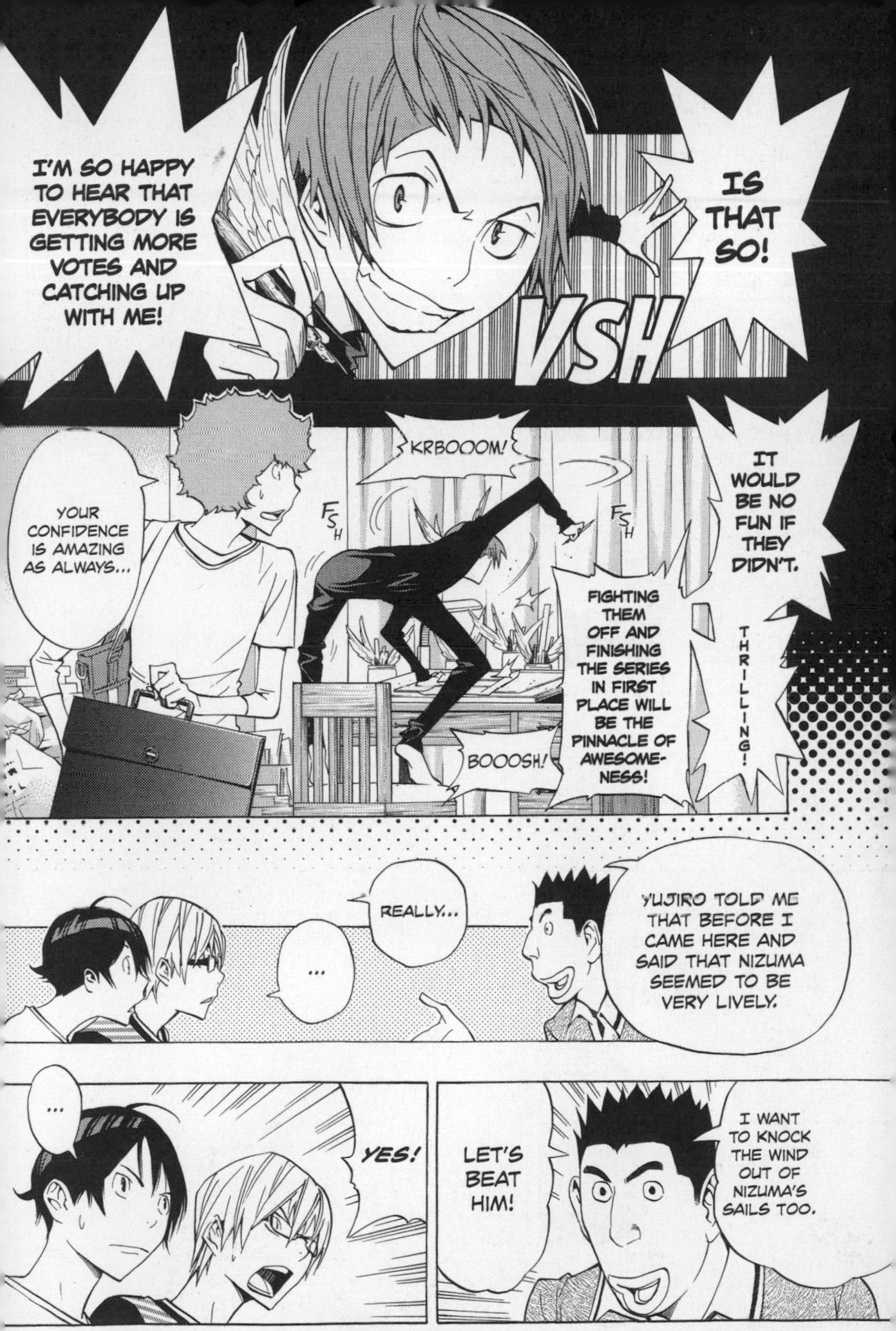
IS THAT SO!
I'M SO HAPPY TO HEAR THAT EVERYBODY IS GETTING MORE VOTES AND CATCHING UP WITH ME!
VSH
IT WOULD BE NO FUN IF THEY DIDN'T.
FIGHTING THEM OFF AND FINISHING THE SERIES IN FIRST PLACE WILL BE THE PINNACLE OF AWESOME-NESS!
THRILLING!
KRBOOOM!
FSH
FSH
BOOOSH!
YOUR CONFIDENCE IS AMAZING AS ALWAYS...
YUJIRO TOLD ME THAT BEFORE I CAME HERE AND SAID THAT NIZUMA SEEMED TO BE VERY LIVELY.
REALLY...
...
I WANT TO KNOCK THE WIND OUT OF NIZUMA'S SAILS TOO.
LET'S BEAT HIM!
YES!
...

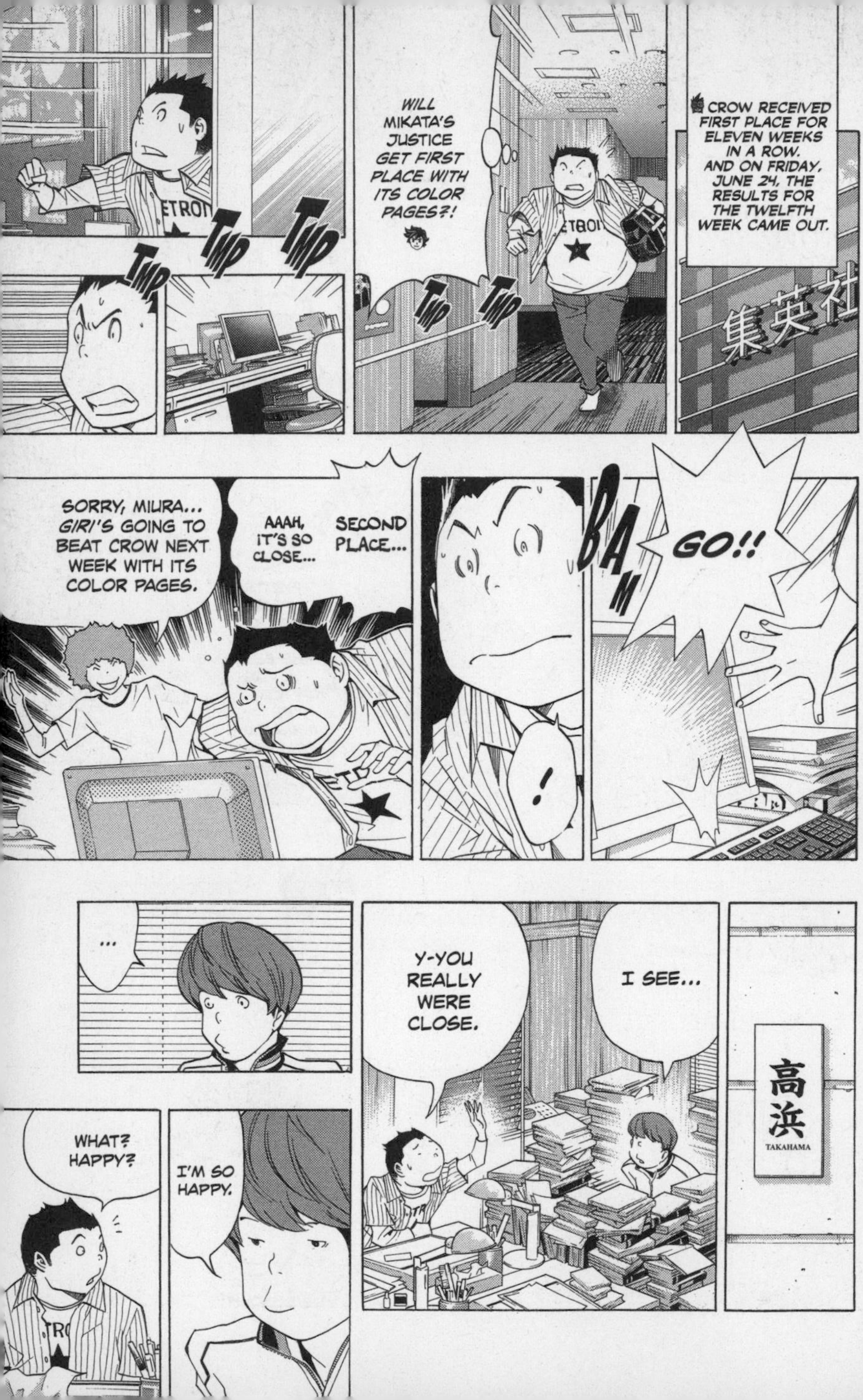

CROW RECEIVED FIRST PLACE FOR ELEVEN WEEKS IN A ROW. AND ON FRIDAY, JUNE 24, THE RESULTS FOR THE TWELFTH WEEK CAME OUT.
集英社
WILL MIKATA'S JUSTICE GET FIRST PLACE WITH ITS COLOR PAGES?!
TMP
TMP
TMP
TMP
TMP
BAM
GO!!
!
SECOND PLACE...
AAAH, IT'S SO CLOSE...
SORRY, MIURA... GIRI'S GOING TO BEAT CROW NEXT WEEK WITH ITS COLOR PAGES.
高浜
TAKAHAMA
I SEE...
Y-YOU REALLY WERE CLOSE.
...
I'M SO HAPPY.
WHAT? HAPPY?

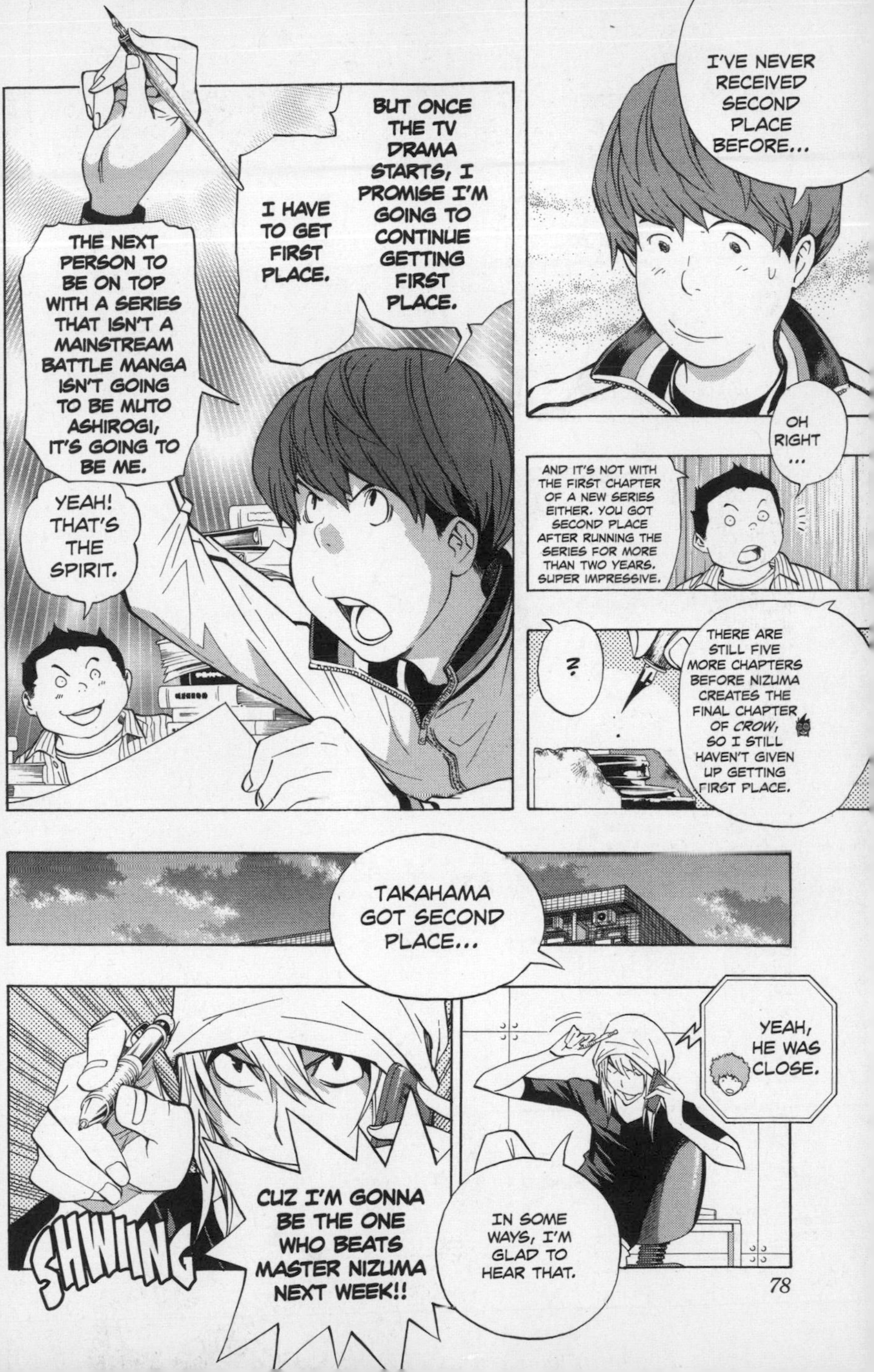

I'VE NEVER RECEIVED SECOND PLACE BEFORE...
OH RIGHT...
AND IT'S NOT WITH THE FIRST CHAPTER OF A NEW SERIES EITHER. YOU GOT SECOND PLACE AFTER RUNNING THE SERIES FOR MORE THAN TWO YEARS. SUPER IMPRESSIVE.
THERE ARE STILL FIVE MORE CHAPTERS BEFORE NIZUMA CREATES THE FINAL CHAPTER OF *CROW*, SO I STILL HAVEN'T GIVEN UP GETTING FIRST PLACE.
?
BUT ONCE THE TV DRAMA STARTS, I PROMISE I'M GOING TO CONTINUE GETTING FIRST PLACE.
I HAVE TO GET FIRST PLACE.
THE NEXT PERSON TO BE ON TOP WITH A SERIES THAT ISN'T A MAINSTREAM BATTLE MANGA ISN'T GOING TO BE MUTO ASHIROGI, IT'S GOING TO BE ME.
YEAH! THAT'S THE SPIRIT.
TAKAHAMA GOT SECOND PLACE...
YEAH, HE WAS CLOSE.
IN SOME WAYS, I'M GLAD TO HEAR THAT.
CUZ I'M GONNA BE THE ONE WHO BEATS MASTER NIZUMA NEXT WEEK!!
SHWIIING

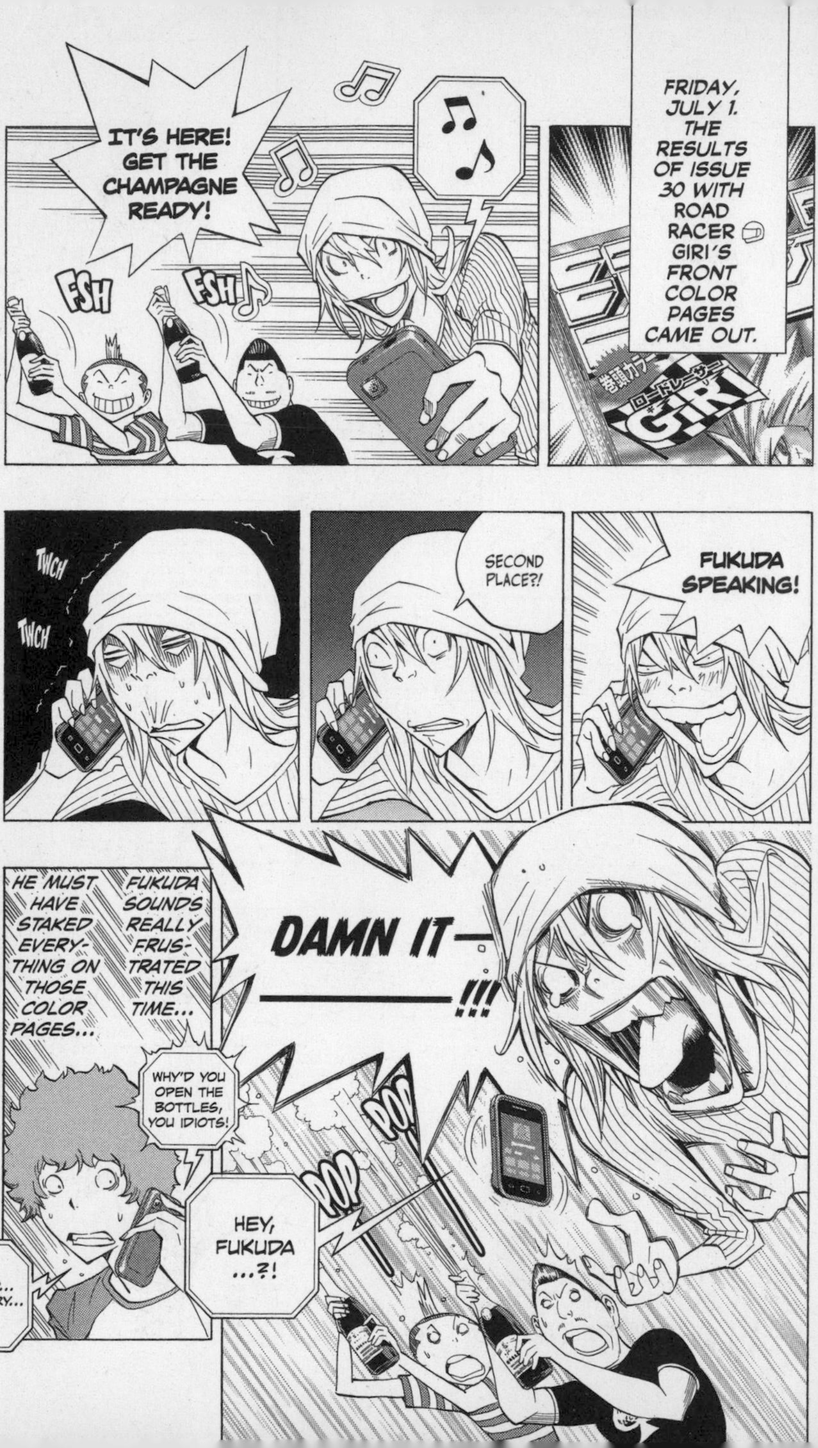
FRIDAY, JULY 1. THE RESULTS OF ISSUE 30 WITH ROAD RACER GIRI'S FRONT COLOR PAGES CAME OUT.
巻頭カラー
ロードレーサー
GIRI
IT'S HERE! GET THE CHAMPAGNE READY!
FSH
FSH
FUKUDA SPEAKING!
SECOND PLACE?!
TWCH
TWCH
DAMN IT———!!!
FUKUDA SOUNDS REALLY FRUS-TRATED THIS TIME...
HE MUST HAVE STAKED EVERY-THING ON THOSE COLOR PAGES...
WHY'D YOU OPEN THE BOTTLES, YOU IDIOTS!
POP
POP
HEY, FUKUDA ...?!
EEP... SORRY...

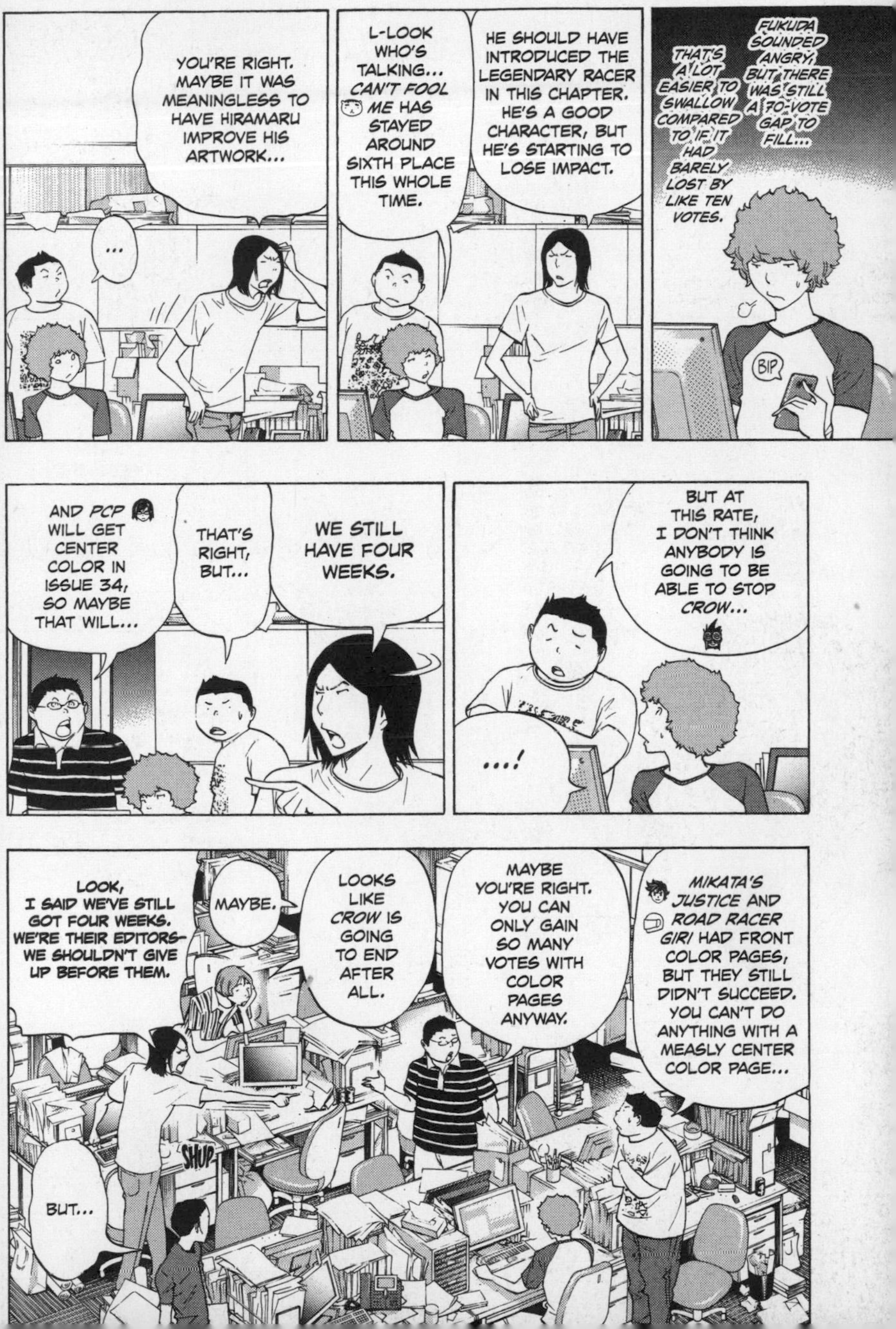
FUKUDA SOUNDED ANGRY, BUT THERE WAS STILL A 70-VOTE GAP TO FILL...
THAT'S A LOT EASIER TO SWALLOW COMPARED TO IF IT HAD BARELY LOST BY LIKE TEN VOTES.
BIP
HE SHOULD HAVE INTRODUCED THE LEGENDARY RACER IN THIS CHAPTER. HE'S A GOOD CHARACTER, BUT HE'S STARTING TO LOSE IMPACT.
L-LOOK WHO'S TALKING... CAN'T FOOL ME HAS STAYED AROUND SIXTH PLACE THIS WHOLE TIME.
YOU'RE RIGHT. MAYBE IT WAS MEANINGLESS TO HAVE HIRAMARU IMPROVE HIS ARTWORK...
...
BUT AT THIS RATE, I DON'T THINK ANYBODY IS GOING TO BE ABLE TO STOP CROW...
...!
WE STILL HAVE FOUR WEEKS.
THAT'S RIGHT, BUT...
AND PCP WILL GET CENTER COLOR IN ISSUE 34, SO MAYBE THAT WILL...
MIKATA'S JUSTICE AND ROAD RACER GIRI HAD FRONT COLOR PAGES, BUT THEY STILL DIDN'T SUCCEED. YOU CAN'T DO ANYTHING WITH A MEASLY CENTER COLOR PAGE...
MAYBE YOU'RE RIGHT. YOU CAN ONLY GAIN SO MANY VOTES WITH COLOR PAGES ANYWAY.
LOOKS LIKE CROW IS GOING TO END AFTER ALL.
MAYBE.
LOOK, I SAID WE'VE STILL GOT FOUR WEEKS. WE'RE THEIR EDITORS- WE SHOULDN'T GIVE UP BEFORE THEM.
SHUP
BUT...

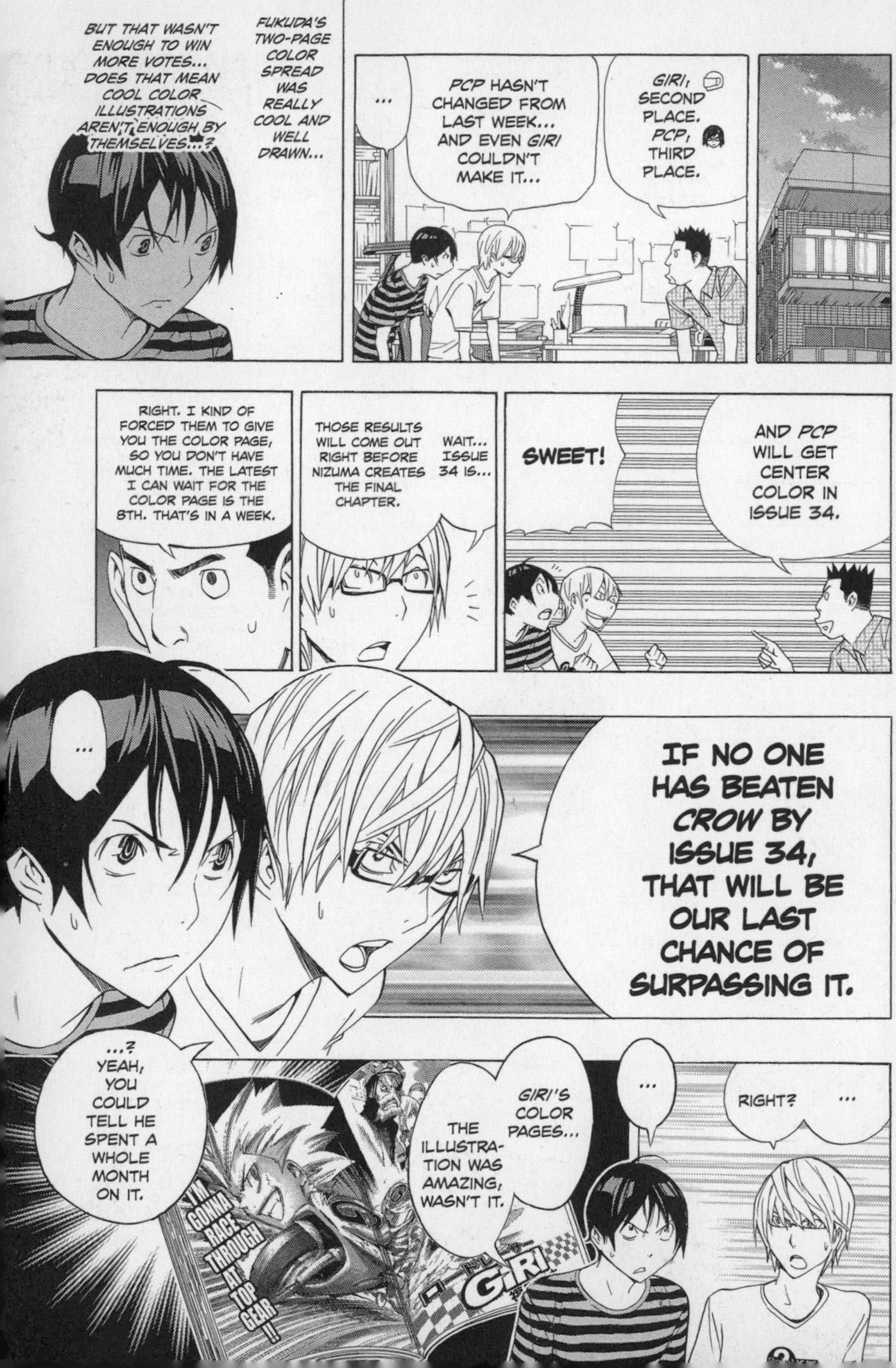
GIRI, SECOND PLACE. PCP, THIRD PLACE.
PCP HASN'T CHANGED FROM LAST WEEK... AND EVEN GIRI COULDN'T MAKE IT...
...
FUKUDA'S TWO-PAGE COLOR SPREAD WAS REALLY COOL AND WELL DRAWN...
BUT THAT WASN'T ENOUGH TO WIN MORE VOTES... DOES THAT MEAN COOL COLOR ILLUSTRATIONS AREN'T ENOUGH BY THEMSELVES...?
AND PCP WILL GET CENTER COLOR IN ISSUE 34.
SWEET!
WAIT... ISSUE 34 IS...
THOSE RESULTS WILL COME OUT RIGHT BEFORE NIZUMA CREATES THE FINAL CHAPTER.
RIGHT. I KIND OF FORCED THEM TO GIVE YOU THE COLOR PAGE, SO YOU DON'T HAVE MUCH TIME. THE LATEST I CAN WAIT FOR THE COLOR PAGE IS THE 8TH. THAT'S IN A WEEK.
IF NO ONE HAS BEATEN CROW BY ISSUE 34, THAT WILL BE OUR LAST CHANCE OF SURPASSING IT.
...
...
RIGHT?
...
GIRI'S COLOR PAGES...
THE ILLUSTRATION WAS AMAZING, WASN'T IT.
...? YEAH, YOU COULD TELL HE SPENT A WHOLE MONTH ON IT.
I'M GONNA RACE THROUGH AT TOP GEAR!!
GIRI

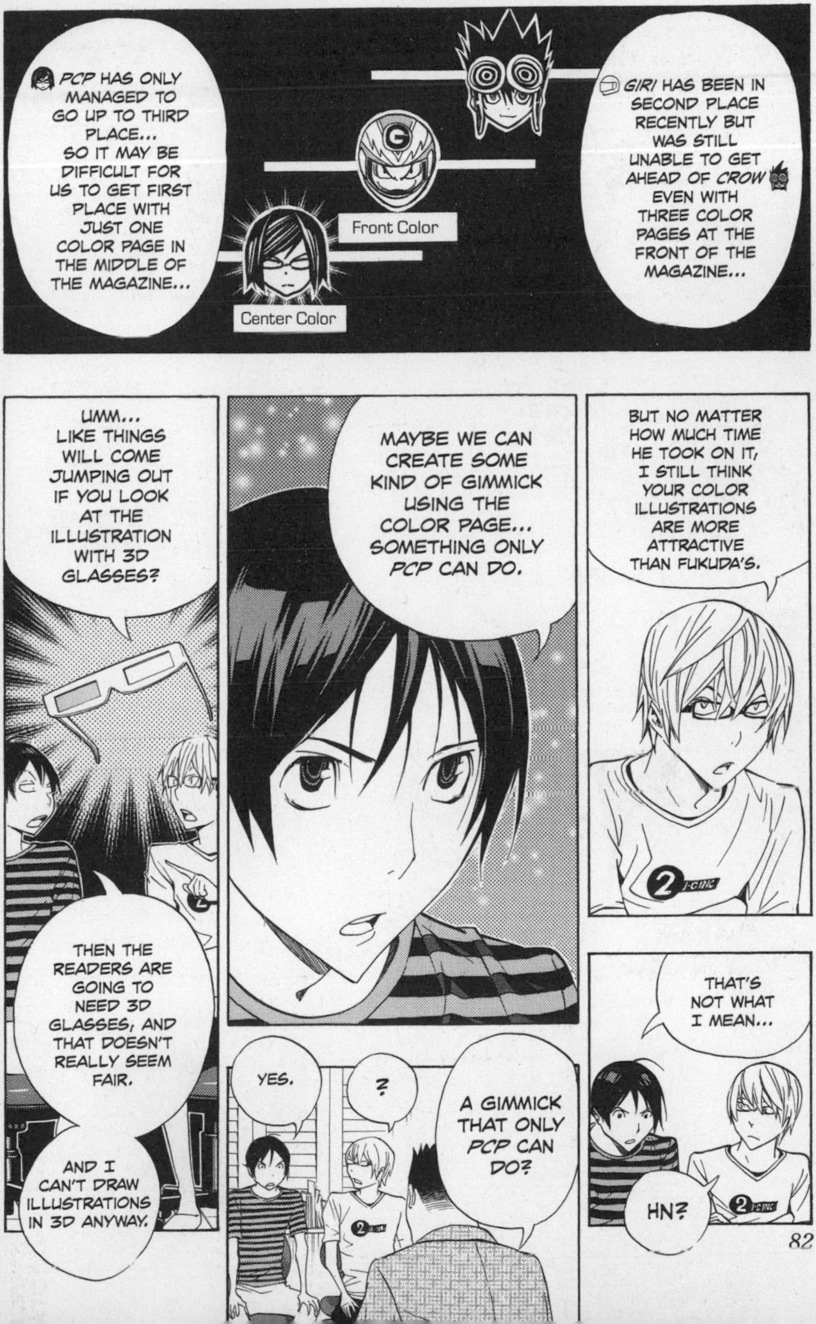
GIRI HAS BEEN IN SECOND PLACE RECENTLY BUT WAS STILL UNABLE TO GET AHEAD OF CROW EVEN WITH THREE COLOR PAGES AT THE FRONT OF THE MAGAZINE...
Front Color
PCP HAS ONLY MANAGED TO GO UP TO THIRD PLACE... SO IT MAY BE DIFFICULT FOR US TO GET FIRST PLACE WITH JUST ONE COLOR PAGE IN THE MIDDLE OF THE MAGAZINE...
Center Color
BUT NO MATTER HOW MUCH TIME HE TOOK ON IT, I STILL THINK YOUR COLOR ILLUSTRATIONS ARE MORE ATTRACTIVE THAN FUKUDA'S.
THAT'S NOT WHAT I MEAN...
HN?
MAYBE WE CAN CREATE SOME KIND OF GIMMICK USING THE COLOR PAGE... SOMETHING ONLY PCP CAN DO.
A GIMMICK THAT ONLY PCP CAN DO?
?
YES.
UMM... LIKE THINGS WILL COME JUMPING OUT IF YOU LOOK AT THE ILLUSTRATION WITH 3D GLASSES?
THEN THE READERS ARE GOING TO NEED 3D GLASSES, AND THAT DOESN'T REALLY SEEM FAIR.
AND I CAN'T DRAW ILLUSTRATIONS IN 3D ANYWAY.

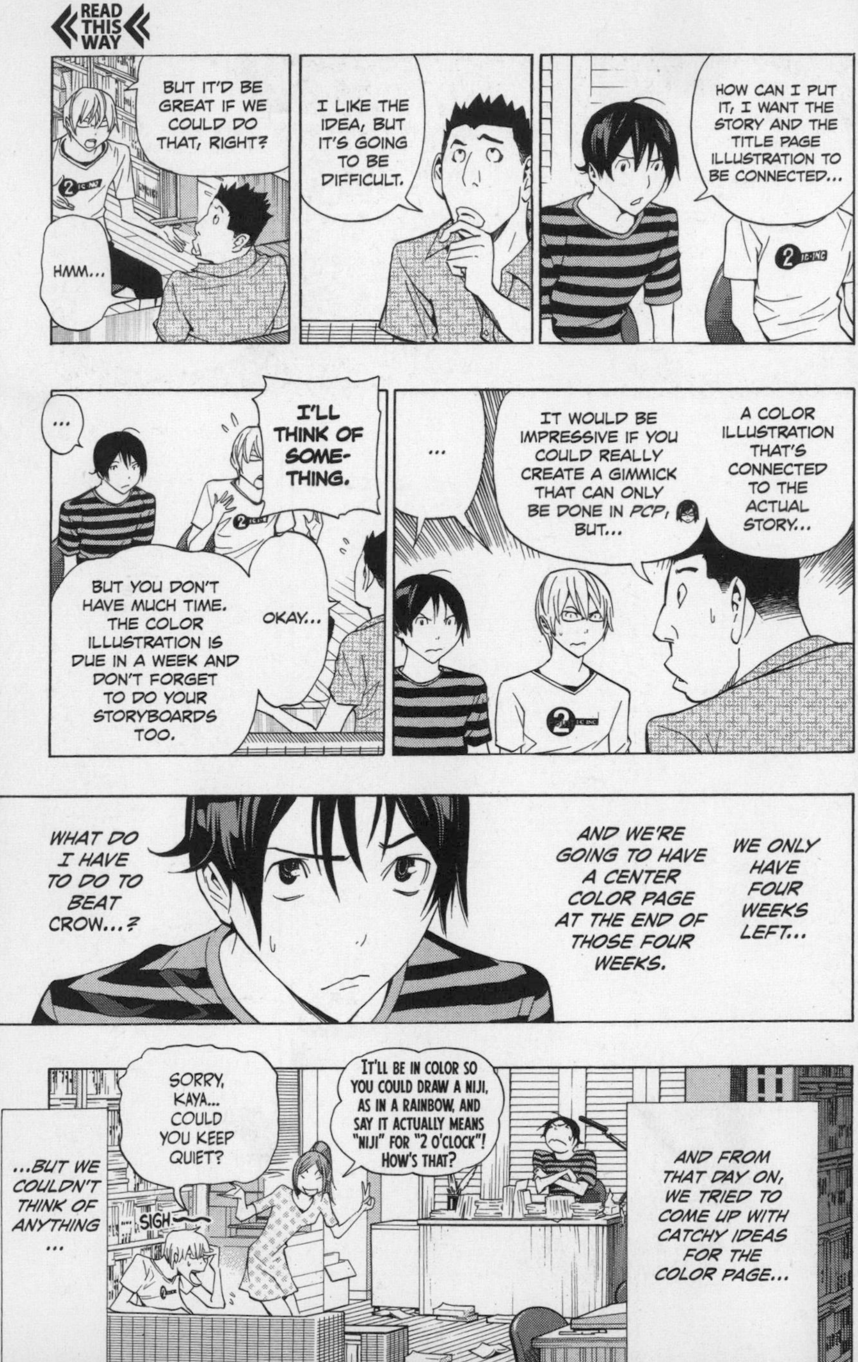
READ THIS WAY
HOW CAN I PUT IT, I WANT THE STORY AND THE TITLE PAGE ILLUSTRATION TO BE CONNECTED...
I LIKE THE IDEA, BUT IT'S GOING TO BE DIFFICULT.
BUT IT'D BE GREAT IF WE COULD DO THAT, RIGHT?
HMM...
A COLOR ILLUSTRATION THAT'S CONNECTED TO THE ACTUAL STORY...
IT WOULD BE IMPRESSIVE IF YOU COULD REALLY CREATE A GIMMICK THAT CAN ONLY BE DONE IN *PCP*, BUT...
...
I'LL THINK OF SOME-THING.
...
BUT YOU DON'T HAVE MUCH TIME. THE COLOR ILLUSTRATION IS DUE IN A WEEK AND DON'T FORGET TO DO YOUR STORYBOARDS TOO.
OKAY...
WE ONLY HAVE FOUR WEEKS LEFT...
AND WE'RE GOING TO HAVE A CENTER COLOR PAGE AT THE END OF THOSE FOUR WEEKS.
WHAT DO I HAVE TO DO TO BEAT CROW...?
AND FROM THAT DAY ON, WE TRIED TO COME UP WITH CATCHY IDEAS FOR THE COLOR PAGE...
IT'LL BE IN COLOR SO YOU COULD DRAW A NIJI, AS IN A RAINBOW, AND SAY IT ACTUALLY MEANS "NIJI" FOR "2 O'CLOCK"! HOW'S THAT?
SORRY, KAYA... COULD YOU KEEP QUIET?
SIGH
...BUT WE COULDN'T THINK OF ANYTHING...

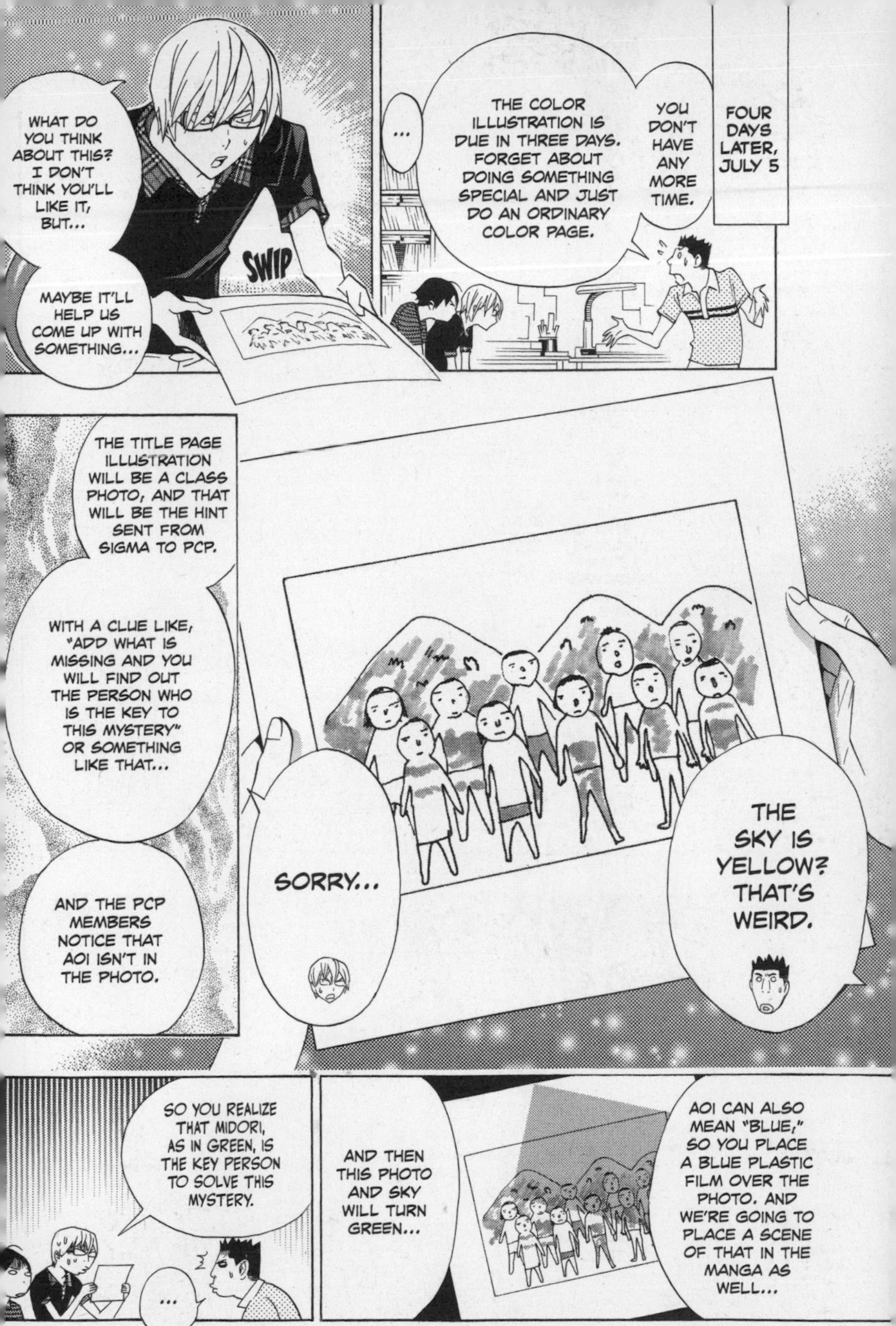
FOUR DAYS LATER, JULY 5
YOU DON'T HAVE ANY MORE TIME.
THE COLOR ILLUSTRATION IS DUE IN THREE DAYS. FORGET ABOUT DOING SOMETHING SPECIAL AND JUST DO AN ORDINARY COLOR PAGE.
...
WHAT DO YOU THINK ABOUT THIS? I DON'T THINK YOU'LL LIKE IT, BUT...
SWIP
MAYBE IT'LL HELP US COME UP WITH SOMETHING...
THE SKY IS YELLOW? THAT'S WEIRD.
SORRY...
THE TITLE PAGE ILLUSTRATION WILL BE A CLASS PHOTO, AND THAT WILL BE THE HINT SENT FROM SIGMA TO PCP.
WITH A CLUE LIKE, "ADD WHAT IS MISSING AND YOU WILL FIND OUT THE PERSON WHO IS THE KEY TO THIS MYSTERY" OR SOMETHING LIKE THAT...
AND THE PCP MEMBERS NOTICE THAT AOI ISN'T IN THE PHOTO.
AOI CAN ALSO MEAN "BLUE," SO YOU PLACE A BLUE PLASTIC FILM OVER THE PHOTO. AND WE'RE GOING TO PLACE A SCENE OF THAT IN THE MANGA AS WELL...
AND THEN THIS PHOTO AND SKY WILL TURN GREEN...
SO YOU REALIZE THAT MIDORI, AS IN GREEN, IS THE KEY PERSON TO SOLVE THIS MYSTERY.
...

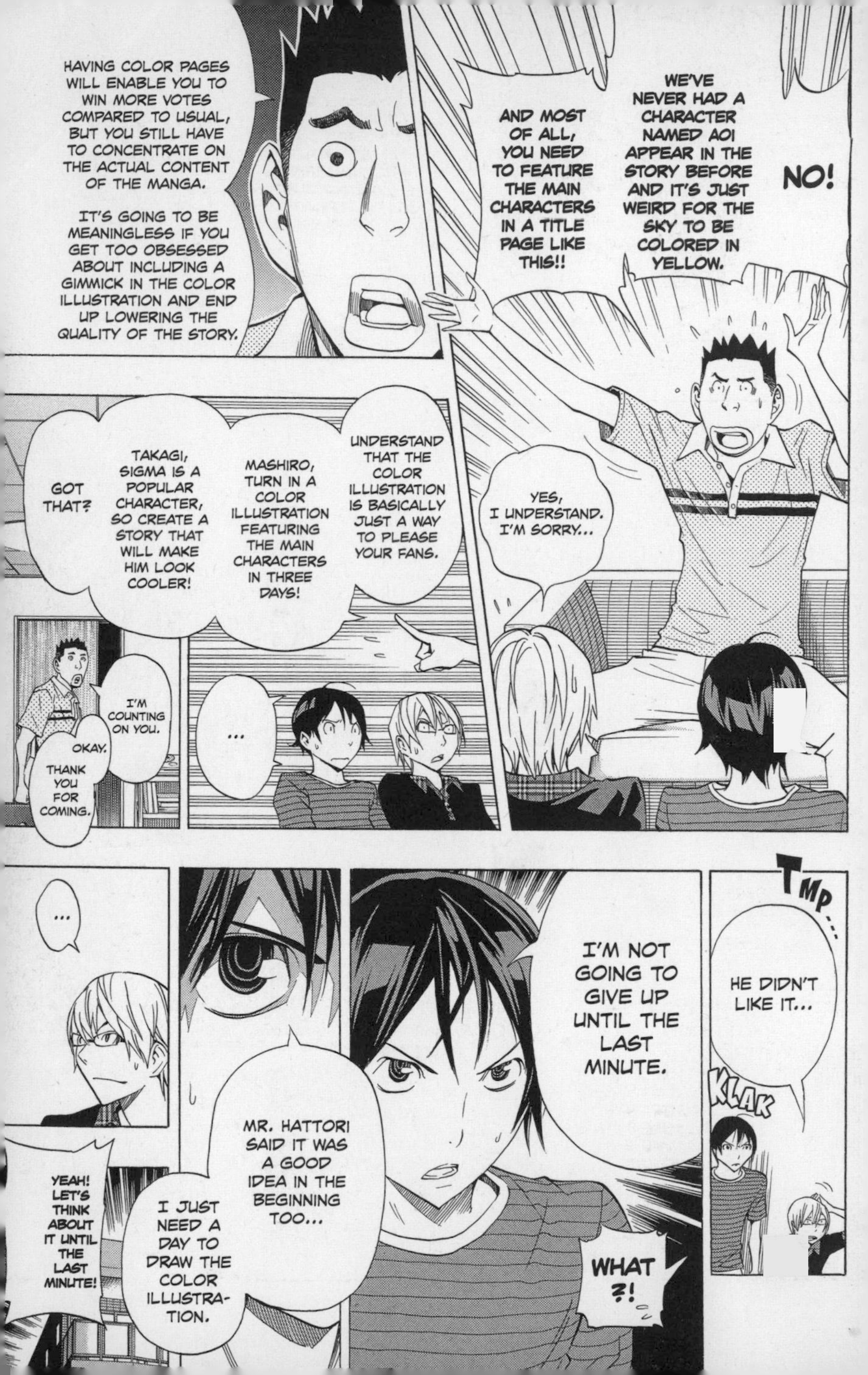

NO!
WE'VE NEVER HAD A CHARACTER NAMED AOI APPEAR IN THE STORY BEFORE AND IT'S JUST WEIRD FOR THE SKY TO BE COLORED IN YELLOW.
AND MOST OF ALL, YOU NEED TO FEATURE THE MAIN CHARACTERS IN A TITLE PAGE LIKE THIS!!
YES, I UNDERSTAND. I'M SORRY...
HAVING COLOR PAGES WILL ENABLE YOU TO WIN MORE VOTES COMPARED TO USUAL, BUT YOU STILL HAVE TO CONCENTRATE ON THE ACTUAL CONTENT OF THE MANGA.
IT'S GOING TO BE MEANINGLESS IF YOU GET TOO OBSESSED ABOUT INCLUDING A GIMMICK IN THE COLOR ILLUSTRATION AND END UP LOWERING THE QUALITY OF THE STORY.
UNDERSTAND THAT THE COLOR ILLUSTRATION IS BASICALLY JUST A WAY TO PLEASE YOUR FANS.
MASHIRO, TURN IN A COLOR ILLUSTRATION FEATURING THE MAIN CHARACTERS IN THREE DAYS!
TAKAGI, SIGMA IS A POPULAR CHARACTER, SO CREATE A STORY THAT WILL MAKE HIM LOOK COOLER!
GOT THAT?
...
I'M COUNTING ON YOU.
OKAY.
THANK YOU FOR COMING.
TMP...
HE DIDN'T LIKE IT...
KLAK
I'M NOT GOING TO GIVE UP UNTIL THE LAST MINUTE.
WHAT?!
MR. HATTORI SAID IT WAS A GOOD IDEA IN THE BEGINNING TOO...
I JUST NEED A DAY TO DRAW THE COLOR ILLUSTRATION.
...
YEAH! LET'S THINK ABOUT IT UNTIL THE LAST MINUTE!

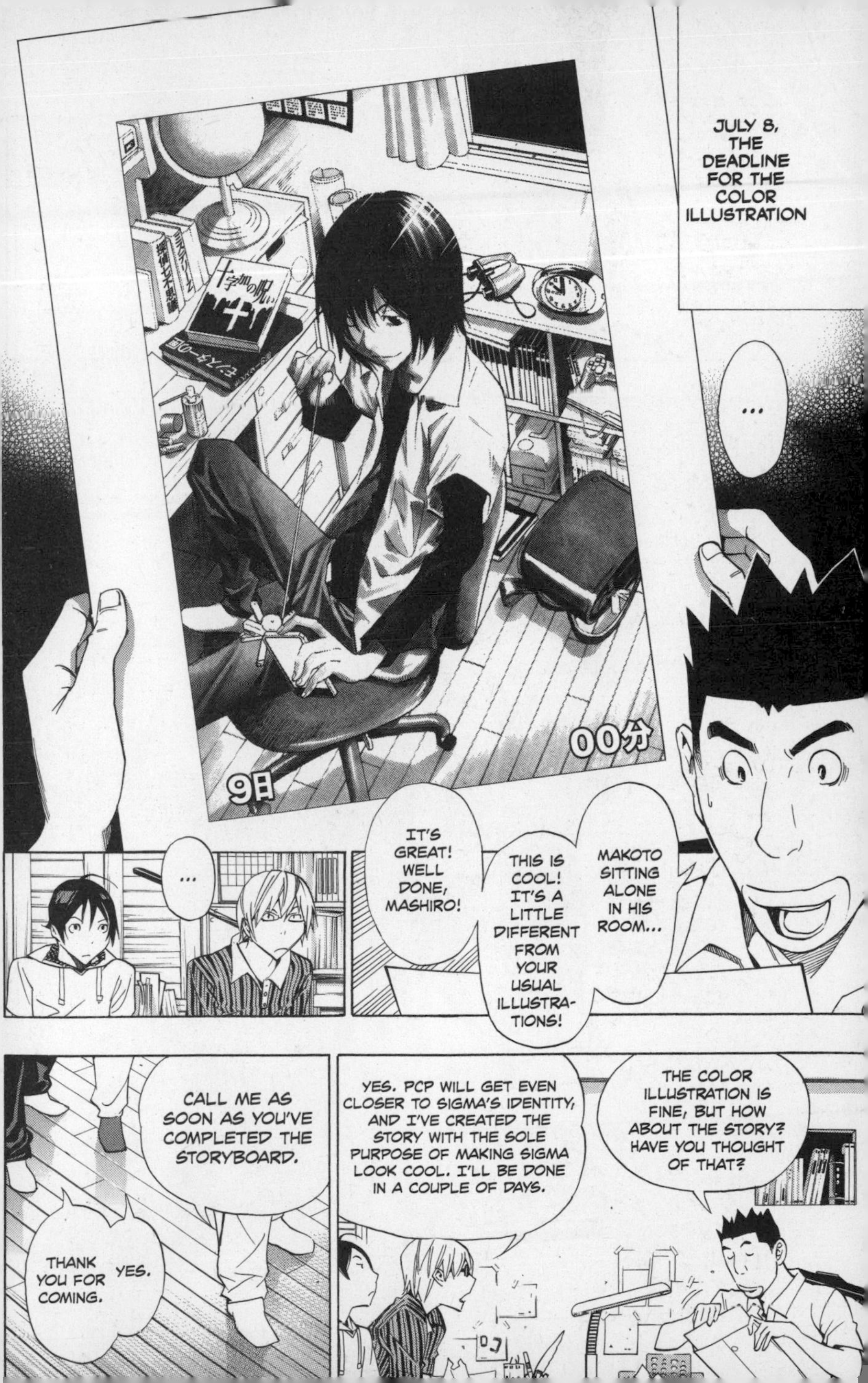

JULY 8, THE DEADLINE FOR THE COLOR ILLUSTRATION
...
00分
9日
MAKOTO SITTING ALONE IN HIS ROOM...
THIS IS COOL! IT'S A LITTLE DIFFERENT FROM YOUR USUAL ILLUSTRATIONS!
IT'S GREAT! WELL DONE, MASHIRO!
...
THE COLOR ILLUSTRATION IS FINE, BUT HOW ABOUT THE STORY? HAVE YOU THOUGHT OF THAT?
YES. PCP WILL GET EVEN CLOSER TO SIGMA'S IDENTITY, AND I'VE CREATED THE STORY WITH THE SOLE PURPOSE OF MAKING SIGMA LOOK COOL. I'LL BE DONE IN A COUPLE OF DAYS.
CALL ME AS SOON AS YOU'VE COMPLETED THE STORYBOARD.
YES.
THANK YOU FOR COMING.

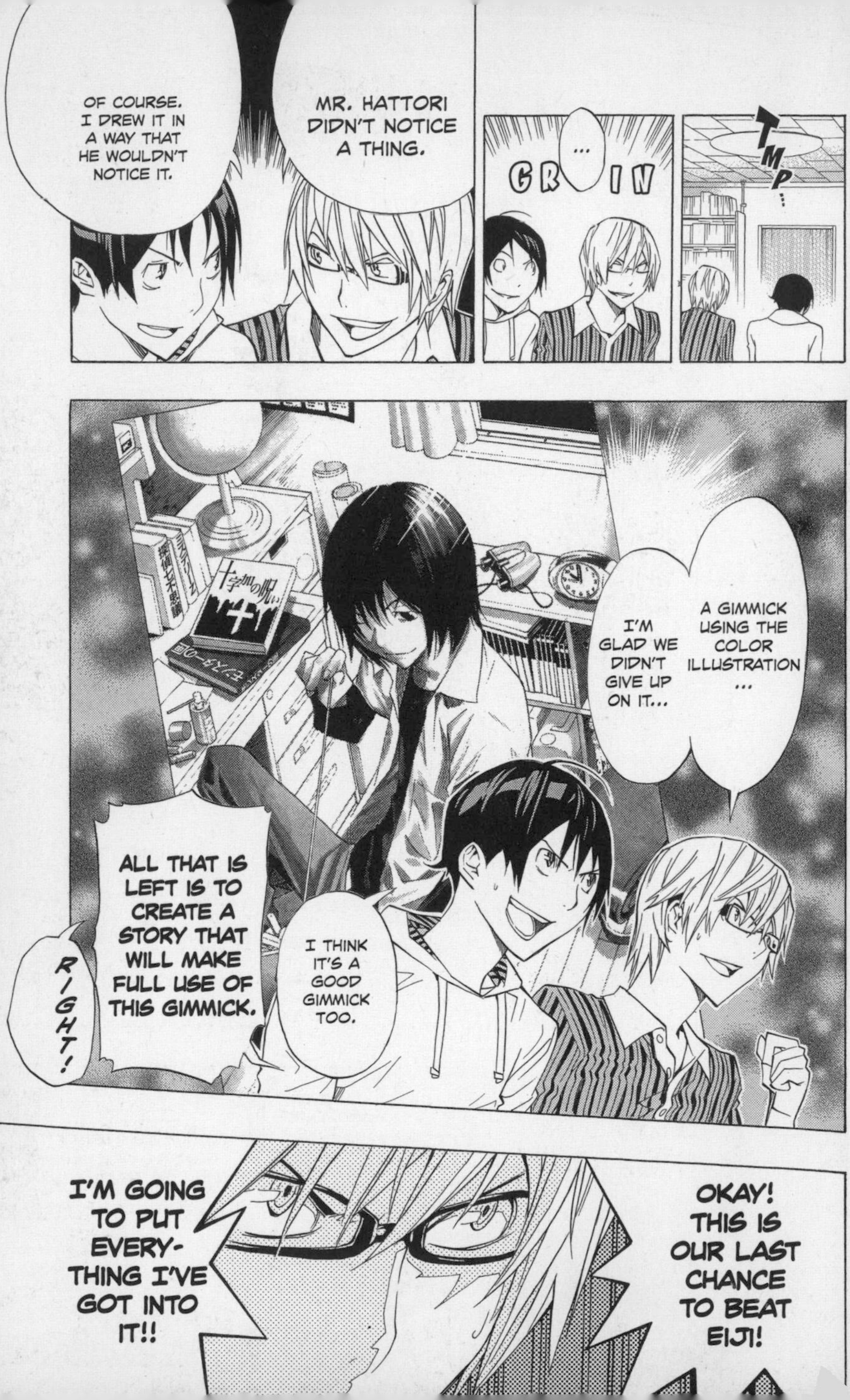
TMP...
...
GRIN
MR. HATTORI DIDN'T NOTICE A THING.
OF COURSE. I DREW IT IN A WAY THAT HE WOULDN'T NOTICE IT.
A GIMMICK USING THE COLOR ILLUSTRATION...
I'M GLAD WE DIDN'T GIVE UP ON IT...
I THINK IT'S A GOOD GIMMICK TOO.
ALL THAT IS LEFT IS TO CREATE A STORY THAT WILL MAKE FULL USE OF THIS GIMMICK.
RIGHT!
OKAY! THIS IS OUR LAST CHANCE TO BEAT EIJI!
I'M GOING TO PUT EVERY-THING I'VE GOT INTO IT!!

OHBA'S STORYBOARD

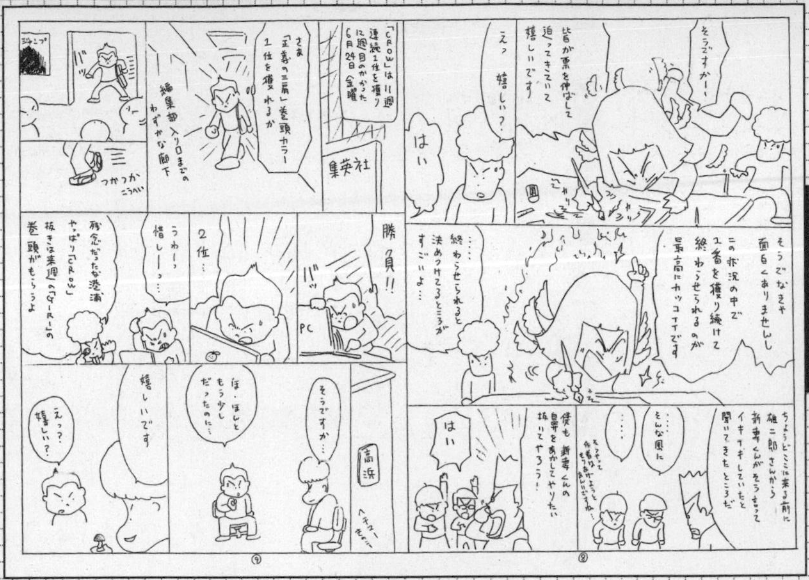
そうですかー
皆が票を伸ばして追ってきていて嬉しいです
えっ 嬉しい?
はい
そうでなきゃ面白くありませんし
この状況の中で1番を獲り続けて終わらせられるのが最高にカッコイイです
…終わらせられると決めつけてるところがすごいよ…
ちょうどここに来る前に雄二郎さんから新妻くんがそう言ってイキイキしていたと聞いてきたところだ
……そんな風に
……
僕も新妻くんの鼻をあかしてやりたい
はい
集英社
「CROW」は11週連続1位を獲り12週目のかかった6月24日金曜
さぁ「正義の三肩」巻頭カラー1位を獲れるか
編集部入り口までのわずかな廊下
バッ
つかつか
勝負!!
バッ
2位…
うわーっ 惜しーっ…
残念だな港浦
そうですか…
高浜
ほ、ほんとにもう少しだったのに…
嬉しいです
えっ? 嬉しい?

OBATA'S STORYBOARD

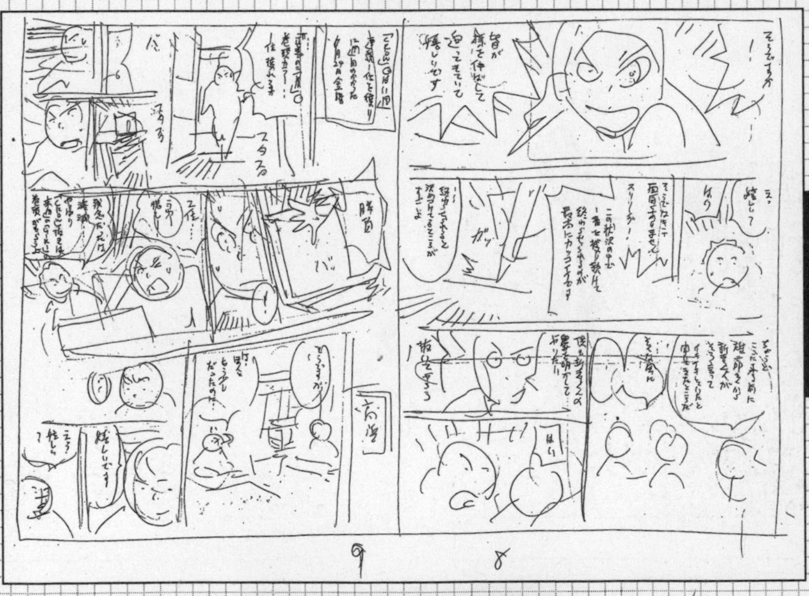

COMPLETE!

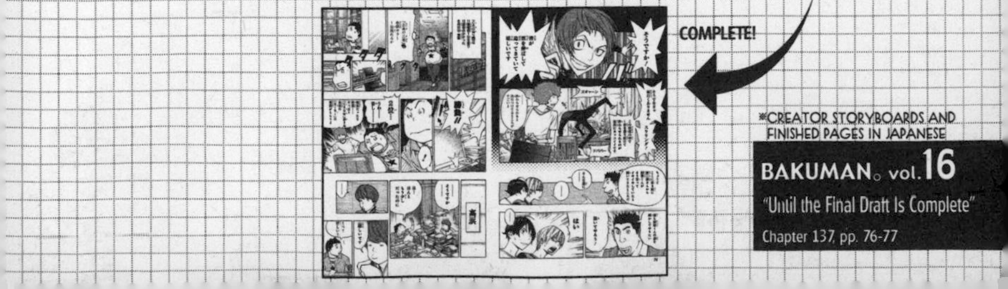

*CREATOR STORYBOARDS AND FINISHED PAGES IN JAPANESE

BAKUMAN。 vol.16

"Until the Final Draft Is Complete"

Chapter 137, pp. 76-77

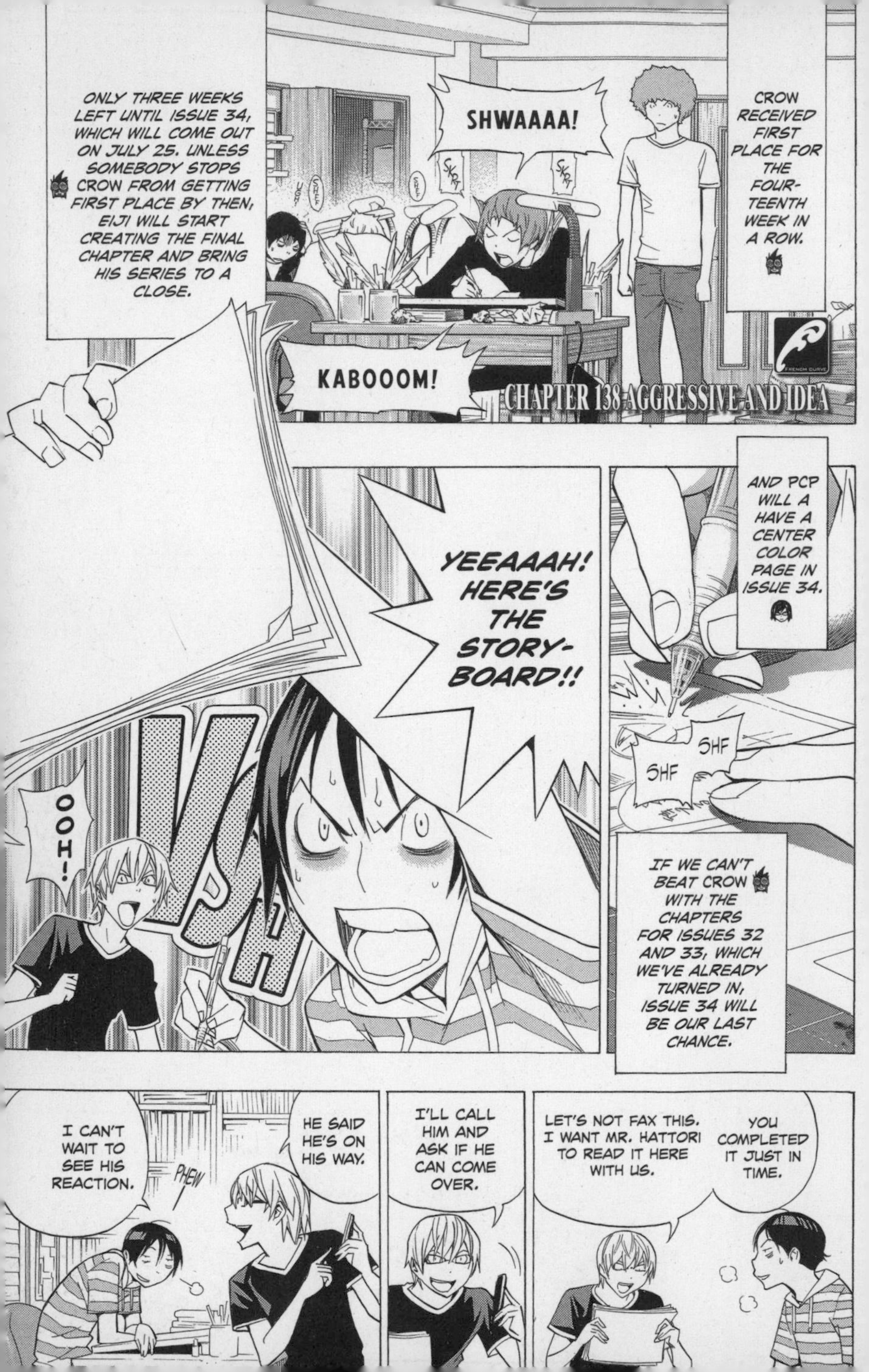
CROW RECEIVED FIRST PLACE FOR THE FOURTEENTH WEEK IN A ROW.
SHWAAAA!
SKRT
SKRT
KABOOOM!
CHAPTER 138 AGGRESSIVE AND IDEA
ONLY THREE WEEKS LEFT UNTIL ISSUE 34, WHICH WILL COME OUT ON JULY 25. UNLESS SOMEBODY STOPS CROW FROM GETTING FIRST PLACE BY THEN, EIJI WILL START CREATING THE FINAL CHAPTER AND BRING HIS SERIES TO A CLOSE.
AND PCP WILL A HAVE A CENTER COLOR PAGE IN ISSUE 34.
SHF
SHF
IF WE CAN'T BEAT CROW WITH THE CHAPTERS FOR ISSUES 32 AND 33, WHICH WE'VE ALREADY TURNED IN, ISSUE 34 WILL BE OUR LAST CHANCE.
YEEAAAH! HERE'S THE STORY-BOARD!!
OOH!
YOU COMPLETED IT JUST IN TIME.
LET'S NOT FAX THIS. I WANT MR. HATTORI TO READ IT HERE WITH US.
I'LL CALL HIM AND ASK IF HE CAN COME OVER.
HE SAID HE'S ON HIS WAY.
PHEW
I CAN'T WAIT TO SEE HIS REACTION.

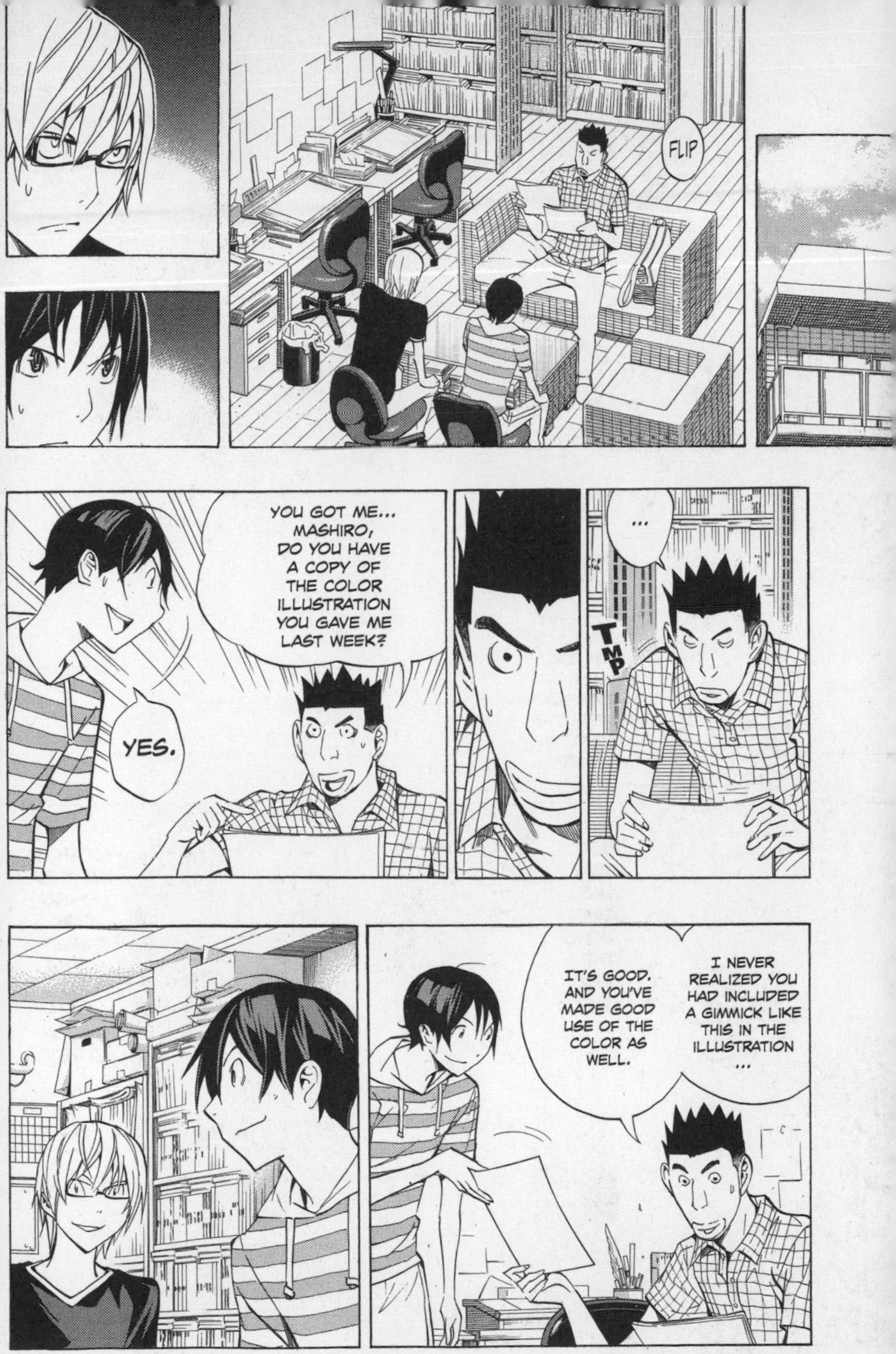
FLIP
...
TMP
YOU GOT ME... MASHIRO, DO YOU HAVE A COPY OF THE COLOR ILLUSTRATION YOU GAVE ME LAST WEEK?
YES.
I NEVER REALIZED YOU HAD INCLUDED A GIMMICK LIKE THIS IN THE ILLUSTRATION ...
IT'S GOOD. AND YOU'VE MADE GOOD USE OF THE COLOR AS WELL.

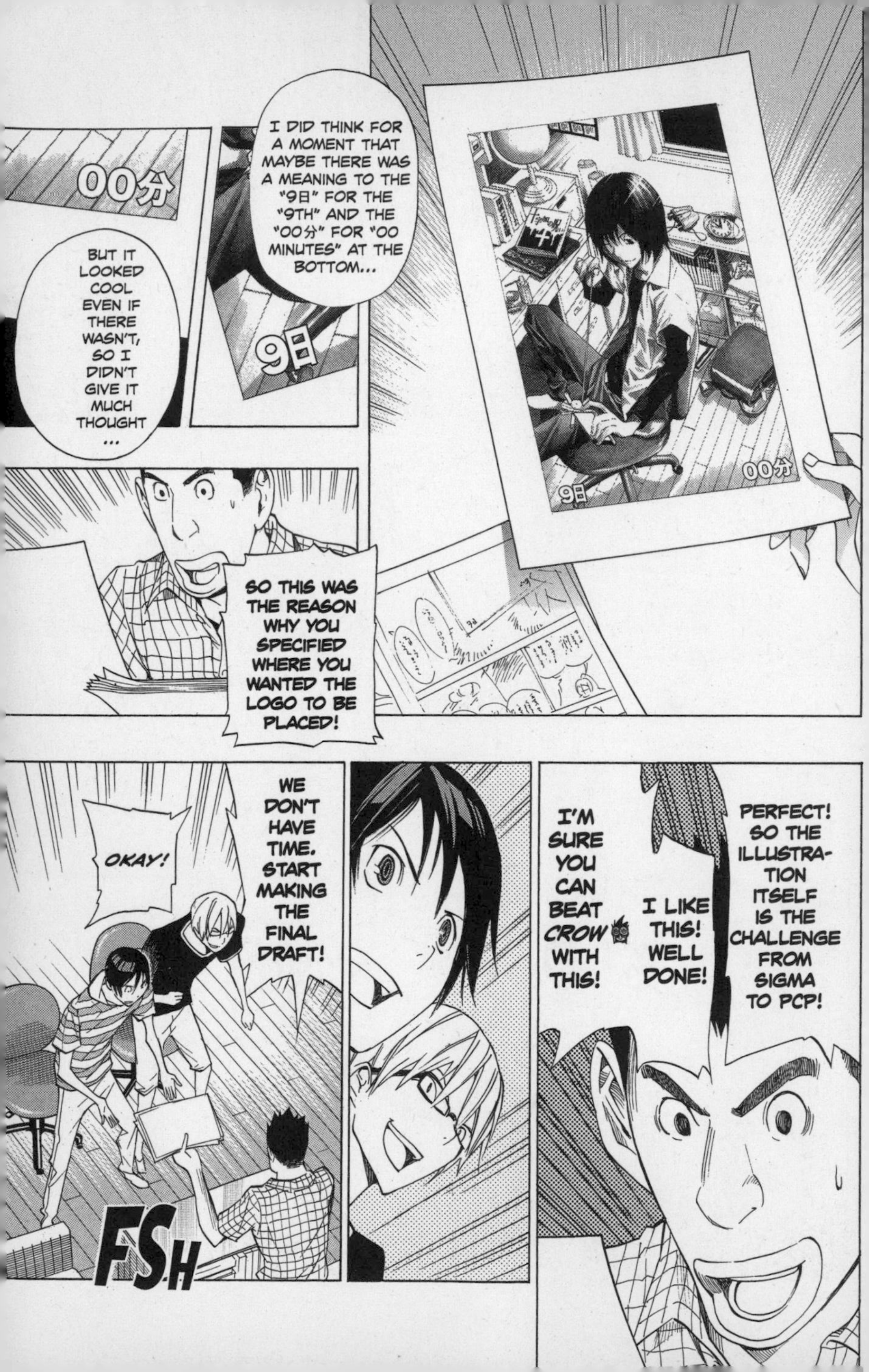
00分
9日
I DID THINK FOR A MOMENT THAT MAYBE THERE WAS A MEANING TO THE "9日" FOR THE "9TH" AND THE "00分" FOR "00 MINUTES" AT THE BOTTOM...
9日
00分
BUT IT LOOKED COOL EVEN IF THERE WASN'T, SO I DIDN'T GIVE IT MUCH THOUGHT...
SO THIS WAS THE REASON WHY YOU SPECIFIED WHERE YOU WANTED THE LOGO TO BE PLACED!
PERFECT! SO THE ILLUSTRATION ITSELF IS THE CHALLENGE FROM SIGMA TO PCP!
I LIKE THIS! WELL DONE!
I'M SURE YOU CAN BEAT CROW WITH THIS!
WE DON'T HAVE TIME. START MAKING THE FINAL DRAFT!
OKAY!
FSH

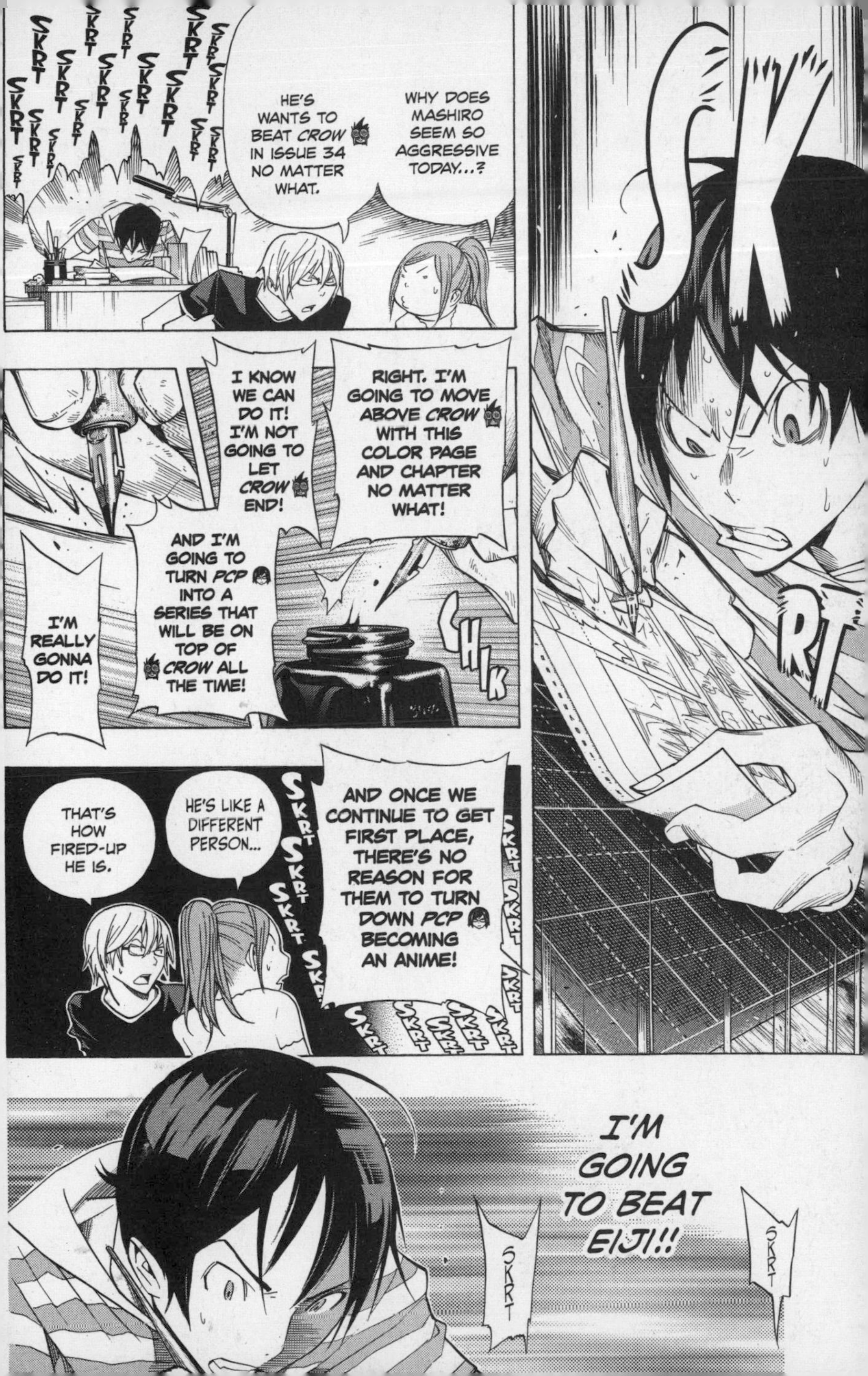
SK
RT
SKRT SKRT SKRT SKRT SKRT
WHY DOES MASHIRO SEEM SO AGGRESSIVE TODAY...?
HE'S WANTS TO BEAT CROW IN ISSUE 34 NO MATTER WHAT.
RIGHT. I'M GOING TO MOVE ABOVE CROW WITH THIS COLOR PAGE AND CHAPTER NO MATTER WHAT!
I KNOW WE CAN DO IT! I'M NOT GOING TO LET CROW END!
CHIK
AND I'M GOING TO TURN PCP INTO A SERIES THAT WILL BE ON TOP OF CROW ALL THE TIME!
I'M REALLY GONNA DO IT!
SKRT SKRT SKRT SKRT
AND ONCE WE CONTINUE TO GET FIRST PLACE, THERE'S NO REASON FOR THEM TO TURN DOWN PCP BECOMING AN ANIME!
HE'S LIKE A DIFFERENT PERSON...
THAT'S HOW FIRED-UP HE IS.
SKRT SKRT SKRT SKRT SKRT
SKRT
I'M GOING TO BEAT EIJI!!
SKRT

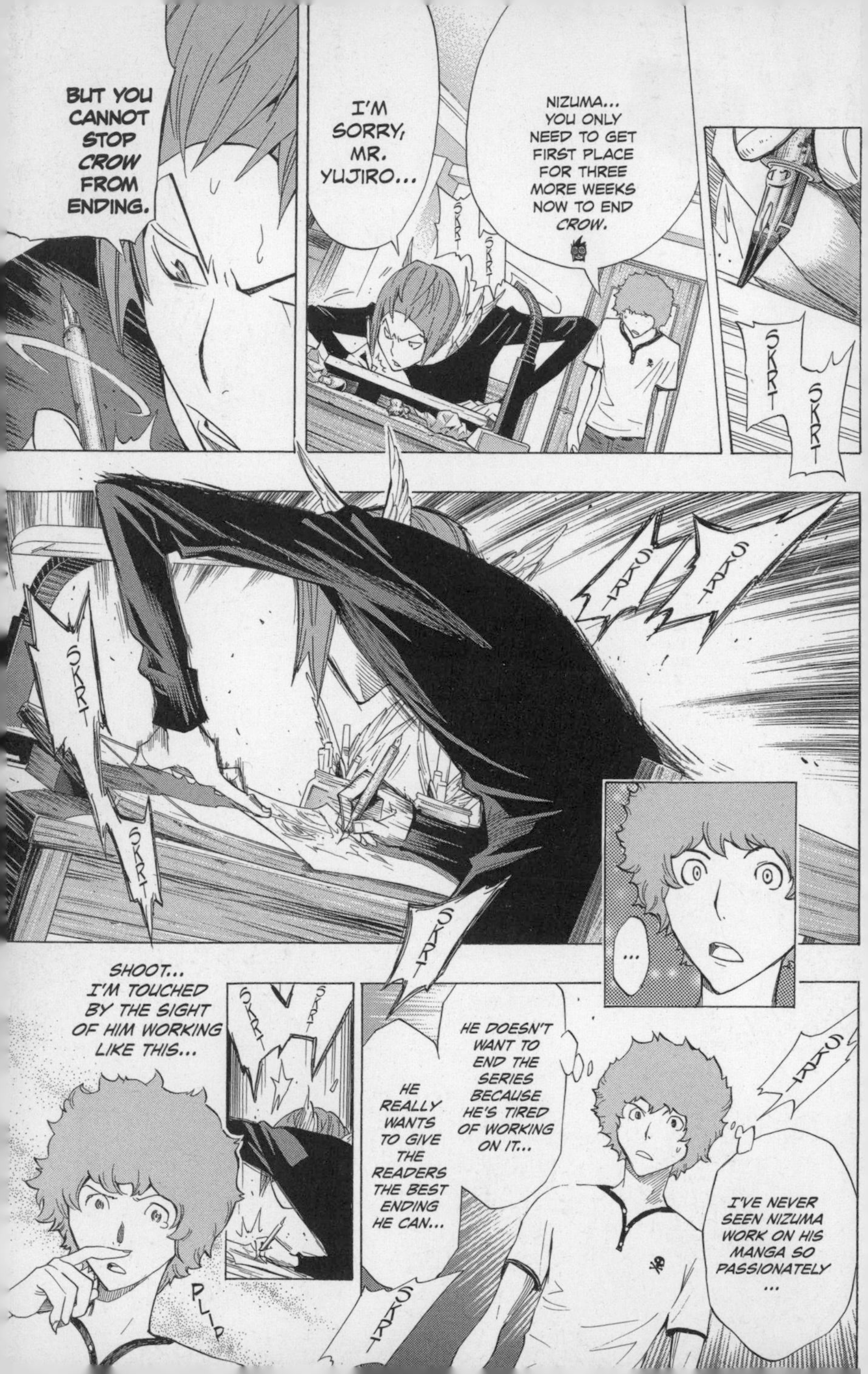
SKRT
SKRT
NIZUMA... YOU ONLY NEED TO GET FIRST PLACE FOR THREE MORE WEEKS NOW TO END *CROW*.
I'M SORRY, MR. YUJIRO...
SKRT
SKRT
BUT YOU CANNOT STOP *CROW* FROM ENDING.
SKRT
SKRT
SKRT
SKRT
SKRT
...
SKRT
I'VE NEVER SEEN NIZUMA WORK ON HIS MANGA SO PASSIONATELY ...
HE DOESN'T WANT TO END THE SERIES BECAUSE HE'S TIRED OF WORKING ON IT...
HE REALLY WANTS TO GIVE THE READERS THE BEST ENDING HE CAN...
SKRT
SKRT
SKRT
SHOOT... I'M TOUCHED BY THE SIGHT OF HIM WORKING LIKE THIS...
PLIP

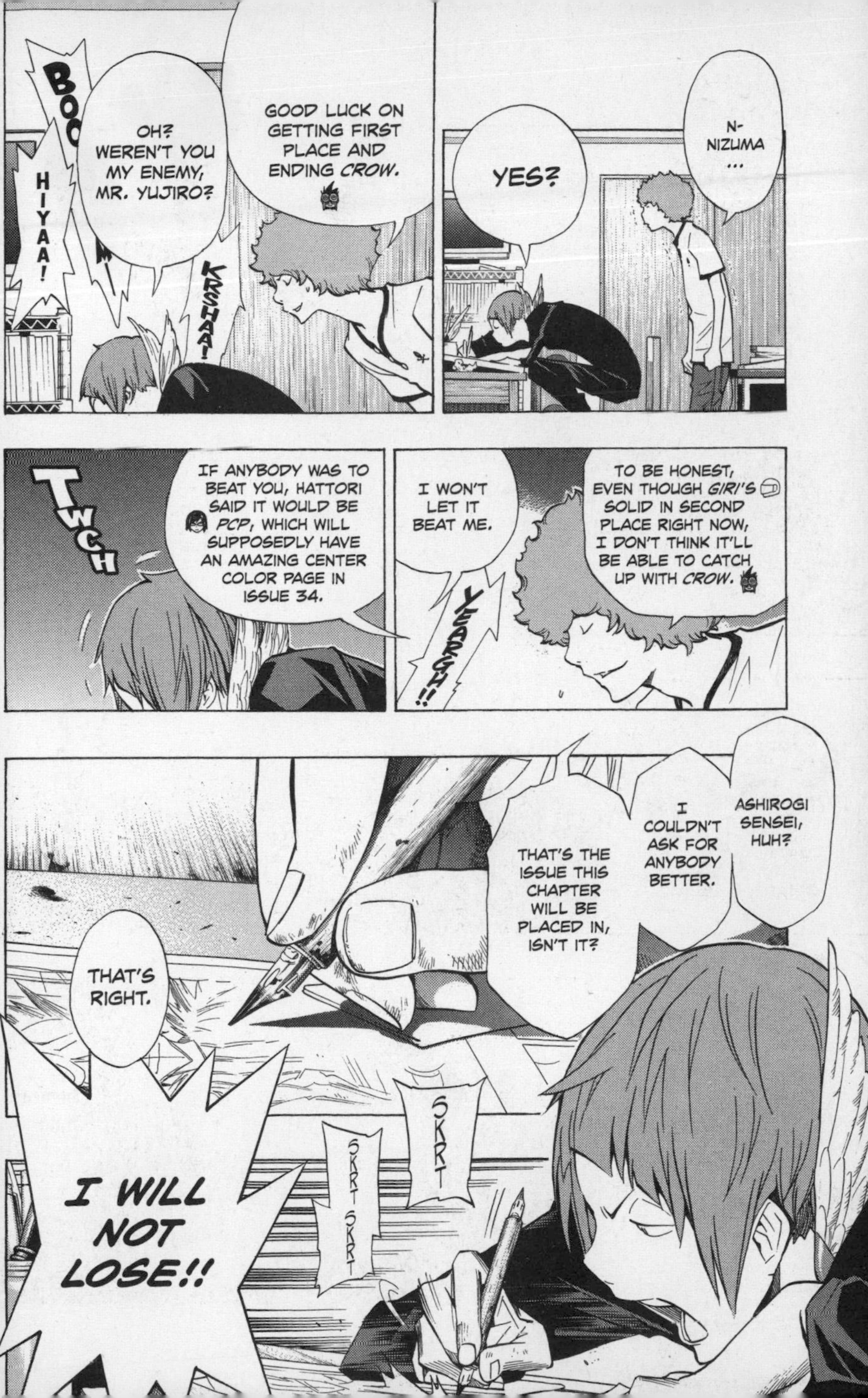
N-NIZUMA ...
YES?
GOOD LUCK ON GETTING FIRST PLACE AND ENDING *CROW*.
OH? WEREN'T YOU MY ENEMY, MR. YUJIRO?
KRSHAA!
BOOM
HIYAA!
TO BE HONEST, EVEN THOUGH *GIRI'S* SOLID IN SECOND PLACE RIGHT NOW, I DON'T THINK IT'LL BE ABLE TO CATCH UP WITH *CROW*.
I WON'T LET IT BEAT ME.
YEARGH!!
IF ANYBODY WAS TO BEAT YOU, HATTORI SAID IT WOULD BE *PCP*, WHICH WILL SUPPOSEDLY HAVE AN AMAZING CENTER COLOR PAGE IN ISSUE 34.
TWCH
ASHIROGI SENSEI, HUH?
I COULDN'T ASK FOR ANYBODY BETTER.
THAT'S THE ISSUE THIS CHAPTER WILL BE PLACED IN, ISN'T IT?
THAT'S RIGHT.
SKRT
SKRT SKRT
I WILL NOT LOSE!!

READ THIS WAY

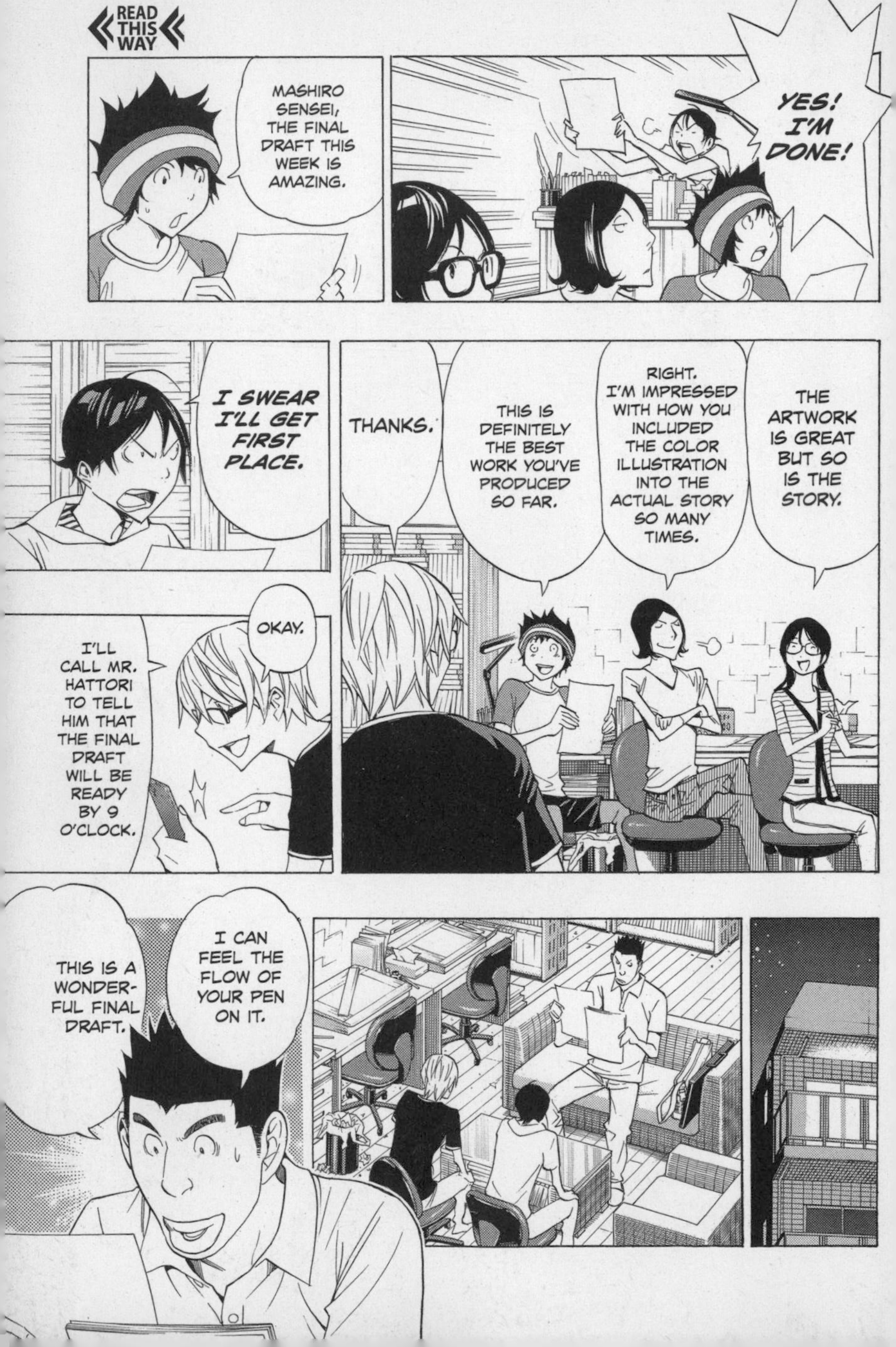

YES! I'M DONE!
MASHIRO SENSEI, THE FINAL DRAFT THIS WEEK IS AMAZING.
THE ARTWORK IS GREAT BUT SO IS THE STORY.
RIGHT. I'M IMPRESSED WITH HOW YOU INCLUDED THE COLOR ILLUSTRATION INTO THE ACTUAL STORY SO MANY TIMES.
THIS IS DEFINITELY THE BEST WORK YOU'VE PRODUCED SO FAR.
THANKS.
I SWEAR I'LL GET FIRST PLACE.
OKAY.
I'LL CALL MR. HATTORI TO TELL HIM THAT THE FINAL DRAFT WILL BE READY BY 9 O'CLOCK.
I CAN FEEL THE FLOW OF YOUR PEN ON IT.
THIS IS A WONDERFUL FINAL DRAFT.

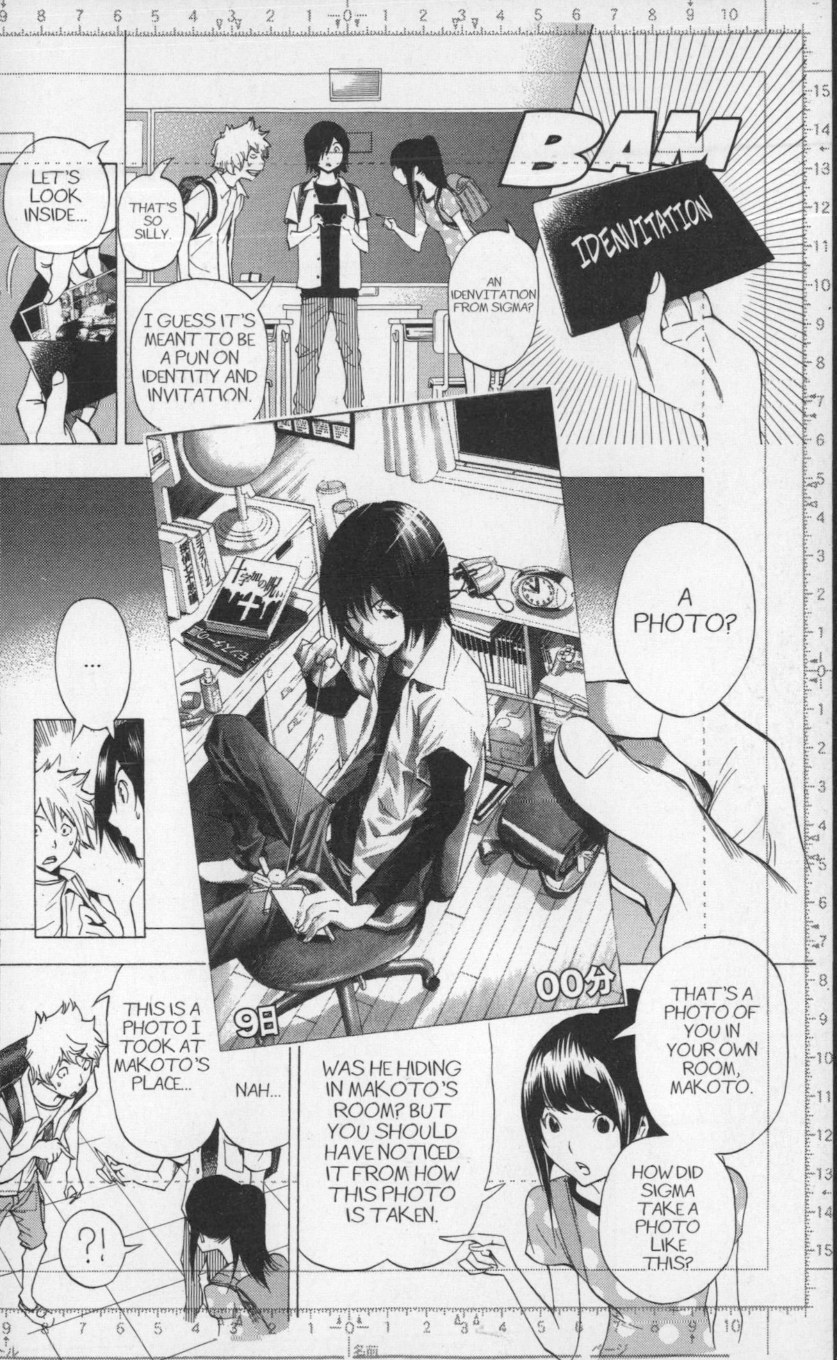
BAM
IDENVITATION
AN IDENVITATION FROM SIGMA?
I GUESS IT'S MEANT TO BE A PUN ON IDENTITY AND INVITATION.
THAT'S SO SILLY.
LET'S LOOK INSIDE...
A PHOTO?
00分
9日
...
THAT'S A PHOTO OF YOU IN YOUR OWN ROOM, MAKOTO.
HOW DID SIGMA TAKE A PHOTO LIKE THIS?
WAS HE HIDING IN MAKOTO'S ROOM? BUT YOU SHOULD HAVE NOTICED IT FROM HOW THIS PHOTO IS TAKEN.
NAH...
THIS IS A PHOTO I TOOK AT MAKOTO'S PLACE...
?!

FOR THE BEST CREATIVE WORK YOU NEED THE BEST MATERIALS & EQUIPMENT.

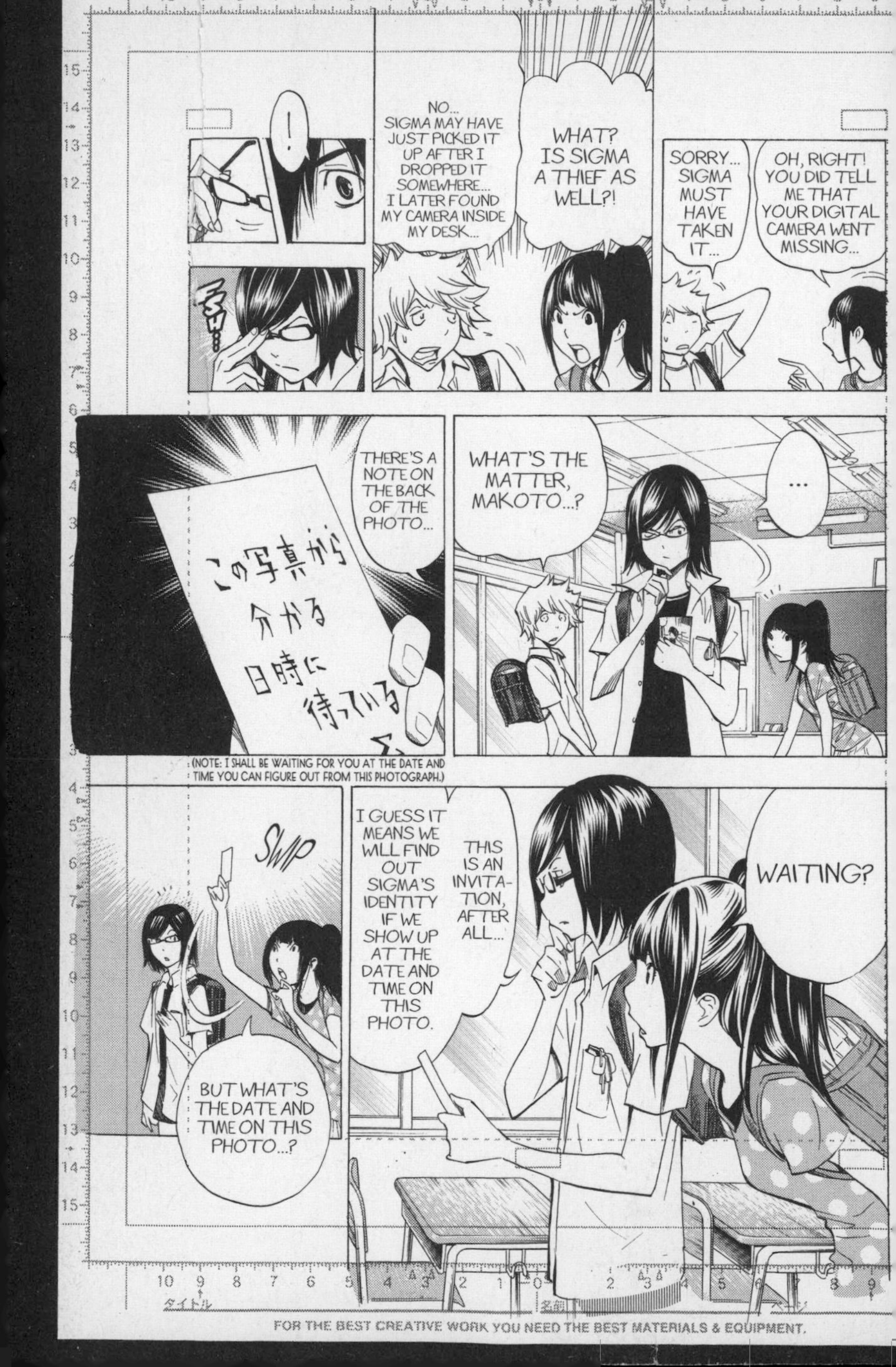
OH, RIGHT! YOU DID TELL ME THAT YOUR DIGITAL CAMERA WENT MISSING...
SORRY... SIGMA MUST HAVE TAKEN IT...
WHAT? IS SIGMA A THIEF AS WELL?!
NO... SIGMA MAY HAVE JUST PICKED IT UP AFTER I DROPPED IT SOMEWHERE... I LATER FOUND MY CAMERA INSIDE MY DESK...
!
...
WHAT'S THE MATTER, MAKOTO...?
THERE'S A NOTE ON THE BACK OF THE PHOTO...
この写真から分かる日時に待っている
Σ
(NOTE: I SHALL BE WAITING FOR YOU AT THE DATE AND TIME YOU CAN FIGURE OUT FROM THIS PHOTOGRAPH.)
WAITING?
THIS IS AN INVITATION, AFTER ALL...
I GUESS IT MEANS WE WILL FIND OUT SIGMA'S IDENTITY IF WE SHOW UP AT THE DATE AND TIME ON THIS PHOTO.
SWIP
BUT WHAT'S THE DATE AND TIME ON THIS PHOTO...?

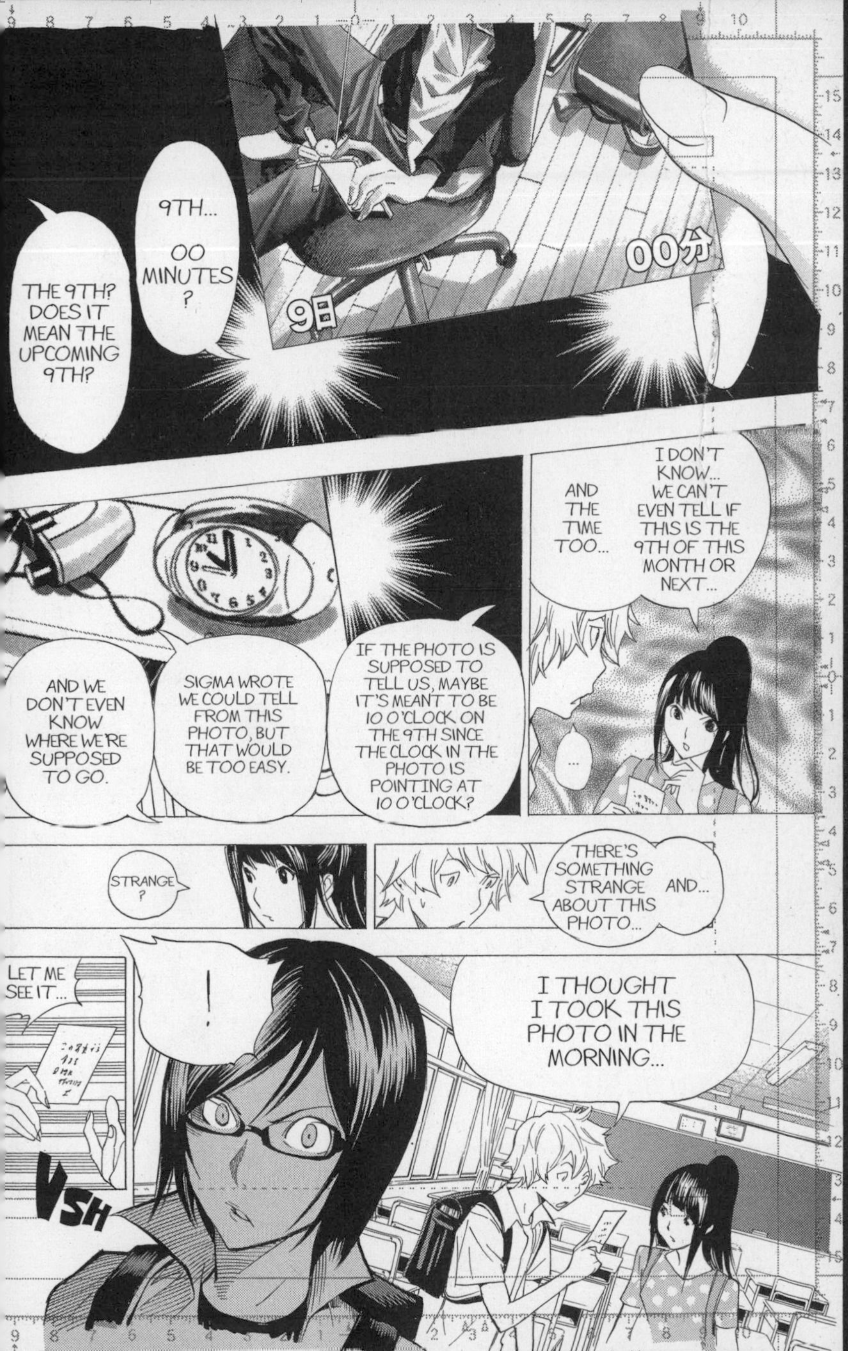
00分
9日
9TH... 00 MINUTES?
THE 9TH? DOES IT MEAN THE UPCOMING 9TH?
I DON'T KNOW... WE CAN'T EVEN TELL IF THIS IS THE 9TH OF THIS MONTH OR NEXT...
AND THE TIME TOO...
...
IF THE PHOTO IS SUPPOSED TO TELL US, MAYBE IT'S MEANT TO BE 10 O'CLOCK ON THE 9TH SINCE THE CLOCK IN THE PHOTO IS POINTING AT 10 O'CLOCK?
SIGMA WROTE WE COULD TELL FROM THIS PHOTO, BUT THAT WOULD BE TOO EASY.
AND WE DON'T EVEN KNOW WHERE WE'RE SUPPOSED TO GO.
THERE'S SOMETHING STRANGE ABOUT THIS PHOTO...
AND...
STRANGE?
I THOUGHT I TOOK THIS PHOTO IN THE MORNING...
!
LET ME SEE IT...
VSH

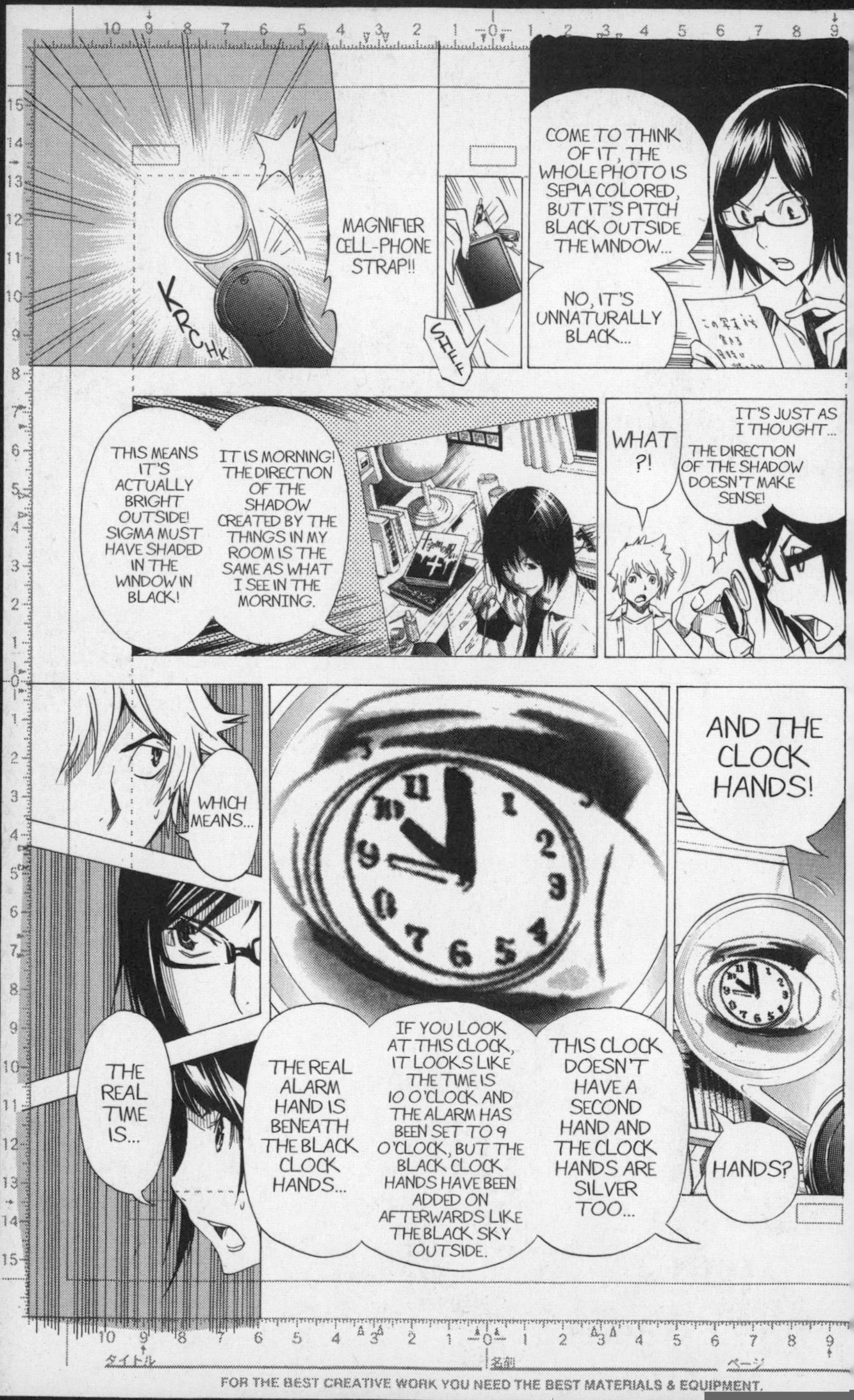
COME TO THINK OF IT, THE WHOLE PHOTO IS SEPIA COLORED, BUT IT'S PITCH BLACK OUTSIDE THE WINDOW...
NO, IT'S UNNATURALLY BLACK...
SHFF
MAGNIFIER CELL-PHONE STRAP!!
KRCHK
IT'S JUST AS I THOUGHT... THE DIRECTION OF THE SHADOW DOESN'T MAKE SENSE!
WHAT?!
IT IS MORNING! THE DIRECTION OF THE SHADOW CREATED BY THE THINGS IN MY ROOM IS THE SAME AS WHAT I SEE IN THE MORNING.
THIS MEANS IT'S ACTUALLY BRIGHT OUTSIDE! SIGMA MUST HAVE SHADED IN THE WINDOW IN BLACK!
AND THE CLOCK HANDS!
HANDS?
THIS CLOCK DOESN'T HAVE A SECOND HAND AND THE CLOCK HANDS ARE SILVER TOO...
IF YOU LOOK AT THIS CLOCK, IT LOOKS LIKE THE TIME IS 10 O'CLOCK AND THE ALARM HAS BEEN SET TO 9 O'CLOCK, BUT THE BLACK CLOCK HANDS HAVE BEEN ADDED ON AFTERWARDS LIKE THE BLACK SKY OUTSIDE.
THE REAL ALARM HAND IS BENEATH THE BLACK CLOCK HANDS...
WHICH MEANS...
THE REAL TIME IS...
タイトル
名前
ページ
FOR THE BEST CREATIVE WORK YOU NEED THE BEST MATERIALS & EQUIPMENT.

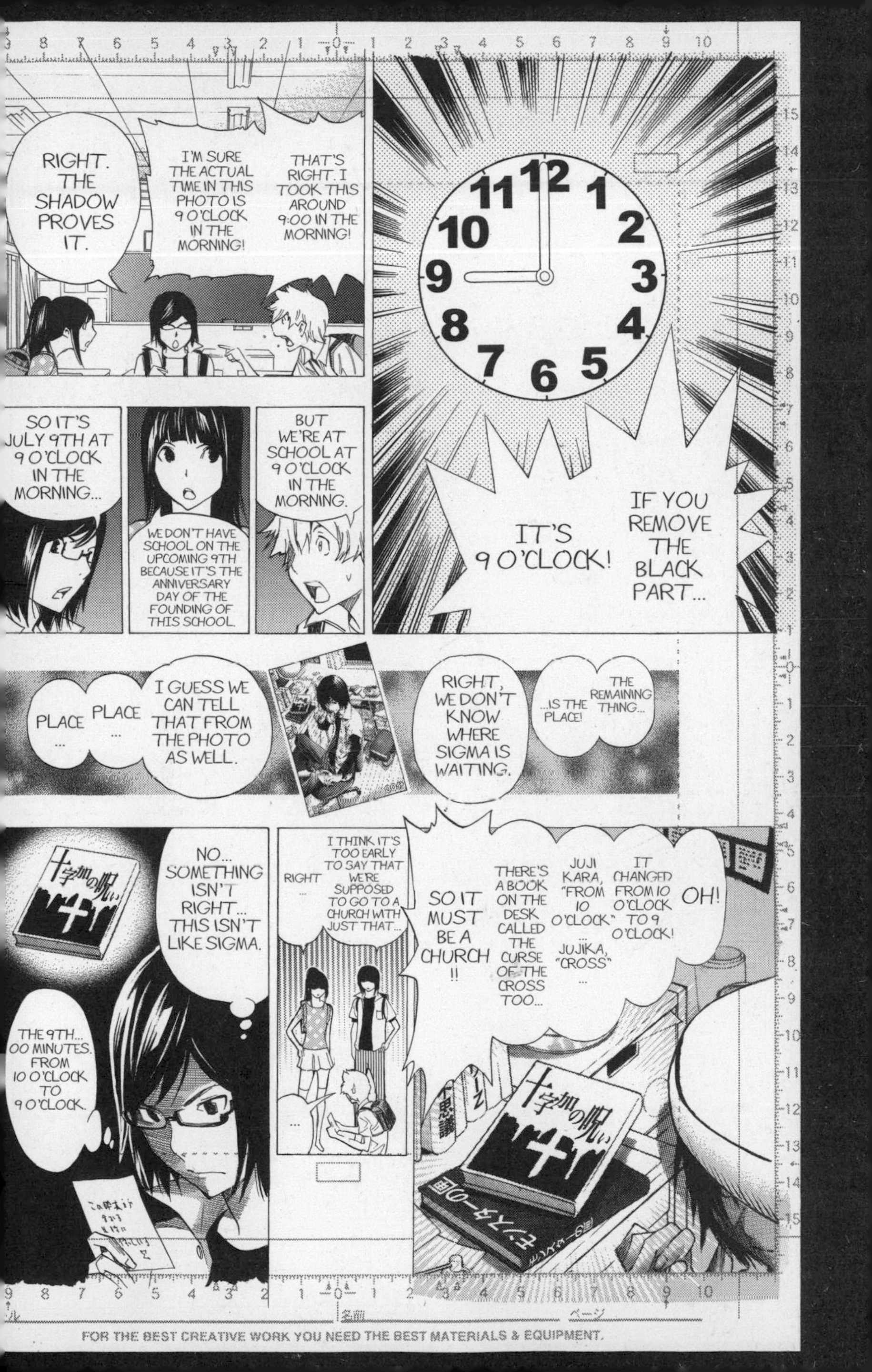
IF YOU REMOVE THE BLACK PART...
IT'S 9 O'CLOCK!
THAT'S RIGHT. I TOOK THIS AROUND 9:00 IN THE MORNING!
I'M SURE THE ACTUAL TIME IN THIS PHOTO IS 9 O'CLOCK IN THE MORNING!
RIGHT. THE SHADOW PROVES IT.
BUT WE'RE AT SCHOOL AT 9 O'CLOCK IN THE MORNING.
WE DON'T HAVE SCHOOL ON THE UPCOMING 9TH BECAUSE IT'S THE ANNIVERSARY DAY OF THE FOUNDING OF THIS SCHOOL.
SO IT'S JULY 9TH AT 9 O'CLOCK IN THE MORNING...
THE REMAINING THING...
...IS THE PLACE!
RIGHT, WE DON'T KNOW WHERE SIGMA IS WAITING.
I GUESS WE CAN TELL THAT FROM THE PHOTO AS WELL.
PLACE ...
PLACE ...
OH!
IT CHANGED FROM 10 O'CLOCK TO 9 O'CLOCK!
JUJI KARA, "FROM 10 O'CLOCK" ... JUJIKA, "CROSS" ...
THERE'S A BOOK ON THE DESK CALLED THE CURSE OF THE CROSS TOO...
SO IT MUST BE A CHURCH!!
I THINK IT'S TOO EARLY TO SAY THAT WE'RE SUPPOSED TO GO TO A CHURCH WITH JUST THAT...
RIGHT ...
...
NO... SOMETHING ISN'T RIGHT... THIS ISN'T LIKE SIGMA.
THE 9TH... 00 MINUTES. FROM 10 O'CLOCK TO 9 O'CLOCK.

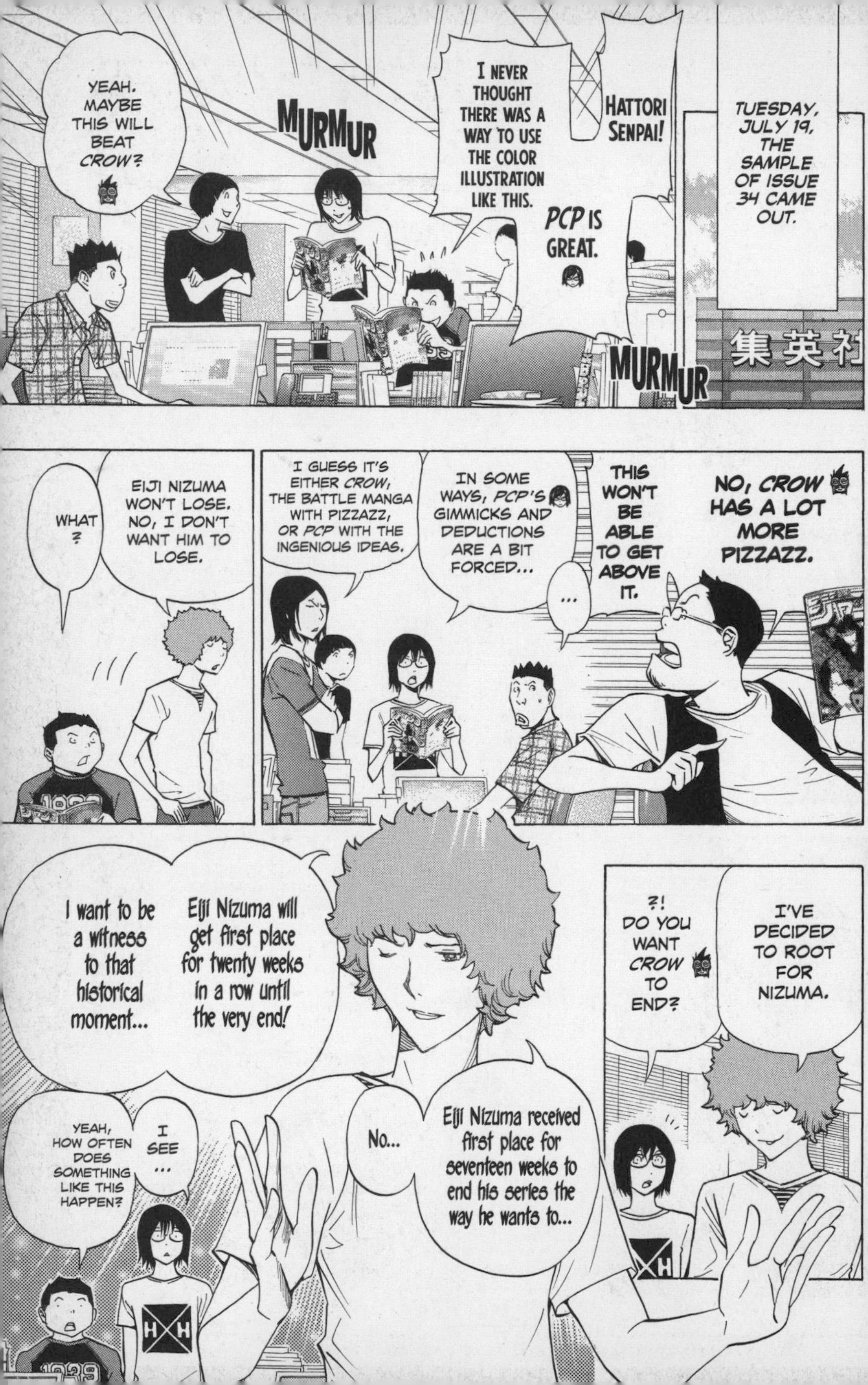
TUESDAY, JULY 19, THE SAMPLE OF ISSUE 34 CAME OUT.
集英社
HATTORI SENPAI!
PCP IS GREAT.
I NEVER THOUGHT THERE WAS A WAY TO USE THE COLOR ILLUSTRATION LIKE THIS.
MURMUR
MURMUR
YEAH. MAYBE THIS WILL BEAT CROW?
NO, CROW HAS A LOT MORE PIZZAZZ.
THIS WON'T BE ABLE TO GET ABOVE IT.
...
IN SOME WAYS, PCP'S GIMMICKS AND DEDUCTIONS ARE A BIT FORCED...
I GUESS IT'S EITHER CROW, THE BATTLE MANGA WITH PIZZAZZ, OR PCP WITH THE INGENIOUS IDEAS.
EIJI NIZUMA WON'T LOSE. NO, I DON'T WANT HIM TO LOSE.
WHAT?
I'VE DECIDED TO ROOT FOR NIZUMA.
?! DO YOU WANT CROW TO END?
Eiji Nizuma will get first place for twenty weeks in a row until the very end!
I want to be a witness to that historical moment...
Eiji Nizuma received first place for seventeen weeks to end his series the way he wants to...
No...
I SEE...
YEAH, HOW OFTEN DOES SOMETHING LIKE THIS HAPPEN?

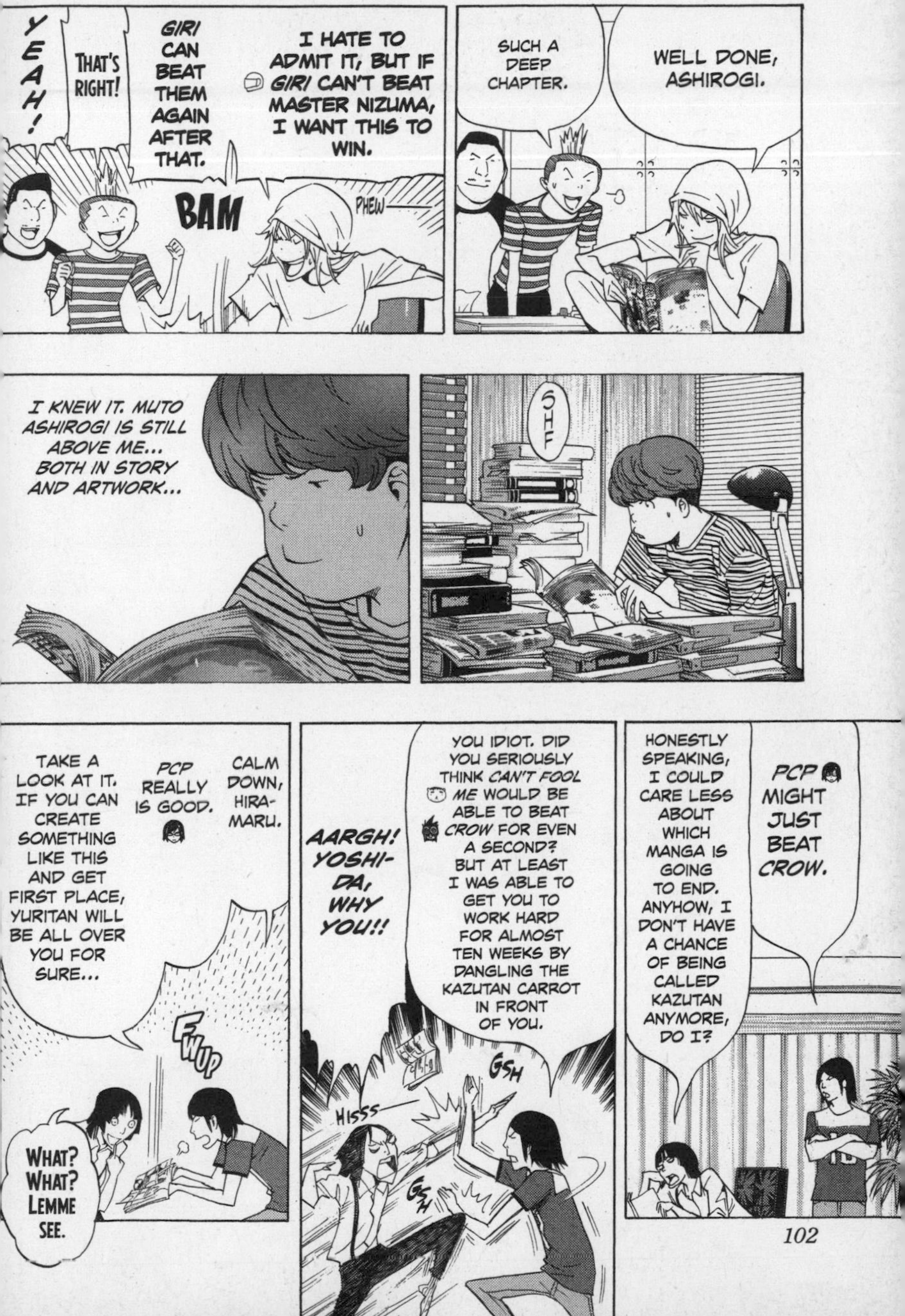
WELL DONE, ASHIROGI.
SUCH A DEEP CHAPTER.
I HATE TO ADMIT IT, BUT IF GIRI CAN'T BEAT MASTER NIZUMA, I WANT THIS TO WIN.
PHEW
BAM
GIRI CAN BEAT THEM AGAIN AFTER THAT.
THAT'S RIGHT!
YEAH!
SHF
I KNEW IT. MUTO ASHIROGI IS STILL ABOVE ME... BOTH IN STORY AND ARTWORK...
PCP MIGHT JUST BEAT CROW.
HONESTLY SPEAKING, I COULD CARE LESS ABOUT WHICH MANGA IS GOING TO END. ANYHOW, I DON'T HAVE A CHANCE OF BEING CALLED KAZUTAN ANYMORE, DO I?
YOU IDIOT. DID YOU SERIOUSLY THINK CAN'T FOOL ME WOULD BE ABLE TO BEAT CROW FOR EVEN A SECOND? BUT AT LEAST I WAS ABLE TO GET YOU TO WORK HARD FOR ALMOST TEN WEEKS BY DANGLING THE KAZUTAN CARROT IN FRONT OF YOU.
AARGH! YOSHIDA, WHY YOU!!
GSH
HISSS
GSH
CALM DOWN, HIRAMARU.
PCP REALLY IS GOOD.
TAKE A LOOK AT IT. IF YOU CAN CREATE SOMETHING LIKE THIS AND GET FIRST PLACE, YURITAN WILL BE ALL OVER YOU FOR SURE...
FWUP
WHAT? WHAT? LEMME SEE.

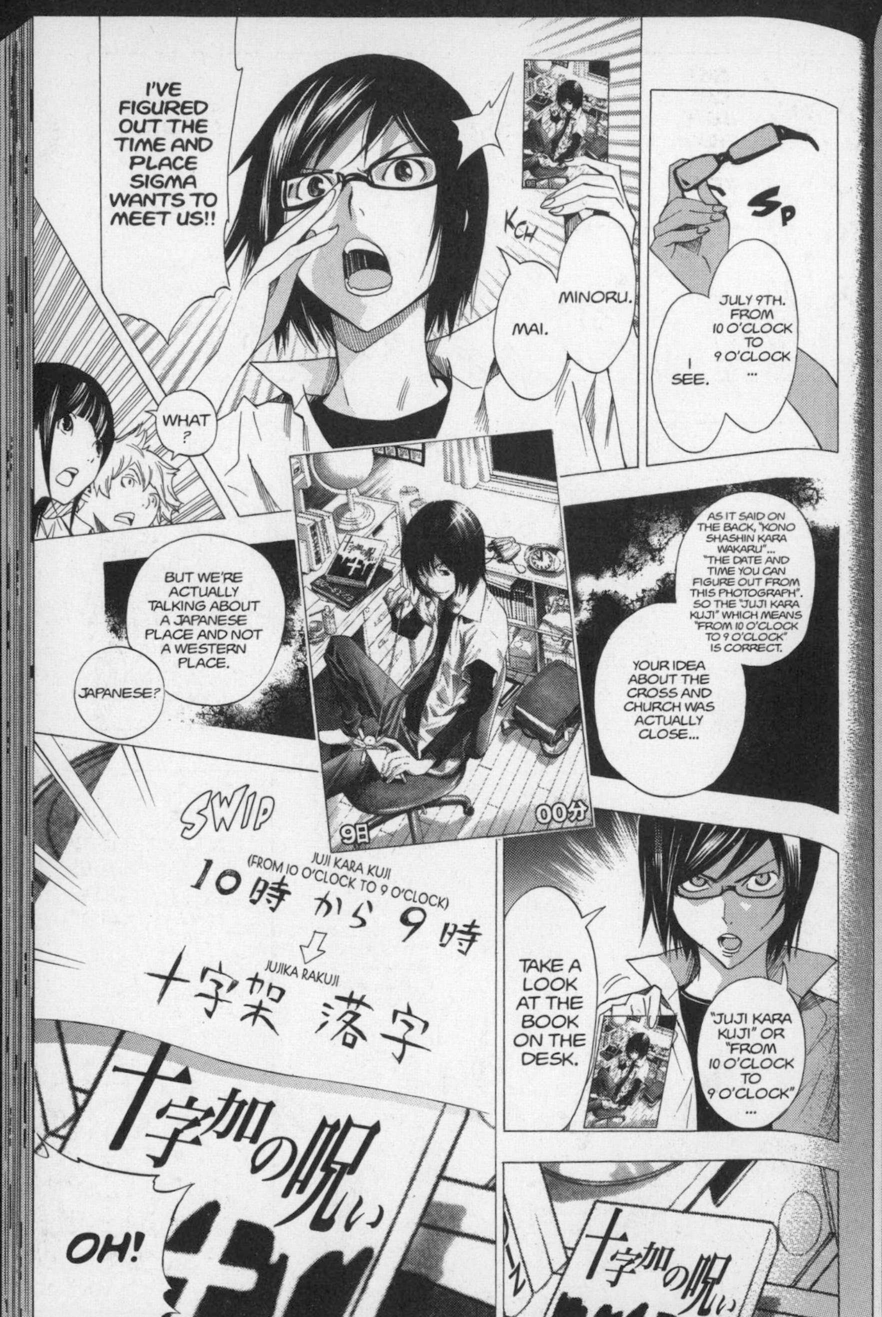
SP
JULY 9TH. FROM 10 O'CLOCK TO 9 O'CLOCK ...
I SEE.
KCH
MINORU.
MAI.
I'VE FIGURED OUT THE TIME AND PLACE SIGMA WANTS TO MEET US!!
WHAT?
AS IT SAID ON THE BACK, "KONO SHASHIN KARA WAKARU"... "THE DATE AND TIME YOU CAN FIGURE OUT FROM THIS PHOTOGRAPH". SO THE "JUJI KARA KUJI" WHICH MEANS "FROM 10 O'CLOCK TO 9 O'CLOCK" IS CORRECT.
YOUR IDEA ABOUT THE CROSS AND CHURCH WAS ACTUALLY CLOSE...
BUT WE'RE ACTUALLY TALKING ABOUT A JAPANESE PLACE AND NOT A WESTERN PLACE.
JAPANESE?
9日
00分
"JUJI KARA KUJI" OR "FROM 10 O'CLOCK TO 9 O'CLOCK" ...
TAKE A LOOK AT THE BOOK ON THE DESK.
SWIP
JUJI KARA KUJI (FROM 10 O'CLOCK TO 9 O'CLOCK)
10時 から 9時
JUJIKA RAKUJI
十字架 落字
十字加の呪い
OH!
十字加の呪い

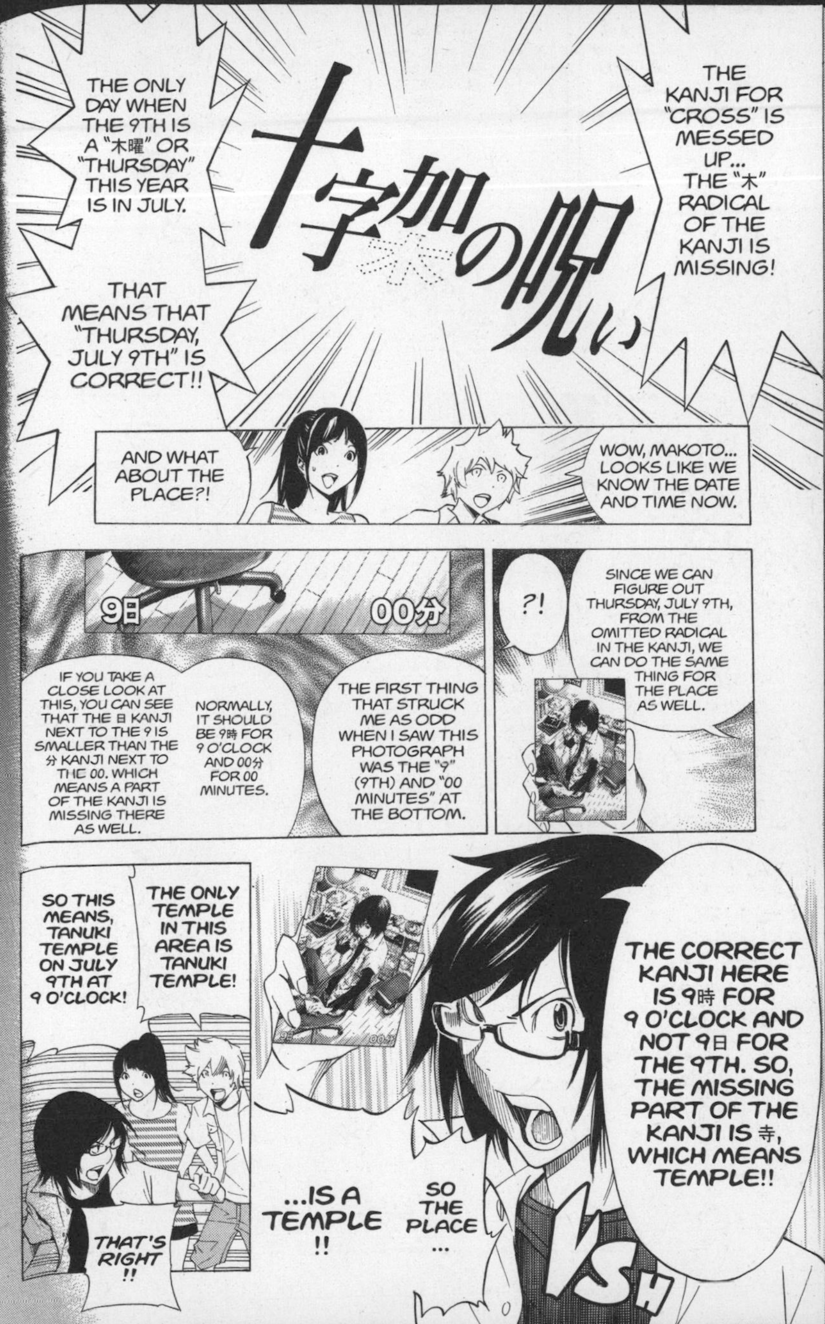
THE KANJI FOR "CROSS" IS MESSED UP... THE "木" RADICAL OF THE KANJI IS MISSING!
十字加の呪い
THE ONLY DAY WHEN THE 9TH IS A "木曜" OR "THURSDAY" THIS YEAR IS IN JULY.
THAT MEANS THAT "THURSDAY, JULY 9TH" IS CORRECT!!
WOW, MAKOTO... LOOKS LIKE WE KNOW THE DATE AND TIME NOW.
AND WHAT ABOUT THE PLACE?!
?!
SINCE WE CAN FIGURE OUT THURSDAY, JULY 9TH, FROM THE OMITTED RADICAL IN THE KANJI, WE CAN DO THE SAME THING FOR THE PLACE AS WELL.
9日
00分
THE FIRST THING THAT STRUCK ME AS ODD WHEN I SAW THIS PHOTOGRAPH WAS THE "9" (9TH) AND "00 MINUTES" AT THE BOTTOM.
NORMALLY, IT SHOULD BE 9時 FOR 9 O'CLOCK AND 00分 FOR 00 MINUTES.
IF YOU TAKE A CLOSE LOOK AT THIS, YOU CAN SEE THAT THE 日 KANJI NEXT TO THE 9 IS SMALLER THAN THE 分 KANJI NEXT TO THE 00. WHICH MEANS A PART OF THE KANJI IS MISSING THERE AS WELL.
THE CORRECT KANJI HERE IS 9時 FOR 9 O'CLOCK AND NOT 9日 FOR THE 9TH. SO, THE MISSING PART OF THE KANJI IS 寺, WHICH MEANS TEMPLE!!
VSH
SO THE PLACE...
...IS A TEMPLE!!
THE ONLY TEMPLE IN THIS AREA IS TANUKI TEMPLE!
SO THIS MEANS, TANUKI TEMPLE ON JULY 9TH AT 9 O'CLOCK!
THAT'S RIGHT!!

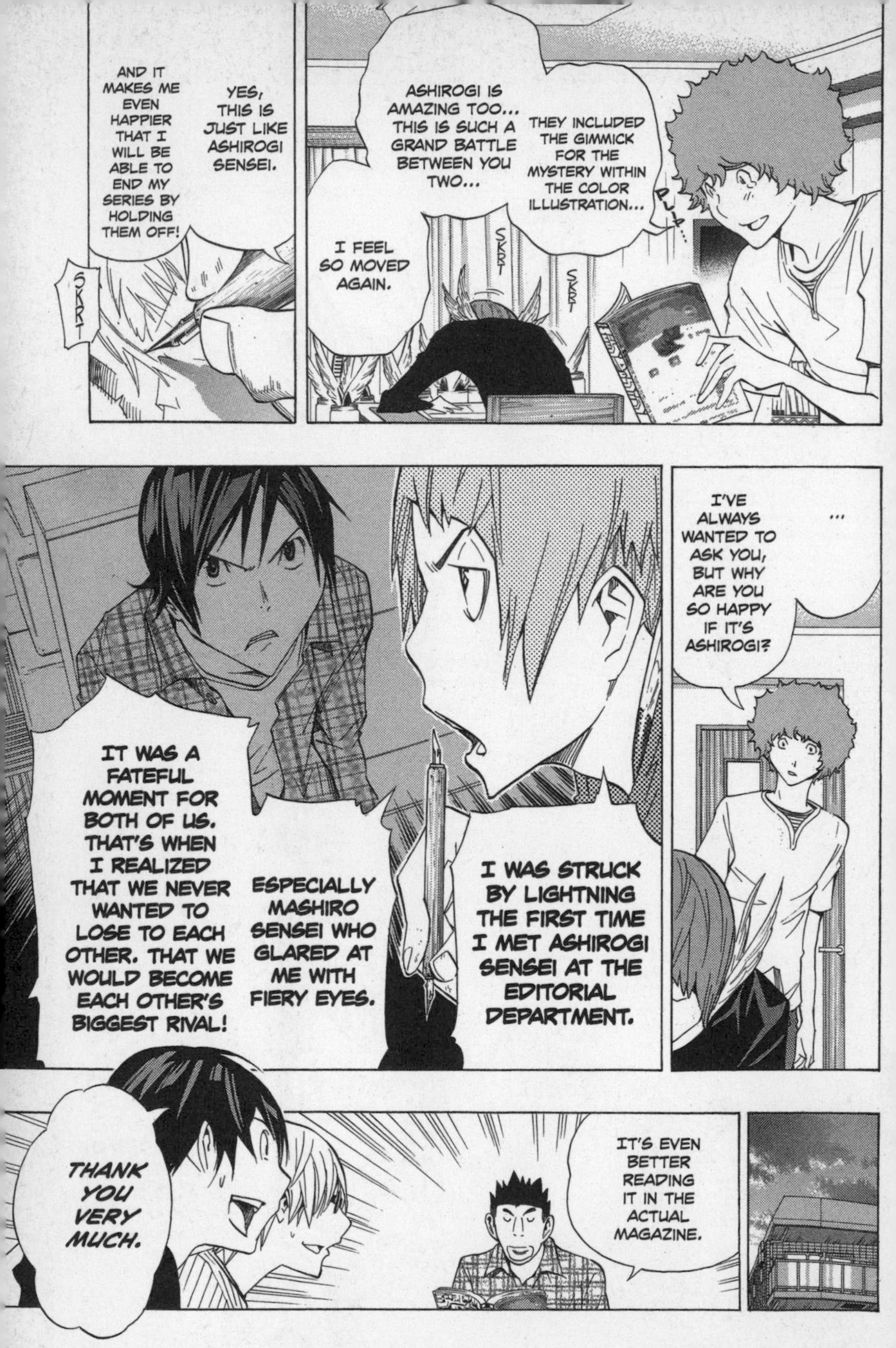
THEY INCLUDED THE GIMMICK FOR THE MYSTERY WITHIN THE COLOR ILLUSTRATION...
ASHIROGI IS AMAZING TOO... THIS IS SUCH A GRAND BATTLE BETWEEN YOU TWO...
I FEEL SO MOVED AGAIN.
SKRT
SKRT
YES, THIS IS JUST LIKE ASHIROGI SENSEI.
AND IT MAKES ME EVEN HAPPIER THAT I WILL BE ABLE TO END MY SERIES BY HOLDING THEM OFF!
SKRT
...
I'VE ALWAYS WANTED TO ASK YOU, BUT WHY ARE YOU SO HAPPY IF IT'S ASHIROGI?
I WAS STRUCK BY LIGHTNING THE FIRST TIME I MET ASHIROGI SENSEI AT THE EDITORIAL DEPARTMENT.
ESPECIALLY MASHIRO SENSEI WHO GLARED AT ME WITH FIERY EYES.
IT WAS A FATEFUL MOMENT FOR BOTH OF US. THAT'S WHEN I REALIZED THAT WE NEVER WANTED TO LOSE TO EACH OTHER. THAT WE WOULD BECOME EACH OTHER'S BIGGEST RIVAL!
IT'S EVEN BETTER READING IT IN THE ACTUAL MAGAZINE.
THANK YOU VERY MUCH.

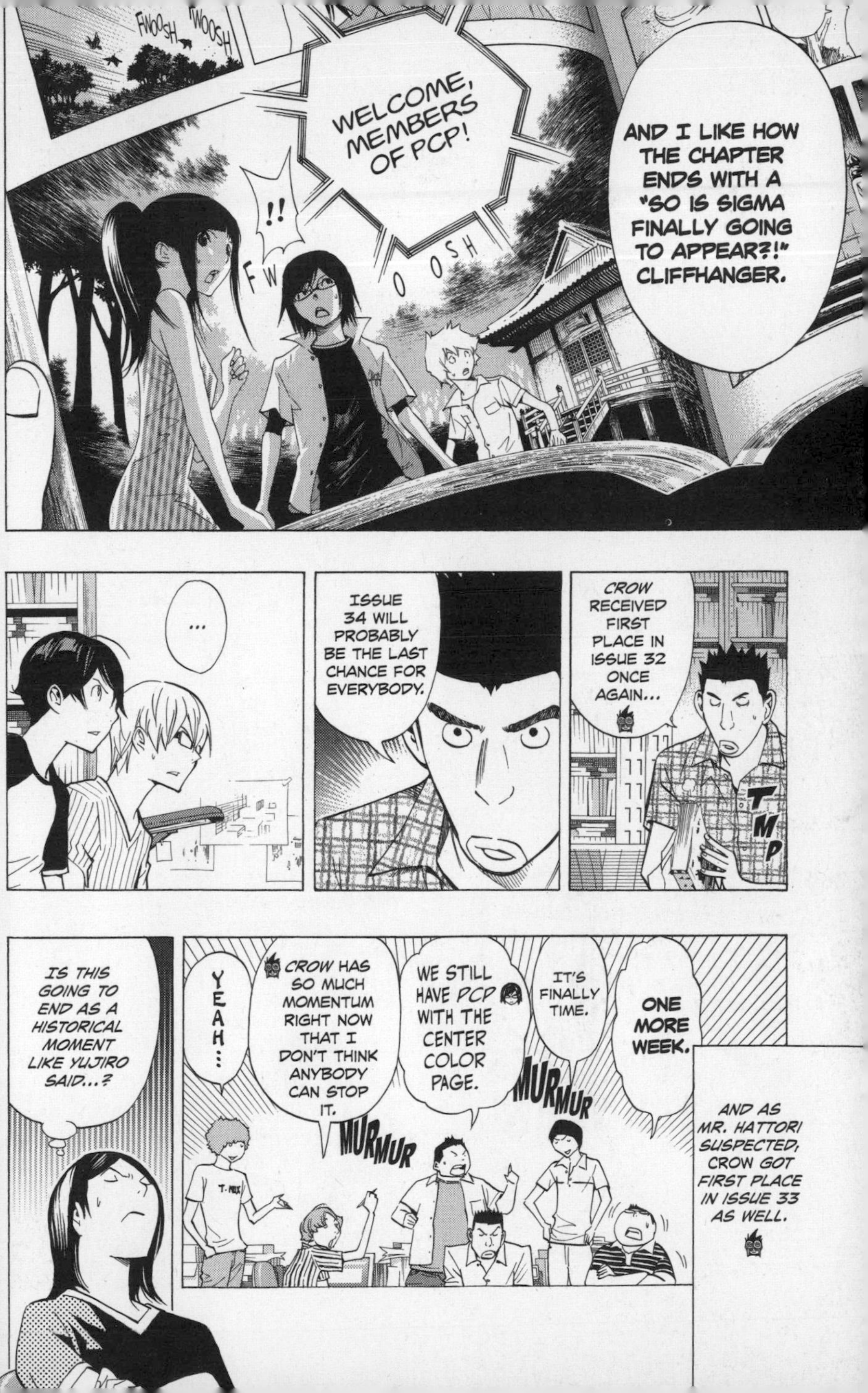
AND I LIKE HOW THE CHAPTER ENDS WITH A "SO IS SIGMA FINALLY GOING TO APPEAR?!" CLIFFHANGER.
FWOOSH
FWOOSH
WELCOME, MEMBERS OF PCP!
!!
FWOOSH
CROW RECEIVED FIRST PLACE IN ISSUE 32 ONCE AGAIN...
TMP
ISSUE 34 WILL PROBABLY BE THE LAST CHANCE FOR EVERYBODY.
...
AND AS MR. HATTORI SUSPECTED, CROW GOT FIRST PLACE IN ISSUE 33 AS WELL.
ONE MORE WEEK.
IT'S FINALLY TIME.
WE STILL HAVE PCP WITH THE CENTER COLOR PAGE.
MURMUR
CROW HAS SO MUCH MOMENTUM RIGHT NOW THAT I DON'T THINK ANYBODY CAN STOP IT.
YEAH...
MURMUR
T. MIX
IS THIS GOING TO END AS A HISTORICAL MOMENT LIKE YUJIRO SAID...?

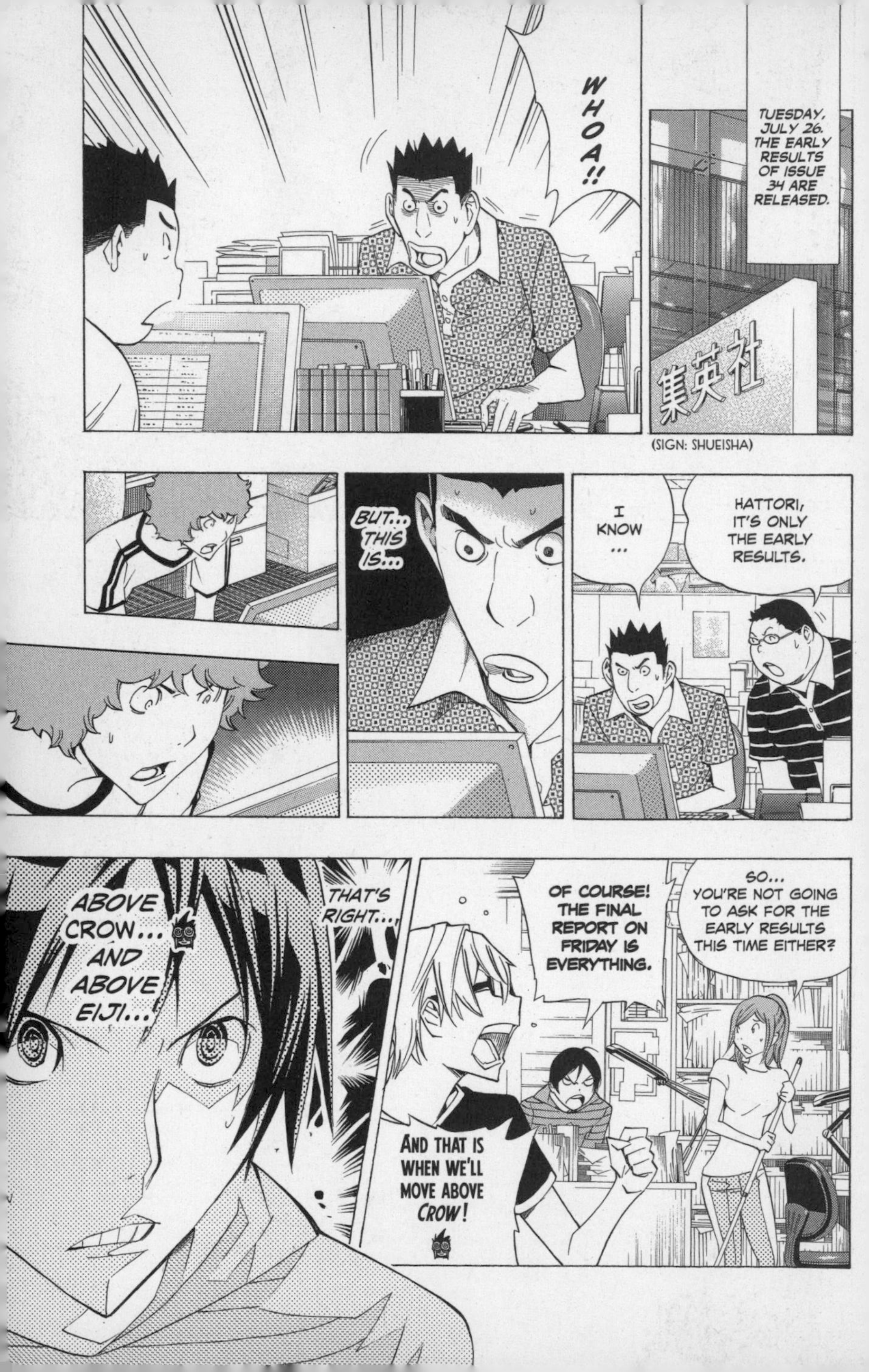
TUESDAY, JULY 26. THE EARLY RESULTS OF ISSUE 34 ARE RELEASED.
(SIGN: SHUEISHA)
WHOA!!
HATTORI, IT'S ONLY THE EARLY RESULTS.
I KNOW...
BUT... THIS IS...
SO... YOU'RE NOT GOING TO ASK FOR THE EARLY RESULTS THIS TIME EITHER?
OF COURSE! THE FINAL REPORT ON FRIDAY IS EVERYTHING.
AND THAT IS WHEN WE'LL MOVE ABOVE CROW!
THAT'S RIGHT...
ABOVE CROW... AND ABOVE EIJI...

OHBA'S STORYBOARD

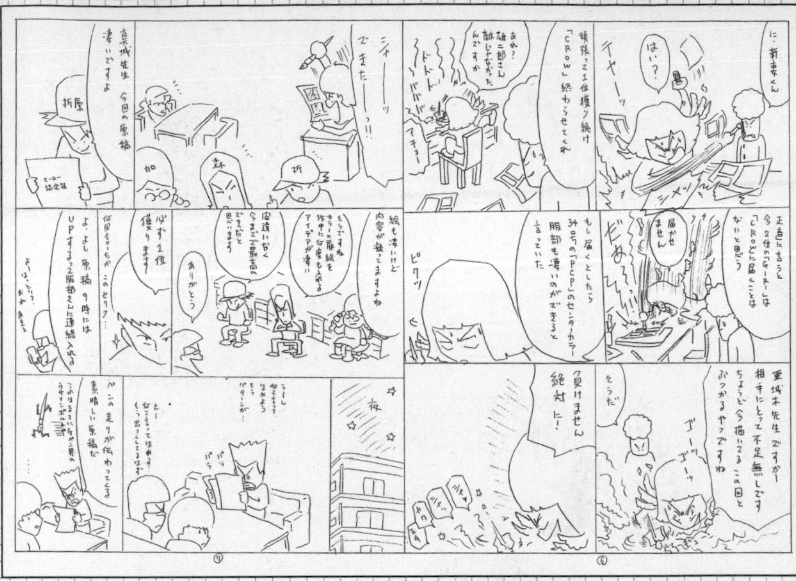

に、新妻くん
はい？
テヤーッ
シメッ
頑張って1位獲り続け「CROW」終わらせてくれ
ドドドドドド
アチョー
正直に言うと今2位の「ぷーぷー」は「CROW」に届くことはないと思う
届かせません
だめっ
もし届くとしたら34号の「PCP」のセンターカラー服部も凄いのができると言っていた
ピクッ
亜城木先生ですが相手にとって不足無しです ちょうど今描いてるこの回とぶつかるヤツですね
ゴーッゴーッ
そうだ
負けません絶対に！
シャーッ できたーっ!!
真城先生今回の原稿凄いですよ
折原
ヒーロー認定証
絵も凄いけど内容が凝ってますよね
ありがとう
必ず1位獲ります
よ、よし原稿9時にはUPするって服部さんに連絡入れる
夜
ペンの走りが伝わってくる素晴しい原稿だ

OBATA'S STORYBOARD

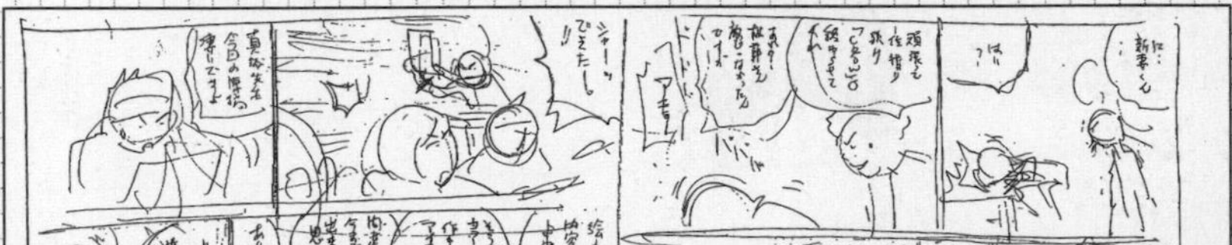

COMPLETE!

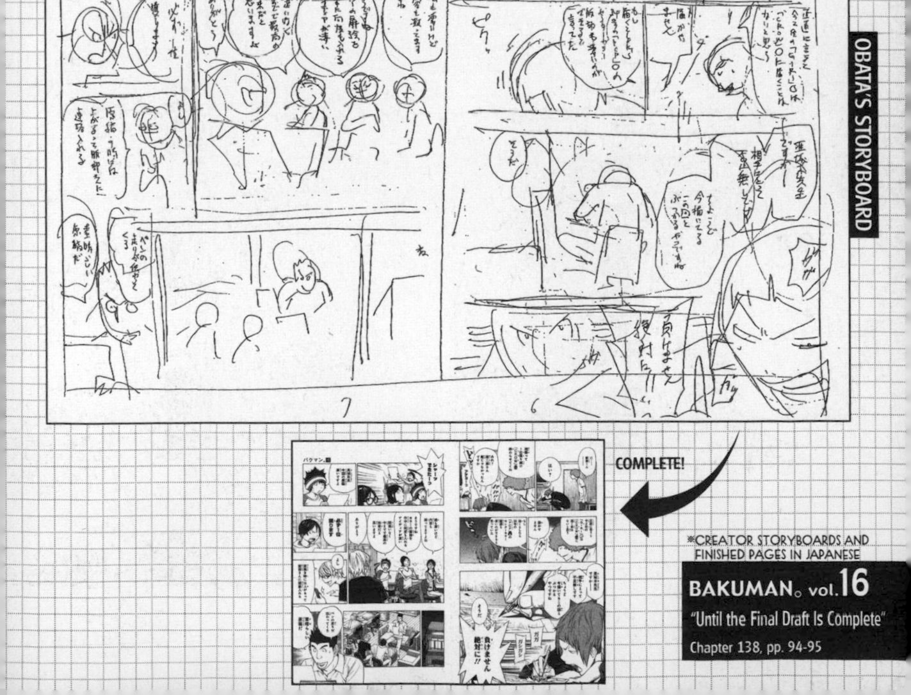

※CREATOR STORYBOARDS AND FINISHED PAGES IN JAPANESE

BAKUMAN。vol.16

"Until the Final Draft Is Complete"

Chapter 138, pp. 94-95

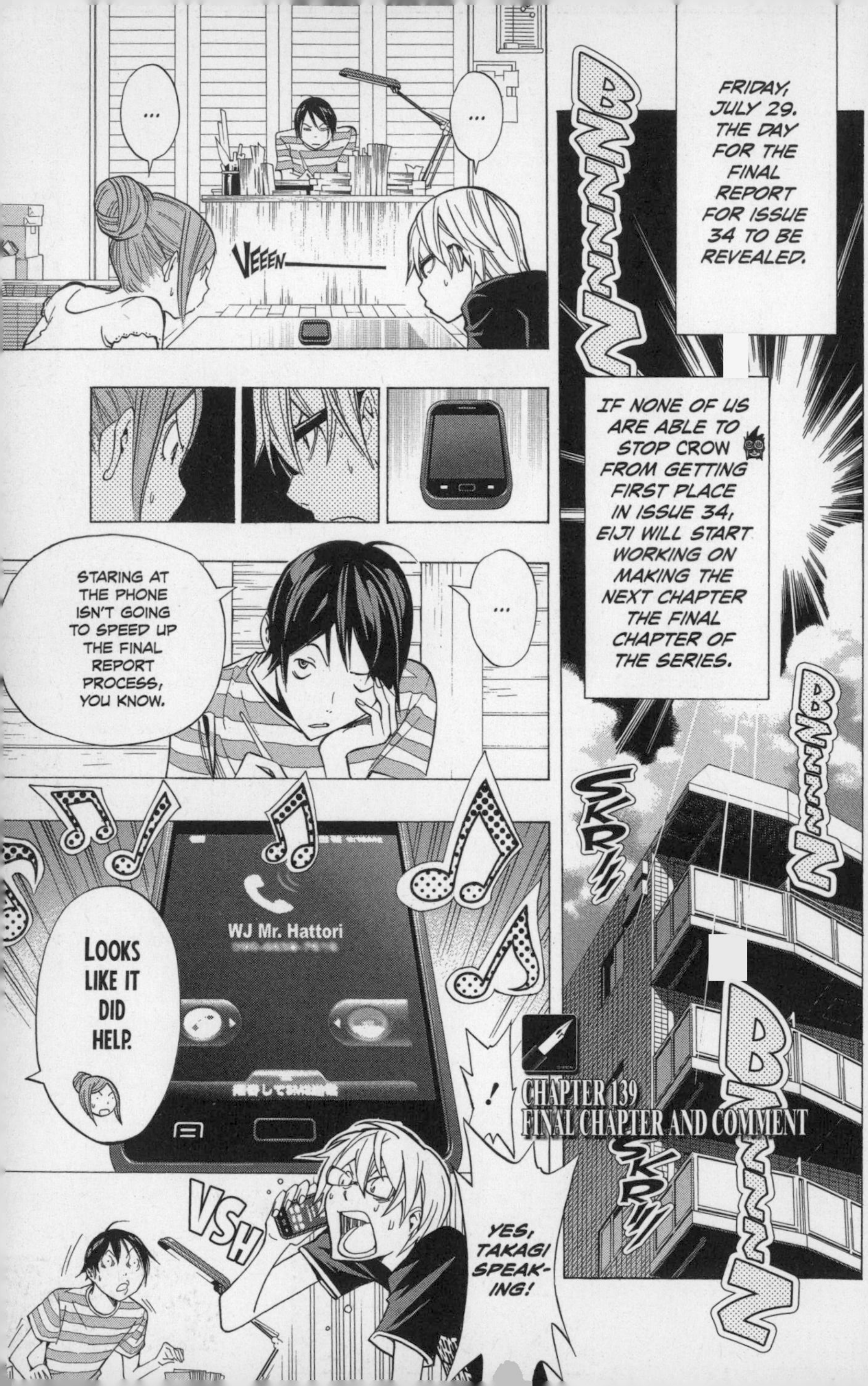
FRIDAY, JULY 29. THE DAY FOR THE FINAL REPORT FOR ISSUE 34 TO BE REVEALED.
IF NONE OF US ARE ABLE TO STOP CROW FROM GETTING FIRST PLACE IN ISSUE 34, EIJI WILL START WORKING ON MAKING THE NEXT CHAPTER THE FINAL CHAPTER OF THE SERIES.
SKRIII
CHAPTER 139
FINAL CHAPTER AND COMMENT
SKRIII
...
...
VEEEN
...
STARING AT THE PHONE ISN'T GOING TO SPEED UP THE FINAL REPORT PROCESS, YOU KNOW.
WJ Mr. Hattori
LOOKS LIKE IT DID HELP.
!
YES, TAKAGI SPEAKING!
VSH

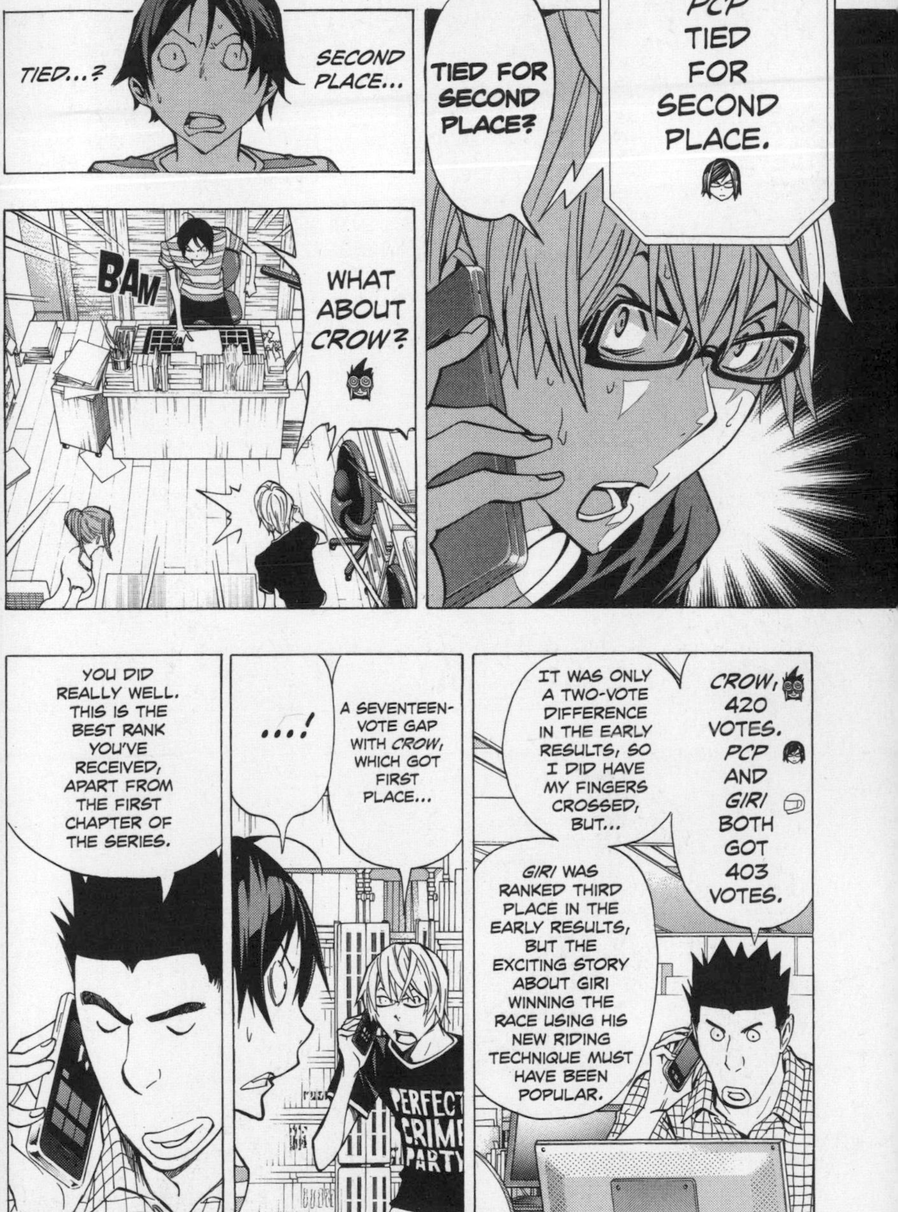
PCP TIED FOR SECOND PLACE.
TIED FOR SECOND PLACE?
SECOND PLACE...
TIED...?
WHAT ABOUT CROW?
BAM
CROW, 420 VOTES. PCP AND GIRI BOTH GOT 403 VOTES.
IT WAS ONLY A TWO-VOTE DIFFERENCE IN THE EARLY RESULTS, SO I DID HAVE MY FINGERS CROSSED, BUT...
GIRI WAS RANKED THIRD PLACE IN THE EARLY RESULTS, BUT THE EXCITING STORY ABOUT GIRI WINNING THE RACE USING HIS NEW RIDING TECHNIQUE MUST HAVE BEEN POPULAR.
A SEVENTEEN-VOTE GAP WITH CROW, WHICH GOT FIRST PLACE...
...!
PERFECT CRIME PARTY
YOU DID REALLY WELL. THIS IS THE BEST RANK YOU'VE RECEIVED, APART FROM THE FIRST CHAPTER OF THE SERIES.

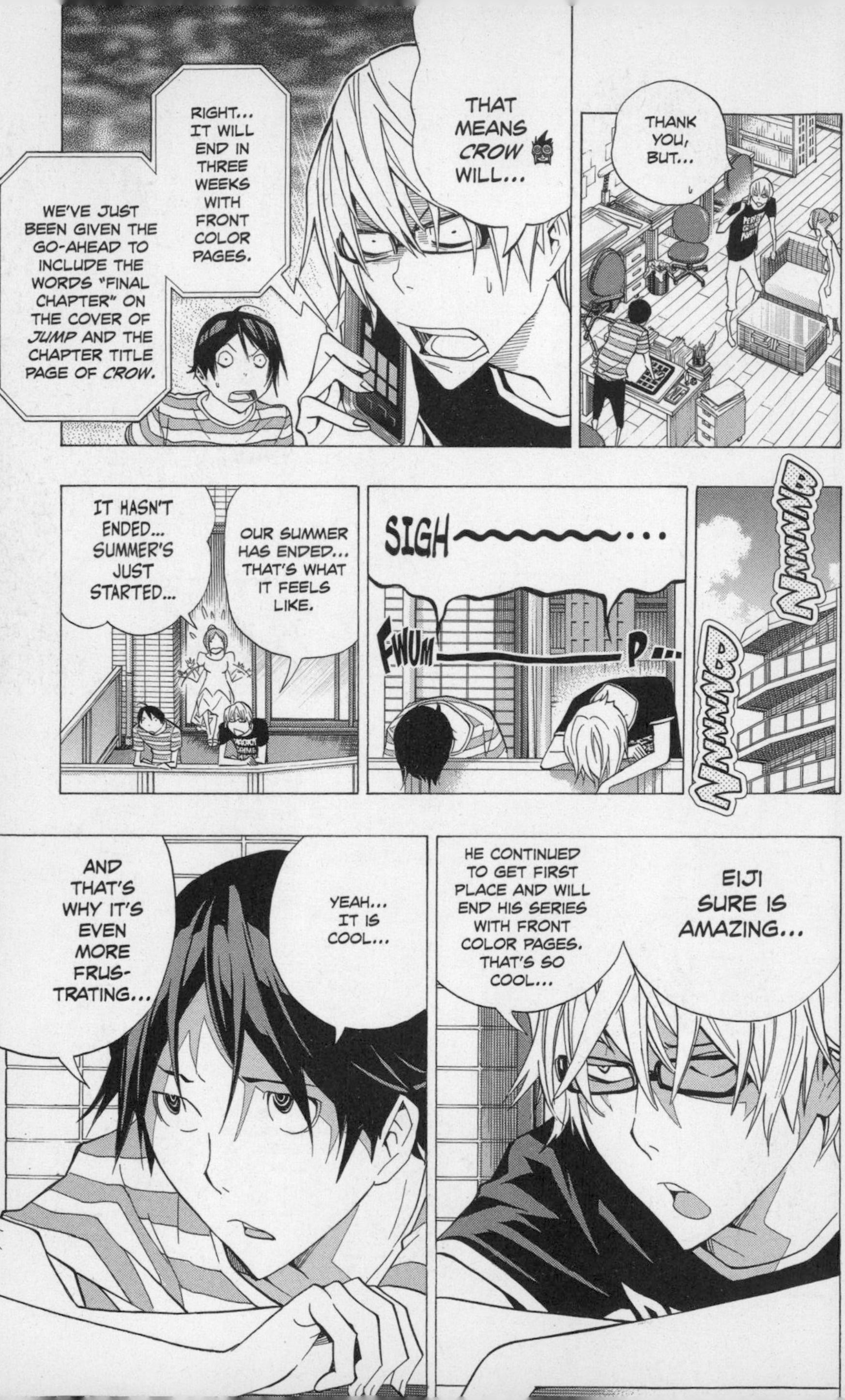
THANK YOU, BUT...
THAT MEANS *CROW* WILL...
RIGHT... IT WILL END IN THREE WEEKS WITH FRONT COLOR PAGES.
WE'VE JUST BEEN GIVEN THE GO-AHEAD TO INCLUDE THE WORDS "FINAL CHAPTER" ON THE COVER OF *JUMP* AND THE CHAPTER TITLE PAGE OF *CROW*.
BNNNNN
BNNNNNN
SIGH~~~~~~~...
FWUM———P...
OUR SUMMER HAS ENDED... THAT'S WHAT IT FEELS LIKE.
IT HASN'T ENDED... SUMMER'S JUST STARTED...
EIJI SURE IS AMAZING...
HE CONTINUED TO GET FIRST PLACE AND WILL END HIS SERIES WITH FRONT COLOR PAGES. THAT'S SO COOL...
YEAH... IT IS COOL...
AND THAT'S WHY IT'S EVEN MORE FRUS-TRATING...

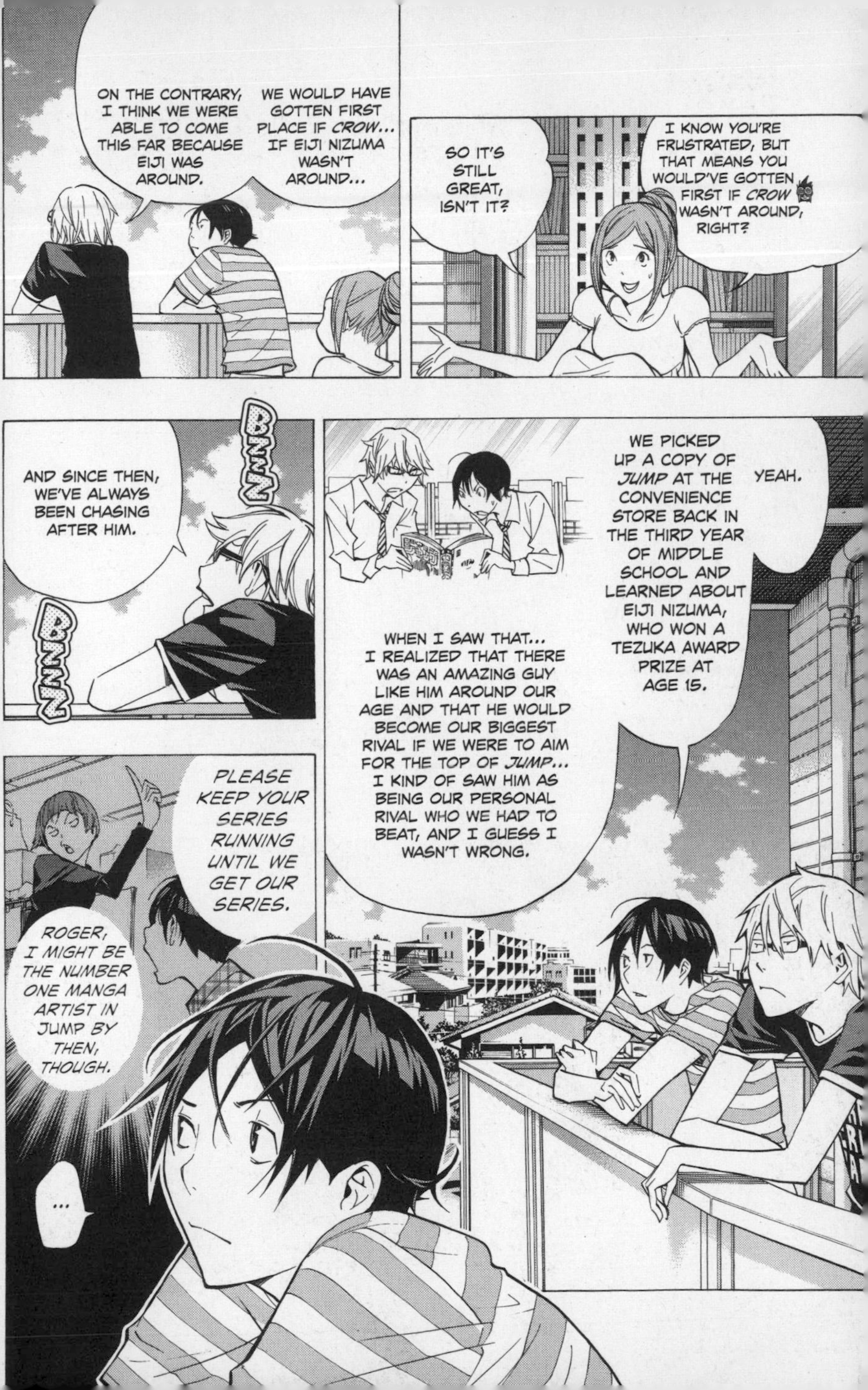
I KNOW YOU'RE FRUSTRATED, BUT THAT MEANS YOU WOULD'VE GOTTEN FIRST IF CROW WASN'T AROUND, RIGHT?
SO IT'S STILL GREAT, ISN'T IT?
WE WOULD HAVE GOTTEN FIRST PLACE IF CROW... IF EIJI NIZUMA WASN'T AROUND...
ON THE CONTRARY, I THINK WE WERE ABLE TO COME THIS FAR BECAUSE EIJI WAS AROUND.
YEAH.
WE PICKED UP A COPY OF JUMP AT THE CONVENIENCE STORE BACK IN THE THIRD YEAR OF MIDDLE SCHOOL AND LEARNED ABOUT EIJI NIZUMA, WHO WON A TEZUKA AWARD PRIZE AT AGE 15.
WHEN I SAW THAT... I REALIZED THAT THERE WAS AN AMAZING GUY LIKE HIM AROUND OUR AGE AND THAT HE WOULD BECOME OUR BIGGEST RIVAL IF WE WERE TO AIM FOR THE TOP OF JUMP... I KIND OF SAW HIM AS BEING OUR PERSONAL RIVAL WHO WE HAD TO BEAT, AND I GUESS I WASN'T WRONG.
BZZZ
AND SINCE THEN, WE'VE ALWAYS BEEN CHASING AFTER HIM.
BZZZ
PLEASE KEEP YOUR SERIES RUNNING UNTIL WE GET OUR SERIES.
ROGER, I MIGHT BE THE NUMBER ONE MANGA ARTIST IN JUMP BY THEN, THOUGH.
...

READ THIS WAY

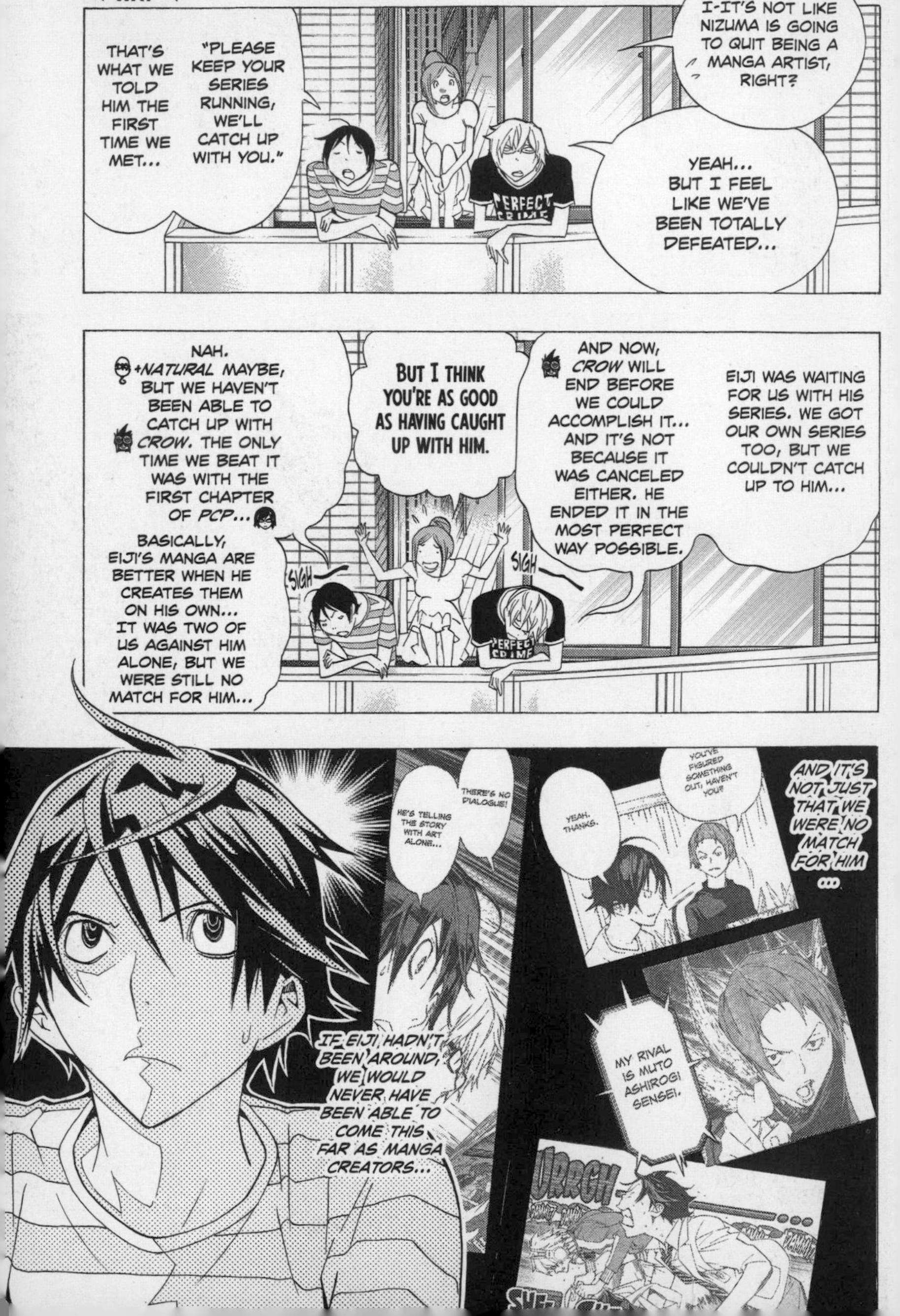
I-IT'S NOT LIKE NIZUMA IS GOING TO QUIT BEING A MANGA ARTIST, RIGHT?
YEAH... BUT I FEEL LIKE WE'VE BEEN TOTALLY DEFEATED...
"PLEASE KEEP YOUR SERIES RUNNING, WE'LL CATCH UP WITH YOU."
THAT'S WHAT WE TOLD HIM THE FIRST TIME WE MET...
EIJI WAS WAITING FOR US WITH HIS SERIES. WE GOT OUR OWN SERIES TOO, BUT WE COULDN'T CATCH UP TO HIM...
AND NOW, CROW WILL END BEFORE WE COULD ACCOMPLISH IT... AND IT'S NOT BECAUSE IT WAS CANCELED EITHER. HE ENDED IT IN THE MOST PERFECT WAY POSSIBLE.
SIGH
BUT I THINK YOU'RE AS GOOD AS HAVING CAUGHT UP WITH HIM.
NAH. +NATURAL MAYBE, BUT WE HAVEN'T BEEN ABLE TO CATCH UP WITH CROW. THE ONLY TIME WE BEAT IT WAS WITH THE FIRST CHAPTER OF PCP...
BASICALLY, EIJI'S MANGA ARE BETTER WHEN HE CREATES THEM ON HIS OWN... IT WAS TWO OF US AGAINST HIM ALONE, BUT WE WERE STILL NO MATCH FOR HIM...
SIGH
AND IT'S NOT JUST THAT WE WERE NO MATCH FOR HIM...
YOU'VE FIGURED SOMETHING OUT, HAVEN'T YOU?
YEAH. THANKS.
MY RIVAL IS MUTO ASHIROGI SENSEI.
URRGH
THERE'S NO DIALOGUE!
HE'S TELLING THE STORY WITH ART ALONE...
IF EIJI HADN'T BEEN AROUND, WE WOULD NEVER HAVE BEEN ABLE TO COME THIS FAR AS MANGA CREATORS...

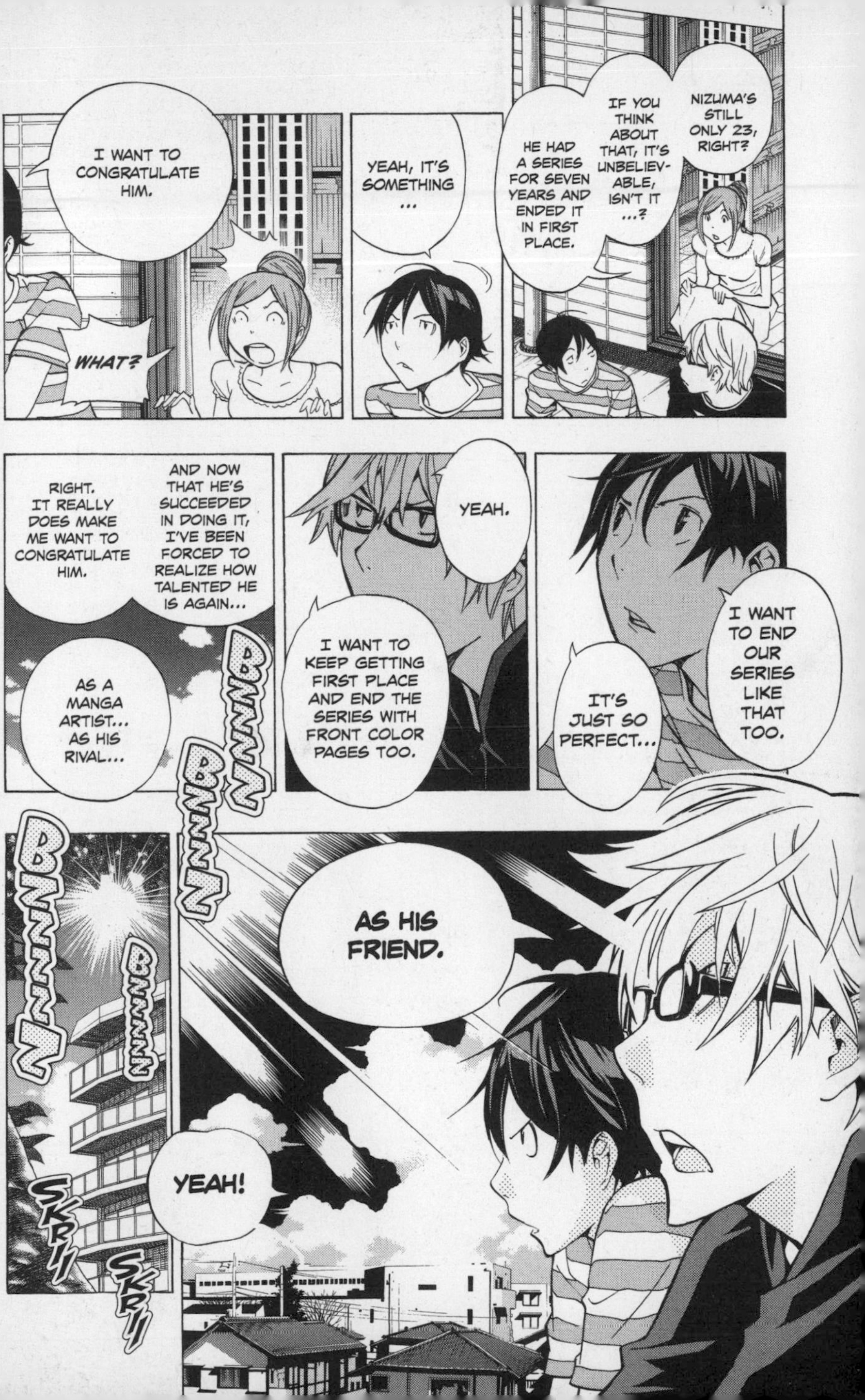
NIZUMA'S STILL ONLY 23, RIGHT?
IF YOU THINK ABOUT THAT, IT'S UNBELIEVABLE, ISN'T IT ...?
HE HAD A SERIES FOR SEVEN YEARS AND ENDED IT IN FIRST PLACE.
YEAH, IT'S SOMETHING ...
I WANT TO CONGRATULATE HIM.
WHAT?
I WANT TO END OUR SERIES LIKE THAT TOO.
IT'S JUST SO PERFECT...
YEAH.
I WANT TO KEEP GETTING FIRST PLACE AND END THE SERIES WITH FRONT COLOR PAGES TOO.
AND NOW THAT HE'S SUCCEEDED IN DOING IT, I'VE BEEN FORCED TO REALIZE HOW TALENTED HE IS AGAIN...
RIGHT. IT REALLY DOES MAKE ME WANT TO CONGRATULATE HIM.
AS A MANGA ARTIST... AS HIS RIVAL...
BZZZZ
AS HIS FRIEND.
YEAH!
SKRII SKRII

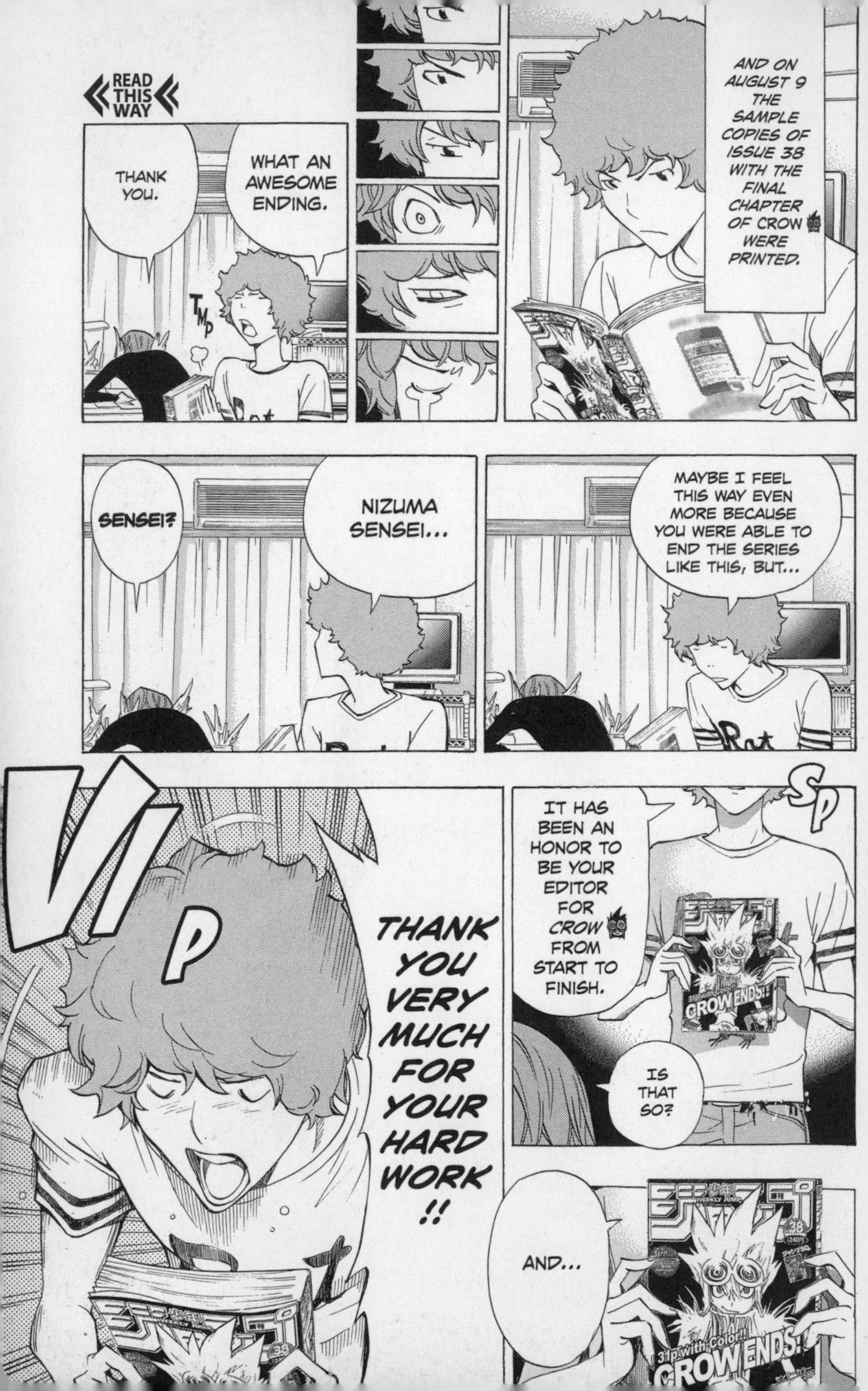
READ THIS WAY
AND ON AUGUST 9 THE SAMPLE COPIES OF ISSUE 38 WITH THE FINAL CHAPTER OF CROW WERE PRINTED.
WHAT AN AWESOME ENDING.
THANK YOU.
TMP
MAYBE I FEEL THIS WAY EVEN MORE BECAUSE YOU WERE ABLE TO END THE SERIES LIKE THIS, BUT...
NIZUMA SENSEI...
SENSEI?
SP
IT HAS BEEN AN HONOR TO BE YOUR EDITOR FOR CROW FROM START TO FINISH.
CROW ENDS!
IS THAT SO?
AND...
WEEKLY JUMP
31p with color!! CROW ENDS!
VIP
THANK YOU VERY MUCH FOR YOUR HARD WORK!!

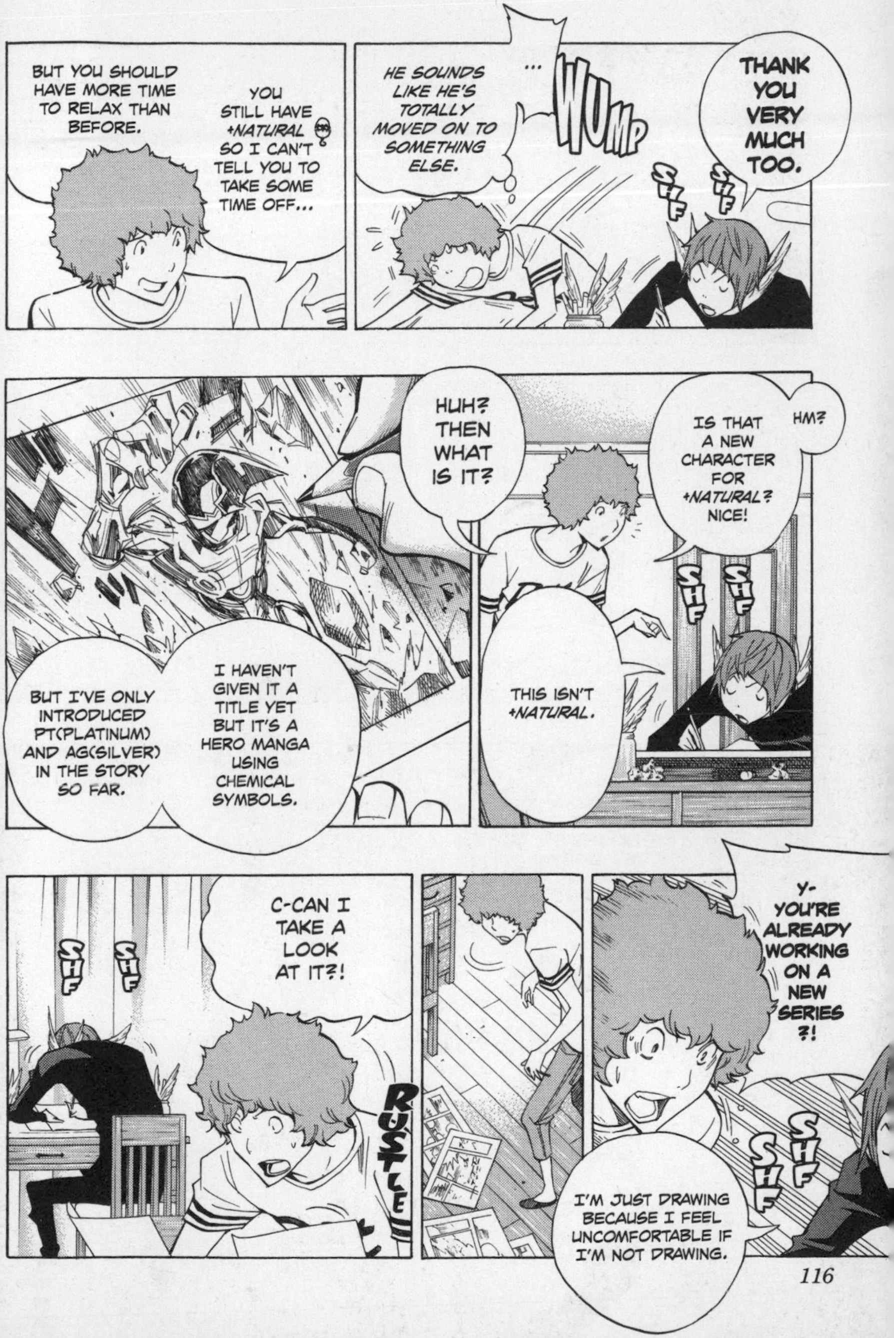
THANK YOU VERY MUCH TOO.
SHF
SHF
WUMP
...
HE SOUNDS LIKE HE'S TOTALLY MOVED ON TO SOMETHING ELSE.
YOU STILL HAVE +NATURAL SO I CAN'T TELL YOU TO TAKE SOME TIME OFF...
BUT YOU SHOULD HAVE MORE TIME TO RELAX THAN BEFORE.
HM?
IS THAT A NEW CHARACTER FOR +NATURAL? NICE!
SHF
SHF
HUH? THEN WHAT IS IT?
THIS ISN'T +NATURAL.
I HAVEN'T GIVEN IT A TITLE YET BUT IT'S A HERO MANGA USING CHEMICAL SYMBOLS.
BUT I'VE ONLY INTRODUCED PT(PLATINUM) AND AG(SILVER) IN THE STORY SO FAR.
Y-YOU'RE ALREADY WORKING ON A NEW SERIES?!
SHF
SHF
I'M JUST DRAWING BECAUSE I FEEL UNCOMFORTABLE IF I'M NOT DRAWING.
C-CAN I TAKE A LOOK AT IT?!
RUSTLE
SHF
SHF

READ THIS WAY

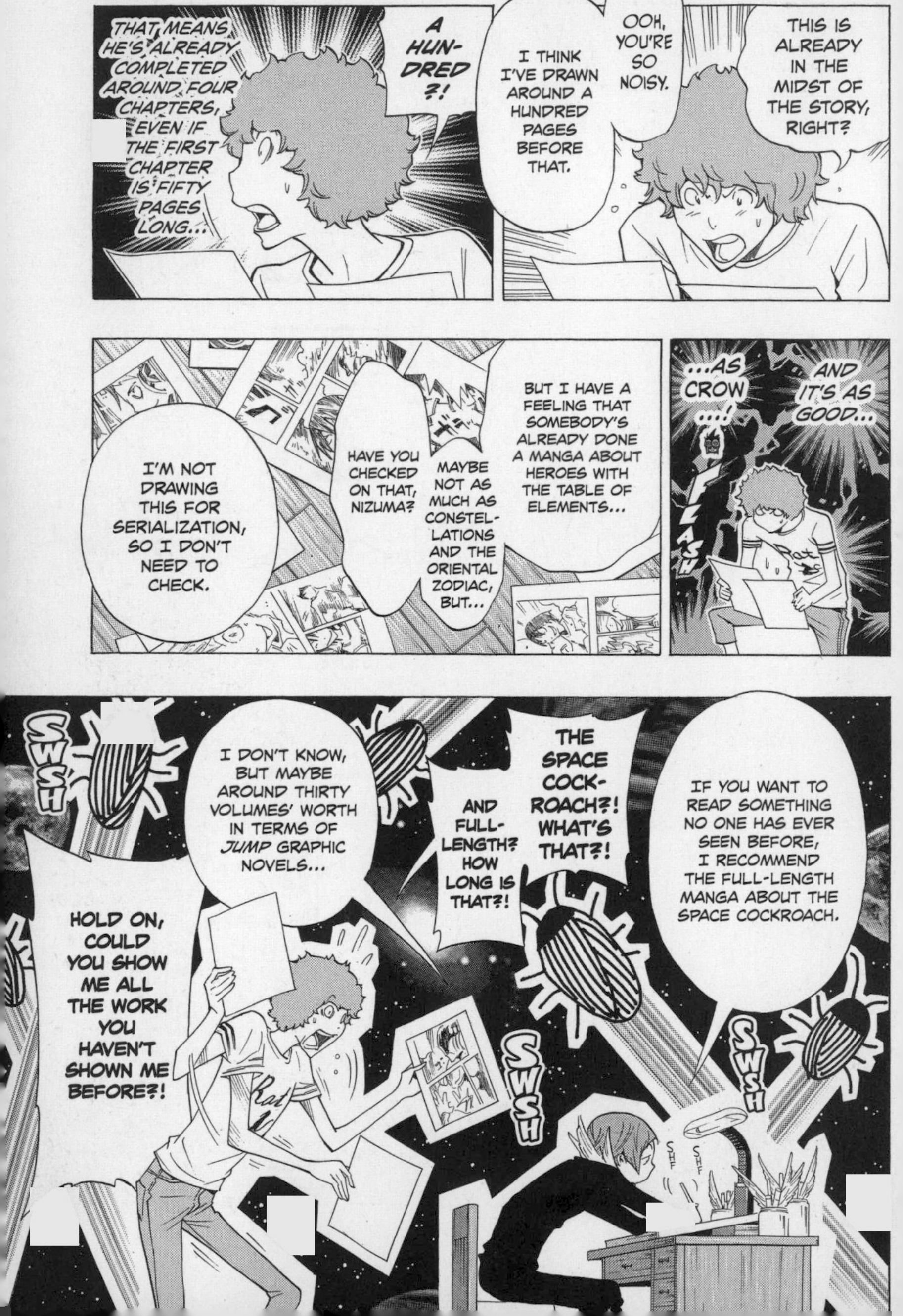
THIS IS ALREADY IN THE MIDST OF THE STORY, RIGHT?
OOH, YOU'RE SO NOISY.
I THINK I'VE DRAWN AROUND A HUNDRED PAGES BEFORE THAT.
A HUNDRED?!
THAT MEANS HE'S ALREADY COMPLETED AROUND FOUR CHAPTERS, EVEN IF THE FIRST CHAPTER IS FIFTY PAGES LONG...
AND IT'S AS GOOD...
...AS CROW...!
BUT I HAVE A FEELING THAT SOMEBODY'S ALREADY DONE A MANGA ABOUT HEROES WITH THE TABLE OF ELEMENTS...
MAYBE NOT AS MUCH AS CONSTELLATIONS AND THE ORIENTAL ZODIAC, BUT...
HAVE YOU CHECKED ON THAT, NIZUMA?
I'M NOT DRAWING THIS FOR SERIALIZATION, SO I DON'T NEED TO CHECK.
IF YOU WANT TO READ SOMETHING NO ONE HAS EVER SEEN BEFORE, I RECOMMEND THE FULL-LENGTH MANGA ABOUT THE SPACE COCKROACH.
SWSH
SHF
SHF
THE SPACE COCKROACH?! WHAT'S THAT?!
AND FULL-LENGTH? HOW LONG IS THAT?!
SWSH
I DON'T KNOW, BUT MAYBE AROUND THIRTY VOLUMES' WORTH IN TERMS OF *JUMP* GRAPHIC NOVELS...
SWSH
HOLD ON, COULD YOU SHOW ME ALL THE WORK YOU HAVEN'T SHOWN ME BEFORE?!

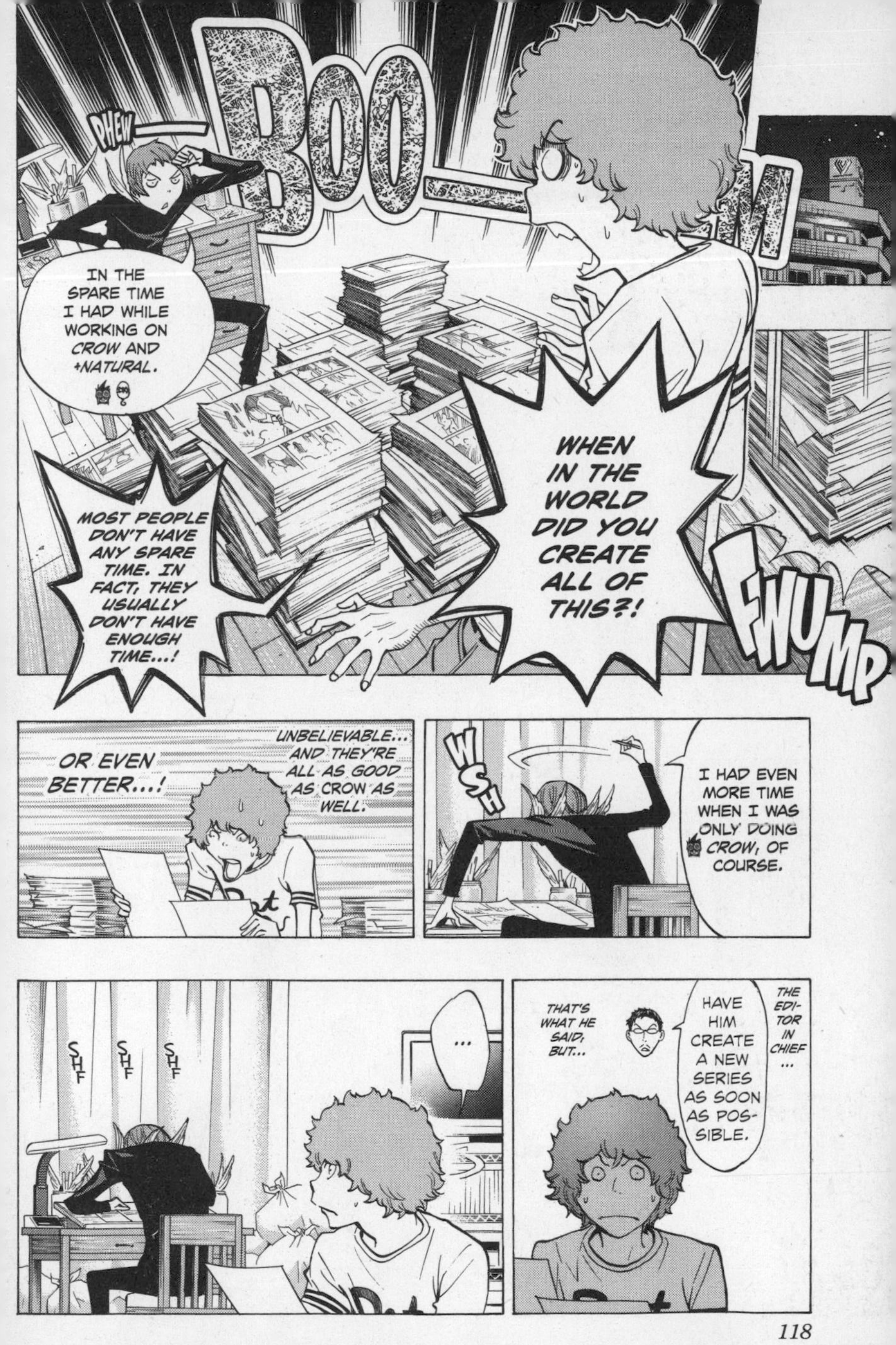
BOO-M
PHEW
WHEN IN THE WORLD DID YOU CREATE ALL OF THIS?!
IN THE SPARE TIME I HAD WHILE WORKING ON CROW AND +NATURAL.
FWUMP
MOST PEOPLE DON'T HAVE ANY SPARE TIME. IN FACT, THEY USUALLY DON'T HAVE ENOUGH TIME...!
WSH
I HAD EVEN MORE TIME WHEN I WAS ONLY DOING CROW, OF COURSE.
UNBELIEVABLE... AND THEY'RE ALL AS GOOD AS CROW AS WELL.
OR EVEN BETTER...!
THE EDITOR IN CHIEF...
HAVE HIM CREATE A NEW SERIES AS SOON AS POSSIBLE.
THAT'S WHAT HE SAID, BUT...
...
SHF SHF SHF

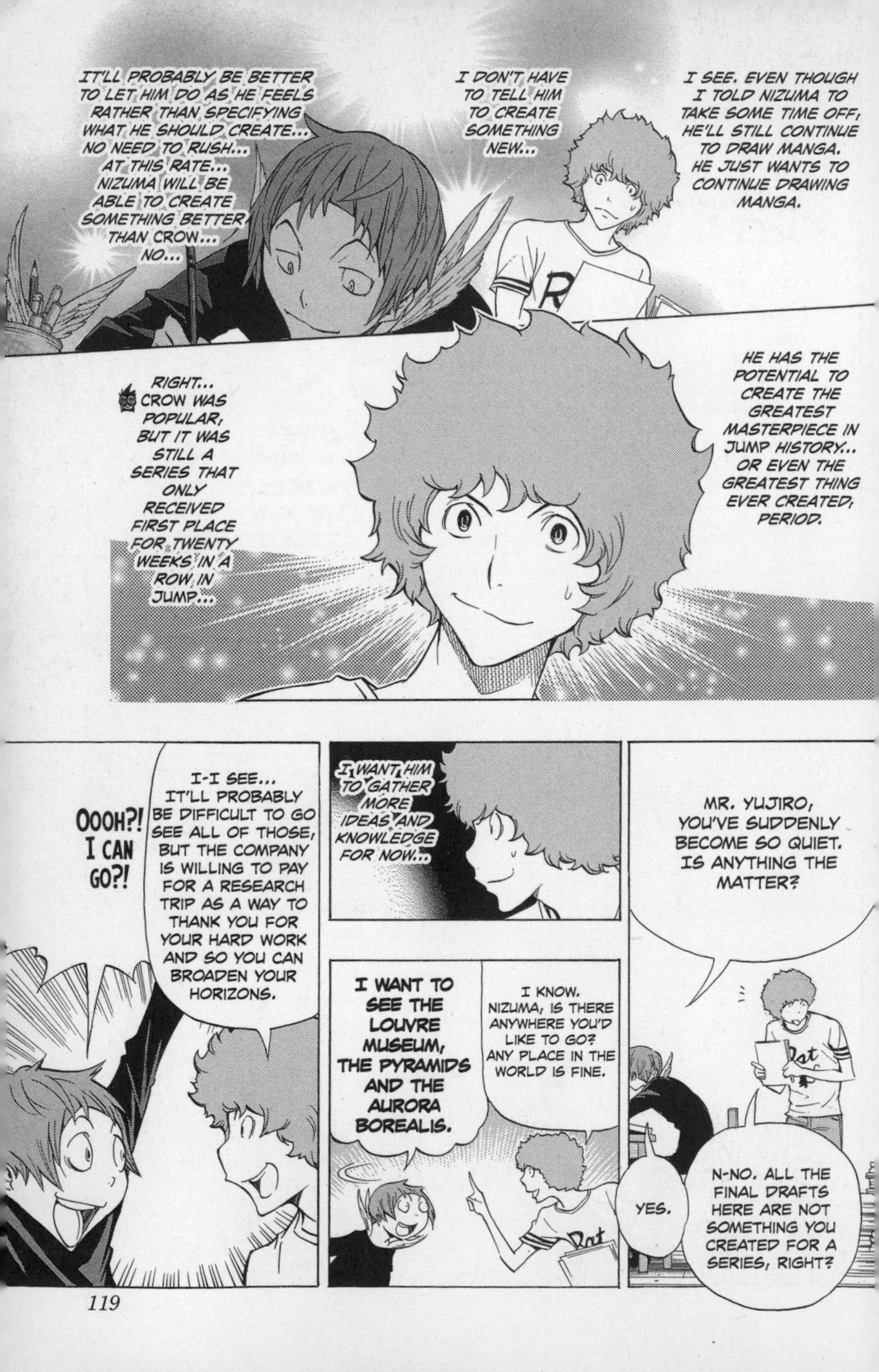
I SEE. EVEN THOUGH I TOLD NIZUMA TO TAKE SOME TIME OFF, HE'LL STILL CONTINUE TO DRAW MANGA. HE JUST WANTS TO CONTINUE DRAWING MANGA.
I DON'T HAVE TO TELL HIM TO CREATE SOMETHING NEW...
IT'LL PROBABLY BE BETTER TO LET HIM DO AS HE FEELS RATHER THAN SPECIFYING WHAT HE SHOULD CREATE... NO NEED TO RUSH... AT THIS RATE... NIZUMA WILL BE ABLE TO CREATE SOMETHING BETTER THAN CROW... NO...
HE HAS THE POTENTIAL TO CREATE THE GREATEST MASTERPIECE IN JUMP HISTORY... OR EVEN THE GREATEST THING EVER CREATED, PERIOD.
RIGHT... CROW WAS POPULAR, BUT IT WAS STILL A SERIES THAT ONLY RECEIVED FIRST PLACE FOR TWENTY WEEKS IN A ROW IN JUMP...
MR. YUJIRO, YOU'VE SUDDENLY BECOME SO QUIET. IS ANYTHING THE MATTER?
N-NO. ALL THE FINAL DRAFTS HERE ARE NOT SOMETHING YOU CREATED FOR A SERIES, RIGHT?
YES.
I WANT HIM TO GATHER MORE IDEAS AND KNOWLEDGE FOR NOW...
I KNOW. NIZUMA, IS THERE ANYWHERE YOU'D LIKE TO GO? ANY PLACE IN THE WORLD IS FINE.
I WANT TO SEE THE LOUVRE MUSEUM, THE PYRAMIDS AND THE AURORA BOREALIS.
I-I SEE... IT'LL PROBABLY BE DIFFICULT TO GO SEE ALL OF THOSE, BUT THE COMPANY IS WILLING TO PAY FOR A RESEARCH TRIP AS A WAY TO THANK YOU FOR YOUR HARD WORK AND SO YOU CAN BROADEN YOUR HORIZONS.
OOOH?! I CAN GO?!

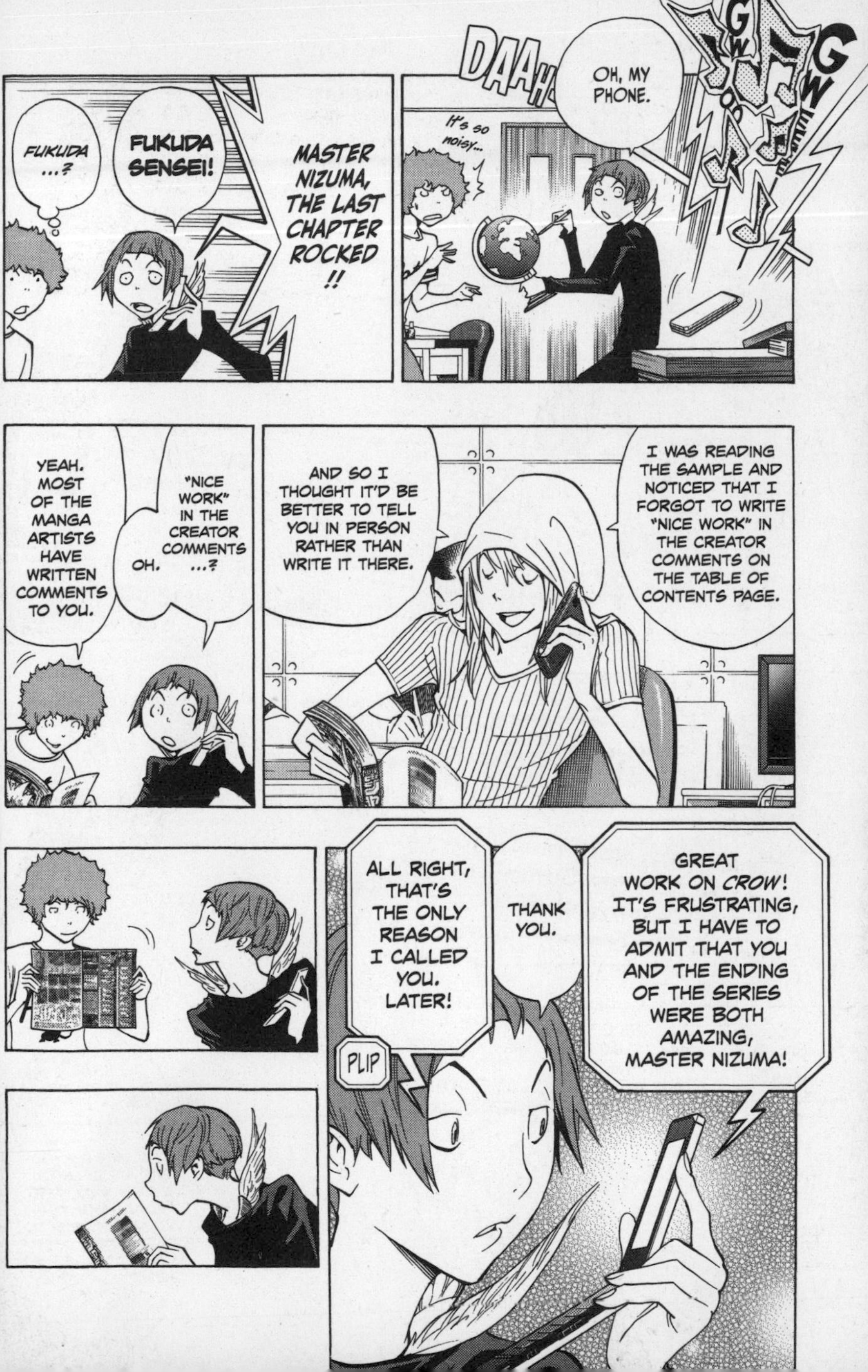
DAAH
OH, MY PHONE.
It's so noisy...
MASTER NIZUMA, THE LAST CHAPTER ROCKED!!
FUKUDA SENSEI!
FUKUDA ...?
I WAS READING THE SAMPLE AND NOTICED THAT I FORGOT TO WRITE "NICE WORK" IN THE CREATOR COMMENTS ON THE TABLE OF CONTENTS PAGE.
AND SO I THOUGHT IT'D BE BETTER TO TELL YOU IN PERSON RATHER THAN WRITE IT THERE.
"NICE WORK" IN THE CREATOR COMMENTS ...?
OH.
YEAH. MOST OF THE MANGA ARTISTS HAVE WRITTEN COMMENTS TO YOU.
GREAT WORK ON CROW! IT'S FRUSTRATING, BUT I HAVE TO ADMIT THAT YOU AND THE ENDING OF THE SERIES WERE BOTH AMAZING, MASTER NIZUMA!
THANK YOU.
ALL RIGHT, THAT'S THE ONLY REASON I CALLED YOU. LATER!
PLIP

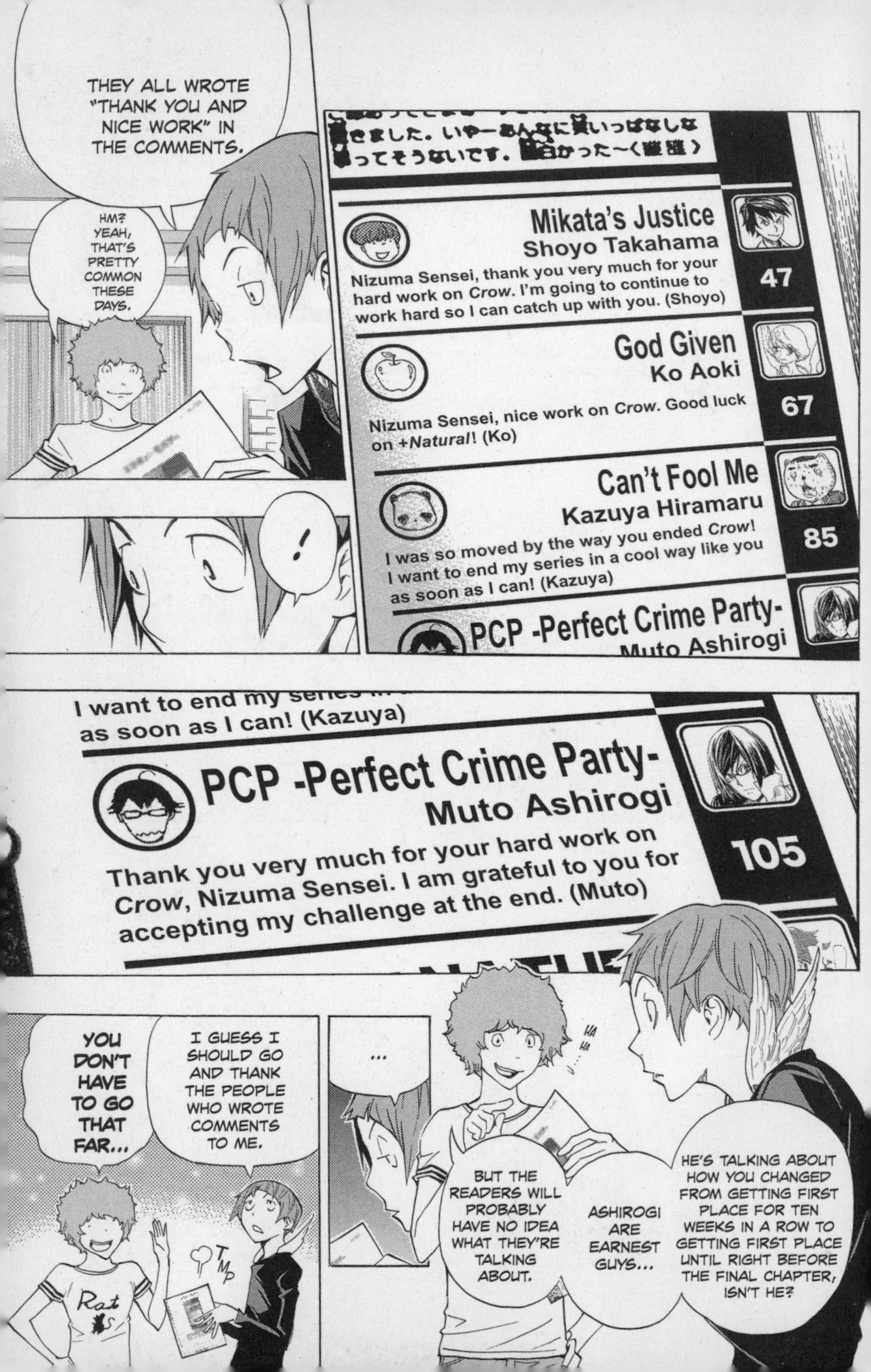

Mikata's Justice
Shoyo Takahama
Nizuma Sensei, thank you very much for your hard work on *Crow*. I'm going to continue to work hard so I can catch up with you. (Shoyo)
47
God Given
Ko Aoki
Nizuma Sensei, nice work on Crow. Good luck on +*Natural*! (Ko)
67
Can't Fool Me
Kazuya Hiramaru
I was so moved by the way you ended *Crow*! I want to end my series in a cool way like you as soon as I can! (Kazuya)
85
PCP -Perfect Crime Party-
Muto Ashirogi
THEY ALL WROTE "THANK YOU AND NICE WORK" IN THE COMMENTS.
HM? YEAH, THAT'S PRETTY COMMON THESE DAYS.
!
I want to end my series in a cool way like you as soon as I can! (Kazuya)
PCP -Perfect Crime Party-
Muto Ashirogi
Thank you very much for your hard work on Crow, Nizuma Sensei. I am grateful to you for accepting my challenge at the end. (Muto)
105
HE'S TALKING ABOUT HOW YOU CHANGED FROM GETTING FIRST PLACE FOR TEN WEEKS IN A ROW TO GETTING FIRST PLACE UNTIL RIGHT BEFORE THE FINAL CHAPTER, ISN'T HE?
ASHIROGI ARE EARNEST GUYS...
HA HA
BUT THE READERS WILL PROBABLY HAVE NO IDEA WHAT THEY'RE TALKING ABOUT.
...
I GUESS I SHOULD GO AND THANK THE PEOPLE WHO WROTE COMMENTS TO ME.
YOU DON'T HAVE TO GO THAT FAR...
TMP
Rat

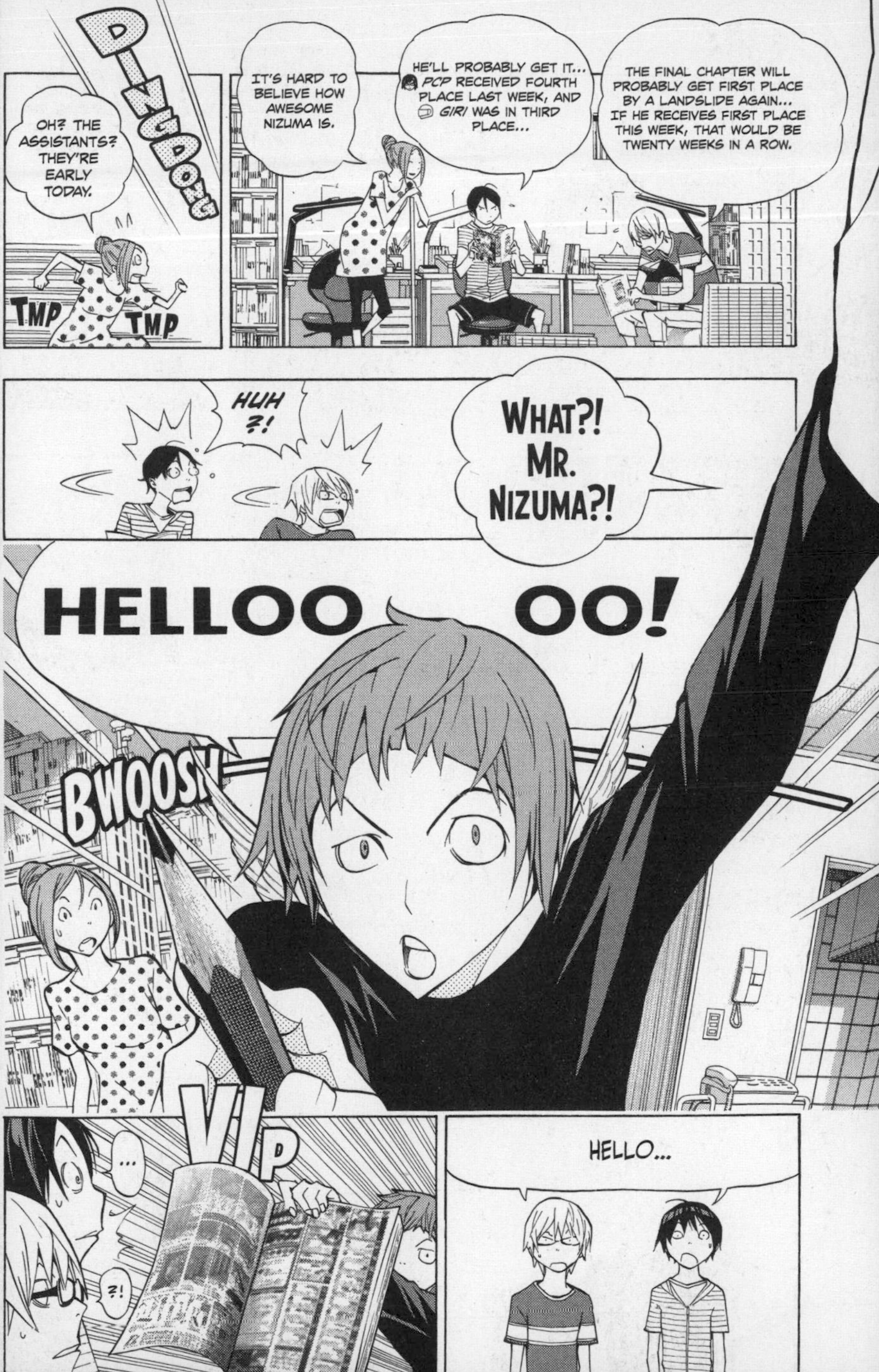
THE FINAL CHAPTER WILL PROBABLY GET FIRST PLACE BY A LANDSLIDE AGAIN... IF HE RECEIVES FIRST PLACE THIS WEEK, THAT WOULD BE TWENTY WEEKS IN A ROW.
HE'LL PROBABLY GET IT... PCP RECEIVED FOURTH PLACE LAST WEEK, AND GIRI WAS IN THIRD PLACE...
IT'S HARD TO BELIEVE HOW AWESOME NIZUMA IS.
DINGDONG
OH? THE ASSISTANTS? THEY'RE EARLY TODAY.
TMP
TMP
WHAT?! MR. NIZUMA?!
HUH ?!
HELLOO OO!
BWOOS
HELLO...
VIP
...
?!

READ THIS WAY

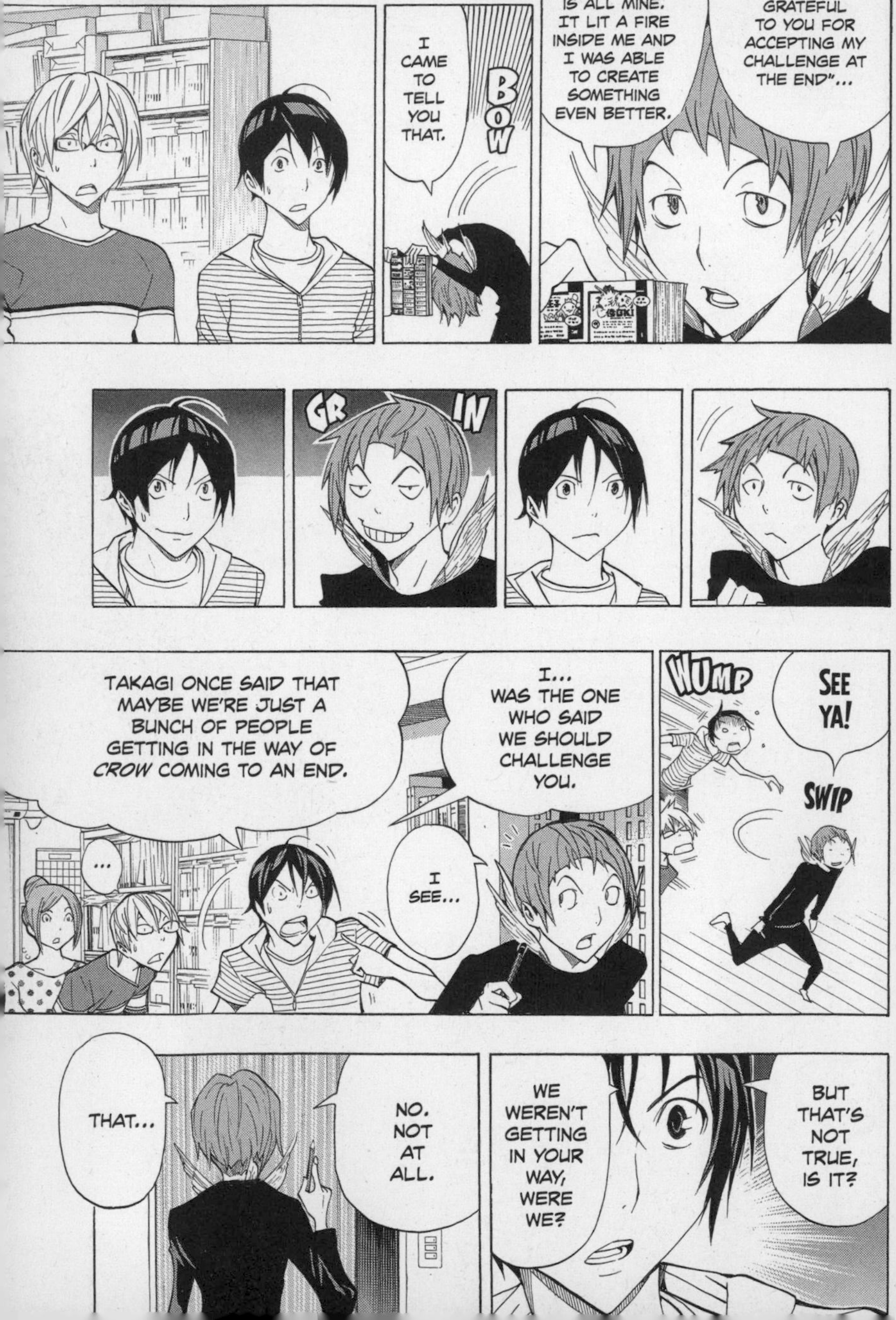
"I AM GRATEFUL TO YOU FOR ACCEPTING MY CHALLENGE AT THE END"...
THE HONOR IS ALL MINE. IT LIT A FIRE INSIDE ME AND I WAS ABLE TO CREATE SOMETHING EVEN BETTER.
I CAME TO TELL YOU THAT.
BOW
GR
IN
SEE YA!
WUMP
SWIP
I... WAS THE ONE WHO SAID WE SHOULD CHALLENGE YOU.
TAKAGI ONCE SAID THAT MAYBE WE'RE JUST A BUNCH OF PEOPLE GETTING IN THE WAY OF *CROW* COMING TO AN END.
I SEE...
...
BUT THAT'S NOT TRUE, IS IT?
WE WEREN'T GETTING IN YOUR WAY, WERE WE?
NO. NOT AT ALL.
THAT...

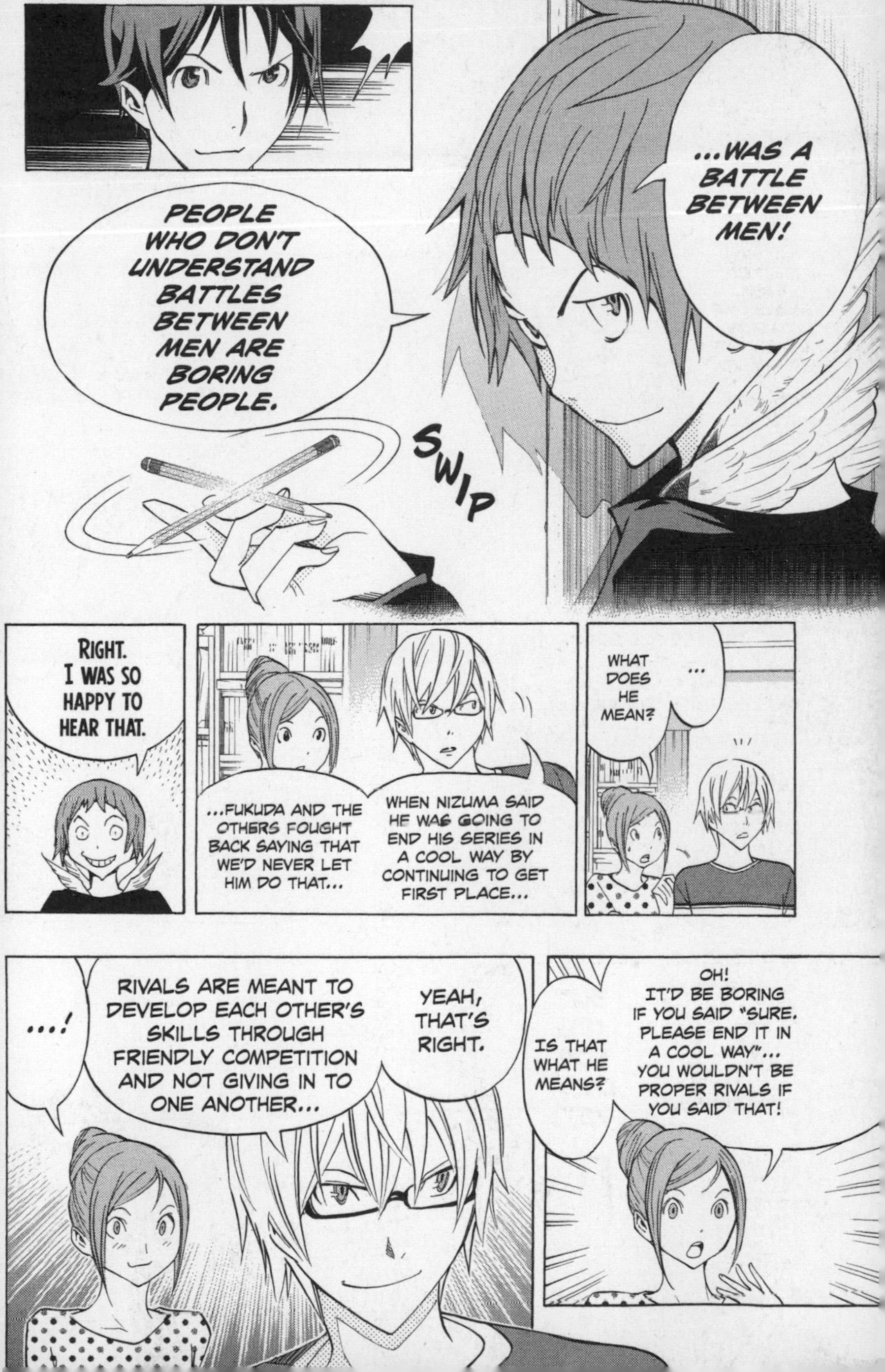
...WAS A BATTLE BETWEEN MEN!
PEOPLE WHO DON'T UNDERSTAND BATTLES BETWEEN MEN ARE BORING PEOPLE.
SWIP
...
WHAT DOES HE MEAN?
WHEN NIZUMA SAID HE WAS GOING TO END HIS SERIES IN A COOL WAY BY CONTINUING TO GET FIRST PLACE...
...FUKUDA AND THE OTHERS FOUGHT BACK SAYING THAT WE'D NEVER LET HIM DO THAT...
RIGHT. I WAS SO HAPPY TO HEAR THAT.
OH! IT'D BE BORING IF YOU SAID "SURE. PLEASE END IT IN A COOL WAY"... YOU WOULDN'T BE PROPER RIVALS IF YOU SAID THAT!
IS THAT WHAT HE MEANS?
YEAH, THAT'S RIGHT.
RIVALS ARE MEANT TO DEVELOP EACH OTHER'S SKILLS THROUGH FRIENDLY COMPETITION AND NOT GIVING IN TO ONE ANOTHER...
...!

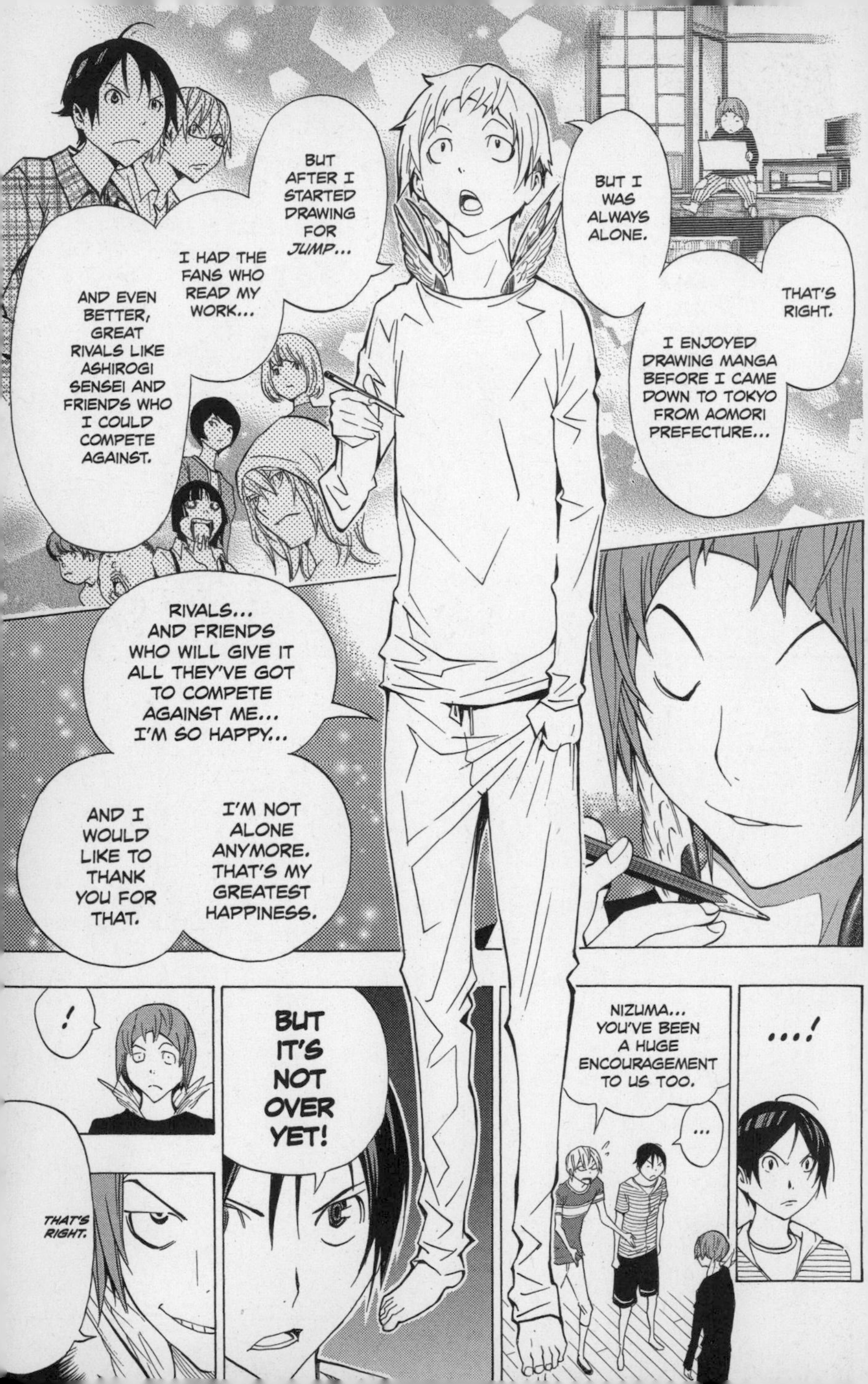
THAT'S RIGHT.
I ENJOYED DRAWING MANGA BEFORE I CAME DOWN TO TOKYO FROM AOMORI PREFECTURE...
BUT I WAS ALWAYS ALONE.
BUT AFTER I STARTED DRAWING FOR *JUMP*...
I HAD THE FANS WHO READ MY WORK...
AND EVEN BETTER, GREAT RIVALS LIKE ASHIROGI SENSEI AND FRIENDS WHO I COULD COMPETE AGAINST.
RIVALS... AND FRIENDS WHO WILL GIVE IT ALL THEY'VE GOT TO COMPETE AGAINST ME... I'M SO HAPPY...
I'M NOT ALONE ANYMORE. THAT'S MY GREATEST HAPPINESS.
AND I WOULD LIKE TO THANK YOU FOR THAT.
...!
NIZUMA... YOU'VE BEEN A HUGE ENCOURAGEMENT TO US TOO.
...
BUT IT'S NOT OVER YET!
!
THAT'S RIGHT.

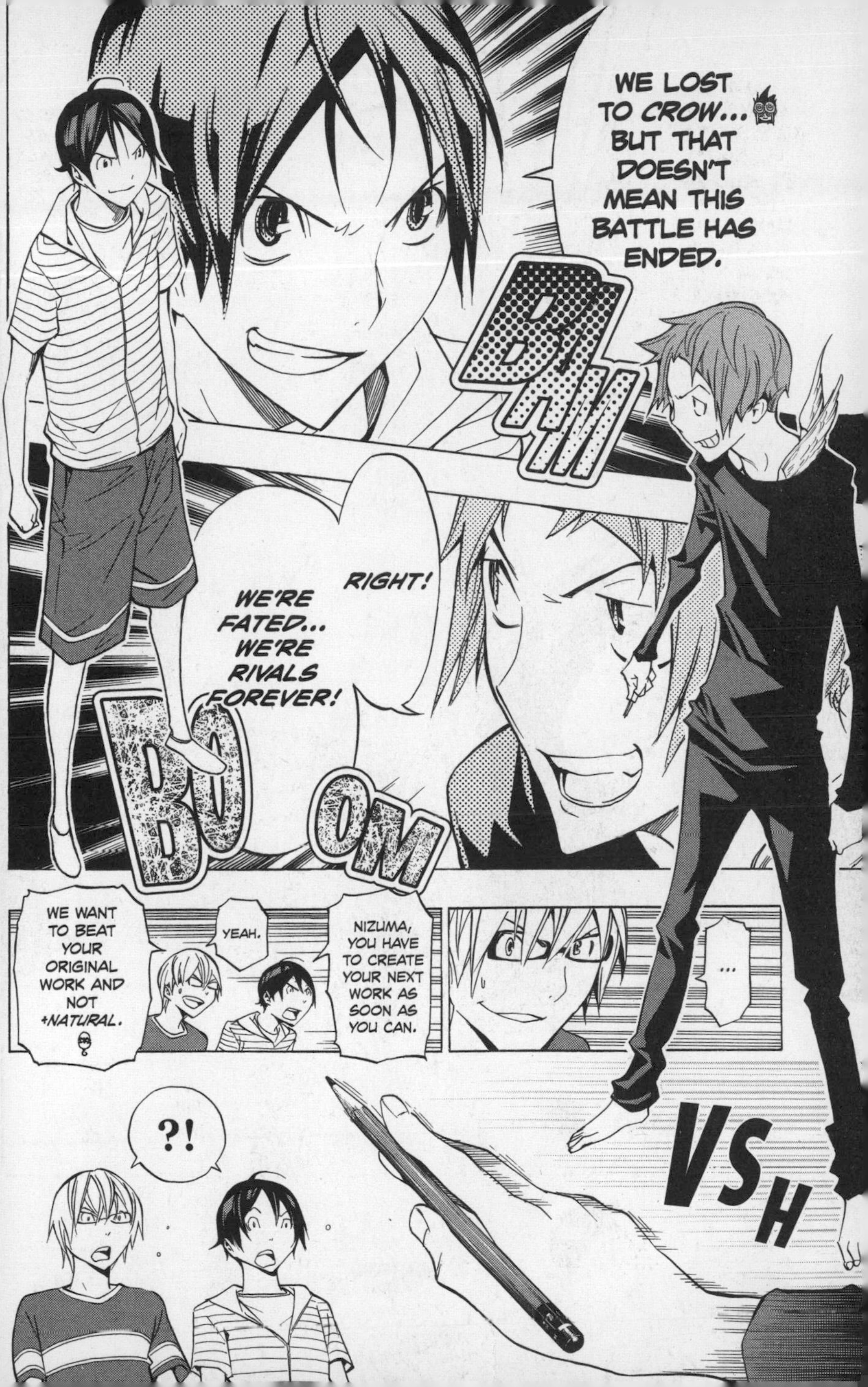
WE LOST TO CROW... BUT THAT DOESN'T MEAN THIS BATTLE HAS ENDED.
BAM
RIGHT!
WE'RE FATED... WE'RE RIVALS FOREVER!
BOOM
...
NIZUMA, YOU HAVE TO CREATE YOUR NEXT WORK AS SOON AS YOU CAN.
YEAH.
WE WANT TO BEAT YOUR ORIGINAL WORK AND NOT +NATURAL.
VSH
?!

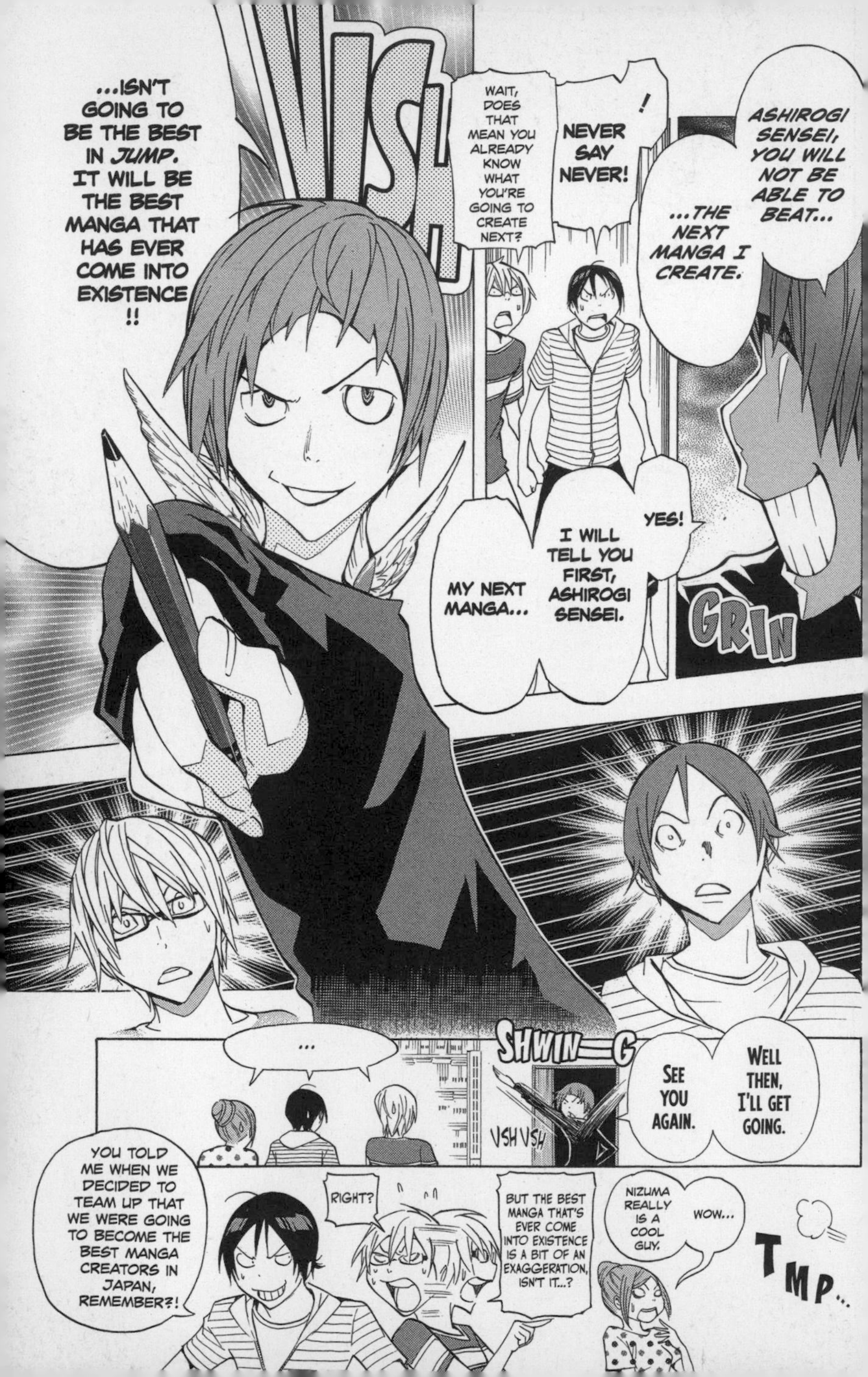
ASHIROGI SENSEI, YOU WILL NOT BE ABLE TO BEAT...
...THE NEXT MANGA I CREATE.
!
NEVER SAY NEVER!
WAIT, DOES THAT MEAN YOU ALREADY KNOW WHAT YOU'RE GOING TO CREATE NEXT?
GRIN
YES!
I WILL TELL YOU FIRST, ASHIROGI SENSEI.
MY NEXT MANGA...
...ISN'T GOING TO BE THE BEST IN *JUMP*. IT WILL BE THE BEST MANGA THAT HAS EVER COME INTO EXISTENCE!!
WELL THEN, I'LL GET GOING.
SEE YOU AGAIN.
SHWIN-G
VSH VSH
...
TMP...
WOW...
NIZUMA REALLY IS A COOL GUY.
BUT THE BEST MANGA THAT'S EVER COME INTO EXISTENCE IS A BIT OF AN EXAGGERATION, ISN'T IT...?
RIGHT?
YOU TOLD ME WHEN WE DECIDED TO TEAM UP THAT WE WERE GOING TO BECOME THE BEST MANGA CREATORS IN JAPAN, REMEMBER?!

OHBA'S STORYBOARD

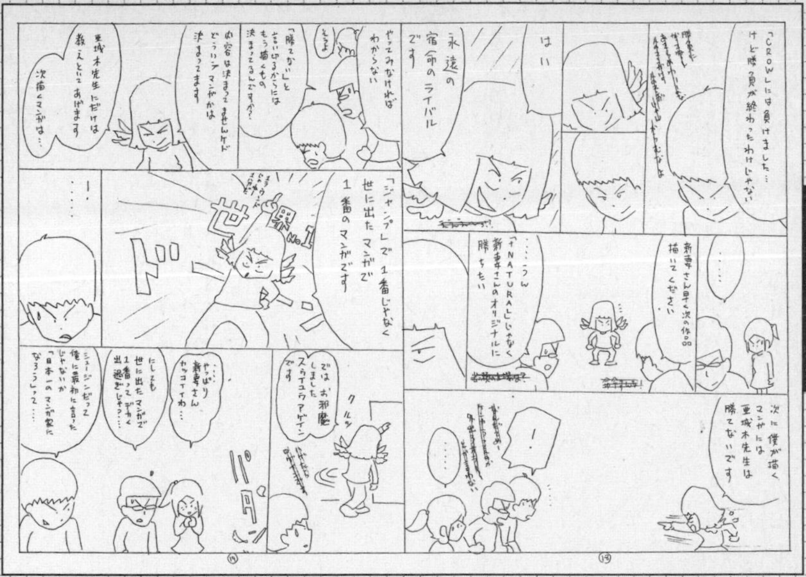
「CROWL」には負けました… けど勝負が終わったわけじゃない
はい
永遠の宿命のライバルです
……
新妻さん早く次の作品描いてください
…うん 「+NATURAL」じゃなく新妻さんのオリジナルに勝ちたい
次に僕が描くマンガには亜城木先生は勝てないです
!
……
13
やってみなければわからない
そうよ
「勝てない」と言い切るからにはもう描くもの決まってるんですか?
内容は決まってませんケドどういうマンガかは決まってます
亜城木先生にだけは教えといてあげます 次描くマンガは…
「ジャンプ」で1番じゃなく世に出たマンガで1番のマンガです
世界No.1
ド
…!
ではお邪魔しましたスライユウアゲインです
クルッ
パタ
…やっぱり新妻さんカッコイイわ…
にしても世に出たマンガで1番ってデカく出過ぎじゃ…
シュージンだって俺に最初に言ったじゃないか「日本一のマンガ家になろう」って…
14

OBATA'S STORYBOARD

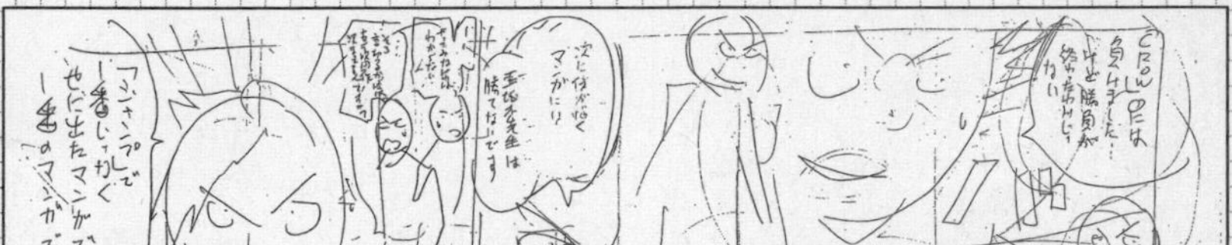
CROWLには負けました… けど勝負が終わったわけじゃない
はい
永遠の宿命のライバルです
次に僕が描くマンガには亜城木先生は勝てないです
「ジャンプ」で一番じゃなく世に出たマンガで一番のマンガです!!
次に描くマンガは…
シュビーン
パタン
19
18

COMPLETE!

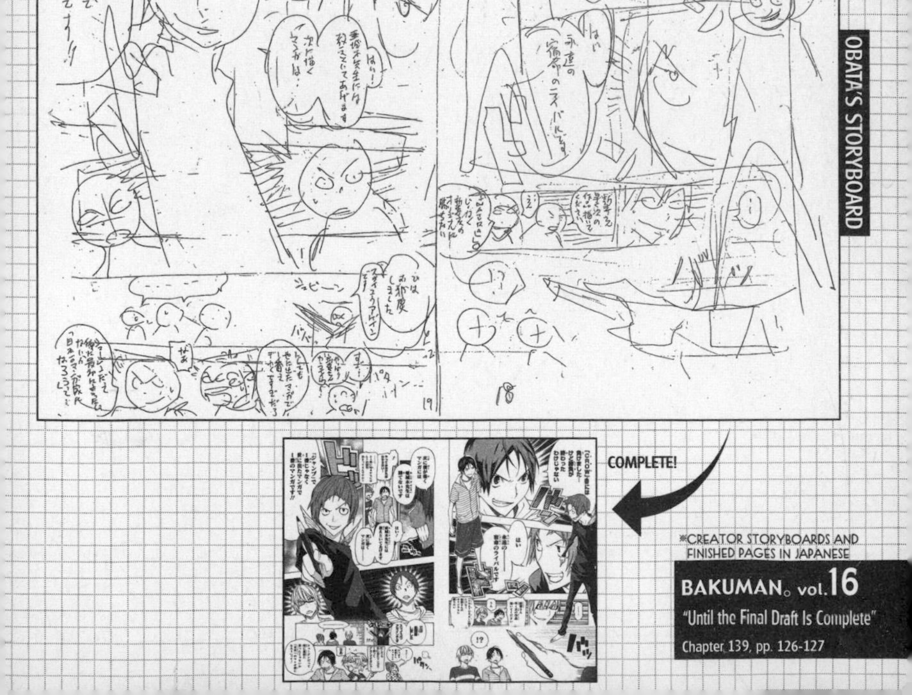

※CREATOR STORYBOARDS AND FINISHED PAGES IN JAPANESE

BAKUMAN。 vol.16

"Until the Final Draft Is Complete"

Chapter 139, pp. 126-127

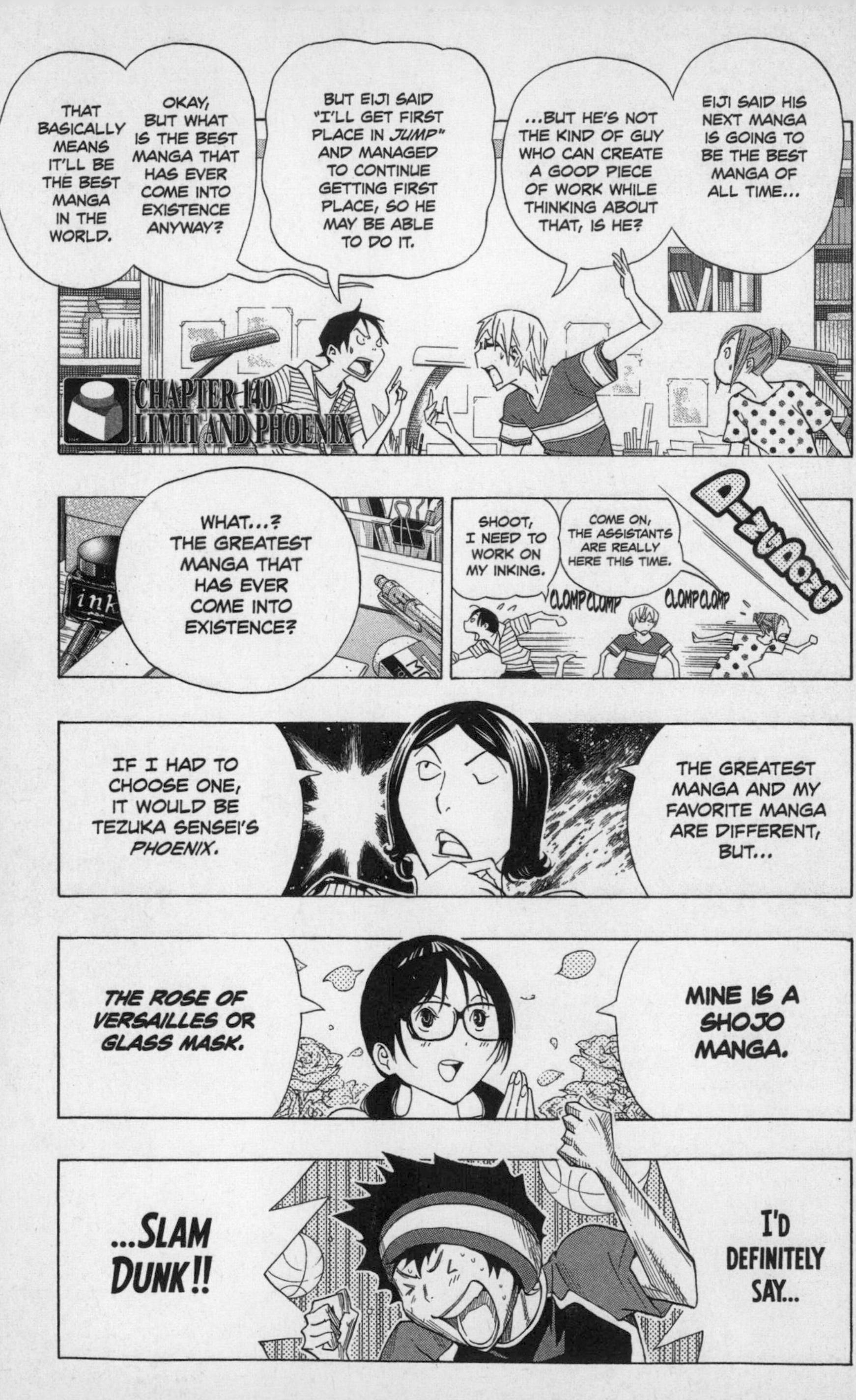
CHAPTER 140
LIMIT AND PHOENIX
EIJI SAID HIS NEXT MANGA IS GOING TO BE THE BEST MANGA OF ALL TIME...
...BUT HE'S NOT THE KIND OF GUY WHO CAN CREATE A GOOD PIECE OF WORK WHILE THINKING ABOUT THAT, IS HE?
BUT EIJI SAID "I'LL GET FIRST PLACE IN *JUMP*" AND MANAGED TO CONTINUE GETTING FIRST PLACE, SO HE MAY BE ABLE TO DO IT.
OKAY, BUT WHAT IS THE BEST MANGA THAT HAS EVER COME INTO EXISTENCE ANYWAY?
THAT BASICALLY MEANS IT'LL BE THE BEST MANGA IN THE WORLD.
A-ZUDOZU
COME ON, THE ASSISTANTS ARE REALLY HERE THIS TIME.
SHOOT, I NEED TO WORK ON MY INKING.
CLOMP CLOMP
CLOMP CLOMP
WHAT...? THE GREATEST MANGA THAT HAS EVER COME INTO EXISTENCE?
ink
THE GREATEST MANGA AND MY FAVORITE MANGA ARE DIFFERENT, BUT...
IF I HAD TO CHOOSE ONE, IT WOULD BE TEZUKA SENSEI'S *PHOENIX*.
MINE IS A SHOJO MANGA.
THE ROSE OF VERSAILLES OR GLASS MASK.
I'D DEFINITELY SAY...
...SLAM DUNK!!

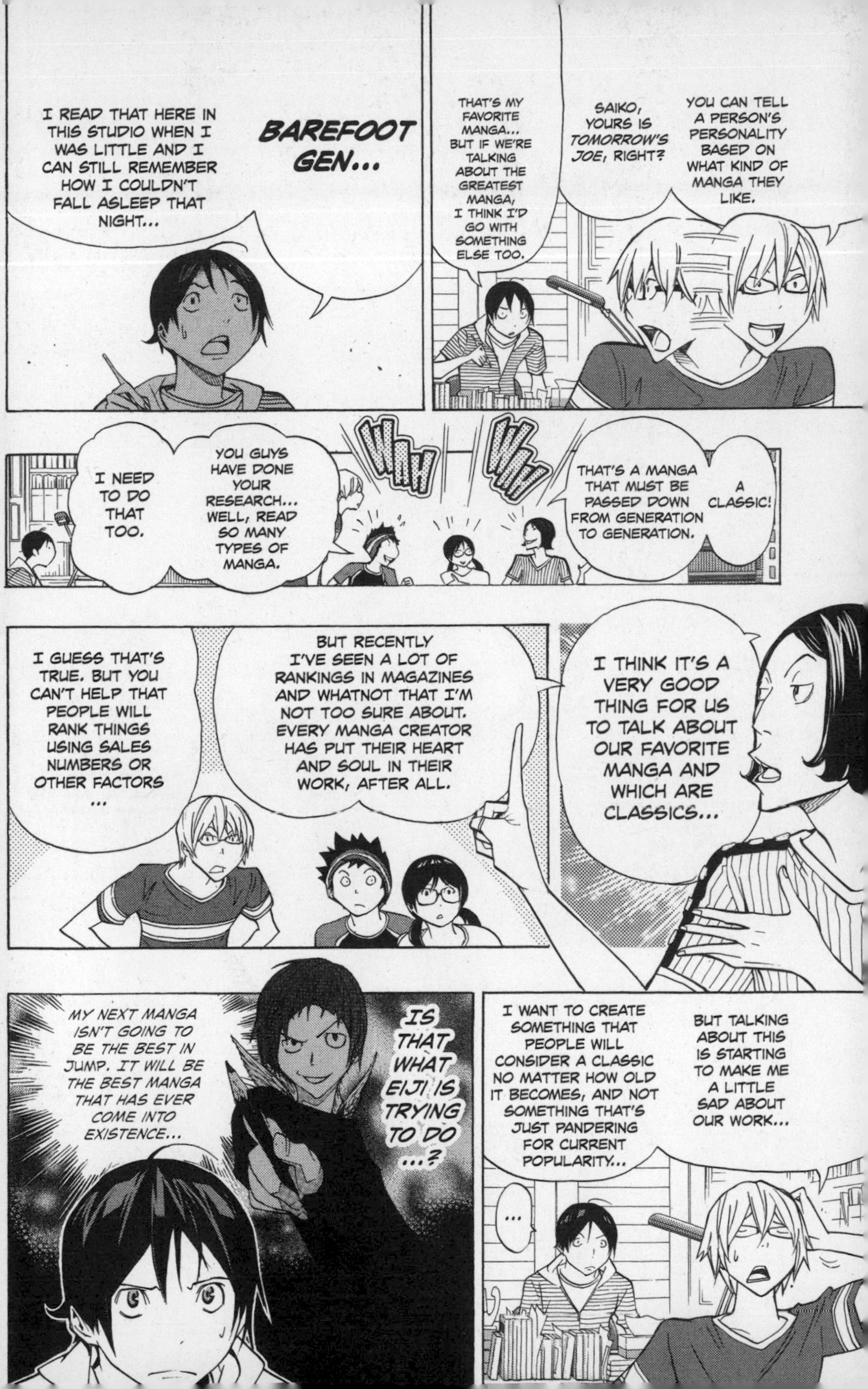
YOU CAN TELL A PERSON'S PERSONALITY BASED ON WHAT KIND OF MANGA THEY LIKE.
SAIKO, YOURS IS *TOMORROW'S JOE*, RIGHT?
THAT'S MY FAVORITE MANGA... BUT IF WE'RE TALKING ABOUT THE GREATEST MANGA, I THINK I'D GO WITH SOMETHING ELSE TOO.
BAREFOOT GEN...
I READ THAT HERE IN THIS STUDIO WHEN I WAS LITTLE AND I CAN STILL REMEMBER HOW I COULDN'T FALL ASLEEP THAT NIGHT...
A CLASSIC!
THAT'S A MANGA THAT MUST BE PASSED DOWN FROM GENERATION TO GENERATION.
YOU GUYS HAVE DONE YOUR RESEARCH... WELL, READ SO MANY TYPES OF MANGA.
I NEED TO DO THAT TOO.
I THINK IT'S A VERY GOOD THING FOR US TO TALK ABOUT OUR FAVORITE MANGA AND WHICH ARE CLASSICS...
BUT RECENTLY I'VE SEEN A LOT OF RANKINGS IN MAGAZINES AND WHATNOT THAT I'M NOT TOO SURE ABOUT. EVERY MANGA CREATOR HAS PUT THEIR HEART AND SOUL IN THEIR WORK, AFTER ALL.
I GUESS THAT'S TRUE. BUT YOU CAN'T HELP THAT PEOPLE WILL RANK THINGS USING SALES NUMBERS OR OTHER FACTORS...
BUT TALKING ABOUT THIS IS STARTING TO MAKE ME A LITTLE SAD ABOUT OUR WORK...
I WANT TO CREATE SOMETHING THAT PEOPLE WILL CONSIDER A CLASSIC NO MATTER HOW OLD IT BECOMES, AND NOT SOMETHING THAT'S JUST PANDERING FOR CURRENT POPULARITY...
...
IS THAT WHAT EIJI IS TRYING TO DO...?
MY NEXT MANGA ISN'T GOING TO BE THE BEST IN *JUMP*. IT WILL BE THE BEST MANGA THAT HAS EVER COME INTO EXISTENCE...

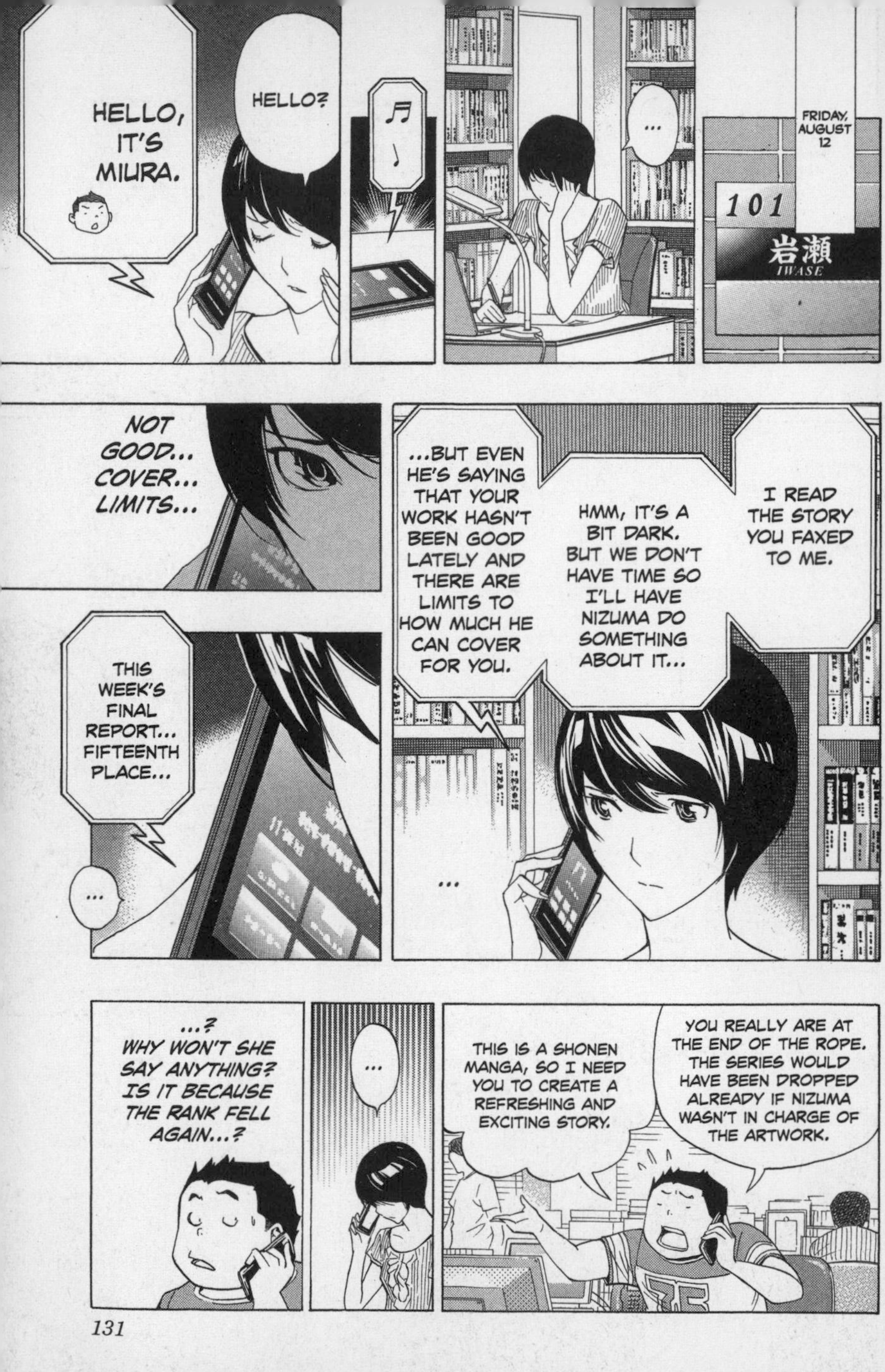
FRIDAY, AUGUST 12
101
岩瀬
IWASE
...
HELLO?
HELLO, IT'S MIURA.
I READ THE STORY YOU FAXED TO ME.
HMM, IT'S A BIT DARK. BUT WE DON'T HAVE TIME SO I'LL HAVE NIZUMA DO SOMETHING ABOUT IT...
...BUT EVEN HE'S SAYING THAT YOUR WORK HASN'T BEEN GOOD LATELY AND THERE ARE LIMITS TO HOW MUCH HE CAN COVER FOR YOU.
...
NOT GOOD... COVER... LIMITS...
THIS WEEK'S FINAL REPORT... FIFTEENTH PLACE...
...
YOU REALLY ARE AT THE END OF THE ROPE. THE SERIES WOULD HAVE BEEN DROPPED ALREADY IF NIZUMA WASN'T IN CHARGE OF THE ARTWORK.
THIS IS A SHONEN MANGA, SO I NEED YOU TO CREATE A REFRESHING AND EXCITING STORY.
...
...? WHY WON'T SHE SAY ANYTHING? IS IT BECAUSE THE RANK FELL AGAIN...?

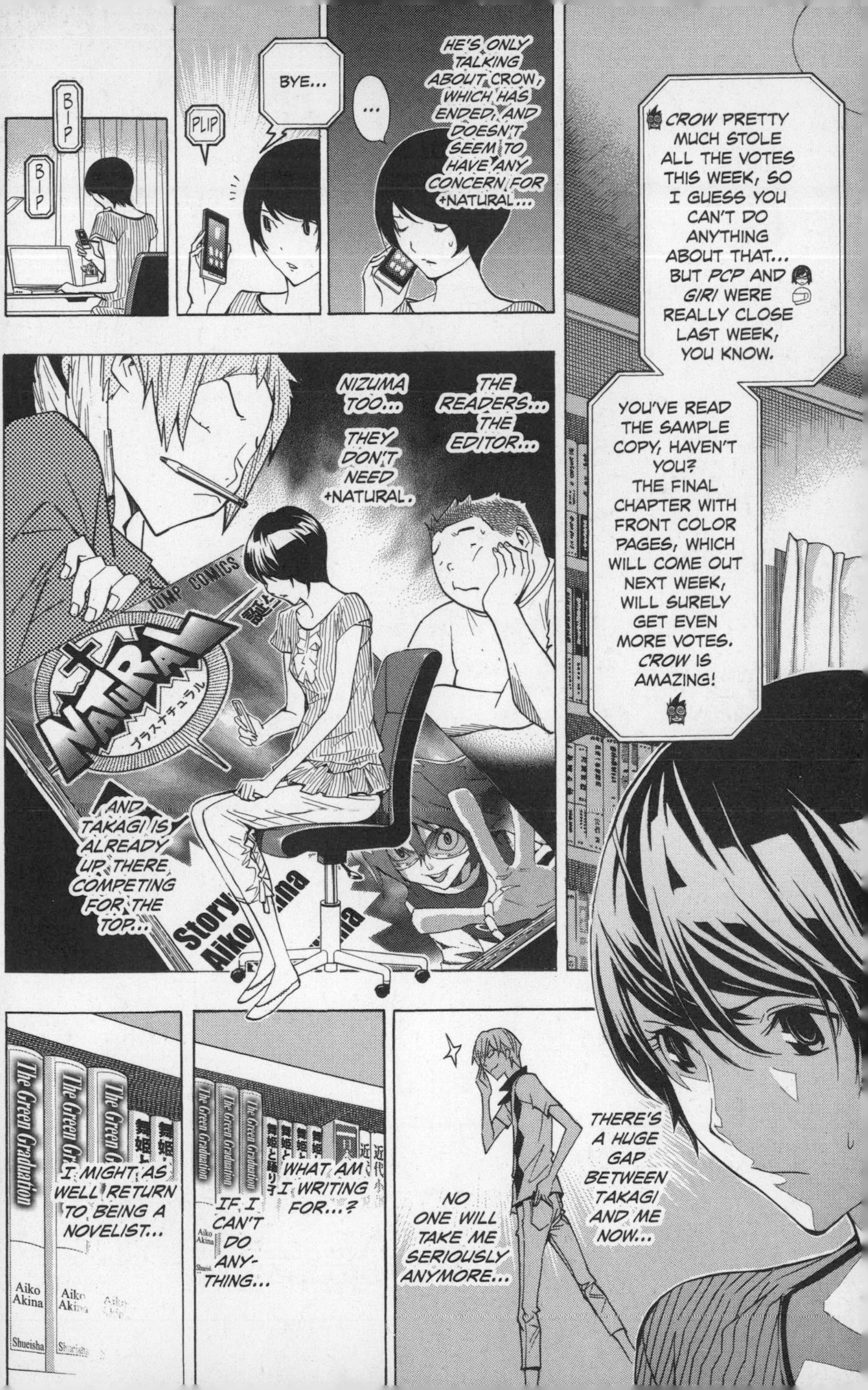
CROW PRETTY MUCH STOLE ALL THE VOTES THIS WEEK, SO I GUESS YOU CAN'T DO ANYTHING ABOUT THAT... BUT PCP AND GIRI WERE REALLY CLOSE LAST WEEK, YOU KNOW.
YOU'VE READ THE SAMPLE COPY, HAVEN'T YOU? THE FINAL CHAPTER WITH FRONT COLOR PAGES, WHICH WILL COME OUT NEXT WEEK, WILL SURELY GET EVEN MORE VOTES. CROW IS AMAZING!
HE'S ONLY TALKING ABOUT CROW, WHICH HAS ENDED, AND DOESN'T SEEM TO HAVE ANY CONCERN FOR +NATURAL...
...
BYE...
PLIP
BIP
BIP
THE READERS... THE EDITOR...
NIZUMA TOO...
THEY DON'T NEED +NATURAL.
JUMP COMICS
+NATURAL
プラスナチュラル
AND TAKAGI IS ALREADY UP THERE COMPETING FOR THE TOP...
THERE'S A HUGE GAP BETWEEN TAKAGI AND ME NOW...
NO ONE WILL TAKE ME SERIOUSLY ANYMORE...
WHAT AM I WRITING FOR...?
IF I CAN'T DO ANYTHING...
The Green Graduation
Aiko Akina
I MIGHT AS WELL RETURN TO BEING A NOVELIST...
The Green Graduation
Aiko Akina
Shueisha

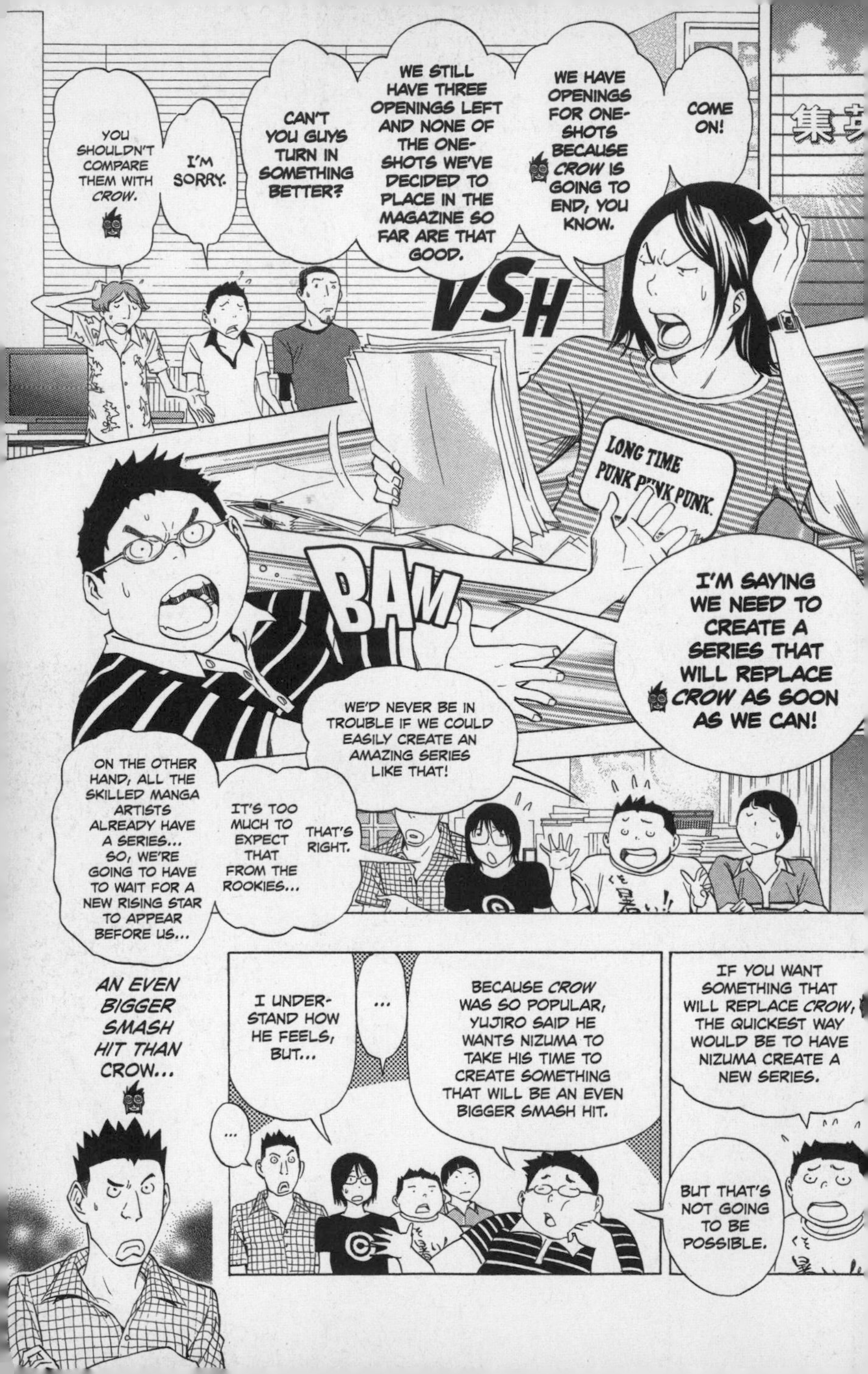
COME ON!
WE HAVE OPENINGS FOR ONE-SHOTS BECAUSE CROW IS GOING TO END, YOU KNOW.
WE STILL HAVE THREE OPENINGS LEFT AND NONE OF THE ONE-SHOTS WE'VE DECIDED TO PLACE IN THE MAGAZINE SO FAR ARE THAT GOOD.
CAN'T YOU GUYS TURN IN SOMETHING BETTER?
I'M SORRY.
YOU SHOULDN'T COMPARE THEM WITH CROW.
VSH
LONG TIME PUNK PUNK PUNK.
I'M SAYING WE NEED TO CREATE A SERIES THAT WILL REPLACE CROW AS SOON AS WE CAN!
BAM
WE'D NEVER BE IN TROUBLE IF WE COULD EASILY CREATE AN AMAZING SERIES LIKE THAT!
THAT'S RIGHT.
IT'S TOO MUCH TO EXPECT THAT FROM THE ROOKIES...
ON THE OTHER HAND, ALL THE SKILLED MANGA ARTISTS ALREADY HAVE A SERIES... SO, WE'RE GOING TO HAVE TO WAIT FOR A NEW RISING STAR TO APPEAR BEFORE US...
IF YOU WANT SOMETHING THAT WILL REPLACE CROW, THE QUICKEST WAY WOULD BE TO HAVE NIZUMA CREATE A NEW SERIES.
BUT THAT'S NOT GOING TO BE POSSIBLE.
BECAUSE CROW WAS SO POPULAR, YUJIRO SAID HE WANTS NIZUMA TO TAKE HIS TIME TO CREATE SOMETHING THAT WILL BE AN EVEN BIGGER SMASH HIT.
...
I UNDER-STAND HOW HE FEELS, BUT...
...
AN EVEN BIGGER SMASH HIT THAN CROW...

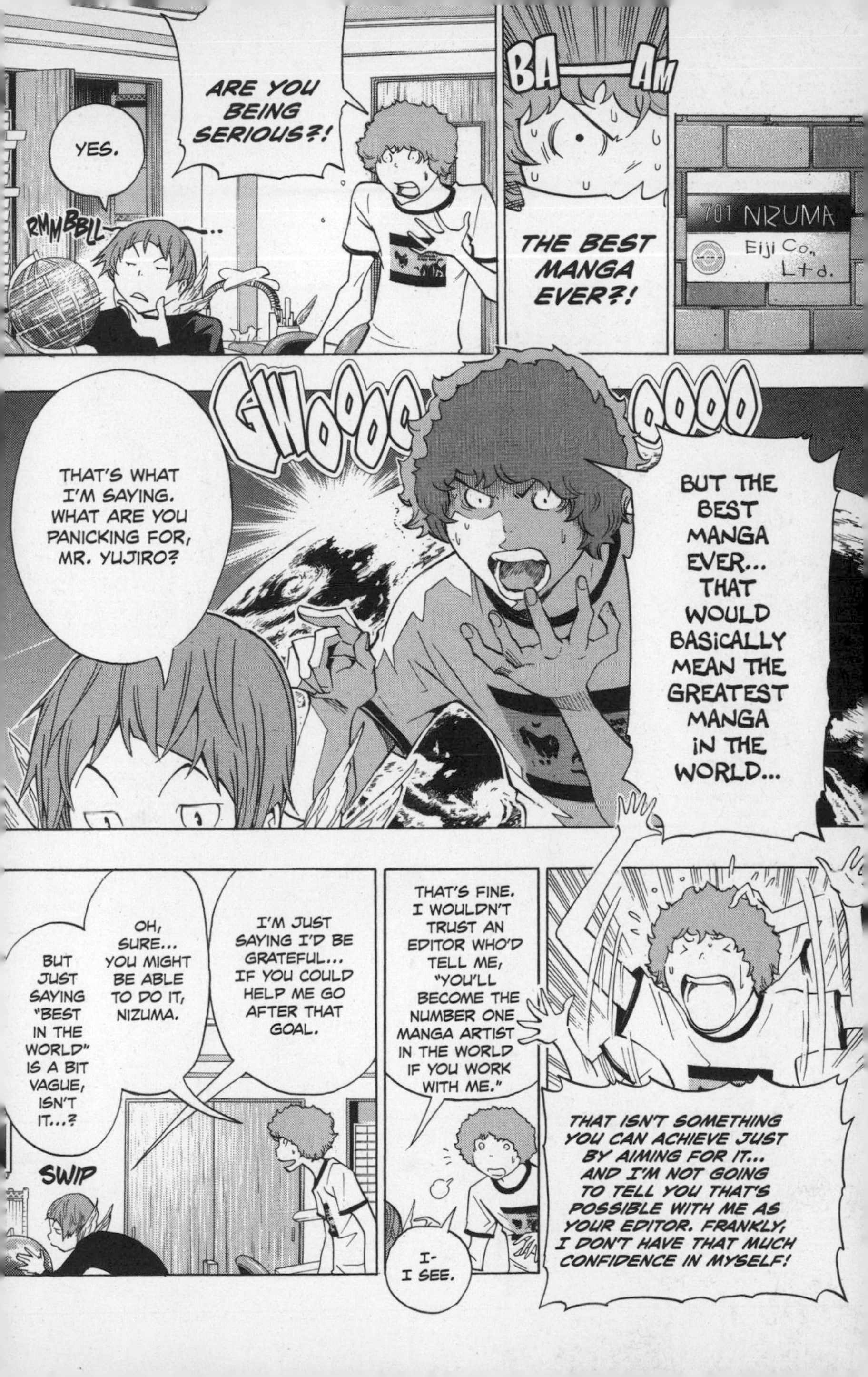
701 NIZUMA
Eiji Co., Ltd.
BA—AM
THE BEST MANGA EVER?!
ARE YOU BEING SERIOUS?!
YES.
RMMBBLL...
GWOOOOOOOOO
BUT THE BEST MANGA EVER... THAT WOULD BASICALLY MEAN THE GREATEST MANGA IN THE WORLD...
THAT'S WHAT I'M SAYING. WHAT ARE YOU PANICKING FOR, MR. YUJIRO?
THAT ISN'T SOMETHING YOU CAN ACHIEVE JUST BY AIMING FOR IT... AND I'M NOT GOING TO TELL YOU THAT'S POSSIBLE WITH ME AS YOUR EDITOR. FRANKLY, I DON'T HAVE THAT MUCH CONFIDENCE IN MYSELF!
THAT'S FINE. I WOULDN'T TRUST AN EDITOR WHO'D TELL ME, "YOU'LL BECOME THE NUMBER ONE MANGA ARTIST IN THE WORLD IF YOU WORK WITH ME."
I- I SEE.
I'M JUST SAYING I'D BE GRATEFUL... IF YOU COULD HELP ME GO AFTER THAT GOAL.
OH, SURE... YOU MIGHT BE ABLE TO DO IT, NIZUMA.
BUT JUST SAYING "BEST IN THE WORLD" IS A BIT VAGUE, ISN'T IT...?
SWIP

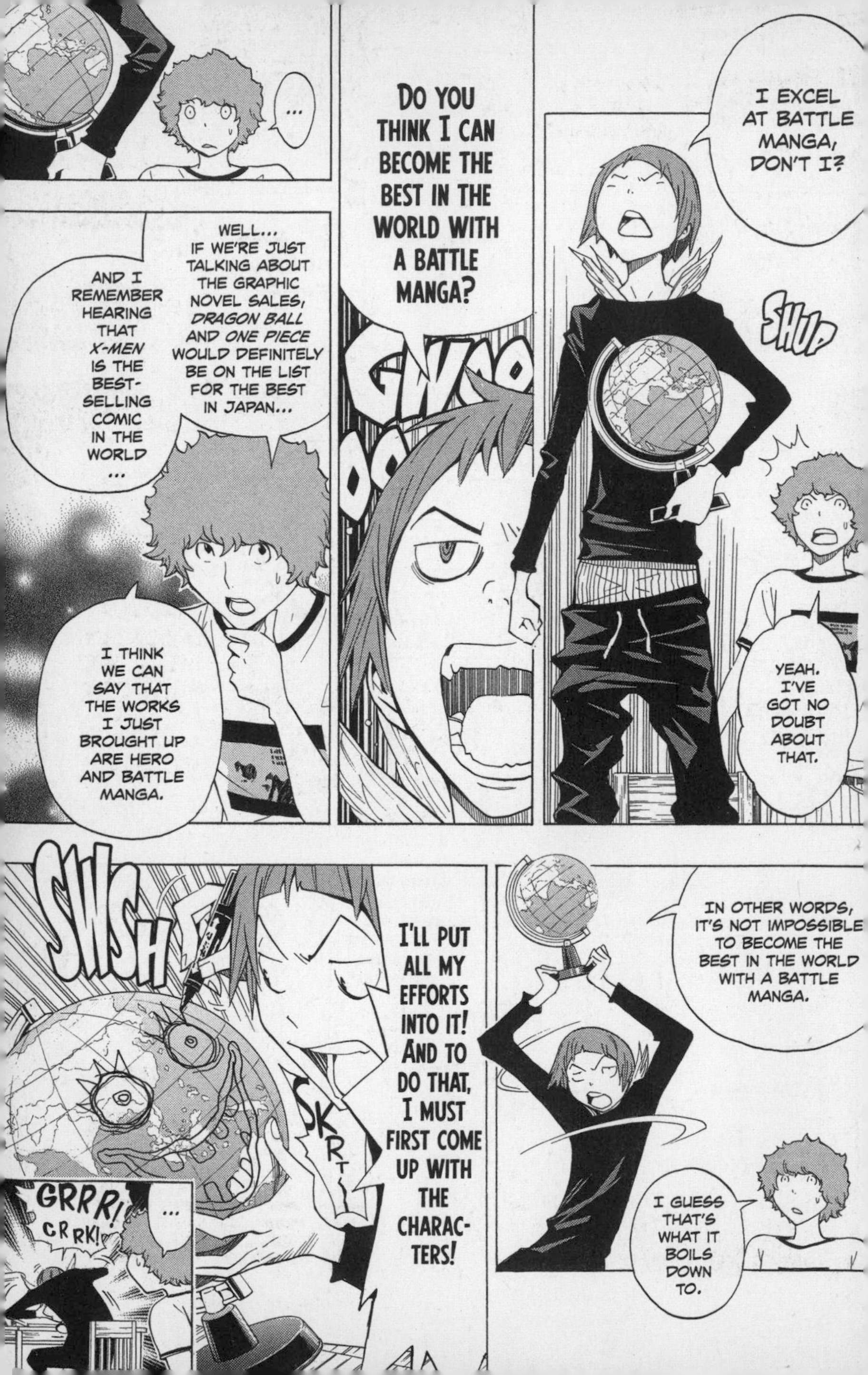
I EXCEL AT BATTLE MANGA, DON'T I?
SHUP
YEAH. I'VE GOT NO DOUBT ABOUT THAT.
DO YOU THINK I CAN BECOME THE BEST IN THE WORLD WITH A BATTLE MANGA?
GWAOOO
...
WELL... IF WE'RE JUST TALKING ABOUT THE GRAPHIC NOVEL SALES, *DRAGON BALL* AND *ONE PIECE* WOULD DEFINITELY BE ON THE LIST FOR THE BEST IN JAPAN...
AND I REMEMBER HEARING THAT *X-MEN* IS THE BEST-SELLING COMIC IN THE WORLD...
I THINK WE CAN SAY THAT THE WORKS I JUST BROUGHT UP ARE HERO AND BATTLE MANGA.
IN OTHER WORDS, IT'S NOT IMPOSSIBLE TO BECOME THE BEST IN THE WORLD WITH A BATTLE MANGA.
I GUESS THAT'S WHAT IT BOILS DOWN TO.
SWSH
I'LL PUT ALL MY EFFORTS INTO IT! AND TO DO THAT, I MUST FIRST COME UP WITH THE CHARACTERS!
SKRT
GRRR!
CRRK!
...

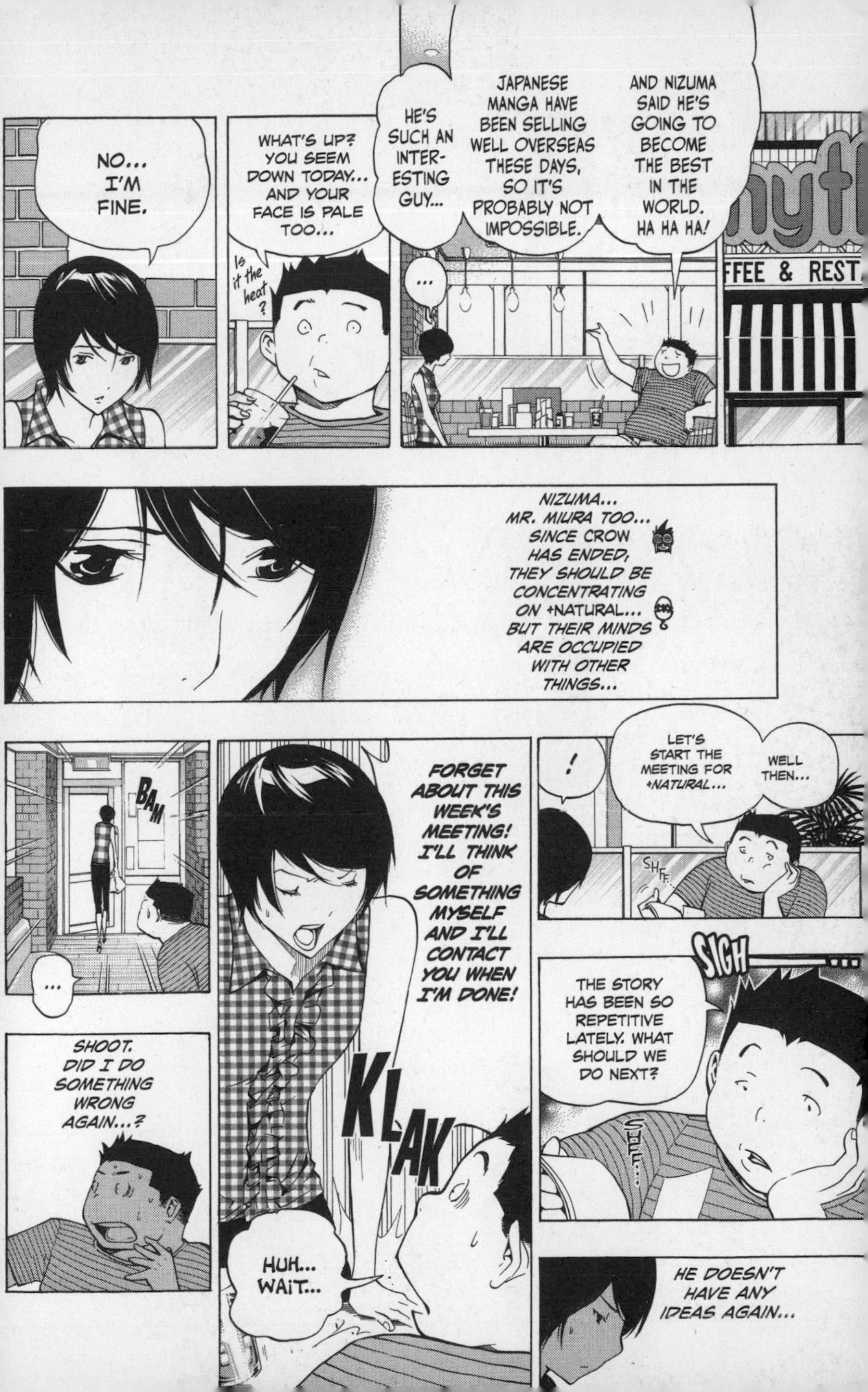
FFEE & REST
AND NIZUMA SAID HE'S GOING TO BECOME THE BEST IN THE WORLD. HA HA HA!
JAPANESE MANGA HAVE BEEN SELLING WELL OVERSEAS THESE DAYS, SO IT'S PROBABLY NOT IMPOSSIBLE.
HE'S SUCH AN INTERESTING GUY...
...
WHAT'S UP? YOU SEEM DOWN TODAY... AND YOUR FACE IS PALE TOO...
Is it the heat?
NO... I'M FINE.
NIZUMA... MR. MIURA TOO... SINCE CROW HAS ENDED, THEY SHOULD BE CONCENTRATING ON +NATURAL... BUT THEIR MINDS ARE OCCUPIED WITH OTHER THINGS...
WELL THEN...
LET'S START THE MEETING FOR +NATURAL...
SHFF...
!
SIGH
THE STORY HAS BEEN SO REPETITIVE LATELY. WHAT SHOULD WE DO NEXT?
SHFF...
HE DOESN'T HAVE ANY IDEAS AGAIN...
FORGET ABOUT THIS WEEK'S MEETING! I'LL THINK OF SOMETHING MYSELF AND I'LL CONTACT YOU WHEN I'M DONE!
KLAK
HUH... WAIT...
BAM
...
SHOOT. DID I DO SOMETHING WRONG AGAIN...?

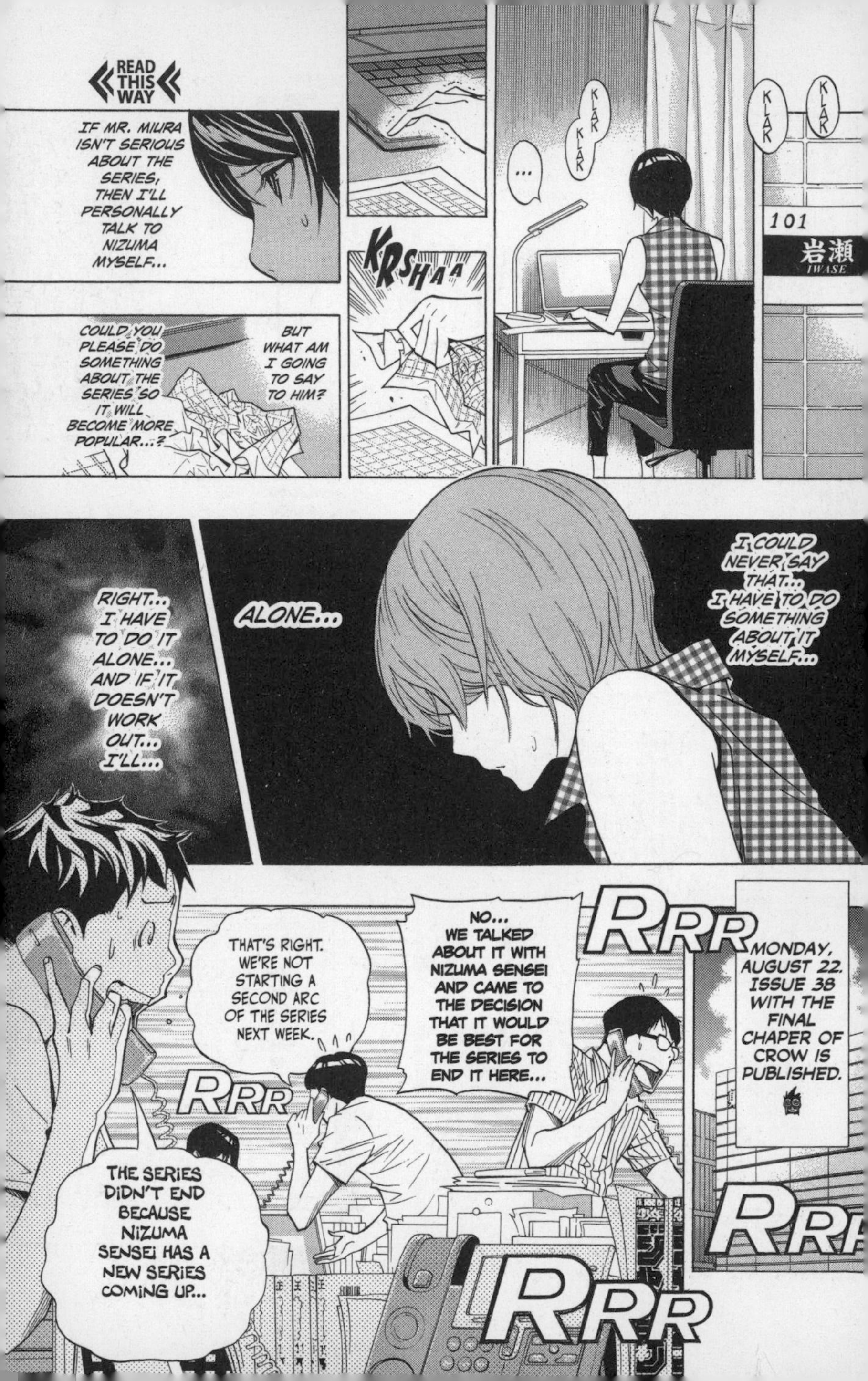
READ THIS WAY
KLAK KLAK
101
岩瀬 IWASE
KLAK KLAK
...
KRSHAA
IF MR. MIURA ISN'T SERIOUS ABOUT THE SERIES, THEN I'LL PERSONALLY TALK TO NIZUMA MYSELF...
BUT WHAT AM I GOING TO SAY TO HIM?
COULD YOU PLEASE DO SOMETHING ABOUT THE SERIES SO IT WILL BECOME MORE POPULAR...?
I COULD NEVER SAY THAT... I HAVE TO DO SOMETHING ABOUT IT MYSELF...
ALONE...
RIGHT... I HAVE TO DO IT ALONE... AND IF IT DOESN'T WORK OUT... I'LL...
MONDAY, AUGUST 22. ISSUE 38 WITH THE FINAL CHAPER OF CROW IS PUBLISHED.
RRR
NO... WE TALKED ABOUT IT WITH NIZUMA SENSEI AND CAME TO THE DECISION THAT IT WOULD BE BEST FOR THE SERIES TO END IT HERE...
RRR
THAT'S RIGHT. WE'RE NOT STARTING A SECOND ARC OF THE SERIES NEXT WEEK.
RRR
THE SERIES DIDN'T END BECAUSE NIZUMA SENSEI HAS A NEW SERIES COMING UP...
RRR

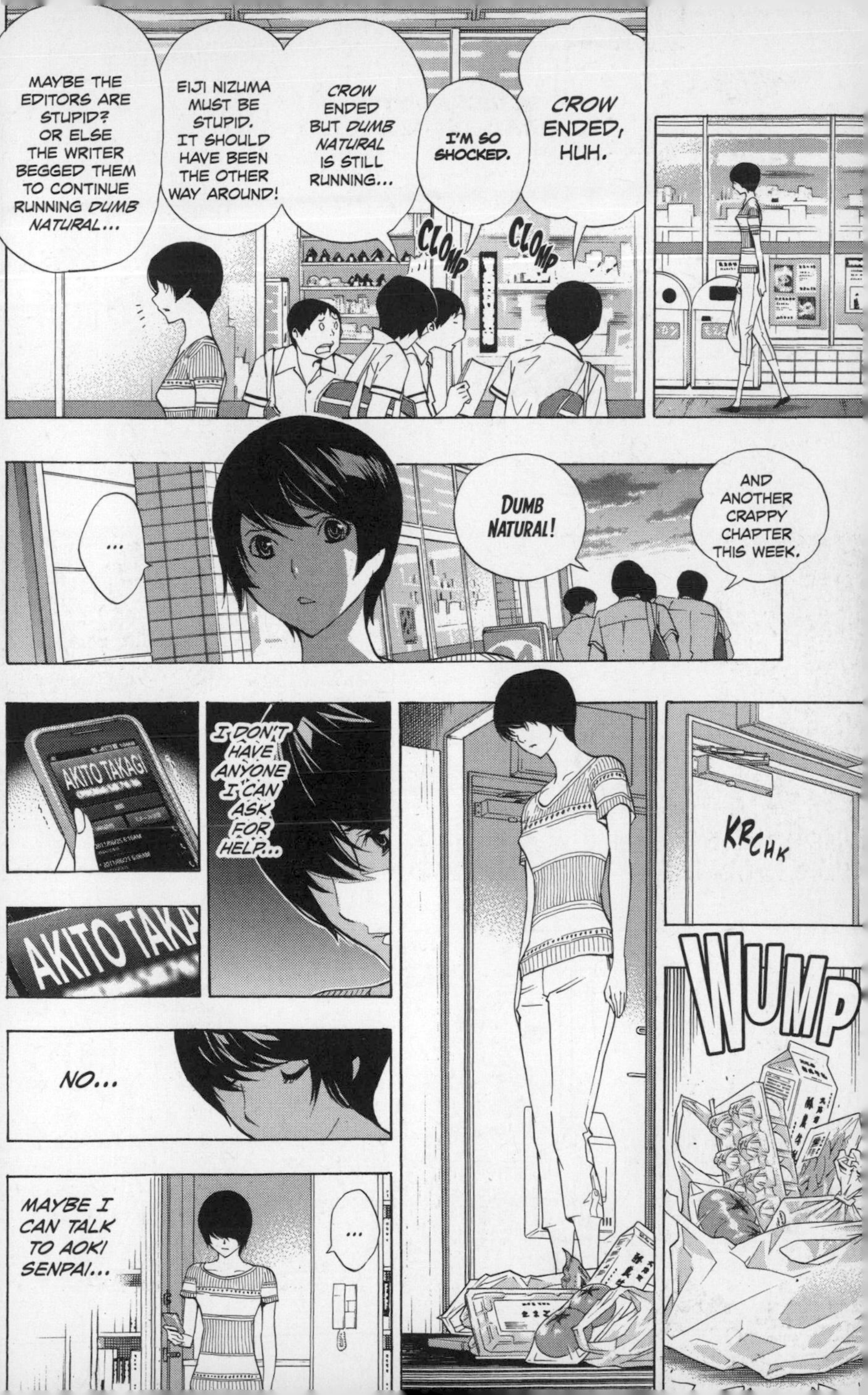
CROW ENDED, HUH.
I'M SO SHOCKED.
CLOMP
CLOMP
CROW ENDED BUT DUMB NATURAL IS STILL RUNNING...
EIJI NIZUMA MUST BE STUPID. IT SHOULD HAVE BEEN THE OTHER WAY AROUND!
MAYBE THE EDITORS ARE STUPID? OR ELSE THE WRITER BEGGED THEM TO CONTINUE RUNNING DUMB NATURAL...
AND ANOTHER CRAPPY CHAPTER THIS WEEK.
DUMB NATURAL!
...
KRCHK
WUMP
I DON'T HAVE ANYONE I CAN ASK FOR HELP...
AKITO TAKAGI
AKITO TAKA
NO...
...
MAYBE I CAN TALK TO AOKI SENPAI...

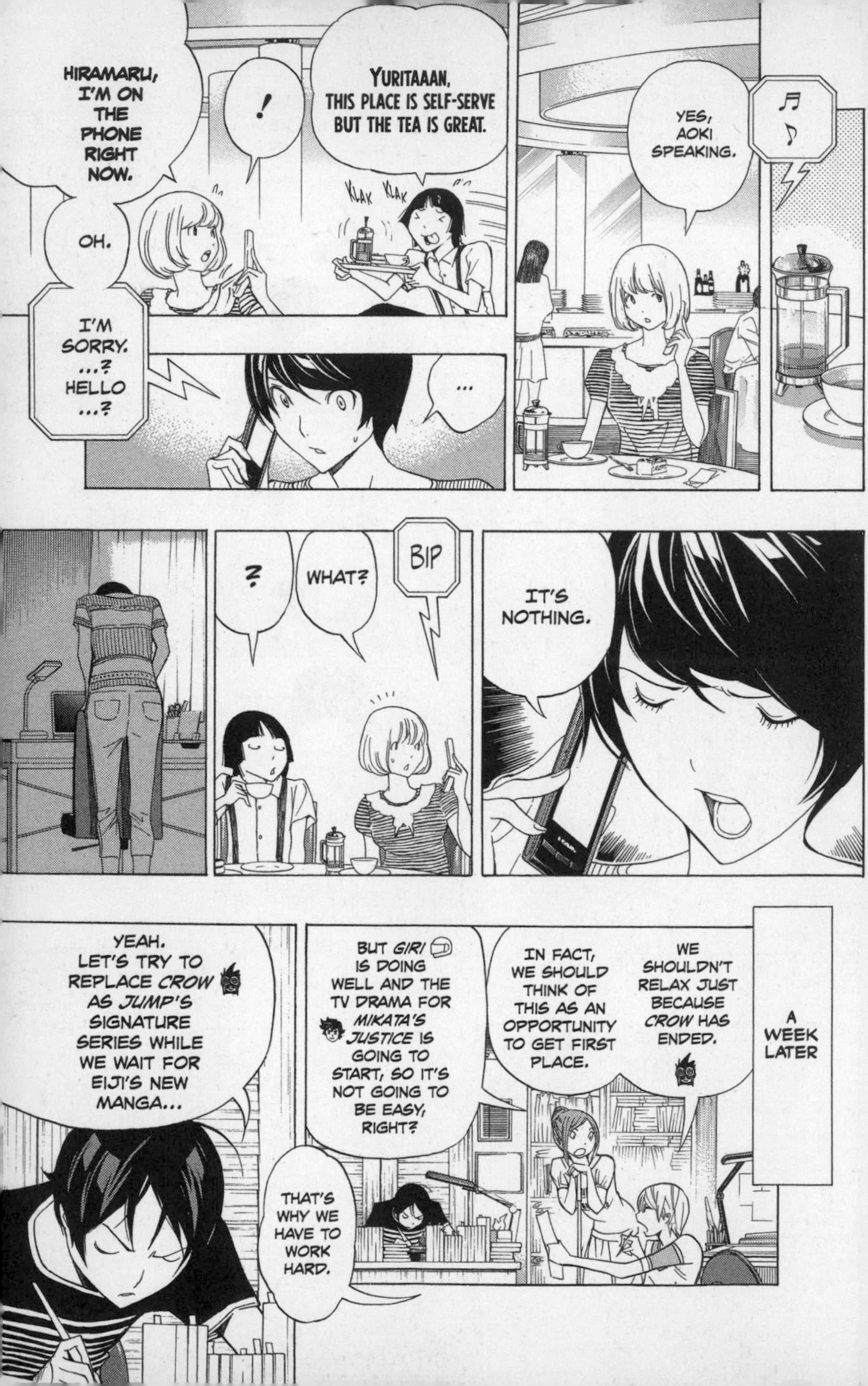
YES, AOKI SPEAKING.
YURITAAAN, THIS PLACE IS SELF-SERVE BUT THE TEA IS GREAT.
KLAK KLAK
!
HIRAMARU, I'M ON THE PHONE RIGHT NOW.
OH.
...
I'M SORRY. ...? HELLO ...?
IT'S NOTHING.
BIP
WHAT?
?
A WEEK LATER
WE SHOULDN'T RELAX JUST BECAUSE CROW HAS ENDED.
IN FACT, WE SHOULD THINK OF THIS AS AN OPPORTUNITY TO GET FIRST PLACE.
BUT GIRI IS DOING WELL AND THE TV DRAMA FOR MIKATA'S JUSTICE IS GOING TO START, SO IT'S NOT GOING TO BE EASY, RIGHT?
THAT'S WHY WE HAVE TO WORK HARD.
YEAH. LET'S TRY TO REPLACE CROW AS JUMP'S SIGNATURE SERIES WHILE WE WAIT FOR EIJI'S NEW MANGA...

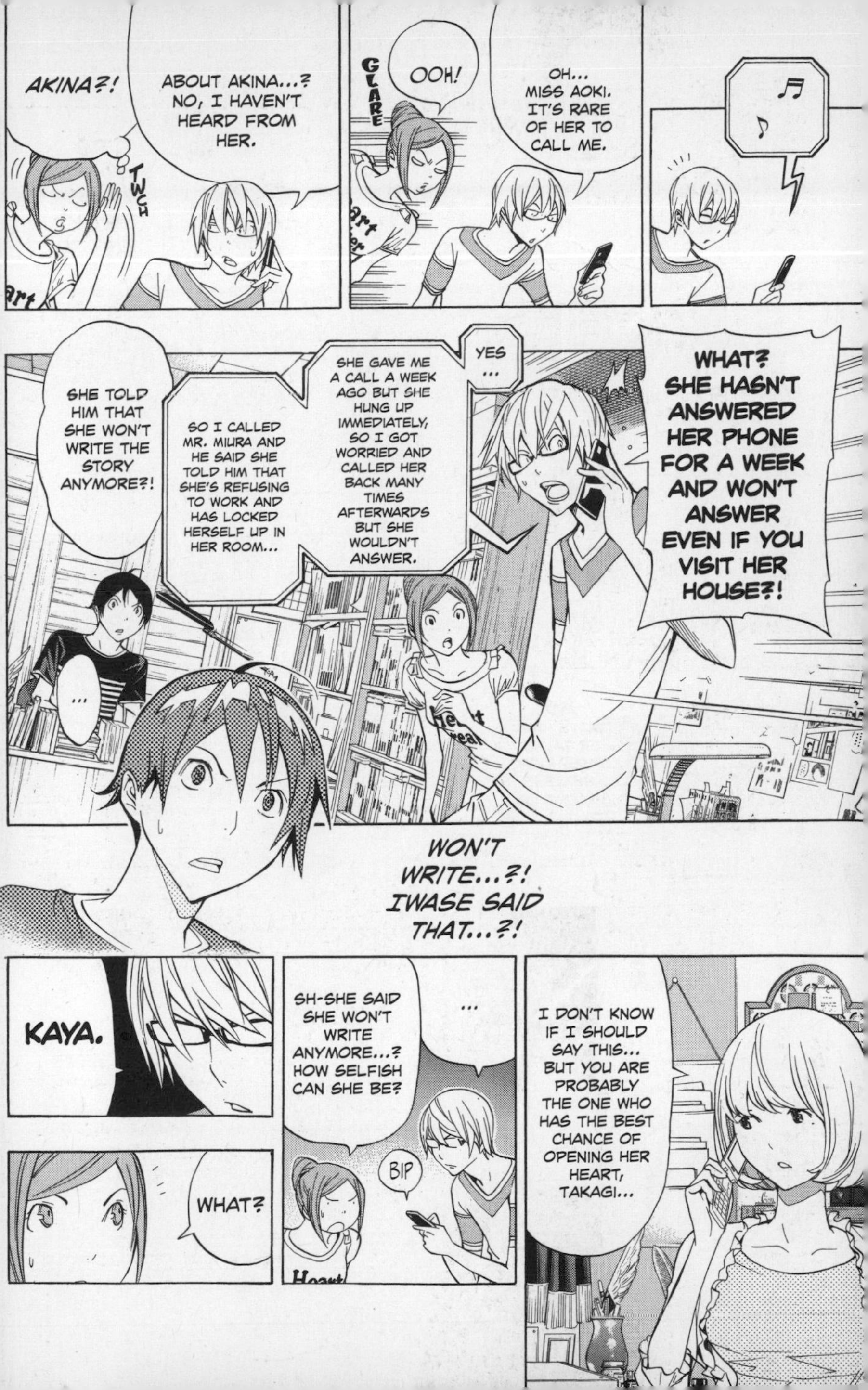
♫ ♪
OH... MISS AOKI. IT'S RARE OF HER TO CALL ME.
OOH!
GLARE
ABOUT AKINA...? NO, I HAVEN'T HEARD FROM HER.
AKINA?!
TWCH
WHAT? SHE HASN'T ANSWERED HER PHONE FOR A WEEK AND WON'T ANSWER EVEN IF YOU VISIT HER HOUSE?!
YES...
SHE GAVE ME A CALL A WEEK AGO BUT SHE HUNG UP IMMEDIATELY, SO I GOT WORRIED AND CALLED HER BACK MANY TIMES AFTERWARDS BUT SHE WOULDN'T ANSWER.
SO I CALLED MR. MIURA AND HE SAID SHE TOLD HIM THAT SHE'S REFUSING TO WORK AND HAS LOCKED HERSELF UP IN HER ROOM...
SHE TOLD HIM THAT SHE WON'T WRITE THE STORY ANYMORE?!
...
WON'T WRITE...?! IWASE SAID THAT...?!
I DON'T KNOW IF I SHOULD SAY THIS... BUT YOU ARE PROBABLY THE ONE WHO HAS THE BEST CHANCE OF OPENING HER HEART, TAKAGI...
...
SH-SHE SAID SHE WON'T WRITE ANYMORE...? HOW SELFISH CAN SHE BE?
BIP
KAYA.
WHAT?

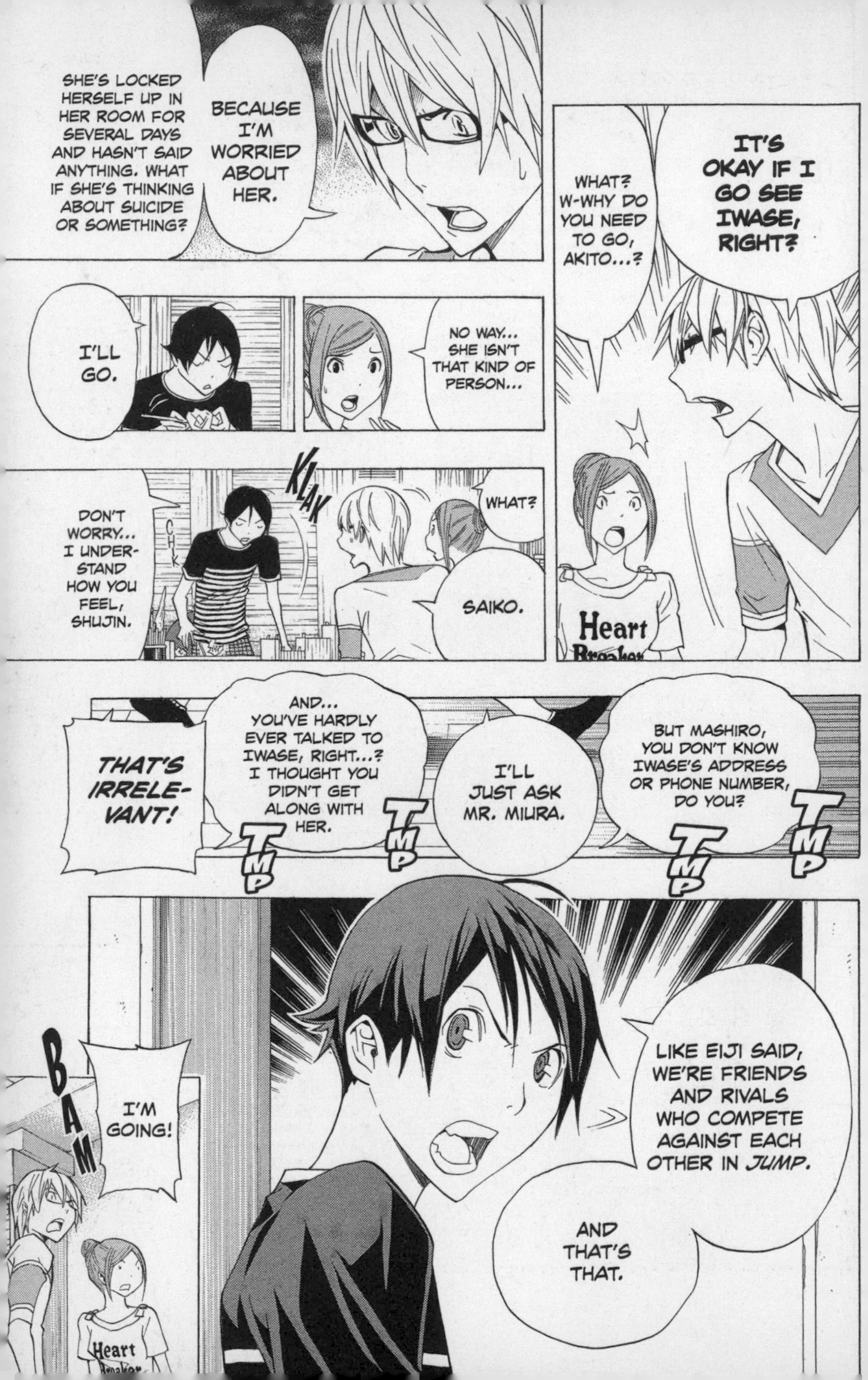
IT'S OKAY IF I GO SEE IWASE, RIGHT?
WHAT? W-WHY DO YOU NEED TO GO, AKITO...?
BECAUSE I'M WORRIED ABOUT HER.
SHE'S LOCKED HERSELF UP IN HER ROOM FOR SEVERAL DAYS AND HASN'T SAID ANYTHING. WHAT IF SHE'S THINKING ABOUT SUICIDE OR SOMETHING?
NO WAY... SHE ISN'T THAT KIND OF PERSON...
I'LL GO.
WHAT?
SAIKO.
KLAK
DON'T WORRY... I UNDERSTAND HOW YOU FEEL, SHUJIN.
CHIK
BUT MASHIRO, YOU DON'T KNOW IWASE'S ADDRESS OR PHONE NUMBER, DO YOU?
TMP
TMP
I'LL JUST ASK MR. MIURA.
TMP
AND... YOU'VE HARDLY EVER TALKED TO IWASE, RIGHT...? I THOUGHT YOU DIDN'T GET ALONG WITH HER.
TMP
THAT'S IRRELEVANT!
LIKE EIJI SAID, WE'RE FRIENDS AND RIVALS WHO COMPETE AGAINST EACH OTHER IN *JUMP*.
AND THAT'S THAT.
I'M GOING!
BAM

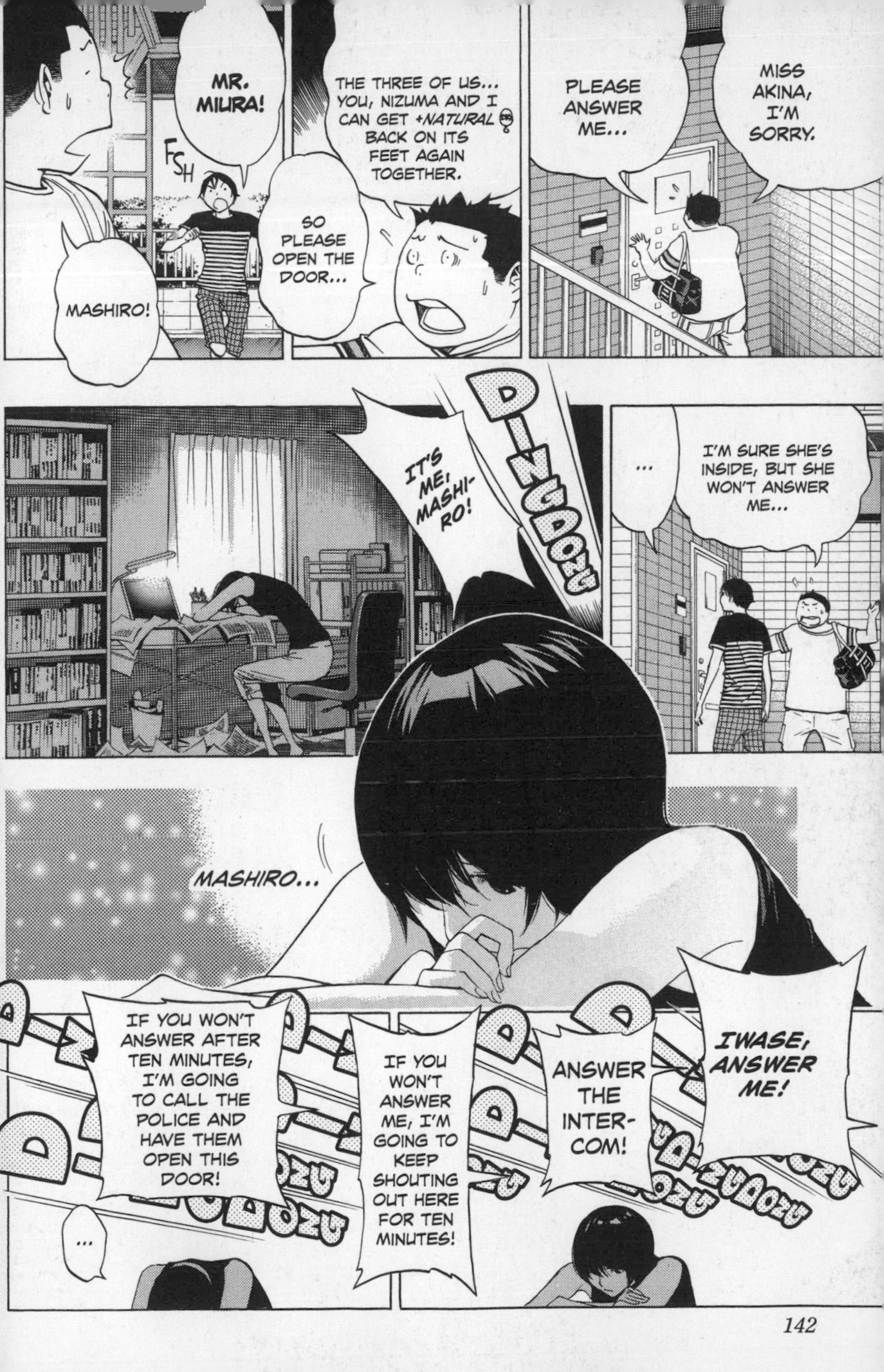
MISS AKINA, I'M SORRY.
PLEASE ANSWER ME...
THE THREE OF US... YOU, NIZUMA AND I CAN GET +NATURAL BACK ON ITS FEET AGAIN TOGETHER.
SO PLEASE OPEN THE DOOR...
MR. MIURA!
FSH
MASHIRO!
I'M SURE SHE'S INSIDE, BUT SHE WON'T ANSWER ME...
...
DINGDONG
IT'S ME, MASHIRO!
MASHIRO...
IWASE, ANSWER ME!
ANSWER THE INTERCOM!
IF YOU WON'T ANSWER ME, I'M GOING TO KEEP SHOUTING OUT HERE FOR TEN MINUTES!
IF YOU WON'T ANSWER AFTER TEN MINUTES, I'M GOING TO CALL THE POLICE AND HAVE THEM OPEN THIS DOOR!
...

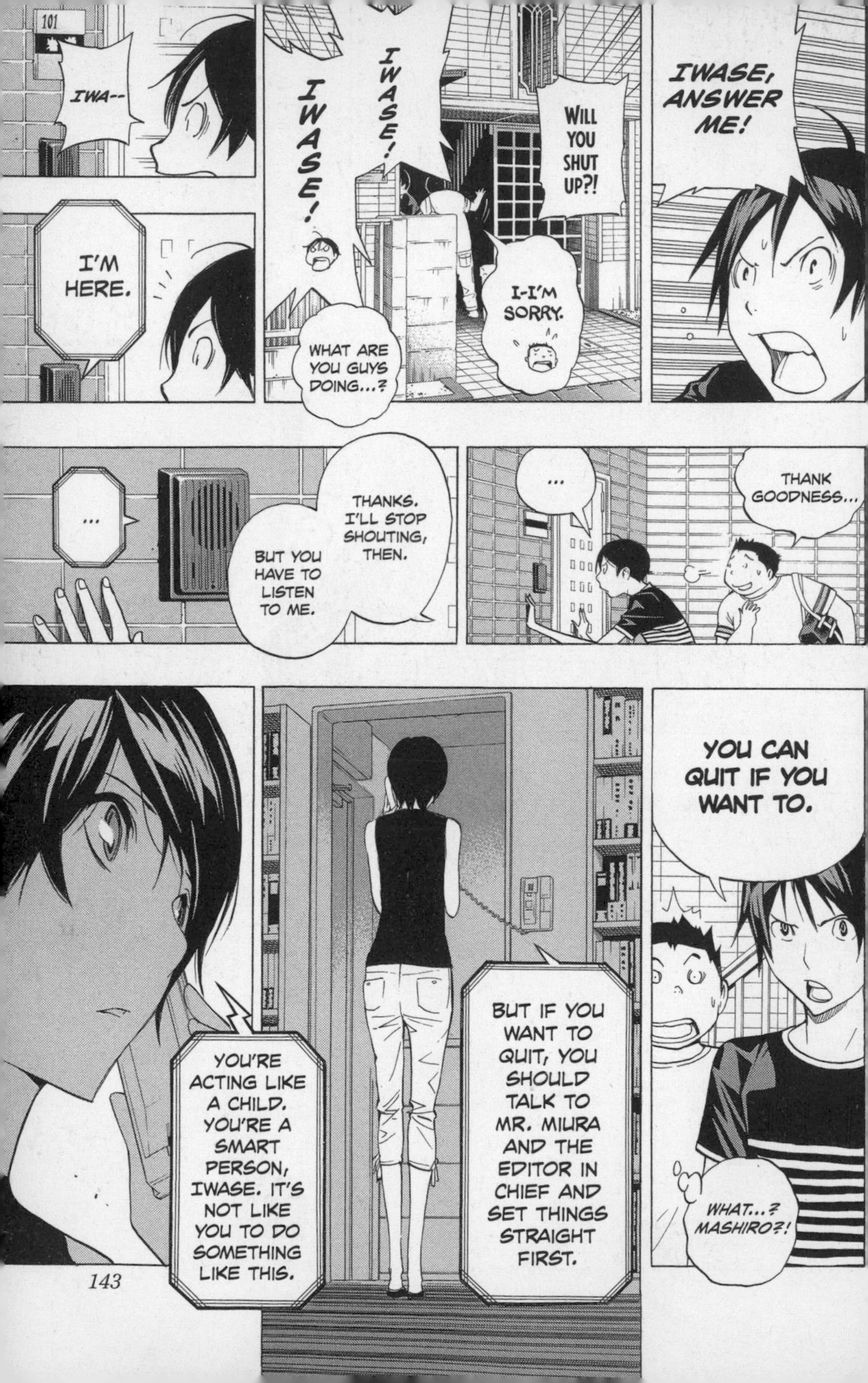
IWASE, ANSWER ME!
IWASE!
IWASE!
WILL YOU SHUT UP?!
I-I'M SORRY.
WHAT ARE YOU GUYS DOING...?
101
IWA--
I'M HERE.
THANK GOODNESS...
...
THANKS. I'LL STOP SHOUTING, THEN.
BUT YOU HAVE TO LISTEN TO ME.
...
YOU CAN QUIT IF YOU WANT TO.
WHAT...? MASHIRO?!
BUT IF YOU WANT TO QUIT, YOU SHOULD TALK TO MR. MIURA AND THE EDITOR IN CHIEF AND SET THINGS STRAIGHT FIRST.
YOU'RE ACTING LIKE A CHILD. YOU'RE A SMART PERSON, IWASE. IT'S NOT LIKE YOU TO DO SOMETHING LIKE THIS.

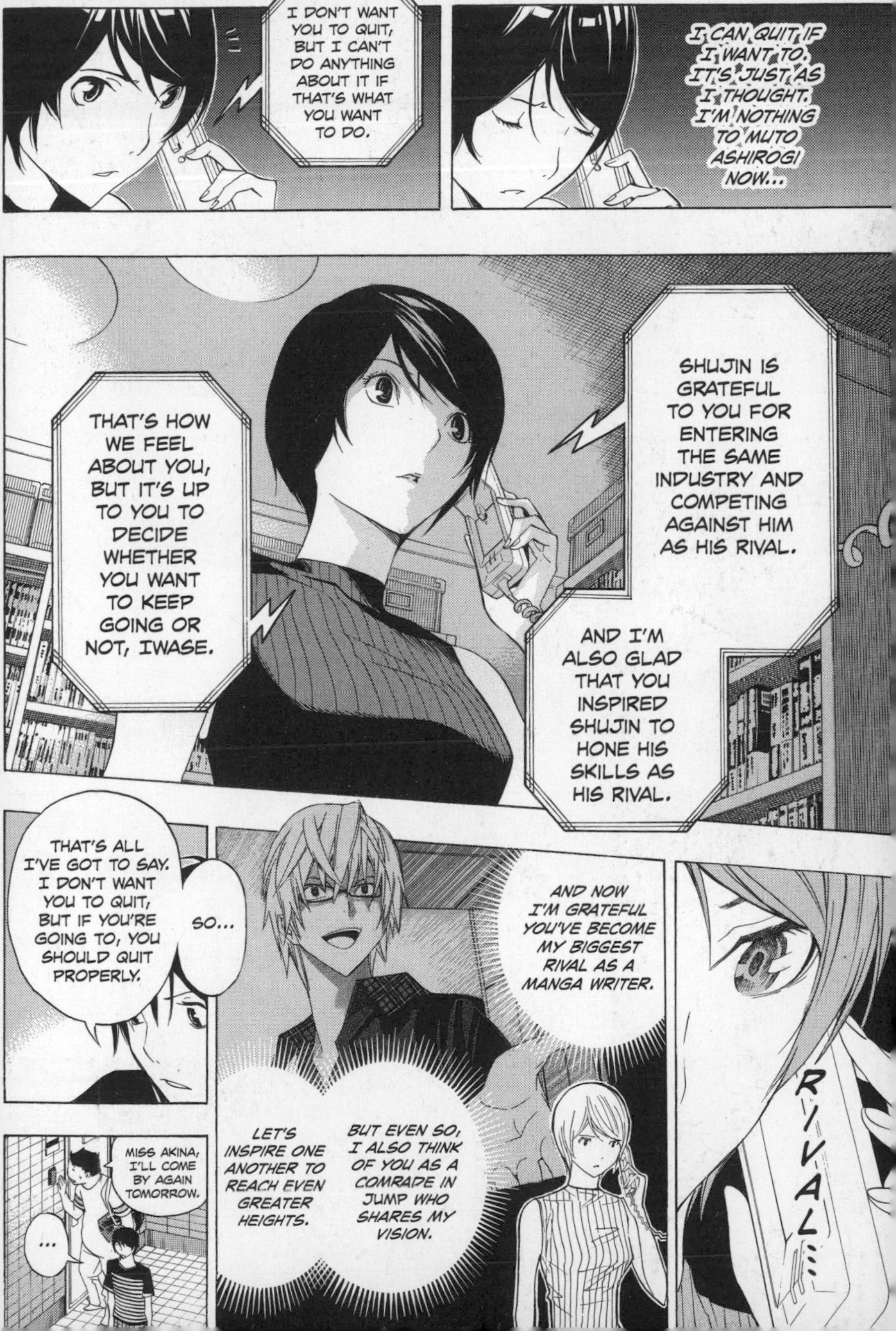
I CAN QUIT IF I WANT TO. IT'S JUST AS I THOUGHT. I'M NOTHING TO MUTO ASHIROGI NOW...
I DON'T WANT YOU TO QUIT, BUT I CAN'T DO ANYTHING ABOUT IT IF THAT'S WHAT YOU WANT TO DO.
SHUJIN IS GRATEFUL TO YOU FOR ENTERING THE SAME INDUSTRY AND COMPETING AGAINST HIM AS HIS RIVAL.
AND I'M ALSO GLAD THAT YOU INSPIRED SHUJIN TO HONE HIS SKILLS AS HIS RIVAL.
THAT'S HOW WE FEEL ABOUT YOU, BUT IT'S UP TO YOU TO DECIDE WHETHER YOU WANT TO KEEP GOING OR NOT, IWASE.
RIVAL...
AND NOW I'M GRATEFUL YOU'VE BECOME MY BIGGEST RIVAL AS A MANGA WRITER.
BUT EVEN SO, I ALSO THINK OF YOU AS A COMRADE IN JUMP WHO SHARES MY VISION.
LET'S INSPIRE ONE ANOTHER TO REACH EVEN GREATER HEIGHTS.
THAT'S ALL I'VE GOT TO SAY. I DON'T WANT YOU TO QUIT, BUT IF YOU'RE GOING TO, YOU SHOULD QUIT PROPERLY.
SO...
MISS AKINA, I'LL COME BY AGAIN TOMORROW.
...

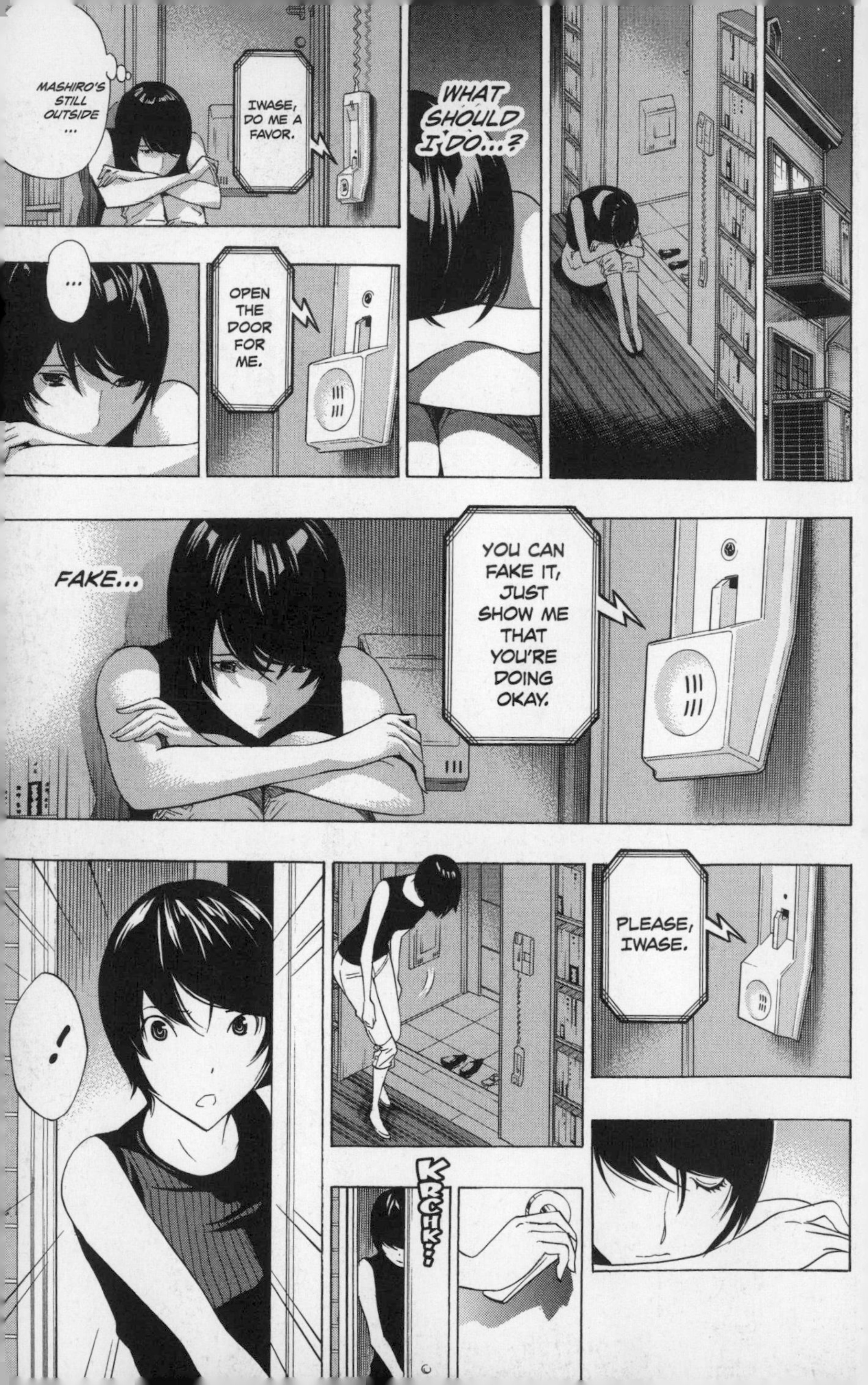
WHAT SHOULD I DO...?
IWASE, DO ME A FAVOR.
MASHIRO'S STILL OUTSIDE ...
OPEN THE DOOR FOR ME.
...
YOU CAN FAKE IT, JUST SHOW ME THAT YOU'RE DOING OKAY.
FAKE...
PLEASE, IWASE.
!
KRCHK...

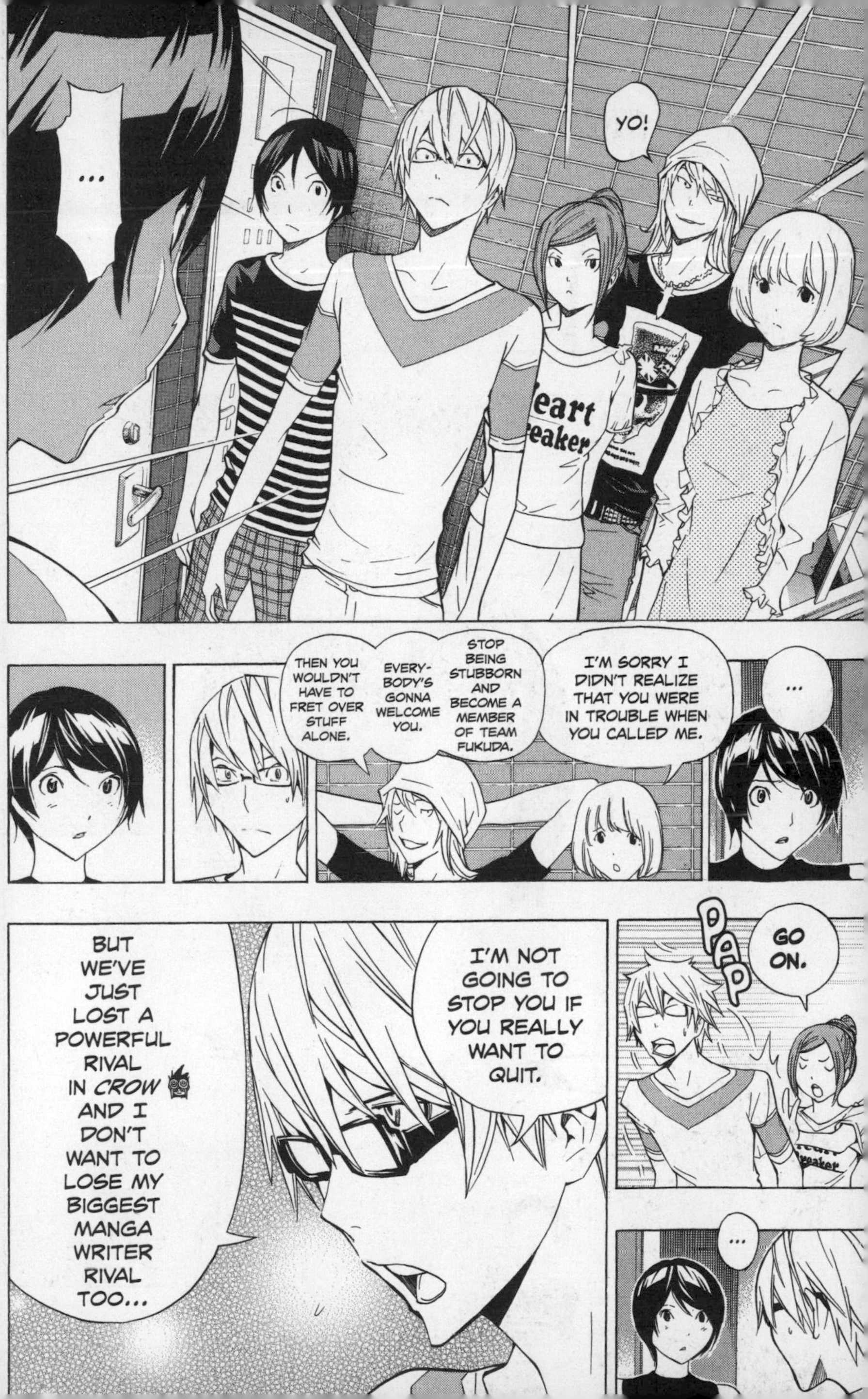
YO!
...
...
I'M SORRY I DIDN'T REALIZE THAT YOU WERE IN TROUBLE WHEN YOU CALLED ME.
STOP BEING STUBBORN AND BECOME A MEMBER OF TEAM FUKUDA.
EVERY-BODY'S GONNA WELCOME YOU.
THEN YOU WOULDN'T HAVE TO FRET OVER STUFF ALONE.
GO ON.
DAP DAP
...
I'M NOT GOING TO STOP YOU IF YOU REALLY WANT TO QUIT.
BUT WE'VE JUST LOST A POWERFUL RIVAL IN *CROW* AND I DON'T WANT TO LOSE MY BIGGEST MANGA WRITER RIVAL TOO...

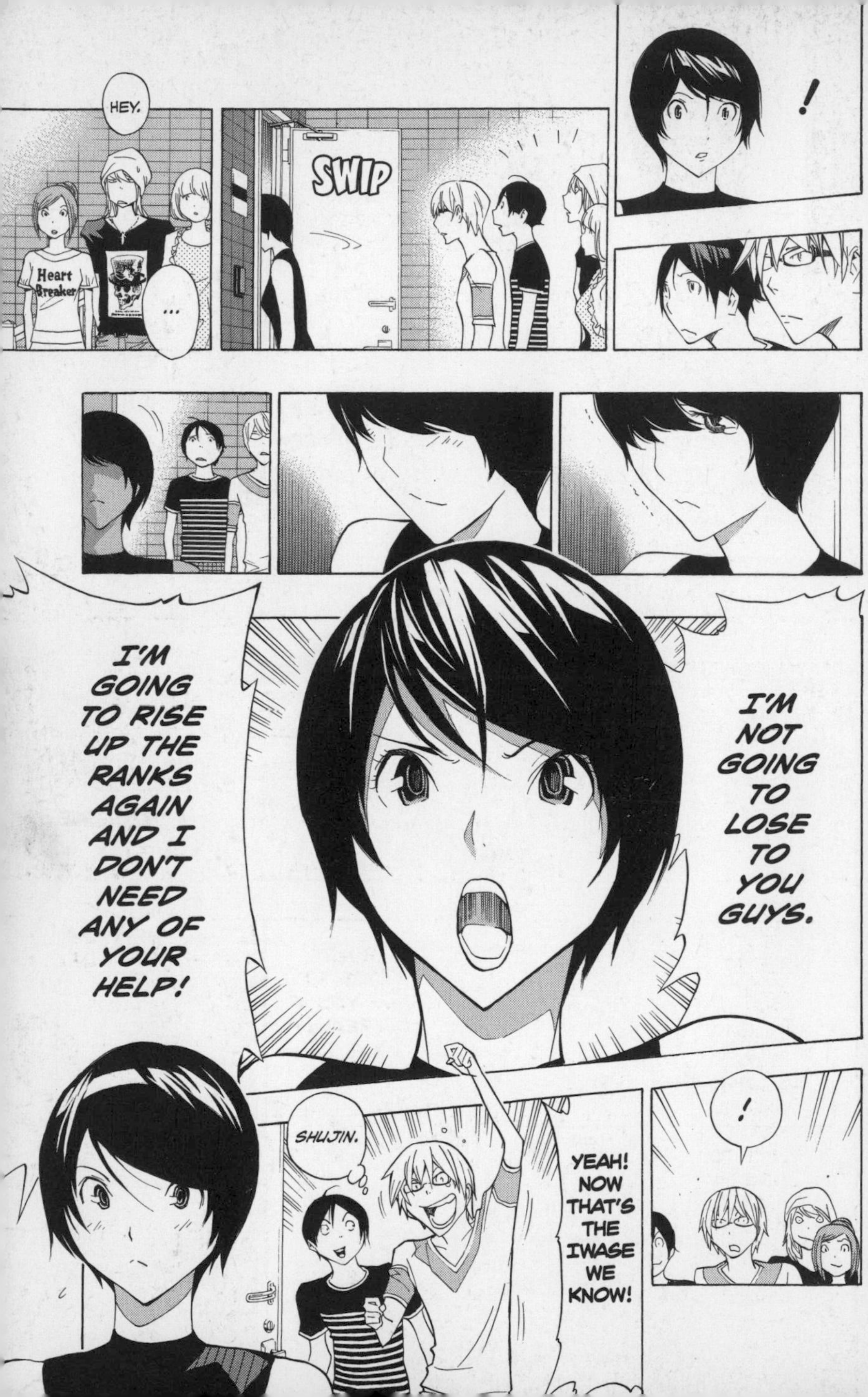
!
SWIP
HEY.
...
I'M NOT GOING TO LOSE TO YOU GUYS.
I'M GOING TO RISE UP THE RANKS AGAIN AND I DON'T NEED ANY OF YOUR HELP!
!
YEAH! NOW THAT'S THE IWASE WE KNOW!
SHUJIN.

OHBA'S STORYBOARD

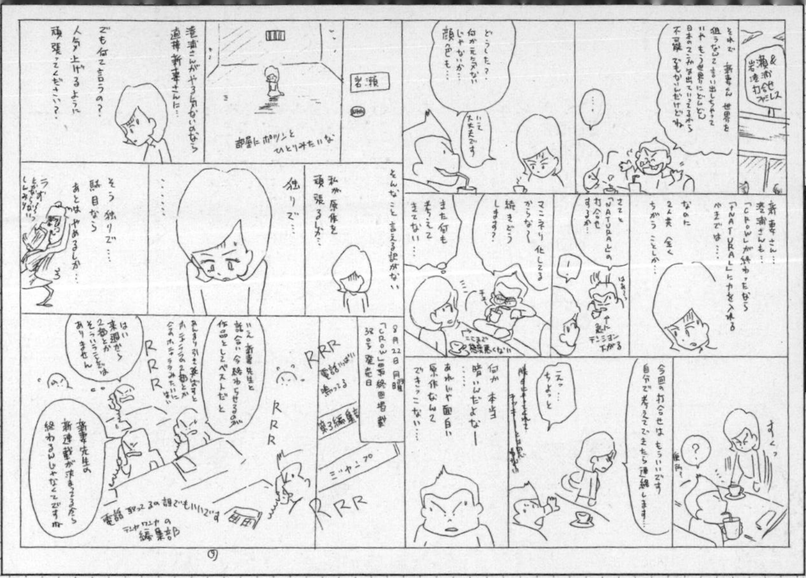

OBATA'S STORYBOARD

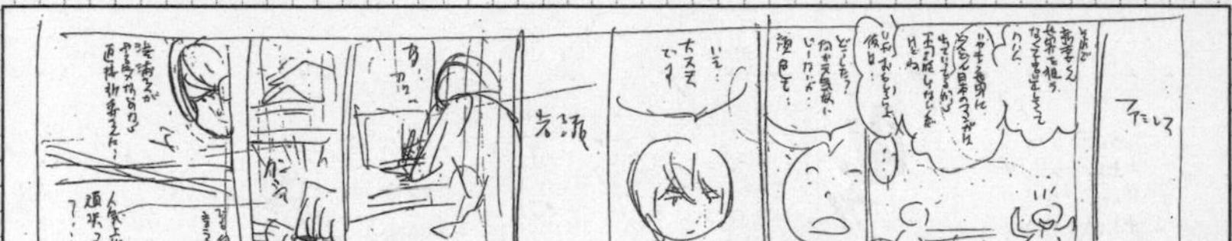

COMPLETE!

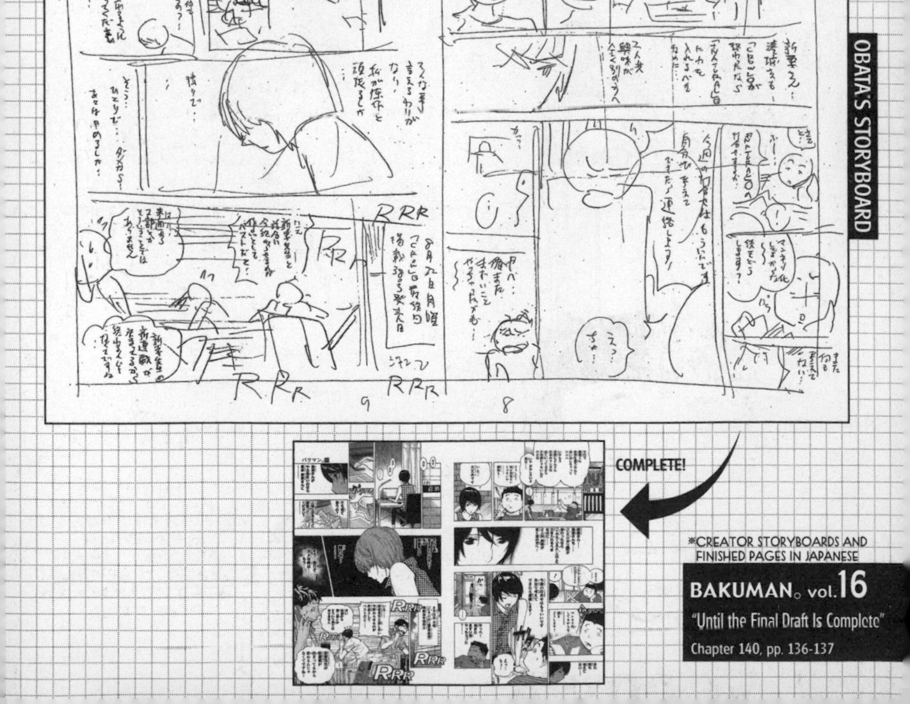

※CREATOR STORYBOARDS AND FINISHED PAGES IN JAPANESE

BAKUMAN。vol.16

"Until the Final Draft Is Complete"

Chapter 140, pp. 136-137

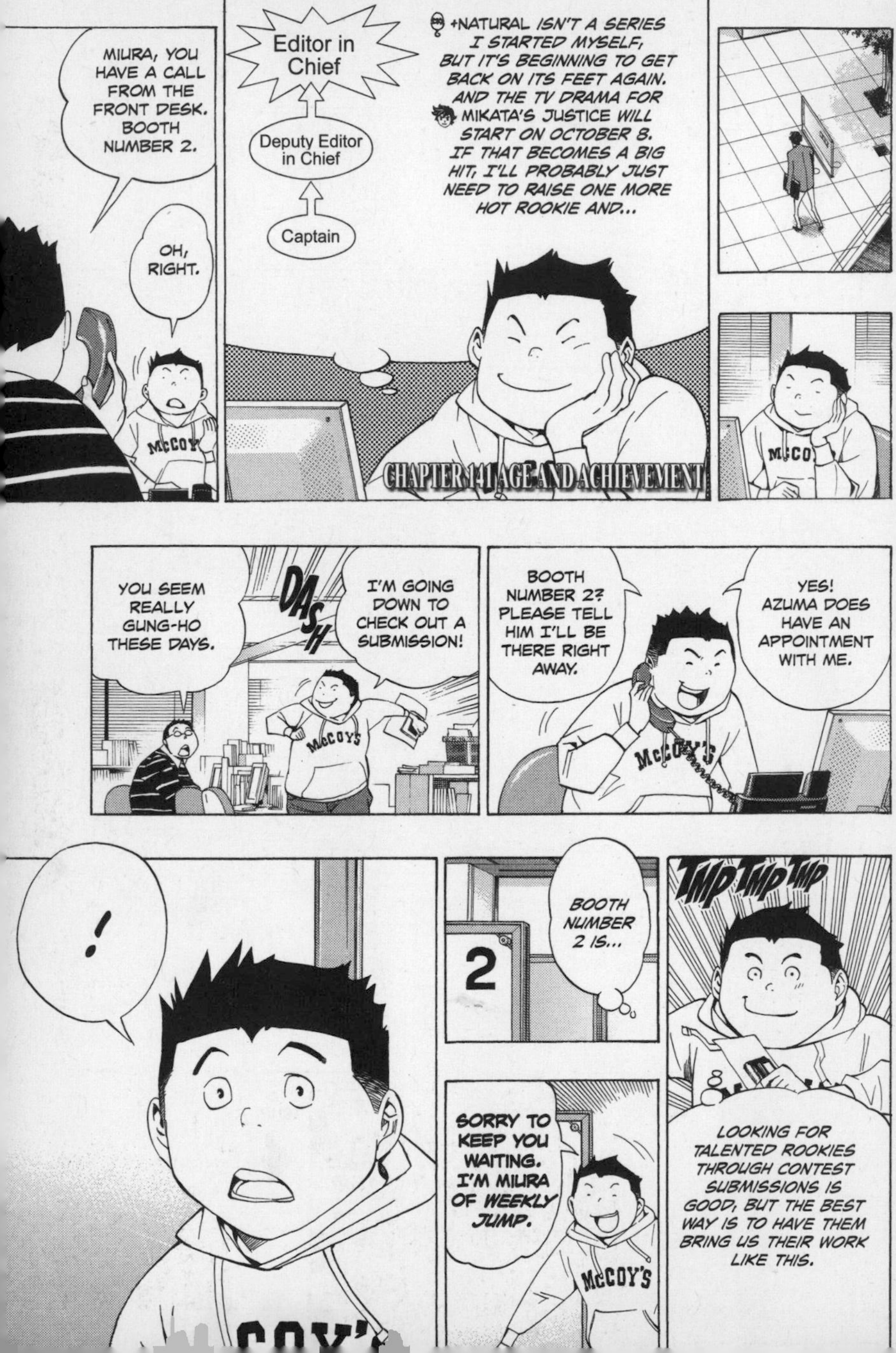
CHAPTER 141 AGE AND ACHIEVEMENT
+NATURAL ISN'T A SERIES I STARTED MYSELF, BUT IT'S BEGINNING TO GET BACK ON ITS FEET AGAIN. AND THE TV DRAMA FOR MIKATA'S JUSTICE WILL START ON OCTOBER 8. IF THAT BECOMES A BIG HIT, I'LL PROBABLY JUST NEED TO RAISE ONE MORE HOT ROOKIE AND...
Editor in Chief
Deputy Editor in Chief
Captain
MIURA, YOU HAVE A CALL FROM THE FRONT DESK. BOOTH NUMBER 2.
OH, RIGHT.
YES! AZUMA DOES HAVE AN APPOINTMENT WITH ME.
BOOTH NUMBER 2? PLEASE TELL HIM I'LL BE THERE RIGHT AWAY.
I'M GOING DOWN TO CHECK OUT A SUBMISSION!
DASH
YOU SEEM REALLY GUNG-HO THESE DAYS.
TMP TMP TMP
LOOKING FOR TALENTED ROOKIES THROUGH CONTEST SUBMISSIONS IS GOOD, BUT THE BEST WAY IS TO HAVE THEM BRING US THEIR WORK LIKE THIS.
2
BOOTH NUMBER 2 IS...
SORRY TO KEEP YOU WAITING. I'M MIURA OF WEEKLY JUMP.
!

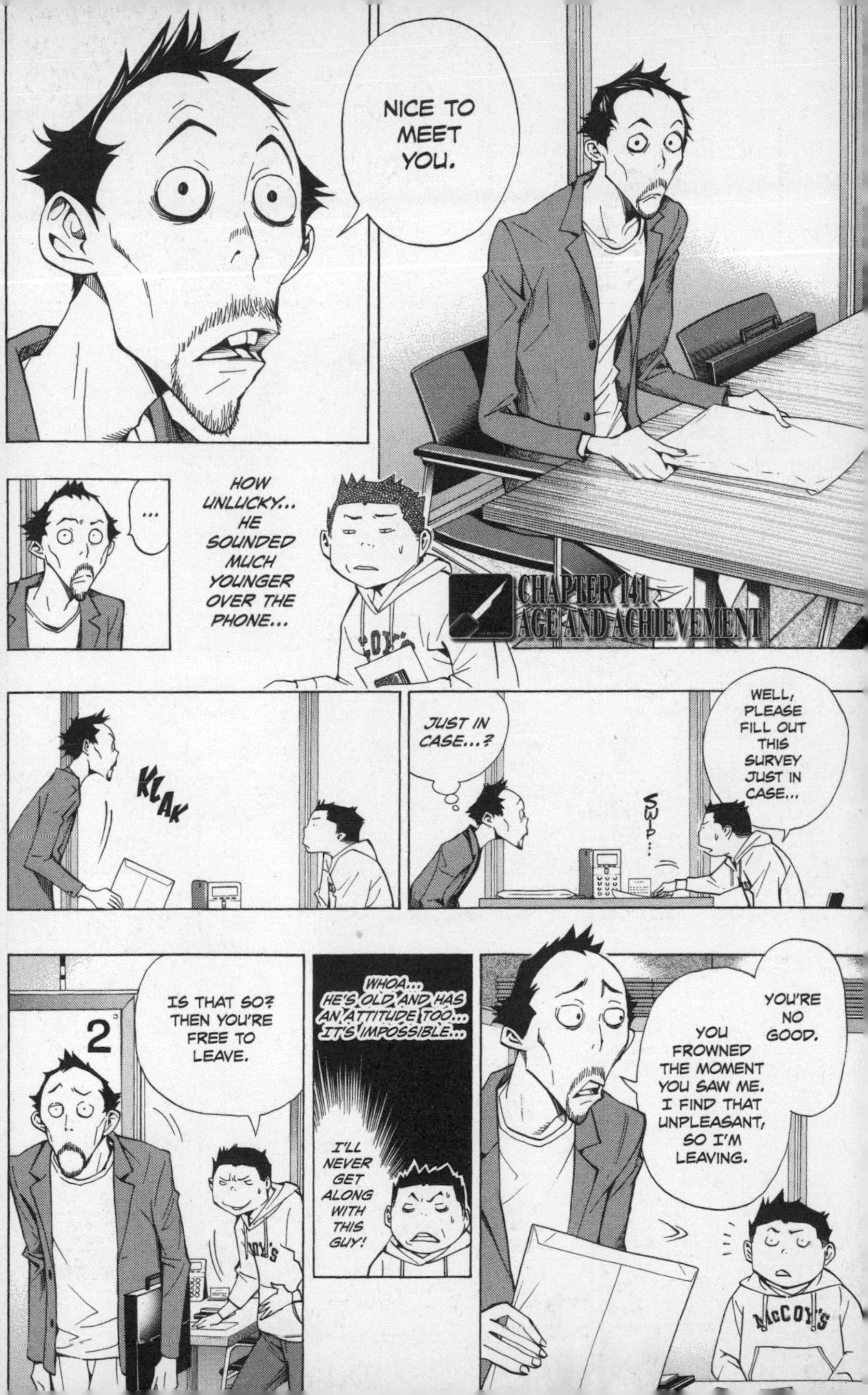
NICE TO MEET YOU.
CHAPTER 141
AGE AND ACHIEVEMENT
HOW UNLUCKY... HE SOUNDED MUCH YOUNGER OVER THE PHONE...
...
WELL, PLEASE FILL OUT THIS SURVEY JUST IN CASE...
SWIP...
JUST IN CASE...?
KLAK
YOU'RE NO GOOD.
YOU FROWNED THE MOMENT YOU SAW ME. I FIND THAT UNPLEASANT, SO I'M LEAVING.
McCOY'S
WHOA... HE'S OLD, AND HAS AN ATTITUDE TOO... IT'S IMPOSSIBLE...
I'LL NEVER GET ALONG WITH THIS GUY!
IS THAT SO? THEN YOU'RE FREE TO LEAVE.
2

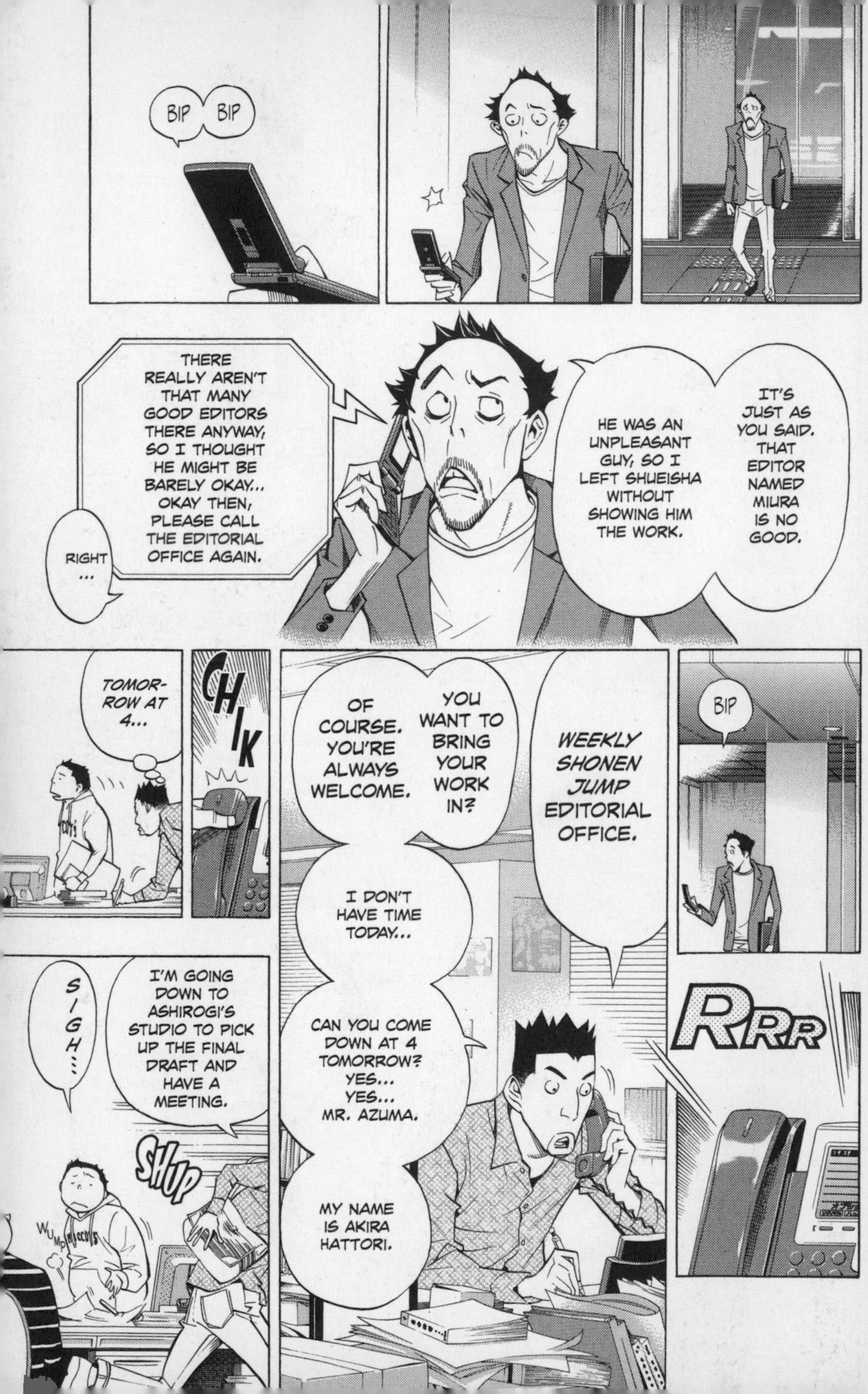
BIP BIP
IT'S JUST AS YOU SAID. THAT EDITOR NAMED MIURA IS NO GOOD.
HE WAS AN UNPLEASANT GUY, SO I LEFT SHUEISHA WITHOUT SHOWING HIM THE WORK.
THERE REALLY AREN'T THAT MANY GOOD EDITORS THERE ANYWAY, SO I THOUGHT HE MIGHT BE BARELY OKAY... OKAY THEN, PLEASE CALL THE EDITORIAL OFFICE AGAIN.
RIGHT...
BIP
RRR
WEEKLY SHONEN JUMP EDITORIAL OFFICE.
YOU WANT TO BRING YOUR WORK IN?
OF COURSE. YOU'RE ALWAYS WELCOME.
I DON'T HAVE TIME TODAY...
CAN YOU COME DOWN AT 4 TOMORROW? YES... YES... MR. AZUMA.
MY NAME IS AKIRA HATTORI.
CHIK
TOMOR-ROW AT 4...
I'M GOING DOWN TO ASHIROGI'S STUDIO TO PICK UP THE FINAL DRAFT AND HAVE A MEETING.
SHUP
SIGH...
WUMP

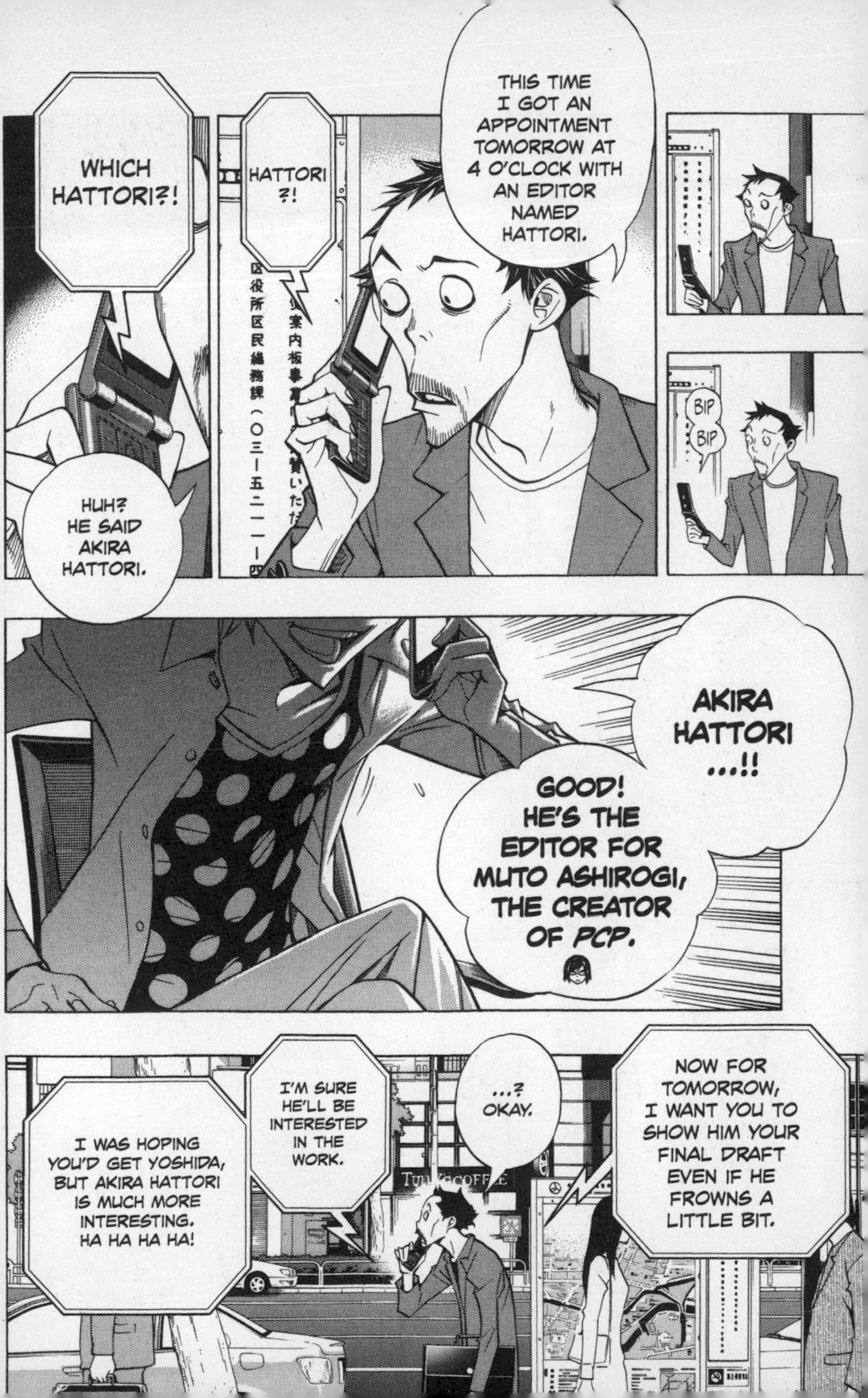
BIP
BIP
THIS TIME I GOT AN APPOINTMENT TOMORROW AT 4 O'CLOCK WITH AN EDITOR NAMED HATTORI.
HATTORI ?!
区役所区民総務課（〇三－五二一一－四
WHICH HATTORI?!
HUH? HE SAID AKIRA HATTORI.
AKIRA HATTORI ...!!
GOOD! HE'S THE EDITOR FOR MUTO ASHIROGI, THE CREATOR OF PCP.
NOW FOR TOMORROW, I WANT YOU TO SHOW HIM YOUR FINAL DRAFT EVEN IF HE FROWNS A LITTLE BIT.
...? OKAY.
I'M SURE HE'LL BE INTERESTED IN THE WORK.
I WAS HOPING YOU'D GET YOSHIDA, BUT AKIRA HATTORI IS MUCH MORE INTERESTING. HA HA HA HA!

READ THIS WAY

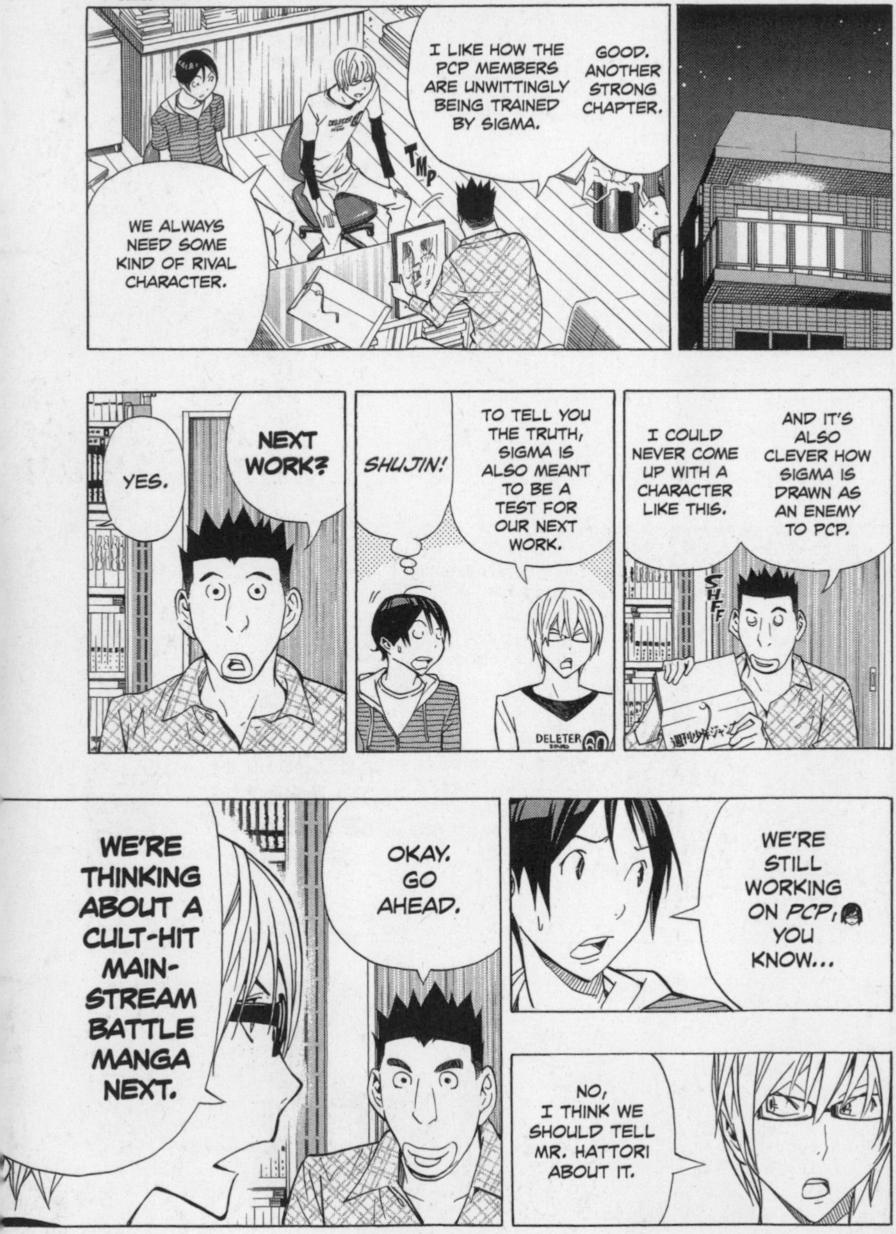
GOOD. ANOTHER STRONG CHAPTER.
I LIKE HOW THE PCP MEMBERS ARE UNWITTINGLY BEING TRAINED BY SIGMA.
TMP
WE ALWAYS NEED SOME KIND OF RIVAL CHARACTER.
AND IT'S ALSO CLEVER HOW SIGMA IS DRAWN AS AN ENEMY TO PCP.
I COULD NEVER COME UP WITH A CHARACTER LIKE THIS.
SHFF
TO TELL YOU THE TRUTH, SIGMA IS ALSO MEANT TO BE A TEST FOR OUR NEXT WORK.
SHUJIN!
DELETER
NEXT WORK?
YES.
WE'RE STILL WORKING ON PCP, YOU KNOW...
NO, I THINK WE SHOULD TELL MR. HATTORI ABOUT IT.
OKAY. GO AHEAD.
WE'RE THINKING ABOUT A CULT-HIT MAIN-STREAM BATTLE MANGA NEXT.

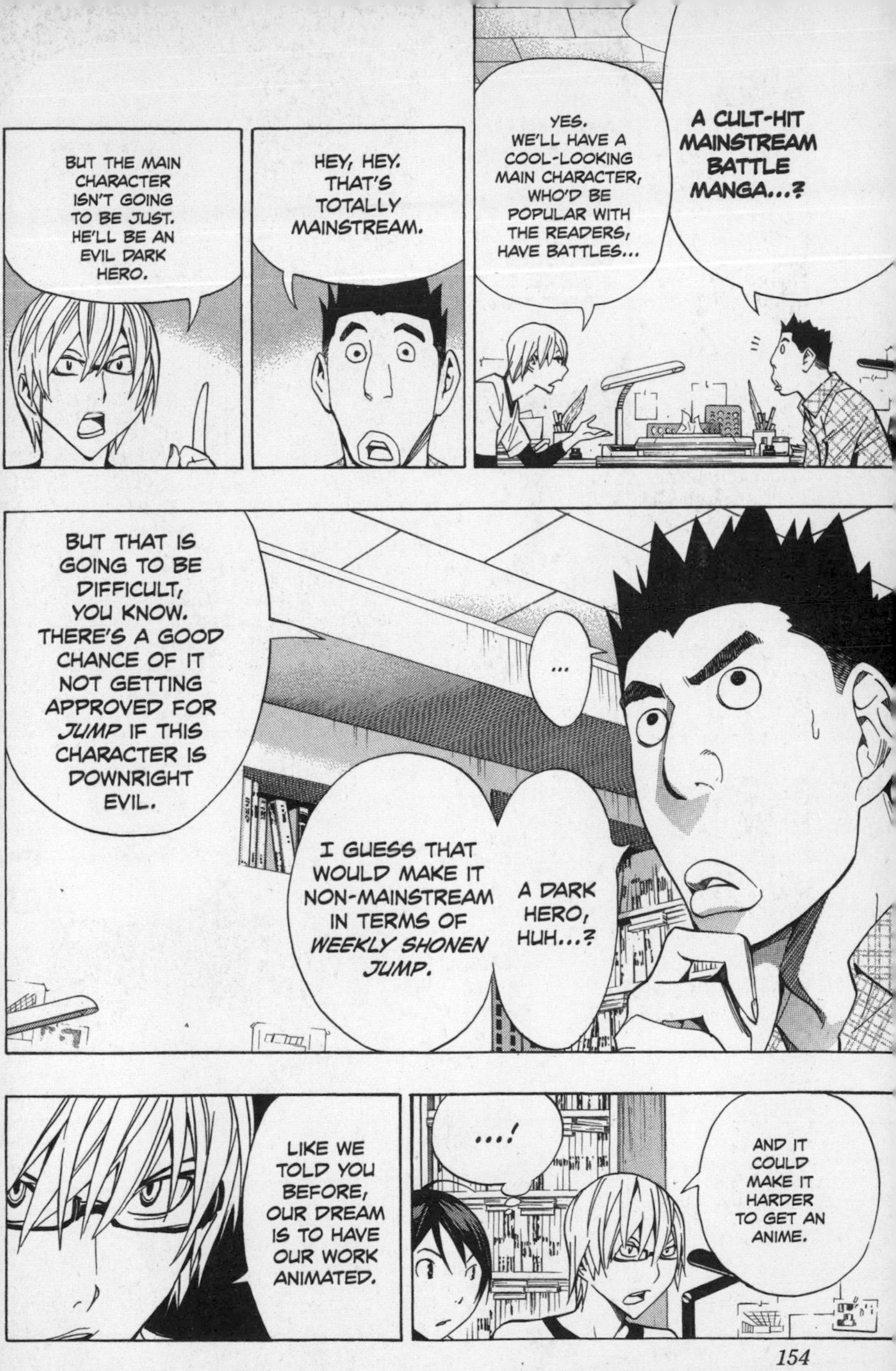
A CULT-HIT MAINSTREAM BATTLE MANGA...?
YES. WE'LL HAVE A COOL-LOOKING MAIN CHARACTER, WHO'D BE POPULAR WITH THE READERS, HAVE BATTLES...
HEY, HEY. THAT'S TOTALLY MAINSTREAM.
BUT THE MAIN CHARACTER ISN'T GOING TO BE JUST. HE'LL BE AN EVIL DARK HERO.
...
A DARK HERO, HUH...?
I GUESS THAT WOULD MAKE IT NON-MAINSTREAM IN TERMS OF *WEEKLY SHONEN JUMP*.
BUT THAT IS GOING TO BE DIFFICULT, YOU KNOW. THERE'S A GOOD CHANCE OF IT NOT GETTING APPROVED FOR *JUMP* IF THIS CHARACTER IS DOWNRIGHT EVIL.
AND IT COULD MAKE IT HARDER TO GET AN ANIME.
...!
LIKE WE TOLD YOU BEFORE, OUR DREAM IS TO HAVE OUR WORK ANIMATED.

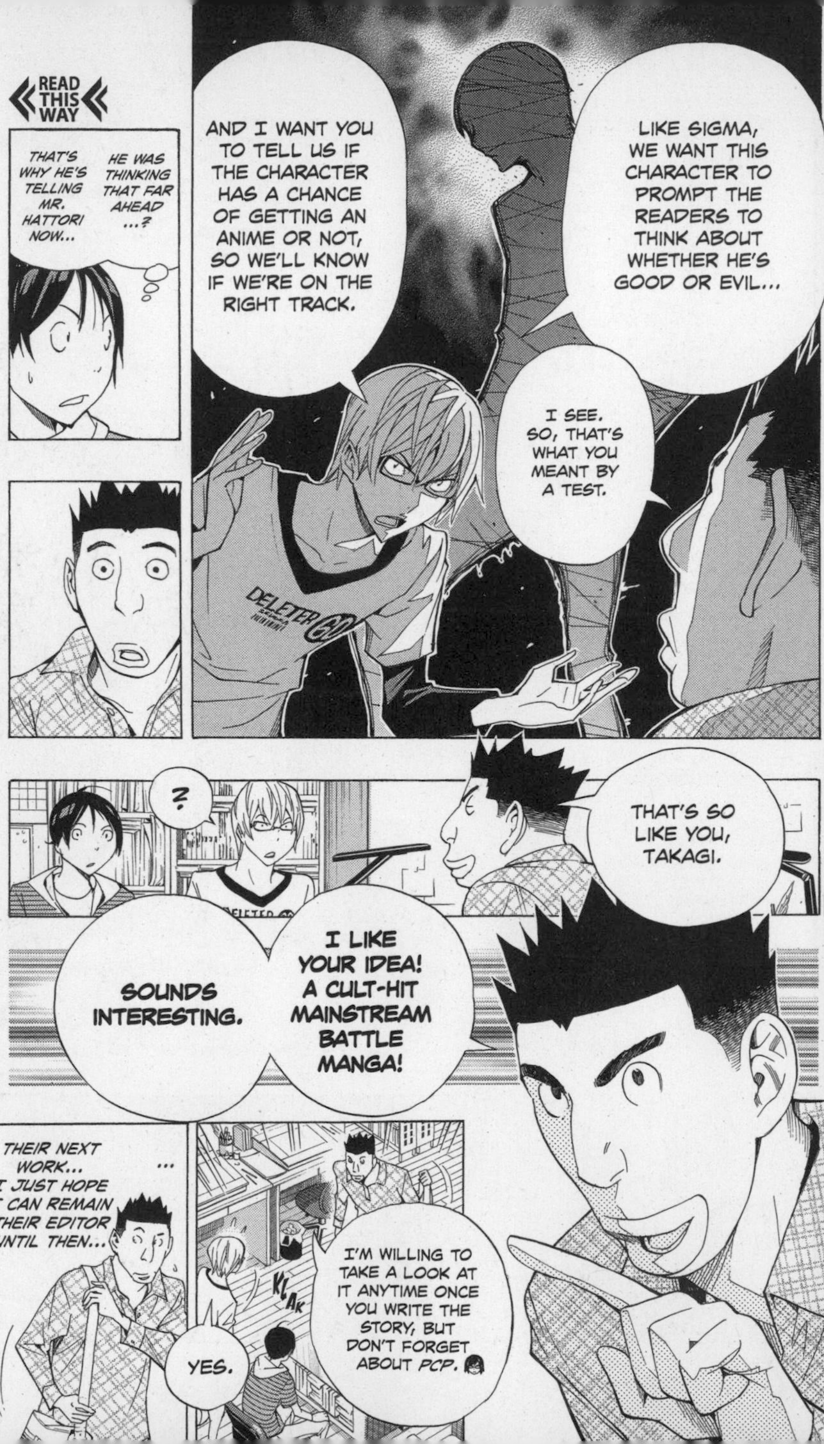
READ THIS WAY
LIKE SIGMA, WE WANT THIS CHARACTER TO PROMPT THE READERS TO THINK ABOUT WHETHER HE'S GOOD OR EVIL...
AND I WANT YOU TO TELL US IF THE CHARACTER HAS A CHANCE OF GETTING AN ANIME OR NOT, SO WE'LL KNOW IF WE'RE ON THE RIGHT TRACK.
I SEE. SO, THAT'S WHAT YOU MEANT BY A TEST.
HE WAS THINKING THAT FAR AHEAD ...?
THAT'S WHY HE'S TELLING MR. HATTORI NOW...
THAT'S SO LIKE YOU, TAKAGI.
?
I LIKE YOUR IDEA! A CULT-HIT MAINSTREAM BATTLE MANGA!
SOUNDS INTERESTING.
I'M WILLING TO TAKE A LOOK AT IT ANYTIME ONCE YOU WRITE THE STORY, BUT DON'T FORGET ABOUT *PCP*.
KLAK
YES.
...
THEIR NEXT WORK... I JUST HOPE I CAN REMAIN THEIR EDITOR UNTIL THEN...

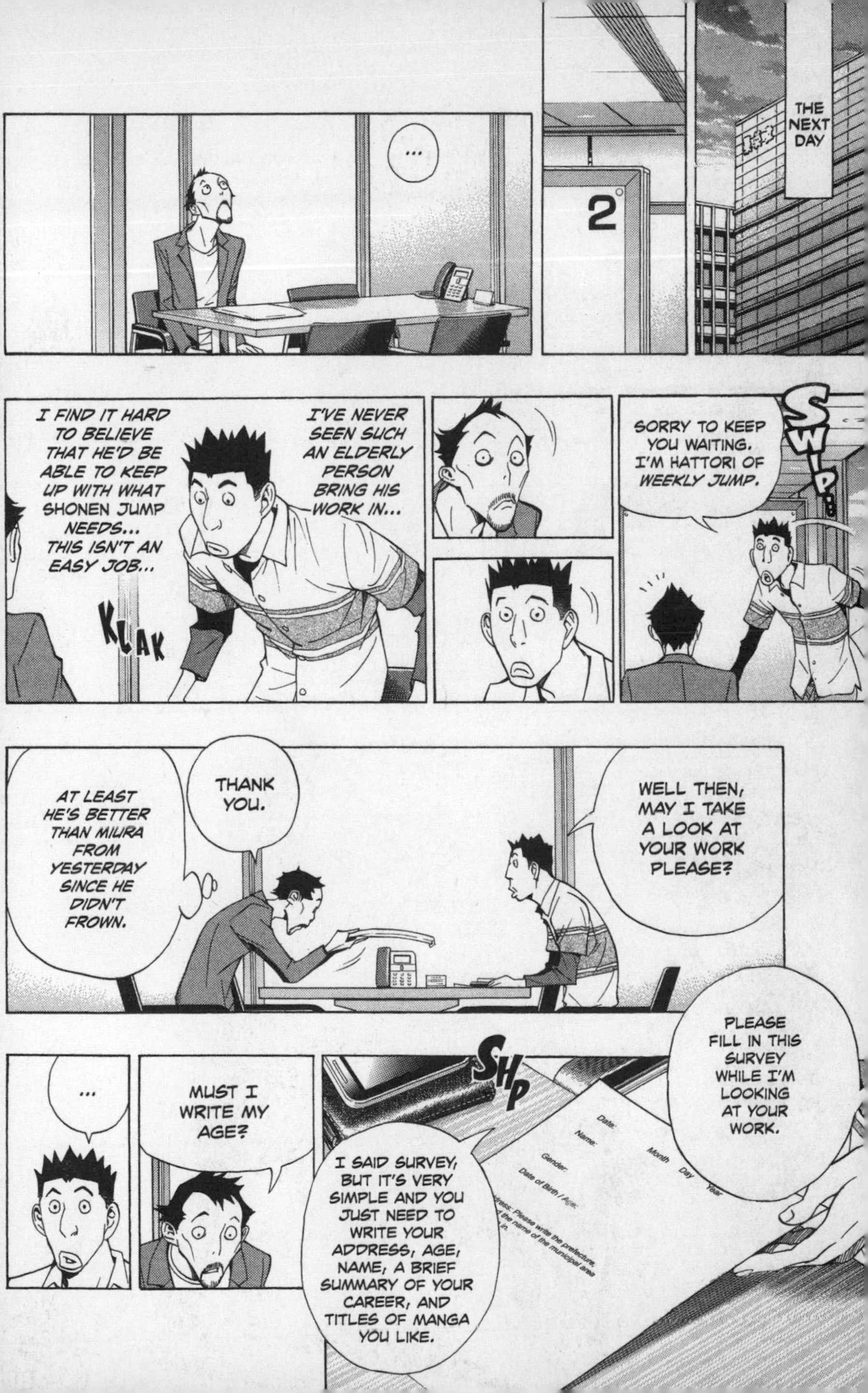
THE NEXT DAY
2
...
SWIP!!
SORRY TO KEEP YOU WAITING. I'M HATTORI OF WEEKLY JUMP.
I'VE NEVER SEEN SUCH AN ELDERLY PERSON BRING HIS WORK IN...
I FIND IT HARD TO BELIEVE THAT HE'D BE ABLE TO KEEP UP WITH WHAT SHONEN JUMP NEEDS... THIS ISN'T AN EASY JOB...
KLAK
WELL THEN, MAY I TAKE A LOOK AT YOUR WORK PLEASE?
THANK YOU.
AT LEAST HE'S BETTER THAN MIURA FROM YESTERDAY SINCE HE DIDN'T FROWN.
SHP
PLEASE FILL IN THIS SURVEY WHILE I'M LOOKING AT YOUR WORK.
Date:
Month
Day
Year
Name:
Gender:
Date of Birth / Age:
I SAID SURVEY, BUT IT'S VERY SIMPLE AND YOU JUST NEED TO WRITE YOUR ADDRESS, AGE, NAME, A BRIEF SUMMARY OF YOUR CAREER, AND TITLES OF MANGA YOU LIKE.
MUST I WRITE MY AGE?
...

READ THIS WAY

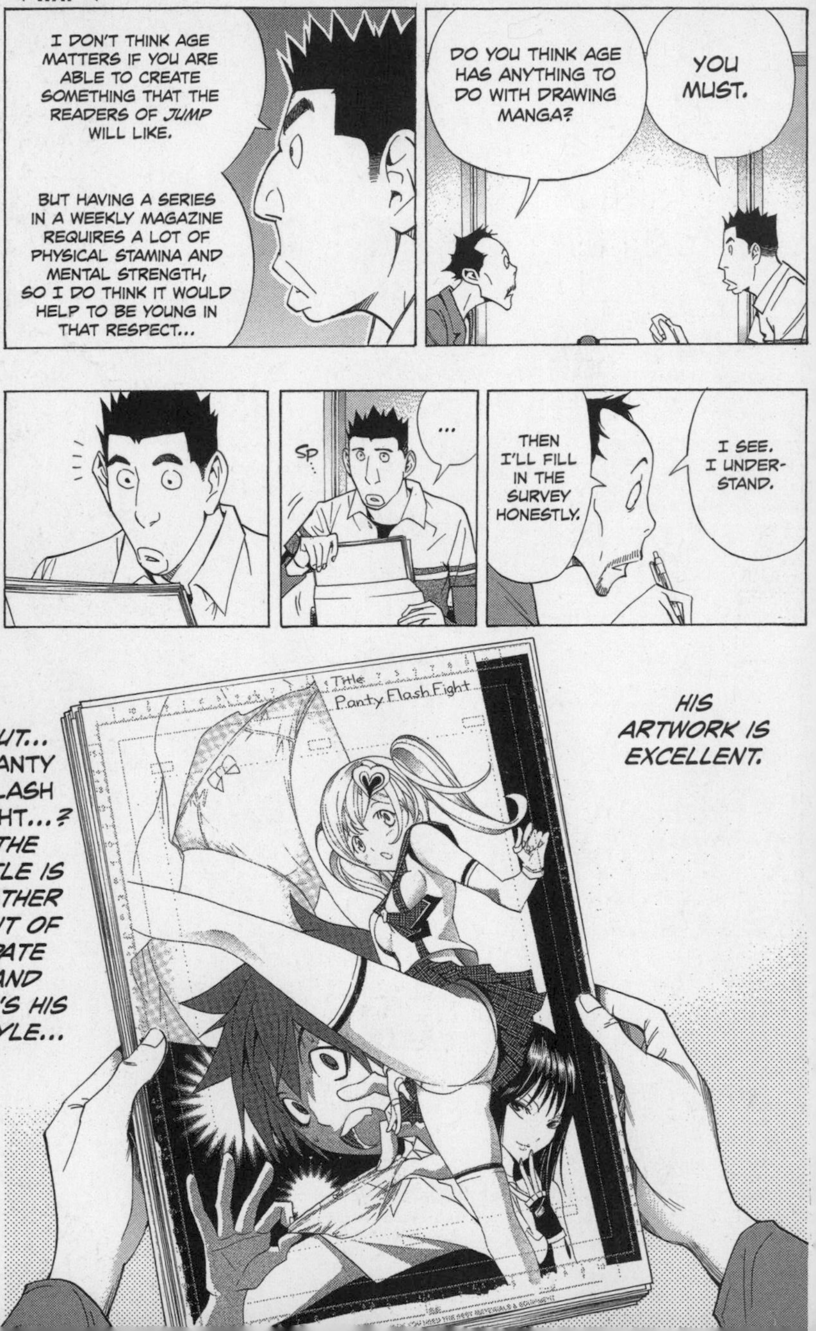
YOU MUST.
DO YOU THINK AGE HAS ANYTHING TO DO WITH DRAWING MANGA?
I DON'T THINK AGE MATTERS IF YOU ARE ABLE TO CREATE SOMETHING THAT THE READERS OF *JUMP* WILL LIKE.
BUT HAVING A SERIES IN A WEEKLY MAGAZINE REQUIRES A LOT OF PHYSICAL STAMINA AND MENTAL STRENGTH, SO I DO THINK IT WOULD HELP TO BE YOUNG IN THAT RESPECT...
I SEE. I UNDERSTAND.
THEN I'LL FILL IN THE SURVEY HONESTLY.
...
SP
Title
Panty Flash Fight
HIS ARTWORK IS EXCELLENT.
BUT... PANTY FLASH FIGHT...? THE TITLE IS RATHER OUT OF DATE AND SO'S HIS STYLE...

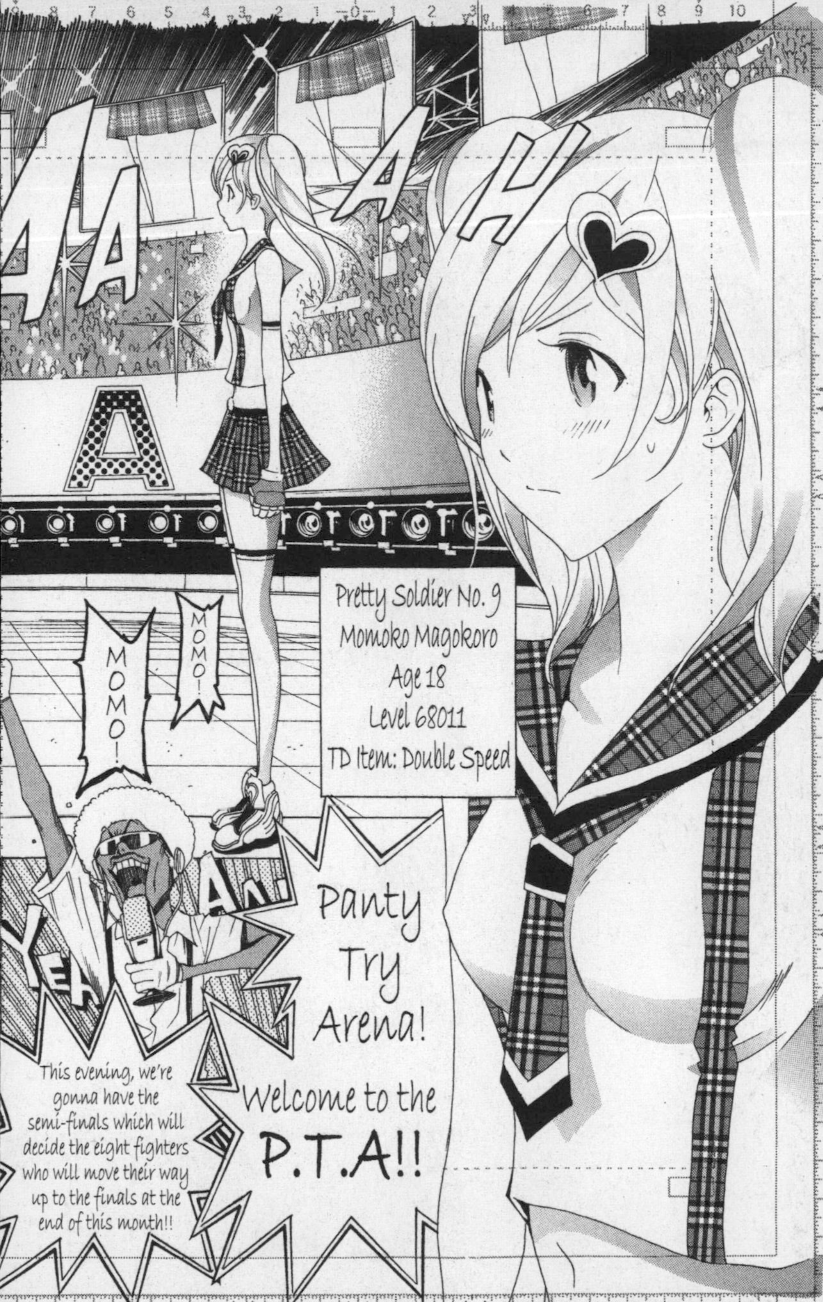
AAAAAH
Pretty Soldier No. 9
Momoko Magokoro
Age 18
Level 68011
TD Item: Double Speed
MOMO!
MOMO!
Panty Try Arena!
Welcome to the P.T.A!!
This evening, we're gonna have the semi-finals which will decide the eight fighters who will move their way up to the finals at the end of this month!!

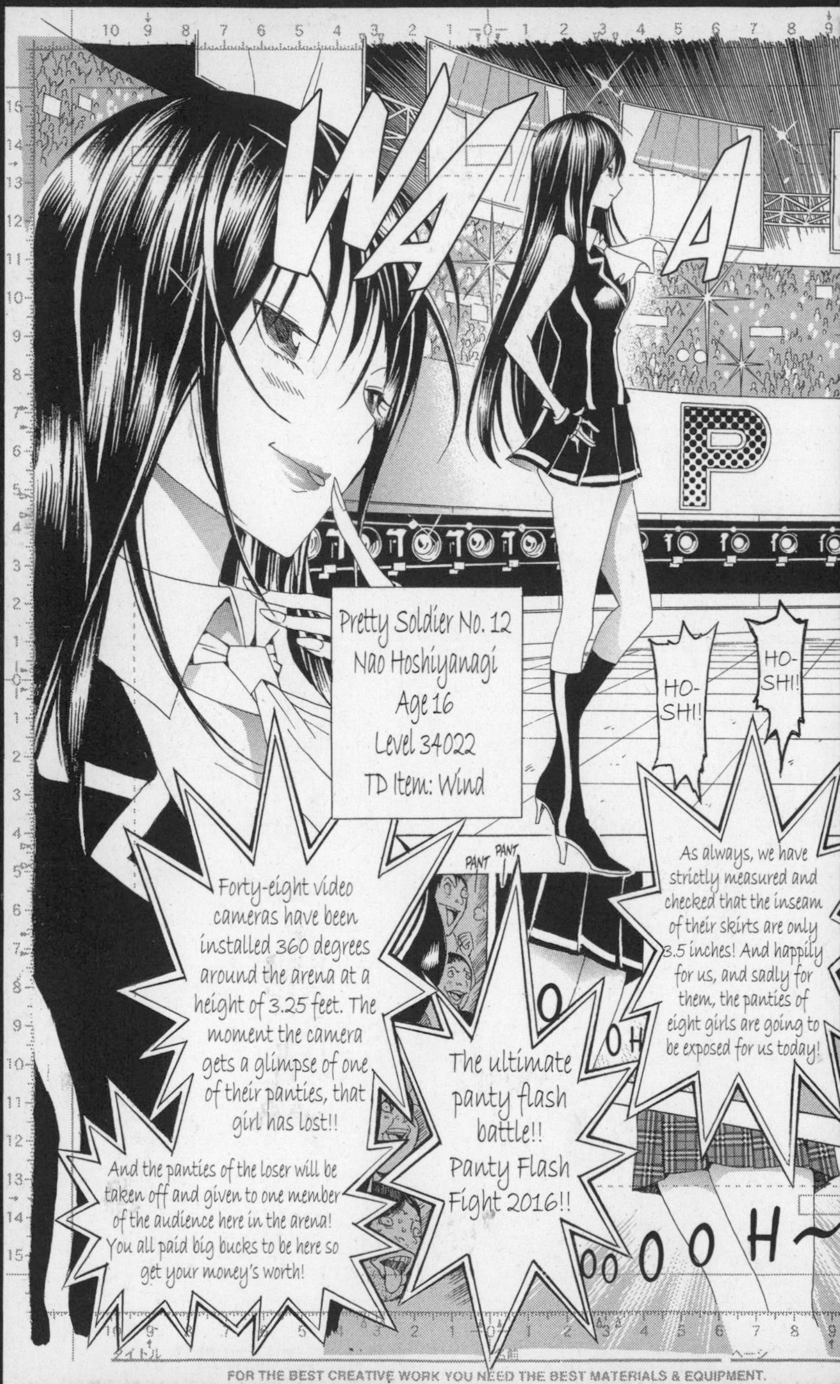
WA A
P
HO-SHI!!
HO-SHI!!
Pretty Soldier No. 12 Nao Hoshiyanagi Age 16 Level 34022 TD Item: Wind
As always, we have strictly measured and checked that the inseam of their skirts are only 3.5 inches! And happily for us, and sadly for them, the panties of eight girls are going to be exposed for us today!
PANT PANT
Forty-eight video cameras have been installed 360 degrees around the arena at a height of 3.25 feet. The moment the camera gets a glimpse of one of their panties, that girl has lost!!
O OH
The ultimate panty flash battle!! Panty Flash Fight 2016!!
And the panties of the loser will be taken off and given to one member of the audience here in the arena! You all paid big bucks to be here so get your money's worth!
oo O O H~
FOR THE BEST CREATIVE WORK YOU NEED THE BEST MATERIALS & EQUIPMENT.

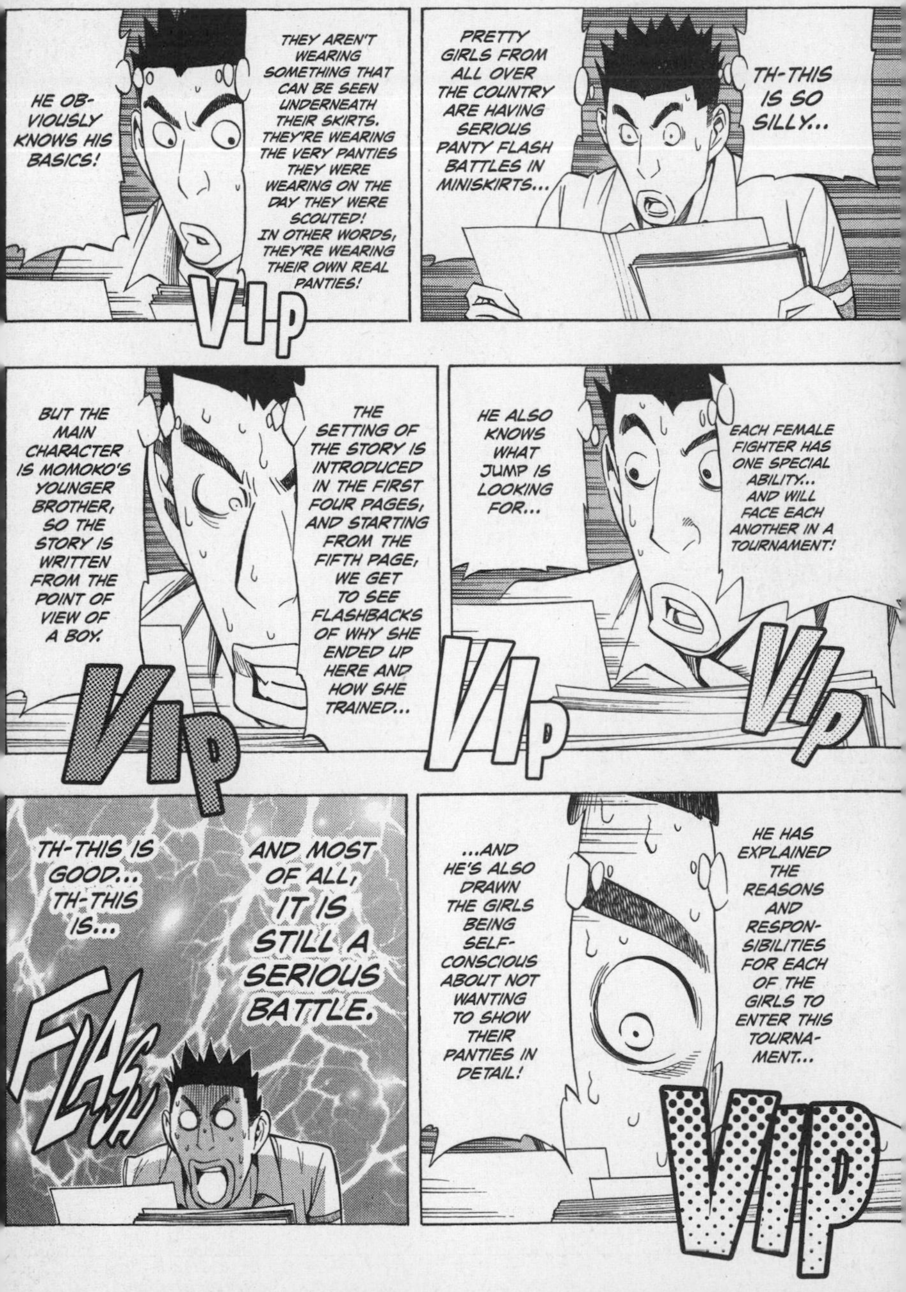
TH-THIS IS SO SILLY...
PRETTY GIRLS FROM ALL OVER THE COUNTRY ARE HAVING SERIOUS PANTY FLASH BATTLES IN MINISKIRTS...
THEY AREN'T WEARING SOMETHING THAT CAN BE SEEN UNDERNEATH THEIR SKIRTS. THEY'RE WEARING THE VERY PANTIES THEY WERE WEARING ON THE DAY THEY WERE SCOUTED! IN OTHER WORDS, THEY'RE WEARING THEIR OWN REAL PANTIES!
HE OBVIOUSLY KNOWS HIS BASICS!
VIP
EACH FEMALE FIGHTER HAS ONE SPECIAL ABILITY... AND WILL FACE EACH ANOTHER IN A TOURNAMENT!
HE ALSO KNOWS WHAT JUMP IS LOOKING FOR...
VIP
VIP
THE SETTING OF THE STORY IS INTRODUCED IN THE FIRST FOUR PAGES, AND STARTING FROM THE FIFTH PAGE, WE GET TO SEE FLASHBACKS OF WHY SHE ENDED UP HERE AND HOW SHE TRAINED...
BUT THE MAIN CHARACTER IS MOMOKO'S YOUNGER BROTHER, SO THE STORY IS WRITTEN FROM THE POINT OF VIEW OF A BOY.
VIP
HE HAS EXPLAINED THE REASONS AND RESPONSIBILITIES FOR EACH OF THE GIRLS TO ENTER THIS TOURNAMENT...
...AND HE'S ALSO DRAWN THE GIRLS BEING SELF-CONSCIOUS ABOUT NOT WANTING TO SHOW THEIR PANTIES IN DETAIL!
VIP
AND MOST OF ALL, IT IS STILL A SERIOUS BATTLE.
TH-THIS IS GOOD... TH-THIS IS...
FLASH

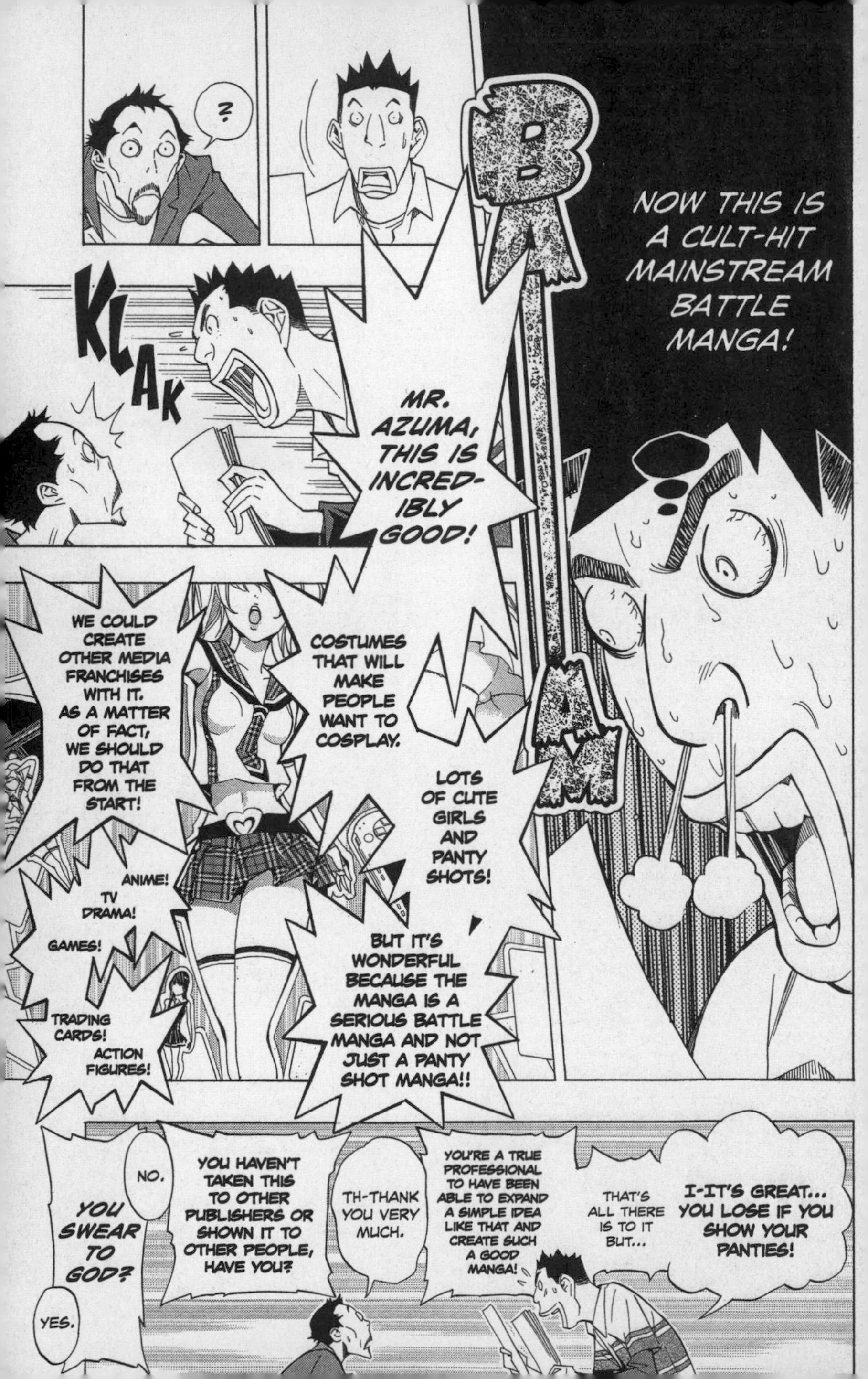
BAM
NOW THIS IS A CULT-HIT MAINSTREAM BATTLE MANGA!
?
KLAK
MR. AZUMA, THIS IS INCREDIBLY GOOD!
COSTUMES THAT WILL MAKE PEOPLE WANT TO COSPLAY.
LOTS OF CUTE GIRLS AND PANTY SHOTS!
WE COULD CREATE OTHER MEDIA FRANCHISES WITH IT. AS A MATTER OF FACT, WE SHOULD DO THAT FROM THE START!
BUT IT'S WONDERFUL BECAUSE THE MANGA IS A SERIOUS BATTLE MANGA AND NOT JUST A PANTY SHOT MANGA!!
ANIME!
TV DRAMA!
GAMES!
TRADING CARDS!
ACTION FIGURES!
I-IT'S GREAT... YOU LOSE IF YOU SHOW YOUR PANTIES!
THAT'S ALL THERE IS TO IT BUT...
YOU'RE A TRUE PROFESSIONAL TO HAVE BEEN ABLE TO EXPAND A SIMPLE IDEA LIKE THAT AND CREATE SUCH A GOOD MANGA!
TH-THANK YOU VERY MUCH.
YOU HAVEN'T TAKEN THIS TO OTHER PUBLISHERS OR SHOWN IT TO OTHER PEOPLE, HAVE YOU?
NO.
YOU SWEAR TO GOD?
YES.

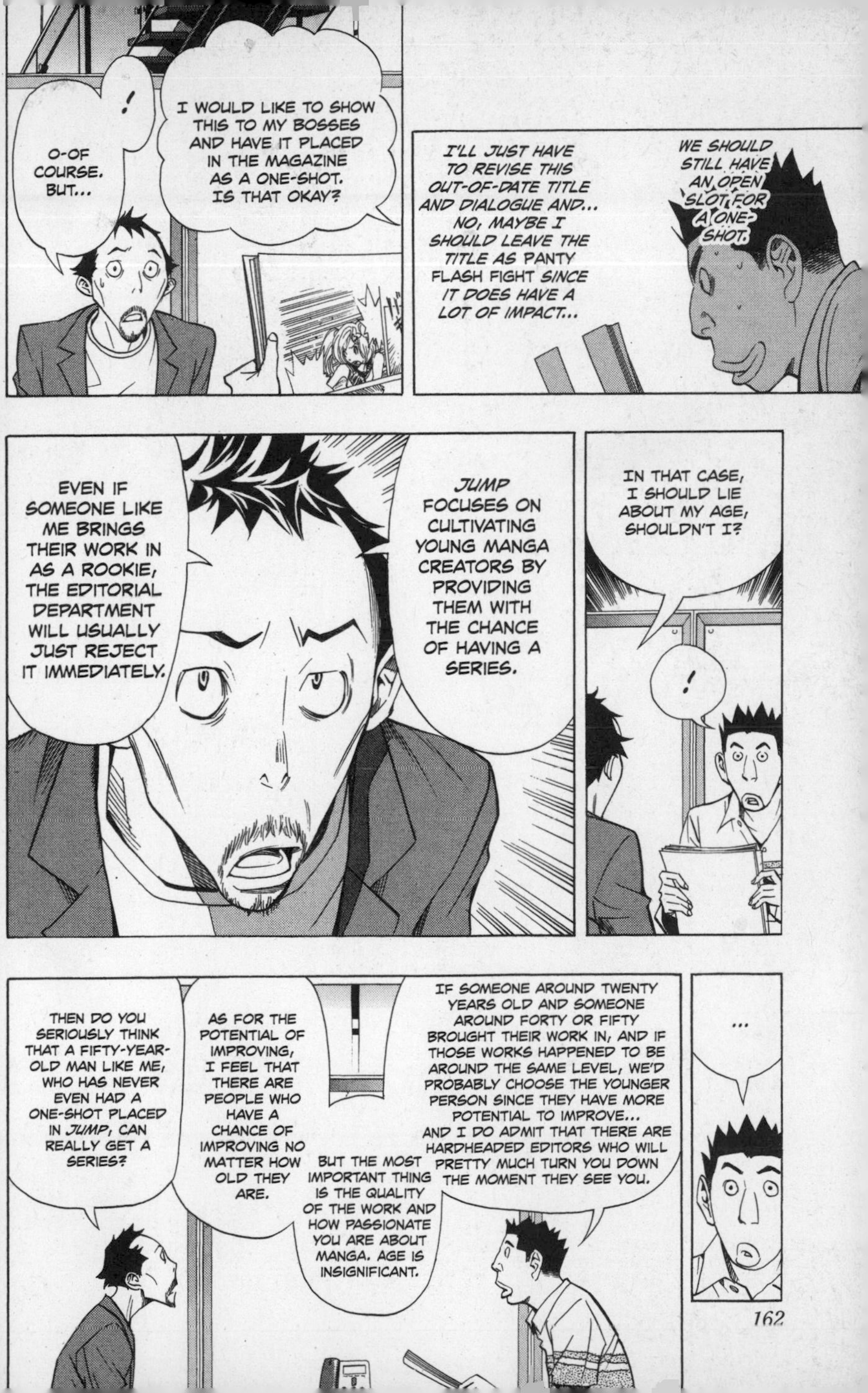
WE SHOULD STILL HAVE AN OPEN SLOT FOR A ONE-SHOT.
I'LL JUST HAVE TO REVISE THIS OUT-OF-DATE TITLE AND DIALOGUE AND... NO, MAYBE I SHOULD LEAVE THE TITLE AS PANTY FLASH FIGHT SINCE IT DOES HAVE A LOT OF IMPACT...
I WOULD LIKE TO SHOW THIS TO MY BOSSES AND HAVE IT PLACED IN THE MAGAZINE AS A ONE-SHOT. IS THAT OKAY?
!
O-OF COURSE. BUT...
IN THAT CASE, I SHOULD LIE ABOUT MY AGE, SHOULDN'T I?
!
JUMP FOCUSES ON CULTIVATING YOUNG MANGA CREATORS BY PROVIDING THEM WITH THE CHANCE OF HAVING A SERIES.
EVEN IF SOMEONE LIKE ME BRINGS THEIR WORK IN AS A ROOKIE, THE EDITORIAL DEPARTMENT WILL USUALLY JUST REJECT IT IMMEDIATELY.
...
IF SOMEONE AROUND TWENTY YEARS OLD AND SOMEONE AROUND FORTY OR FIFTY BROUGHT THEIR WORK IN, AND IF THOSE WORKS HAPPENED TO BE AROUND THE SAME LEVEL, WE'D PROBABLY CHOOSE THE YOUNGER PERSON SINCE THEY HAVE MORE POTENTIAL TO IMPROVE... AND I DO ADMIT THAT THERE ARE HARDHEADED EDITORS WHO WILL PRETTY MUCH TURN YOU DOWN THE MOMENT THEY SEE YOU.
BUT THE MOST IMPORTANT THING IS THE QUALITY OF THE WORK AND HOW PASSIONATE YOU ARE ABOUT MANGA. AGE IS INSIGNIFICANT.
AS FOR THE POTENTIAL OF IMPROVING, I FEEL THAT THERE ARE PEOPLE WHO HAVE A CHANCE OF IMPROVING NO MATTER HOW OLD THEY ARE.
THEN DO YOU SERIOUSLY THINK THAT A FIFTY-YEAR-OLD MAN LIKE ME, WHO HAS NEVER EVEN HAD A ONE-SHOT PLACED IN JUMP, CAN REALLY GET A SERIES?

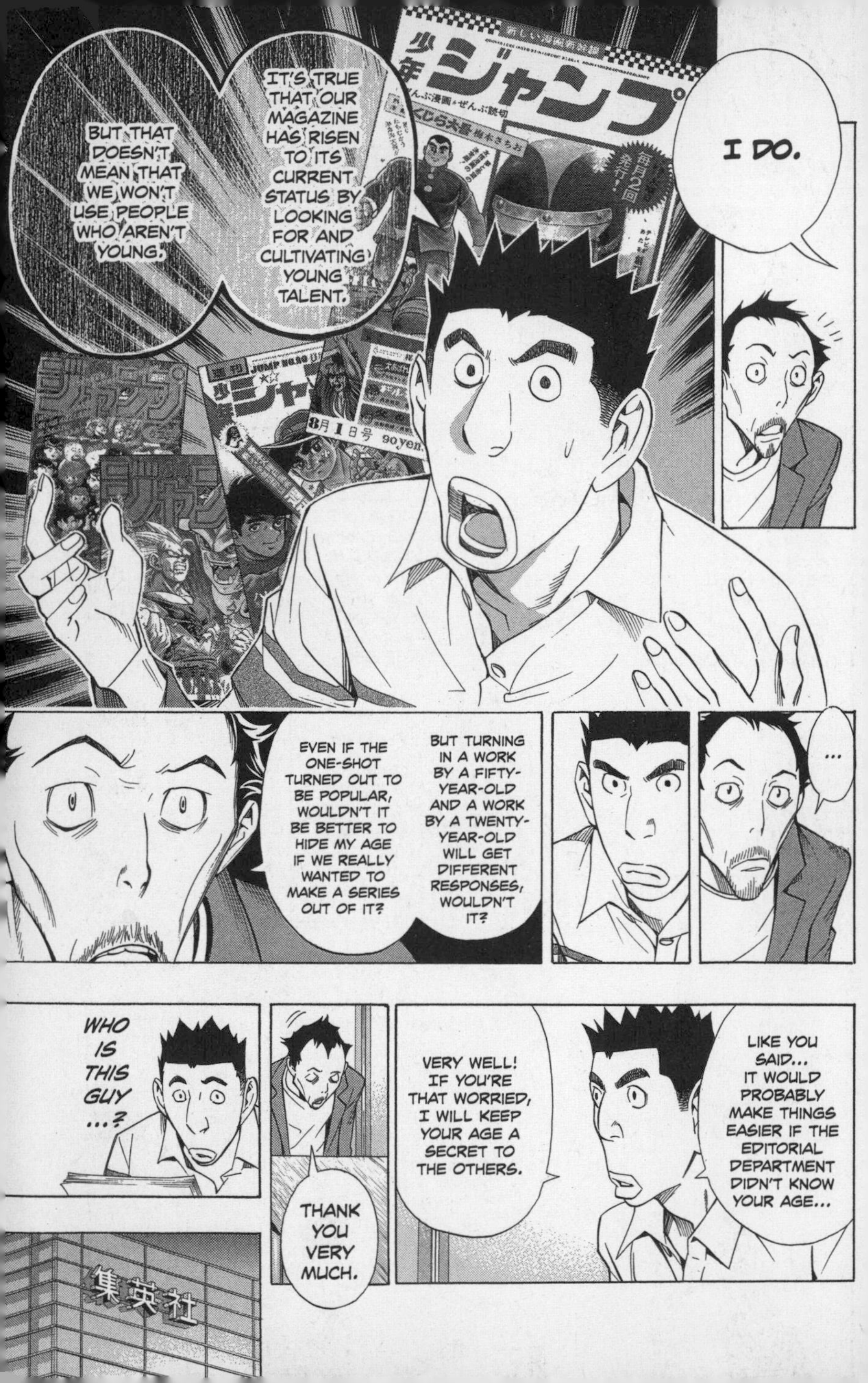

I DO.
少年ジャンプ
毎月2回発行!
IT'S TRUE THAT OUR MAGAZINE HAS RISEN TO ITS CURRENT STATUS BY LOOKING FOR AND CULTIVATING YOUNG TALENT.
BUT THAT DOESN'T MEAN THAT WE WON'T USE PEOPLE WHO AREN'T YOUNG.
8月1日号 90yen.
...
BUT TURNING IN A WORK BY A FIFTY-YEAR-OLD AND A WORK BY A TWENTY-YEAR-OLD WILL GET DIFFERENT RESPONSES, WOULDN'T IT?
EVEN IF THE ONE-SHOT TURNED OUT TO BE POPULAR, WOULDN'T IT BE BETTER TO HIDE MY AGE IF WE REALLY WANTED TO MAKE A SERIES OUT OF IT?
LIKE YOU SAID... IT WOULD PROBABLY MAKE THINGS EASIER IF THE EDITORIAL DEPARTMENT DIDN'T KNOW YOUR AGE...
VERY WELL! IF YOU'RE THAT WORRIED, I WILL KEEP YOUR AGE A SECRET TO THE OTHERS.
THANK YOU VERY MUCH.
WHO IS THIS GUY ...?
集英社

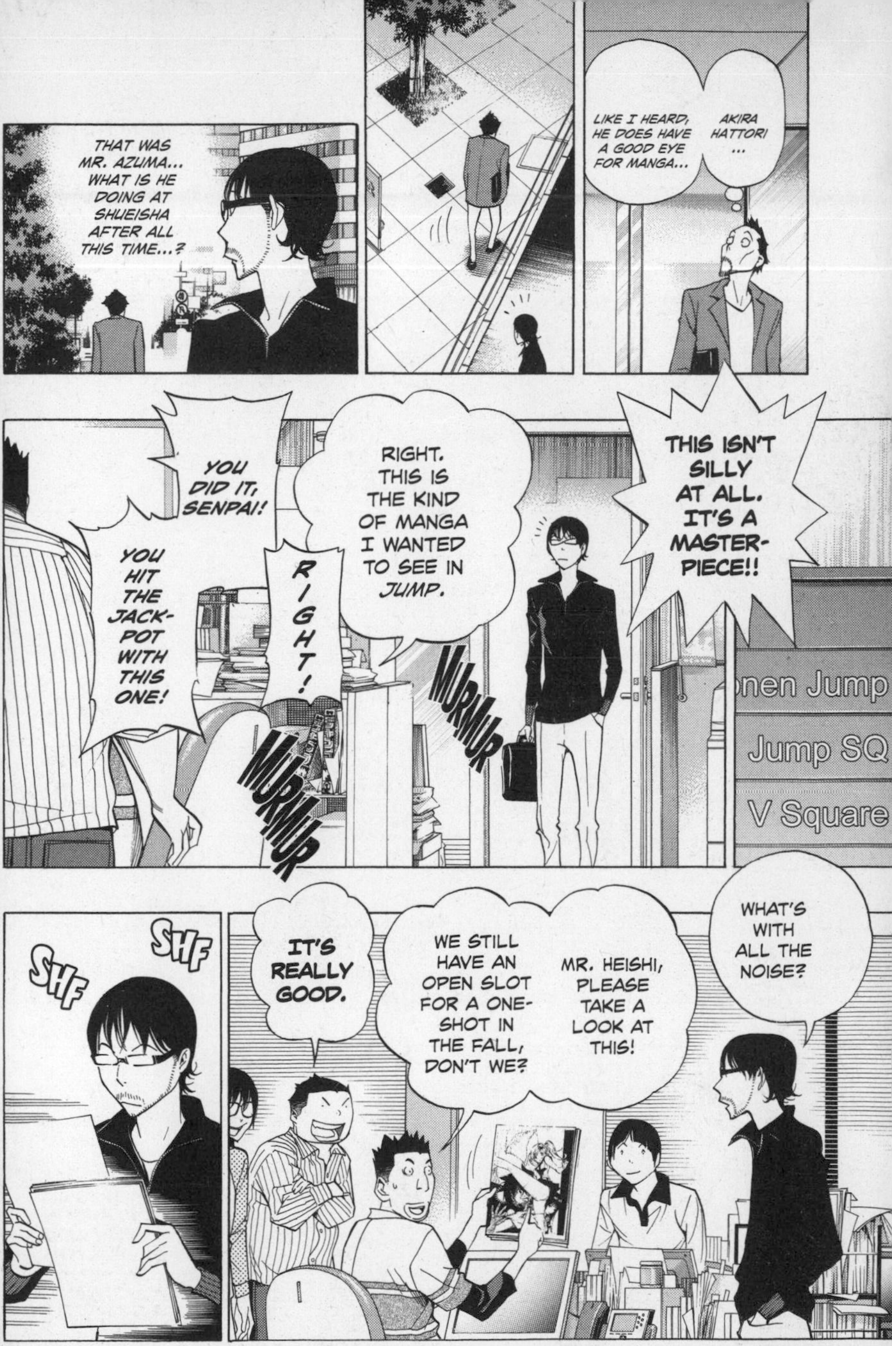
AKIRA HATTORI ...
LIKE I HEARD, HE DOES HAVE A GOOD EYE FOR MANGA...
THAT WAS MR. AZUMA... WHAT IS HE DOING AT SHUEISHA AFTER ALL THIS TIME...?
THIS ISN'T SILLY AT ALL. IT'S A MASTERPIECE!!
Jump SQ
V Square
RIGHT. THIS IS THE KIND OF MANGA I WANTED TO SEE IN JUMP.
MURMUR
RIGHT!
YOU DID IT, SENPAI!
YOU HIT THE JACKPOT WITH THIS ONE!
MURMUR
WHAT'S WITH ALL THE NOISE?
MR. HEISHI, PLEASE TAKE A LOOK AT THIS!
WE STILL HAVE AN OPEN SLOT FOR A ONE-SHOT IN THE FALL, DON'T WE?
IT'S REALLY GOOD.
SHF
SHF

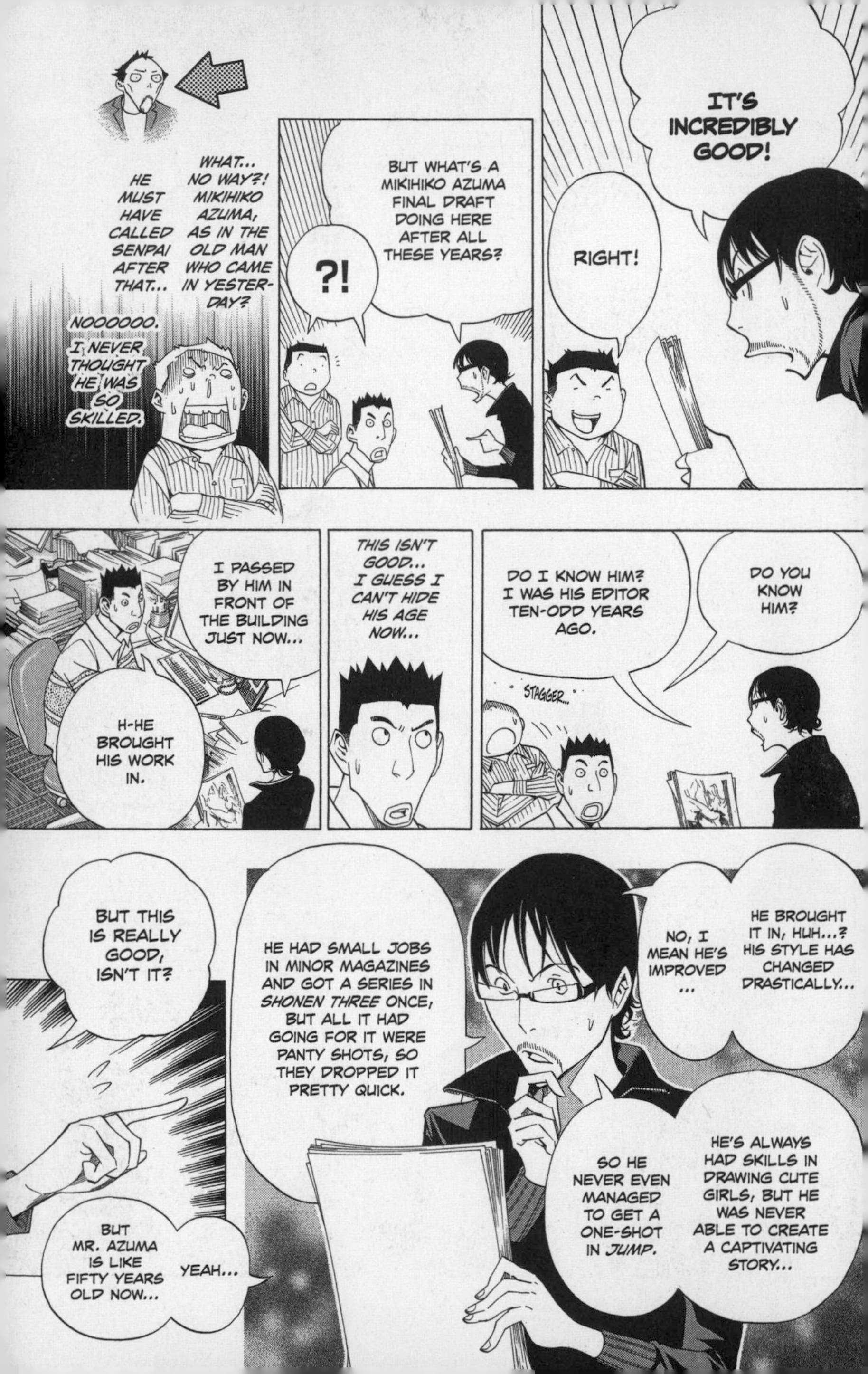
IT'S INCREDIBLY GOOD!
RIGHT!
BUT WHAT'S A MIKIHIKO AZUMA FINAL DRAFT DOING HERE AFTER ALL THESE YEARS?
?!
WHAT... NO WAY?! MIKIHIKO AZUMA, AS IN THE OLD MAN WHO CAME IN YESTERDAY?
HE MUST HAVE CALLED SENPAI AFTER THAT...
NOOOOOO. I NEVER THOUGHT HE WAS SO SKILLED.
DO YOU KNOW HIM?
DO I KNOW HIM? I WAS HIS EDITOR TEN-ODD YEARS AGO.
STAGGER...
THIS ISN'T GOOD... I GUESS I CAN'T HIDE HIS AGE NOW...
I PASSED BY HIM IN FRONT OF THE BUILDING JUST NOW...
H-HE BROUGHT HIS WORK IN.
HE BROUGHT IT IN, HUH...? HIS STYLE HAS CHANGED DRASTICALLY...
NO, I MEAN HE'S IMPROVED...
HE HAD SMALL JOBS IN MINOR MAGAZINES AND GOT A SERIES IN *SHONEN THREE* ONCE, BUT ALL IT HAD GOING FOR IT WERE PANTY SHOTS, SO THEY DROPPED IT PRETTY QUICK.
BUT THIS IS REALLY GOOD, ISN'T IT?
HE'S ALWAYS HAD SKILLS IN DRAWING CUTE GIRLS, BUT HE WAS NEVER ABLE TO CREATE A CAPTIVATING STORY...
SO HE NEVER EVEN MANAGED TO GET A ONE-SHOT IN *JUMP*.
YEAH...
BUT MR. AZUMA IS LIKE FIFTY YEARS OLD NOW...

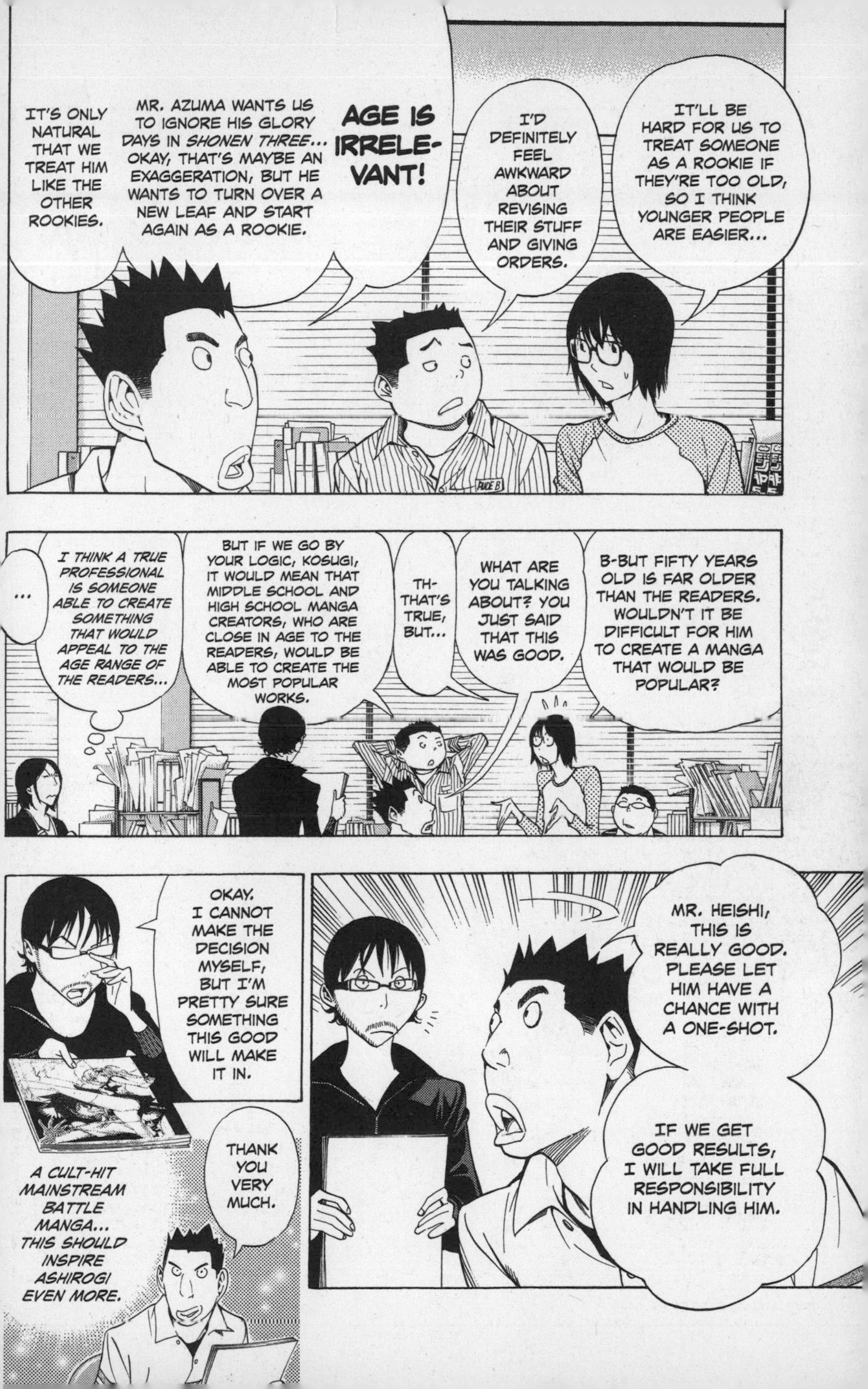
IT'LL BE HARD FOR US TO TREAT SOMEONE AS A ROOKIE IF THEY'RE TOO OLD, SO I THINK YOUNGER PEOPLE ARE EASIER...
I'D DEFINITELY FEEL AWKWARD ABOUT REVISING THEIR STUFF AND GIVING ORDERS.
AGE IS IRRELE-VANT!
MR. AZUMA WANTS US TO IGNORE HIS GLORY DAYS IN *SHONEN THREE*... OKAY, THAT'S MAYBE AN EXAGGERATION, BUT HE WANTS TO TURN OVER A NEW LEAF AND START AGAIN AS A ROOKIE.
IT'S ONLY NATURAL THAT WE TREAT HIM LIKE THE OTHER ROOKIES.
B-BUT FIFTY YEARS OLD IS FAR OLDER THAN THE READERS. WOULDN'T IT BE DIFFICULT FOR HIM TO CREATE A MANGA THAT WOULD BE POPULAR?
WHAT ARE YOU TALKING ABOUT? YOU JUST SAID THAT THIS WAS GOOD.
TH-THAT'S TRUE, BUT...
BUT IF WE GO BY YOUR LOGIC, KOSUGI, IT WOULD MEAN THAT MIDDLE SCHOOL AND HIGH SCHOOL MANGA CREATORS, WHO ARE CLOSE IN AGE TO THE READERS, WOULD BE ABLE TO CREATE THE MOST POPULAR WORKS.
I THINK A TRUE PROFESSIONAL IS SOMEONE ABLE TO CREATE SOMETHING THAT WOULD APPEAL TO THE AGE RANGE OF THE READERS...
...
MR. HEISHI, THIS IS REALLY GOOD. PLEASE LET HIM HAVE A CHANCE WITH A ONE-SHOT.
IF WE GET GOOD RESULTS, I WILL TAKE FULL RESPONSIBILITY IN HANDLING HIM.
OKAY. I CANNOT MAKE THE DECISION MYSELF, BUT I'M PRETTY SURE SOMETHING THIS GOOD WILL MAKE IT IN.
THANK YOU VERY MUCH.
A CULT-HIT MAINSTREAM BATTLE MANGA... THIS SHOULD INSPIRE ASHIROGI EVEN MORE.

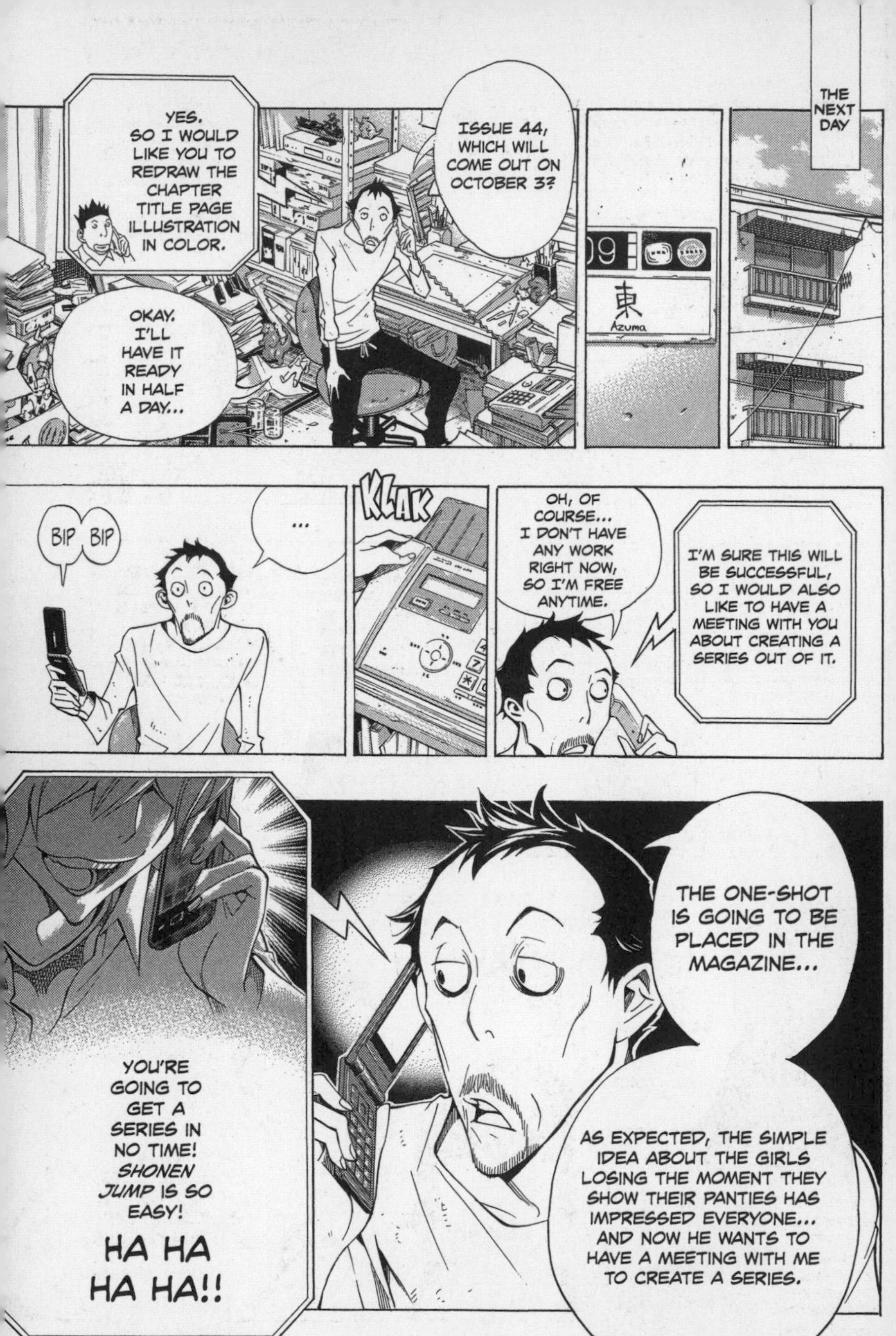
THE NEXT DAY
東
Azuma
ISSUE 44, WHICH WILL COME OUT ON OCTOBER 3?
YES. SO I WOULD LIKE YOU TO REDRAW THE CHAPTER TITLE PAGE ILLUSTRATION IN COLOR.
OKAY. I'LL HAVE IT READY IN HALF A DAY...
I'M SURE THIS WILL BE SUCCESSFUL, SO I WOULD ALSO LIKE TO HAVE A MEETING WITH YOU ABOUT CREATING A SERIES OUT OF IT.
OH, OF COURSE... I DON'T HAVE ANY WORK RIGHT NOW, SO I'M FREE ANYTIME.
KLAK
...
BIP BIP
THE ONE-SHOT IS GOING TO BE PLACED IN THE MAGAZINE...
AS EXPECTED, THE SIMPLE IDEA ABOUT THE GIRLS LOSING THE MOMENT THEY SHOW THEIR PANTIES HAS IMPRESSED EVERYONE... AND NOW HE WANTS TO HAVE A MEETING WITH ME TO CREATE A SERIES.
YOU'RE GOING TO GET A SERIES IN NO TIME! *SHONEN JUMP* IS SO EASY!
HA HA HA HA!!

OHBA'S STORYBOARD

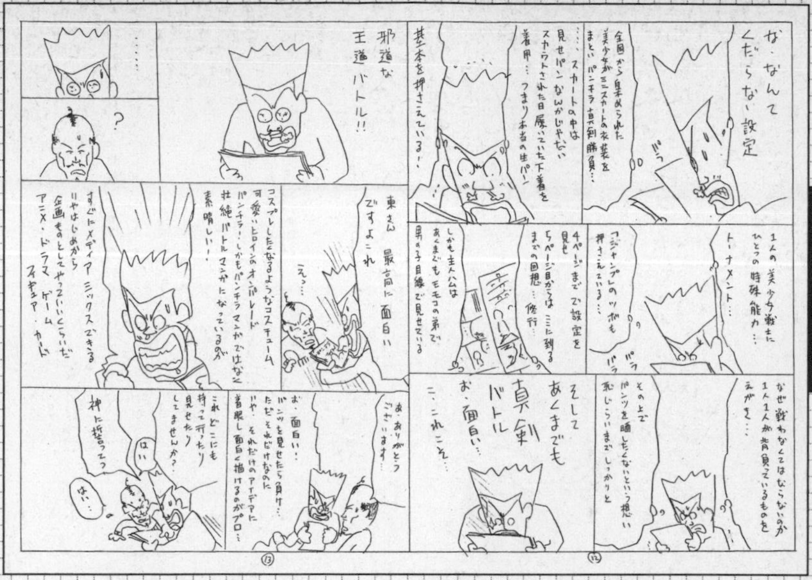
な・なんてくだらない設定
全国から集められた美少女がミニスカートの衣装をまといパンチラ真剣勝負…
…スカートの中は見せパンなんかじゃない スカウトされた日履いていた下着を着用… つまり本当の生パン
基本を押さえている…
1人の美少女戦士はひとつの特殊能力…
トーナメント…
パラ パラ
4ページまで設定を見せ 5ページ目からはここに到るまでの回想… 修行…
しかも主人公はあくまでもモモコの弟で男の子目線で見せている
なぜ戦わなくてはならないのか 1人1人が背負っているものをえがき…
その上でパンツを晒したくないという想い 恥じらいまでしっかりと
そしてあくまでも真剣バトル
お、面白い… こ、これこそ…
12
邪道な王道バトル!!
……
?
東さん 最高に面白いですよこれ
え…
コスプレしたくなるようなコスチューム 可愛いヒロインのオンパレード パンチラ！しかもパンチラマンガではなく壮絶バトルマンガになっているのが素晴しい！
すぐにメディアミックスできる アニメ・ドラマ・ゲーム・フィギュア・カード いやはじめから企画ものとしてやっていいくらいだ
あ・ありがとうございます…
お、面白い… パンツを見せたら負け… ただそれだけなのに いや、それだけのアイデアに着眼し面白く描けるのがプロ…
これどこにも持って行ったり見せたりしてませんか？
はい
神に誓って？
はい…
13

OBATA'S STORYBOARD

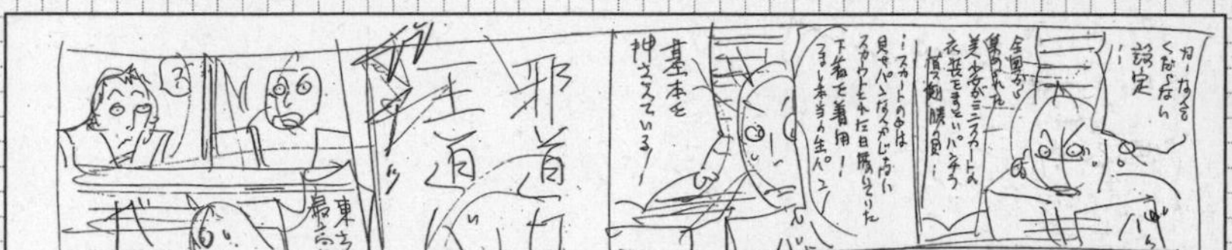

COMPLETE!

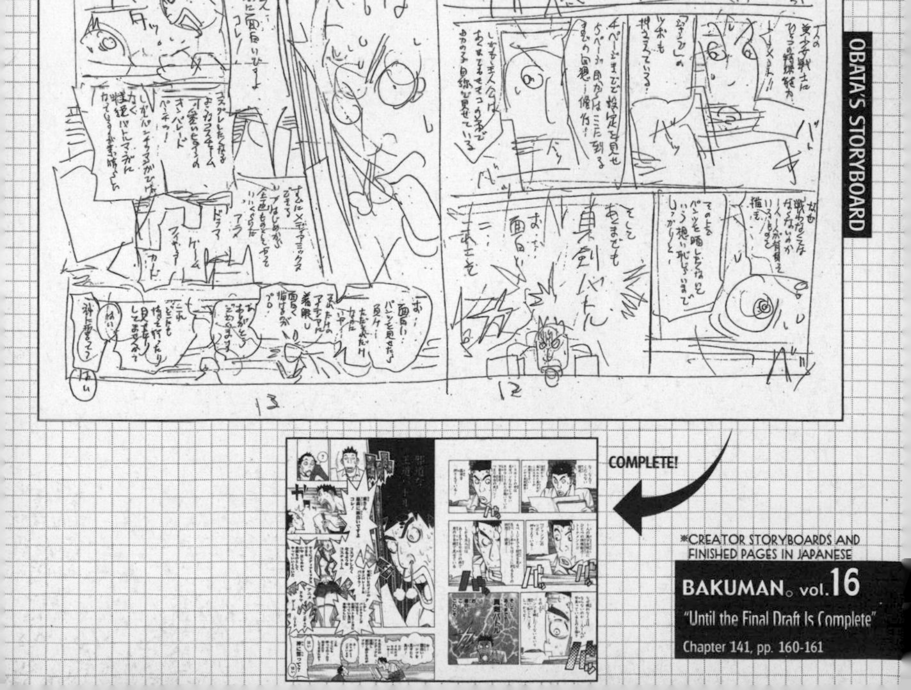

※CREATOR STORYBOARDS AND FINISHED PAGES IN JAPANESE

BAKUMAN。 vol.16

"Until the Final Draft Is Complete"

Chapter 141, pp. 160-161

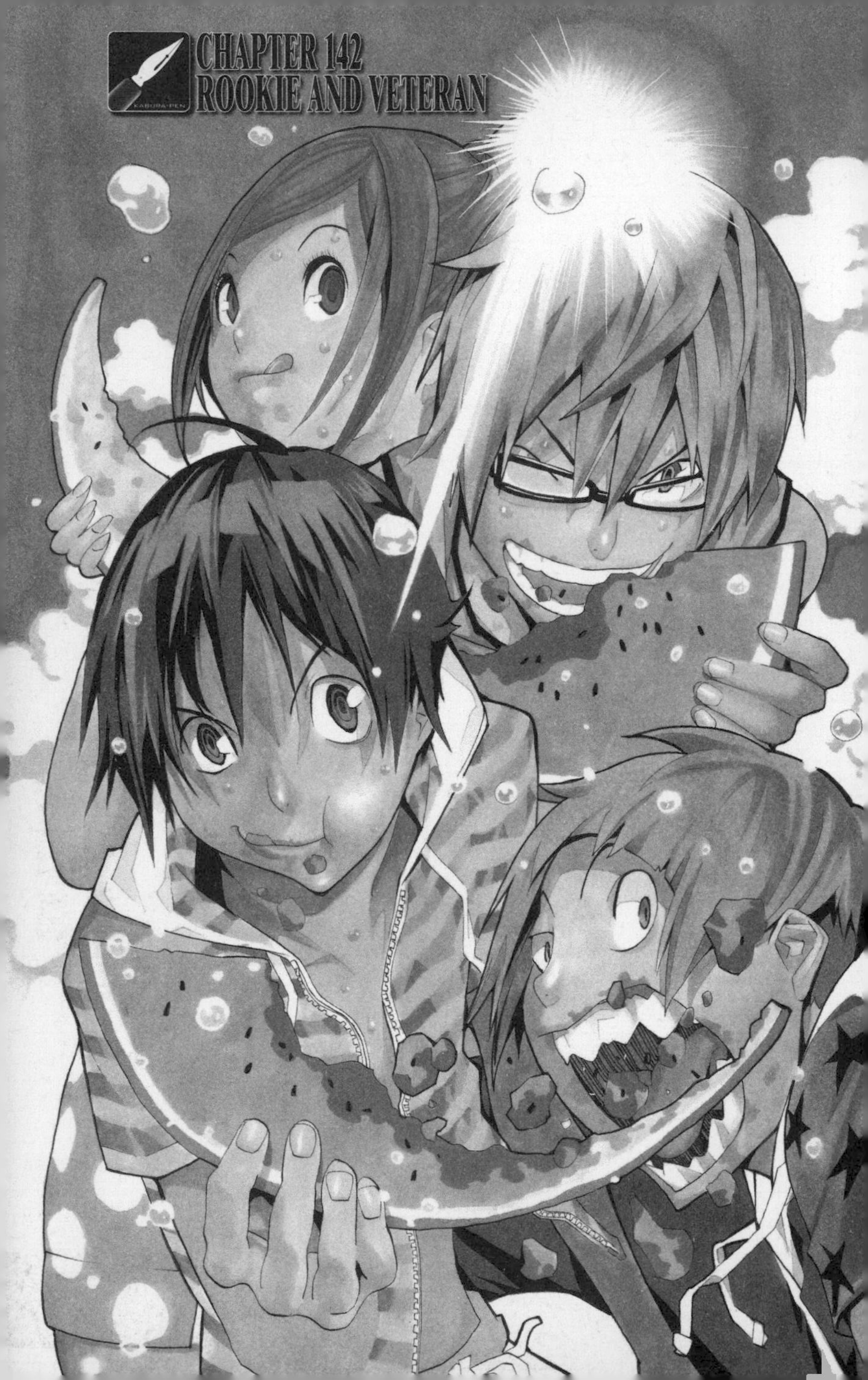
CHAPTER 142
ROOKIE AND VETERAN

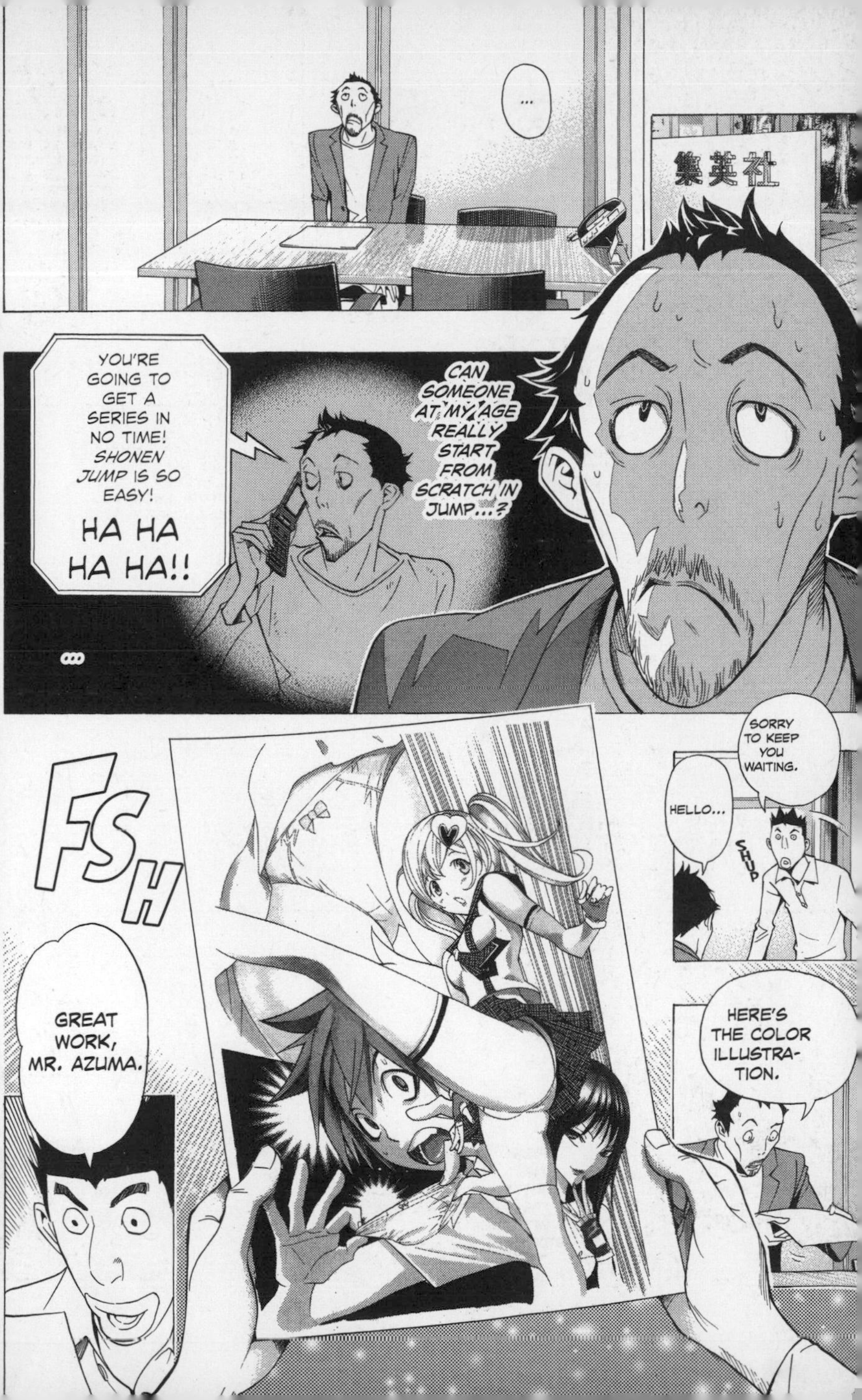
...
集英社
CAN SOMEONE AT MY AGE REALLY START FROM SCRATCH IN JUMP...?
YOU'RE GOING TO GET A SERIES IN NO TIME! SHONEN JUMP IS SO EASY!
HA HA HA HA!!
SORRY TO KEEP YOU WAITING.
HELLO...
SHUP
HERE'S THE COLOR ILLUSTRATION.
FSH
GREAT WORK, MR. AZUMA.

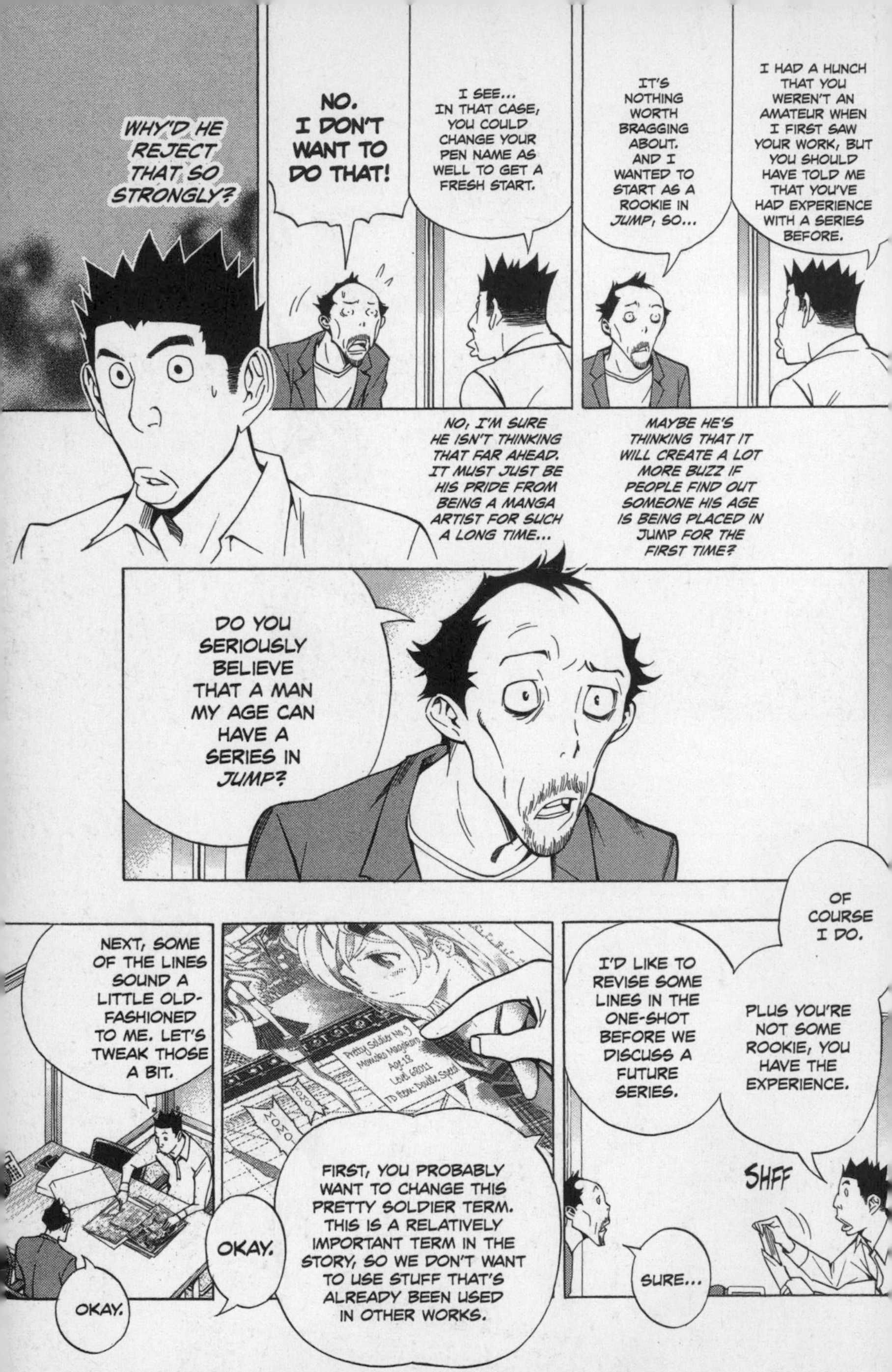
I HAD A HUNCH THAT YOU WEREN'T AN AMATEUR WHEN I FIRST SAW YOUR WORK, BUT YOU SHOULD HAVE TOLD ME THAT YOU'VE HAD EXPERIENCE WITH A SERIES BEFORE.
IT'S NOTHING WORTH BRAGGING ABOUT. AND I WANTED TO START AS A ROOKIE IN *JUMP*, SO...
I SEE... IN THAT CASE, YOU COULD CHANGE YOUR PEN NAME AS WELL TO GET A FRESH START.
NO. I DON'T WANT TO DO THAT!
WHY'D HE REJECT THAT SO STRONGLY?
MAYBE HE'S THINKING THAT IT WILL CREATE A LOT MORE BUZZ IF PEOPLE FIND OUT SOMEONE HIS AGE IS BEING PLACED IN JUMP FOR THE FIRST TIME?
NO, I'M SURE HE ISN'T THINKING THAT FAR AHEAD. IT MUST JUST BE HIS PRIDE FROM BEING A MANGA ARTIST FOR SUCH A LONG TIME...
DO YOU SERIOUSLY BELIEVE THAT A MAN MY AGE CAN HAVE A SERIES IN *JUMP*?
OF COURSE I DO.
PLUS YOU'RE NOT SOME ROOKIE, YOU HAVE THE EXPERIENCE.
I'D LIKE TO REVISE SOME LINES IN THE ONE-SHOT BEFORE WE DISCUSS A FUTURE SERIES.
SHFF
SURE...
FIRST, YOU PROBABLY WANT TO CHANGE THIS PRETTY SOLDIER TERM. THIS IS A RELATIVELY IMPORTANT TERM IN THE STORY, SO WE DON'T WANT TO USE STUFF THAT'S ALREADY BEEN USED IN OTHER WORKS.
OKAY.
NEXT, SOME OF THE LINES SOUND A LITTLE OLD-FASHIONED TO ME. LET'S TWEAK THOSE A BIT.
OKAY.

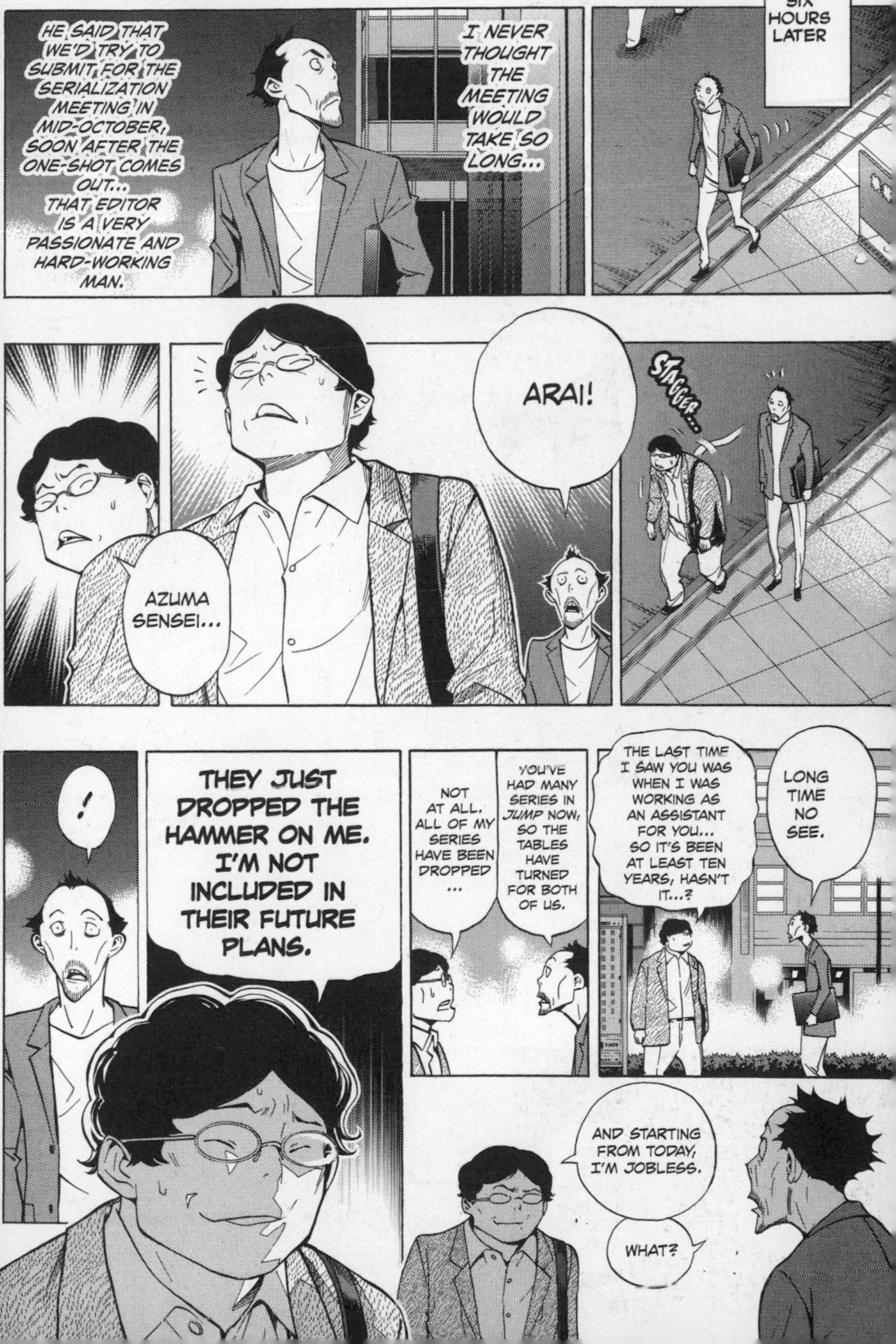
SIX HOURS LATER
I NEVER THOUGHT THE MEETING WOULD TAKE SO LONG...
HE SAID THAT WE'D TRY TO SUBMIT FOR THE SERIALIZATION MEETING IN MID-OCTOBER, SOON AFTER THE ONE-SHOT COMES OUT... THAT EDITOR IS A VERY PASSIONATE AND HARD-WORKING MAN.
STAGGER...
ARAI!
AZUMA SENSEI...
LONG TIME NO SEE.
THE LAST TIME I SAW YOU WAS WHEN I WAS WORKING AS AN ASSISTANT FOR YOU... SO IT'S BEEN AT LEAST TEN YEARS, HASN'T IT...?
YOU'VE HAD MANY SERIES IN JUMP NOW, SO THE TABLES HAVE TURNED FOR BOTH OF US.
NOT AT ALL. ALL OF MY SERIES HAVE BEEN DROPPED...
AND STARTING FROM TODAY, I'M JOBLESS.
WHAT?
THEY JUST DROPPED THE HAMMER ON ME. I'M NOT INCLUDED IN THEIR FUTURE PLANS.
!

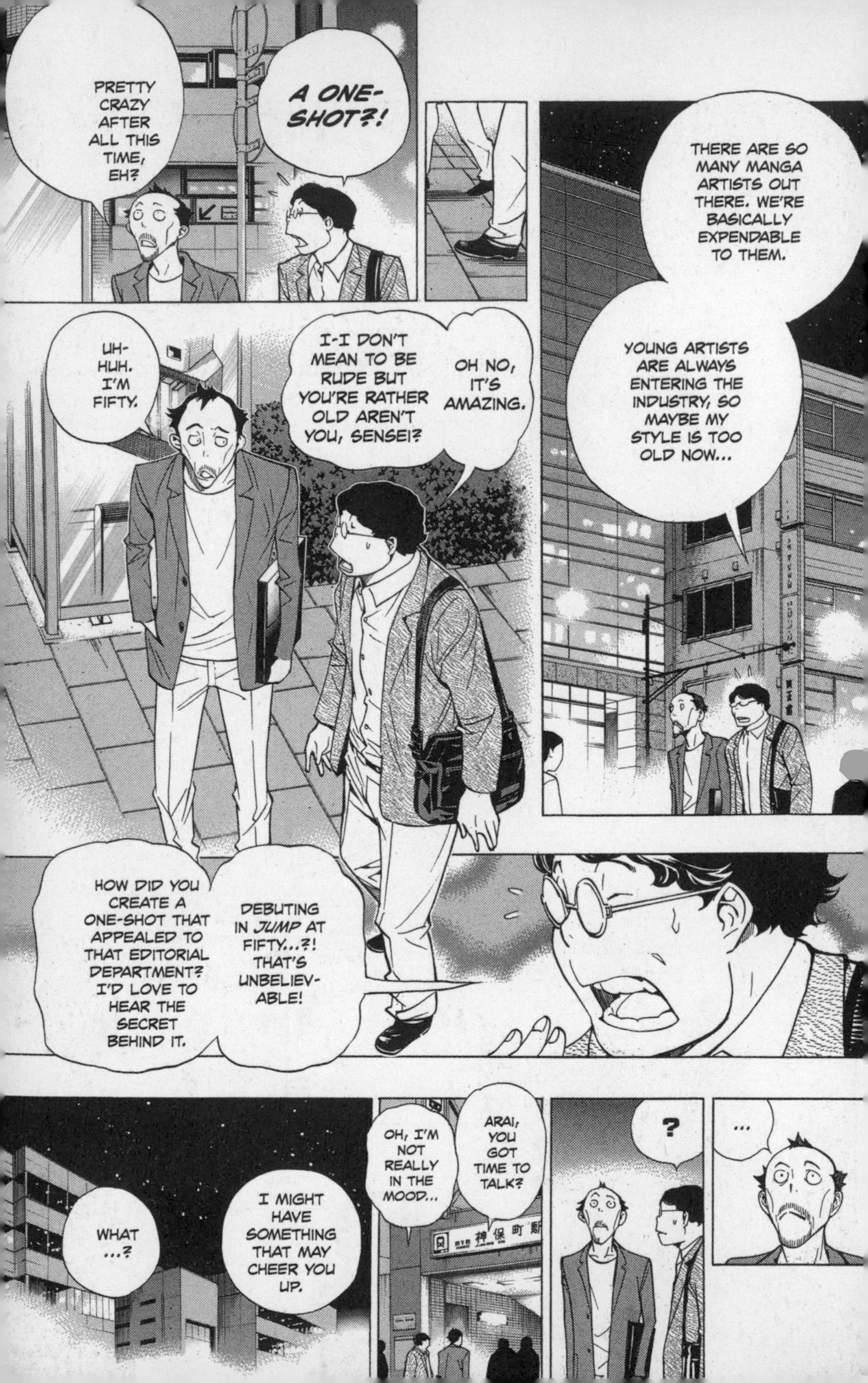
THERE ARE SO MANY MANGA ARTISTS OUT THERE. WE'RE BASICALLY EXPENDABLE TO THEM.
YOUNG ARTISTS ARE ALWAYS ENTERING THE INDUSTRY, SO MAYBE MY STYLE IS TOO OLD NOW...
A ONE-SHOT?!
PRETTY CRAZY AFTER ALL THIS TIME, EH?
I-I DON'T MEAN TO BE RUDE BUT YOU'RE RATHER OLD AREN'T YOU, SENSEI?
OH NO, IT'S AMAZING.
UH-HUH. I'M FIFTY.
DEBUTING IN *JUMP* AT FIFTY...?! THAT'S UNBELIEVABLE!
HOW DID YOU CREATE A ONE-SHOT THAT APPEALED TO THAT EDITORIAL DEPARTMENT? I'D LOVE TO HEAR THE SECRET BEHIND IT.
...
?
ARAI, YOU GOT TIME TO TALK?
OH, I'M NOT REALLY IN THE MOOD...
神保町駅
I MIGHT HAVE SOMETHING THAT MAY CHEER YOU UP.
WHAT ...?

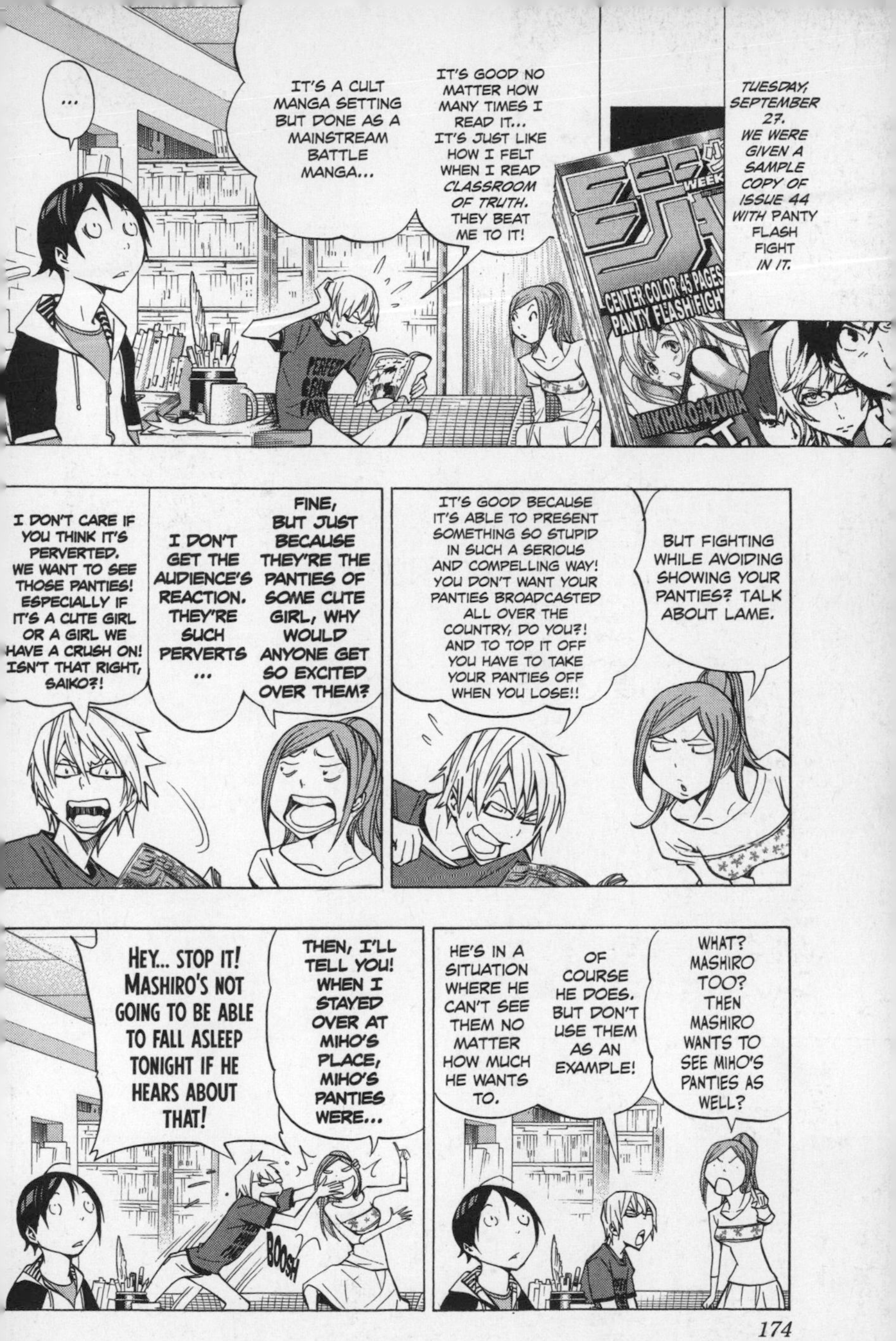
TUESDAY, SEPTEMBER 27. WE WERE GIVEN A SAMPLE COPY OF ISSUE 44 WITH PANTY FLASH FIGHT IN IT.
CENTER COLOR 45 PAGES
PANTY FLASH FIGHT
IT'S GOOD NO MATTER HOW MANY TIMES I READ IT... IT'S JUST LIKE HOW I FELT WHEN I READ CLASSROOM OF TRUTH. THEY BEAT ME TO IT!
IT'S A CULT MANGA SETTING BUT DONE AS A MAINSTREAM BATTLE MANGA...
...
BUT FIGHTING WHILE AVOIDING SHOWING YOUR PANTIES? TALK ABOUT LAME.
IT'S GOOD BECAUSE IT'S ABLE TO PRESENT SOMETHING SO STUPID IN SUCH A SERIOUS AND COMPELLING WAY! YOU DON'T WANT YOUR PANTIES BROADCASTED ALL OVER THE COUNTRY, DO YOU?! AND TO TOP IT OFF YOU HAVE TO TAKE YOUR PANTIES OFF WHEN YOU LOSE!!
FINE, BUT JUST BECAUSE THEY'RE THE PANTIES OF SOME CUTE GIRL, WHY WOULD ANYONE GET SO EXCITED OVER THEM?
I DON'T GET THE AUDIENCE'S REACTION. THEY'RE SUCH PERVERTS...
I DON'T CARE IF YOU THINK IT'S PERVERTED. WE WANT TO SEE THOSE PANTIES! ESPECIALLY IF IT'S A CUTE GIRL OR A GIRL WE HAVE A CRUSH ON! ISN'T THAT RIGHT, SAIKO?!
WHAT? MASHIRO TOO? THEN MASHIRO WANTS TO SEE MIHO'S PANTIES AS WELL?
OF COURSE HE DOES. BUT DON'T USE THEM AS AN EXAMPLE!
HE'S IN A SITUATION WHERE HE CAN'T SEE THEM NO MATTER HOW MUCH HE WANTS TO.
THEN, I'LL TELL YOU! WHEN I STAYED OVER AT MIHO'S PLACE, MIHO'S PANTIES WERE...
HEY... STOP IT! MASHIRO'S NOT GOING TO BE ABLE TO FALL ASLEEP TONIGHT IF HE HEARS ABOUT THAT!
BOOSH

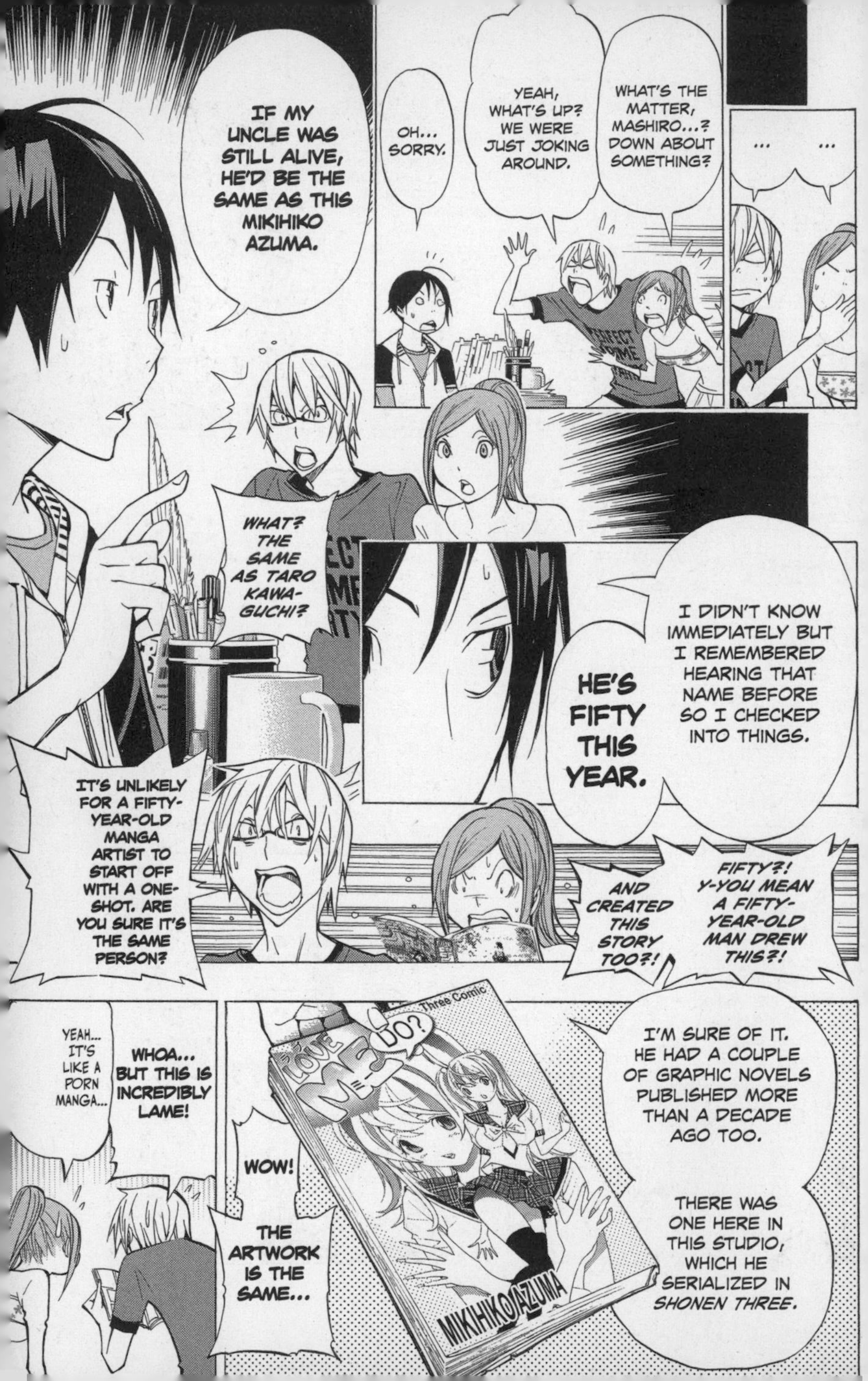
... ...
WHAT'S THE MATTER, MASHIRO...? DOWN ABOUT SOMETHING?
YEAH, WHAT'S UP? WE WERE JUST JOKING AROUND.
OH... SORRY.
IF MY UNCLE WAS STILL ALIVE, HE'D BE THE SAME AS THIS MIKIHIKO AZUMA.
WHAT? THE SAME AS TARO KAWAGUCHI?
I DIDN'T KNOW IMMEDIATELY BUT I REMEMBERED HEARING THAT NAME BEFORE SO I CHECKED INTO THINGS.
HE'S FIFTY THIS YEAR.
FIFTY?! Y-YOU MEAN A FIFTY-YEAR-OLD MAN DREW THIS?!
AND CREATED THIS STORY TOO?!
IT'S UNLIKELY FOR A FIFTY-YEAR-OLD MANGA ARTIST TO START OFF WITH A ONE-SHOT. ARE YOU SURE IT'S THE SAME PERSON?
I'M SURE OF IT. HE HAD A COUPLE OF GRAPHIC NOVELS PUBLISHED MORE THAN A DECADE AGO TOO.
THERE WAS ONE HERE IN THIS STUDIO, WHICH HE SERIALIZED IN *SHONEN THREE*.
Three Comic
LOVE ME DO?
MIKIHIKO AZUMA
WOW!
THE ARTWORK IS THE SAME...
WHOA... BUT THIS IS INCREDIBLY LAME!
YEAH... IT'S LIKE A PORN MANGA...

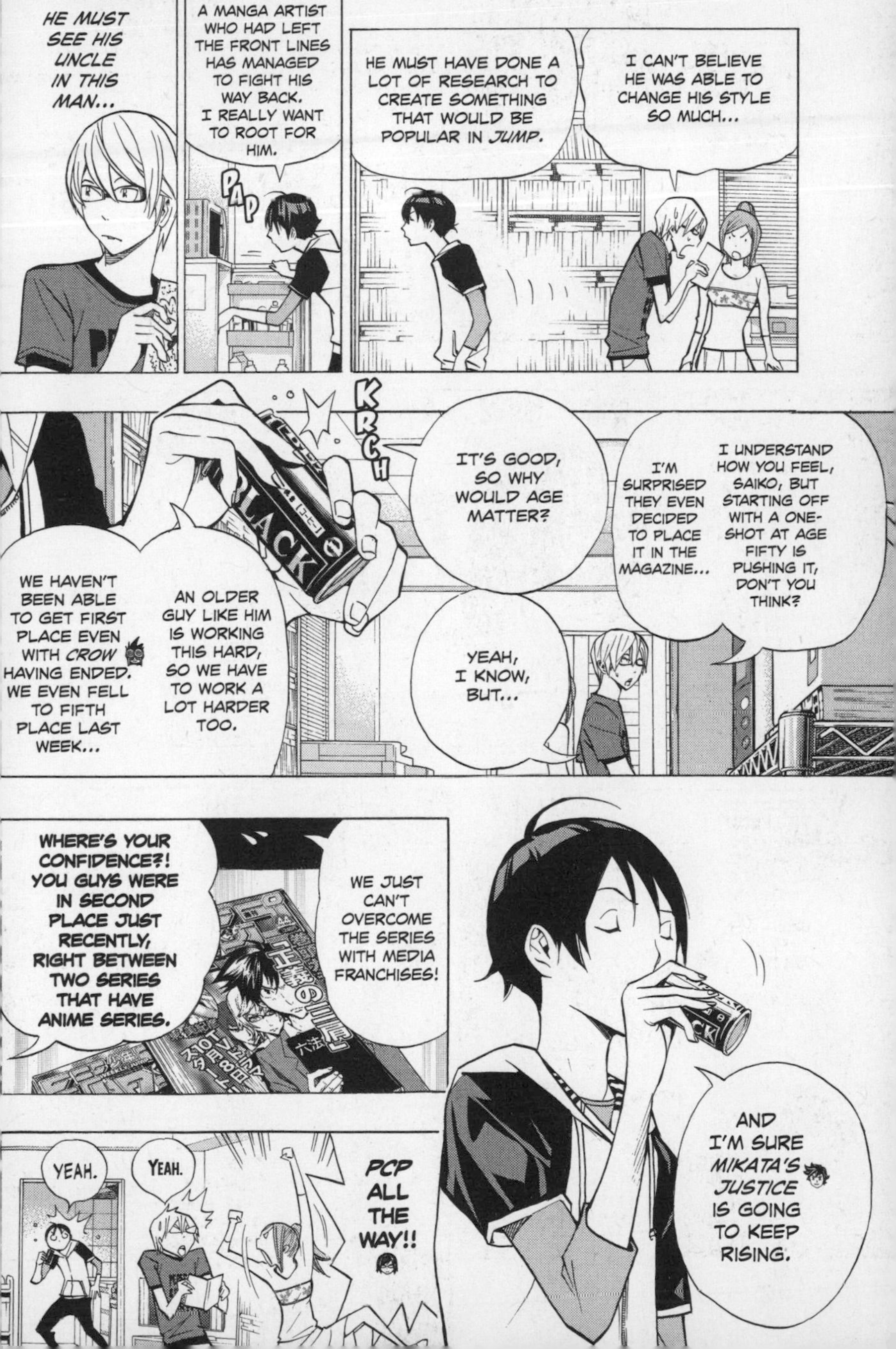
I CAN'T BELIEVE HE WAS ABLE TO CHANGE HIS STYLE SO MUCH...
HE MUST HAVE DONE A LOT OF RESEARCH TO CREATE SOMETHING THAT WOULD BE POPULAR IN *JUMP*.
A MANGA ARTIST WHO HAD LEFT THE FRONT LINES HAS MANAGED TO FIGHT HIS WAY BACK. I REALLY WANT TO ROOT FOR HIM.
PAP
HE MUST SEE HIS UNCLE IN THIS MAN...
I UNDERSTAND HOW YOU FEEL, SAIKO, BUT STARTING OFF WITH A ONE-SHOT AT AGE FIFTY IS PUSHING IT, DON'T YOU THINK?
I'M SURPRISED THEY EVEN DECIDED TO PLACE IT IN THE MAGAZINE...
IT'S GOOD, SO WHY WOULD AGE MATTER?
YEAH, I KNOW, BUT...
KRCH
BLACK
AN OLDER GUY LIKE HIM IS WORKING THIS HARD, SO WE HAVE TO WORK A LOT HARDER TOO.
WE HAVEN'T BEEN ABLE TO GET FIRST PLACE EVEN WITH *CROW* HAVING ENDED. WE EVEN FELL TO FIFTH PLACE LAST WEEK...
AND I'M SURE *MIKATA'S JUSTICE* IS GOING TO KEEP RISING.
WE JUST CAN'T OVERCOME THE SERIES WITH MEDIA FRANCHISES!
WHERE'S YOUR CONFIDENCE?! YOU GUYS WERE IN SECOND PLACE JUST RECENTLY, RIGHT BETWEEN TWO SERIES THAT HAVE ANIME SERIES.
PCP ALL THE WAY!!
YEAH.
YEAH.

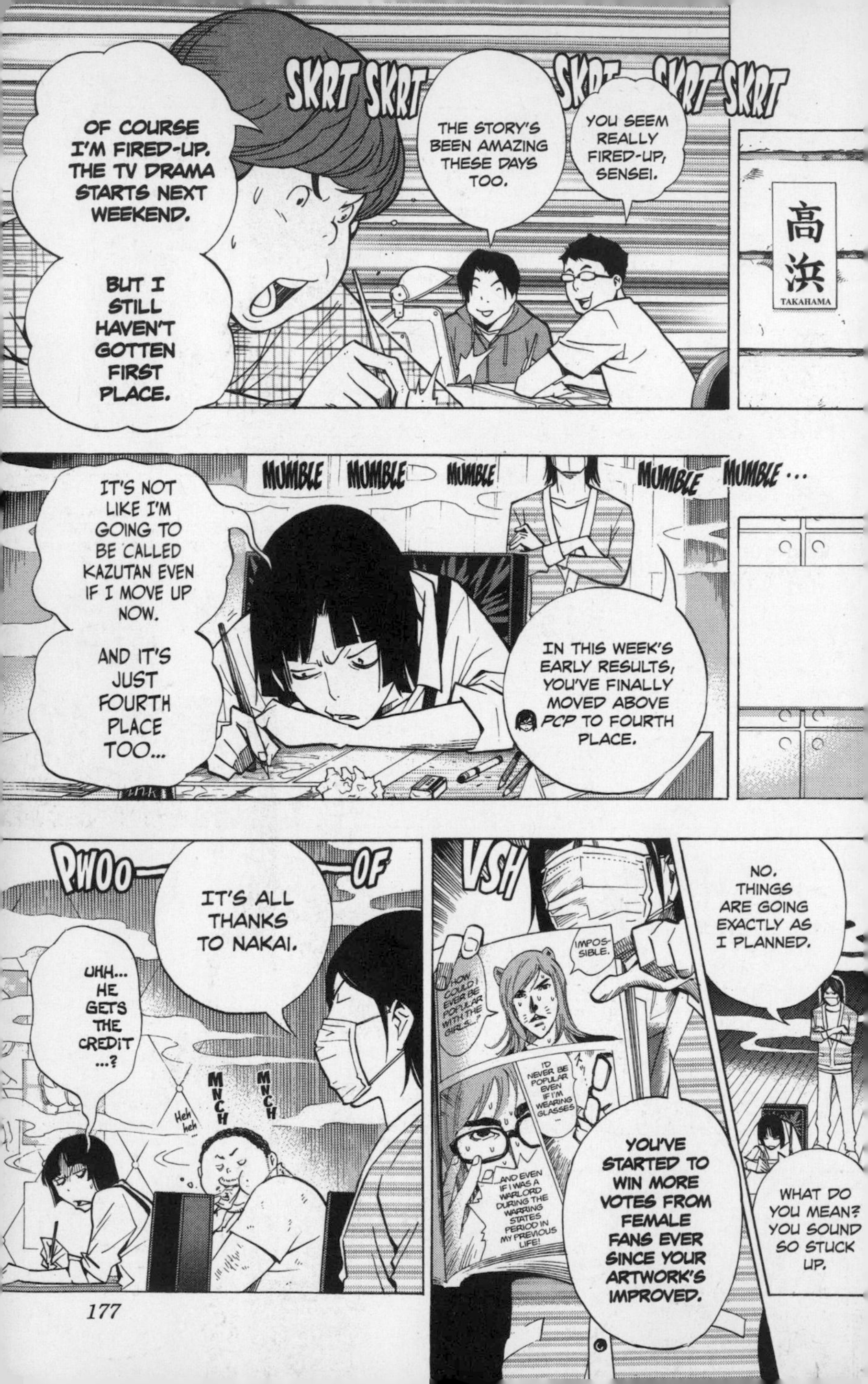

SKRT SKRT
高浜
TAKAHAMA
YOU SEEM REALLY FIRED-UP, SENSEI.
SKRT SKRT SKRT
THE STORY'S BEEN AMAZING THESE DAYS TOO.
SKRT SKRT
OF COURSE I'M FIRED-UP. THE TV DRAMA STARTS NEXT WEEKEND.
BUT I STILL HAVEN'T GOTTEN FIRST PLACE.
MUMBLE MUMBLE ...
MUMBLE
MUMBLE MUMBLE
IN THIS WEEK'S EARLY RESULTS, YOU'VE FINALLY MOVED ABOVE *PCP* TO FOURTH PLACE.
IT'S NOT LIKE I'M GOING TO BE CALLED KAZUTAN EVEN IF I MOVE UP NOW.
AND IT'S JUST FOURTH PLACE TOO...
NO. THINGS ARE GOING EXACTLY AS I PLANNED.
WHAT DO YOU MEAN? YOU SOUND SO STUCK UP.
VSH
IMPOSSIBLE.
HOW COULD I EVER BE POPULAR WITH THE GIRLS...?
I'D NEVER BE POPULAR EVEN IF I'M WEARING GLASSES...
...AND EVEN IF I WAS A WARLORD DURING THE WARRING STATES PERIOD IN MY PREVIOUS LIFE!
YOU'VE STARTED TO WIN MORE VOTES FROM FEMALE FANS EVER SINCE YOUR ARTWORK'S IMPROVED.
PWOO—OF
IT'S ALL THANKS TO NAKAI.
MNCH MNCH
Heh heh
UHH... HE GETS THE CREDIT ...?

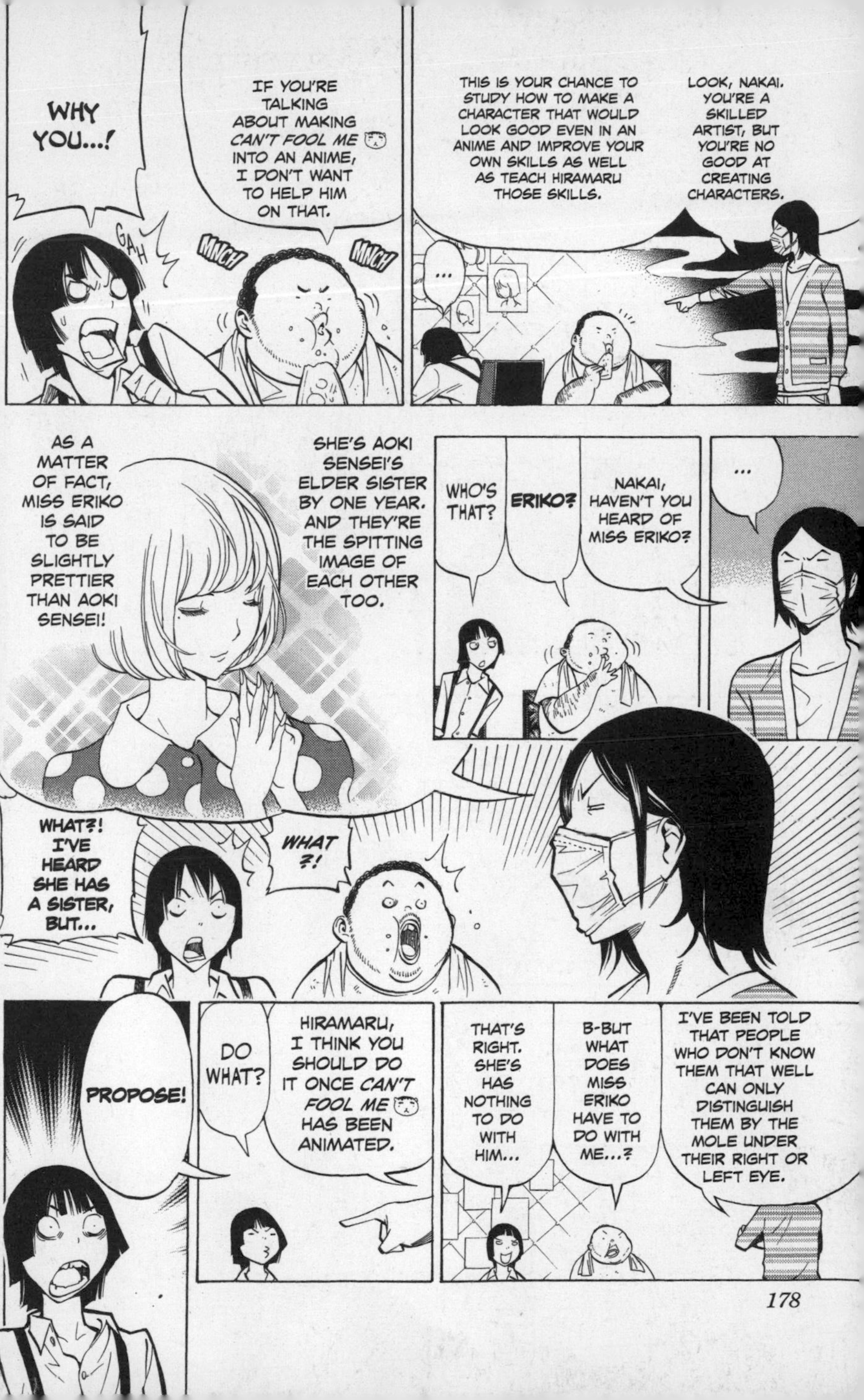
LOOK, NAKAI. YOU'RE A SKILLED ARTIST, BUT YOU'RE NO GOOD AT CREATING CHARACTERS.
THIS IS YOUR CHANCE TO STUDY HOW TO MAKE A CHARACTER THAT WOULD LOOK GOOD EVEN IN AN ANIME AND IMPROVE YOUR OWN SKILLS AS WELL AS TEACH HIRAMARU THOSE SKILLS.
...
IF YOU'RE TALKING ABOUT MAKING *CAN'T FOOL ME* INTO AN ANIME, I DON'T WANT TO HELP HIM ON THAT.
MNCH
MNCH
WHY YOU...!
GAH
...
NAKAI, HAVEN'T YOU HEARD OF MISS ERIKO?
ERIKO?
WHO'S THAT?
SHE'S AOKI SENSEI'S ELDER SISTER BY ONE YEAR. AND THEY'RE THE SPITTING IMAGE OF EACH OTHER TOO.
AS A MATTER OF FACT, MISS ERIKO IS SAID TO BE SLIGHTLY PRETTIER THAN AOKI SENSEI!
WHAT?!
WHAT?! I'VE HEARD SHE HAS A SISTER, BUT...
I'VE BEEN TOLD THAT PEOPLE WHO DON'T KNOW THEM THAT WELL CAN ONLY DISTINGUISH THEM BY THE MOLE UNDER THEIR RIGHT OR LEFT EYE.
B-BUT WHAT DOES MISS ERIKO HAVE TO DO WITH ME...?
THAT'S RIGHT. SHE'S HAS NOTHING TO DO WITH HIM...
HIRAMARU, I THINK YOU SHOULD DO IT ONCE *CAN'T FOOL ME* HAS BEEN ANIMATED.
DO WHAT?
PROPOSE!

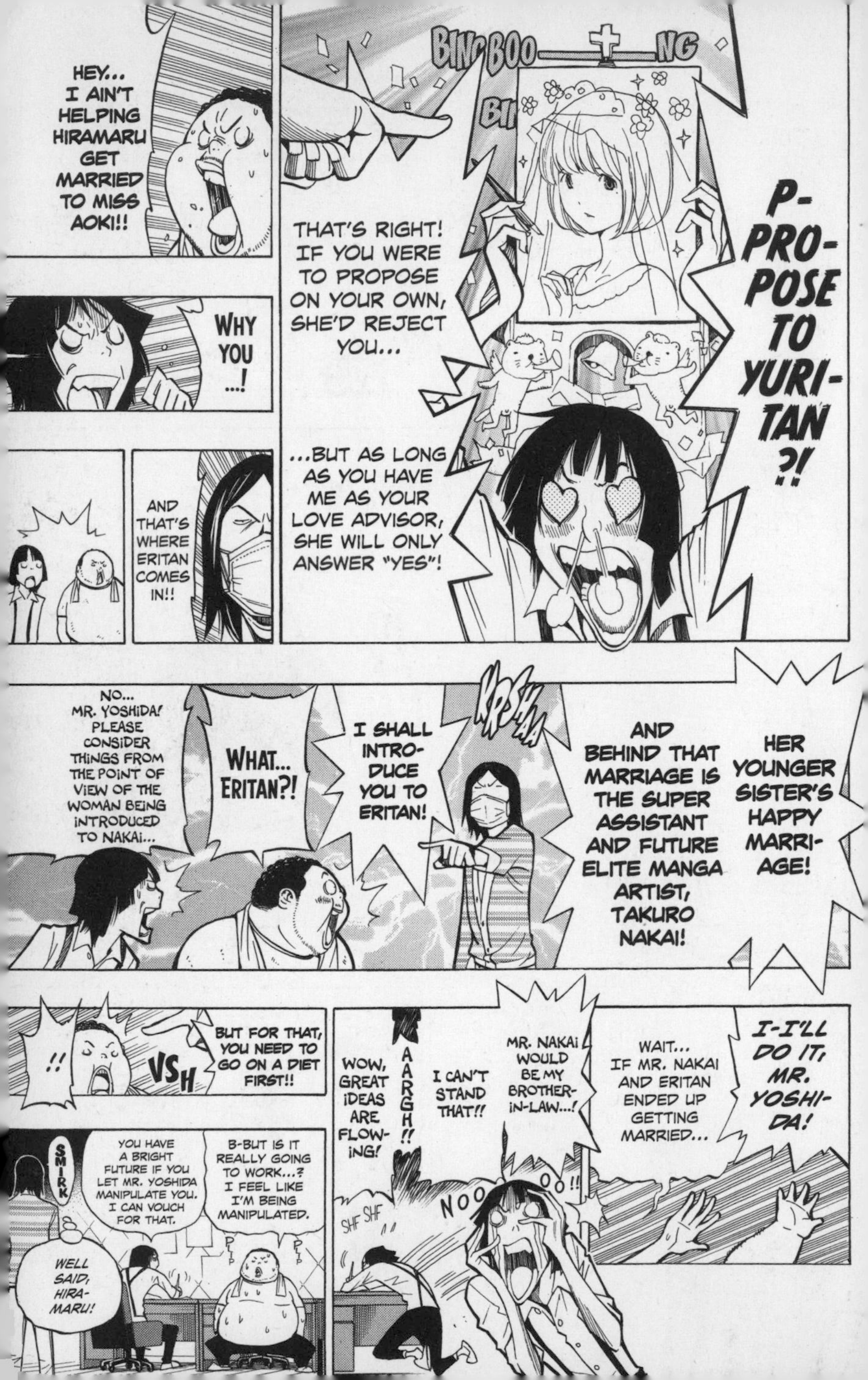
BING BOO—NG
BI
P-PRO-POSE TO YURI-TAN?!
THAT'S RIGHT! IF YOU WERE TO PROPOSE ON YOUR OWN, SHE'D REJECT YOU...
...BUT AS LONG AS YOU HAVE ME AS YOUR LOVE ADVISOR, SHE WILL ONLY ANSWER "YES"!
HEY... I AIN'T HELPING HIRAMARU GET MARRIED TO MISS AOKI!!
WHY YOU ...!
AND THAT'S WHERE ERITAN COMES IN!!
HER YOUNGER SISTER'S HAPPY MARRI-AGE!
AND BEHIND THAT MARRIAGE IS THE SUPER ASSISTANT AND FUTURE ELITE MANGA ARTIST, TAKURO NAKAI!
KRSHAA
I SHALL INTRO-DUCE YOU TO ERITAN!
WHAT... ERITAN?!
NO... MR. YOSHIDA! PLEASE CONSIDER THINGS FROM THE POINT OF VIEW OF THE WOMAN BEING INTRODUCED TO NAKAI...
I-I'LL DO IT, MR. YOSHI-DA!
WAIT... IF MR. NAKAI AND ERITAN ENDED UP GETTING MARRIED...
MR. NAKAI WOULD BE MY BROTHER-IN-LAW...!
I CAN'T STAND THAT!!
AARGH!!
WOW, GREAT IDEAS ARE FLOW-ING!
NOOOO!!
SHF SHF
BUT FOR THAT, YOU NEED TO GO ON A DIET FIRST!!
VSH
!!
B-BUT IS IT REALLY GOING TO WORK...? I FEEL LIKE I'M BEING MANIPULATED.
YOU HAVE A BRIGHT FUTURE IF YOU LET MR. YOSHIDA MANIPULATE YOU. I CAN VOUCH FOR THAT.
SMIRK
PLIP
PLIP
WELL SAID, HIRA-MARU!

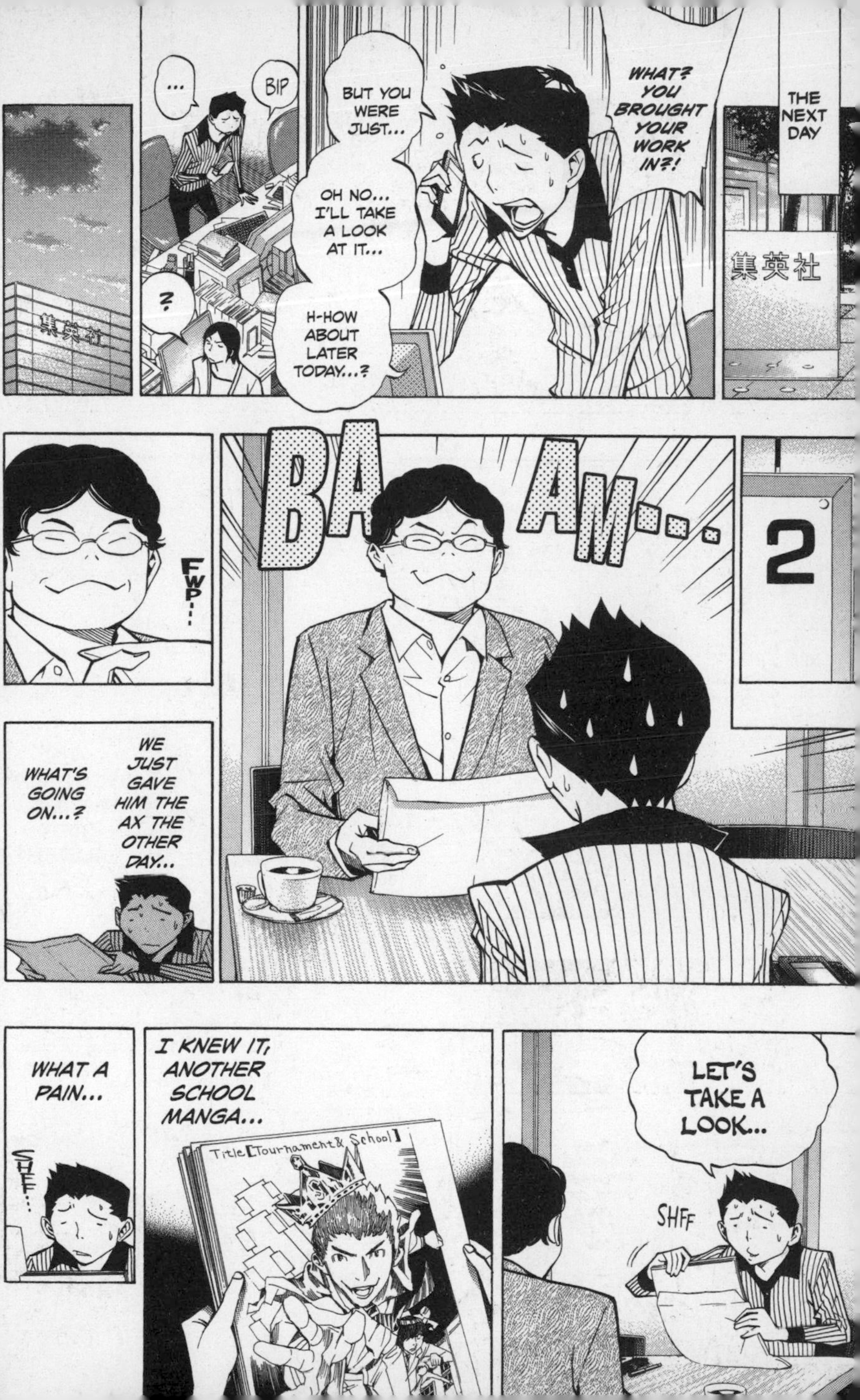
THE NEXT DAY
集英社
WHAT? YOU BROUGHT YOUR WORK IN?!
BUT YOU WERE JUST...
BIP
...
OH NO... I'LL TAKE A LOOK AT IT...
?
H-HOW ABOUT LATER TODAY...?
集英社
2
BAAM...
FWP...
WE JUST GAVE HIM THE AX THE OTHER DAY...
WHAT'S GOING ON...?
LET'S TAKE A LOOK...
SHFF
I KNEW IT, ANOTHER SCHOOL MANGA...
Title [Tournament & School]
WHAT A PAIN...
SHFF...

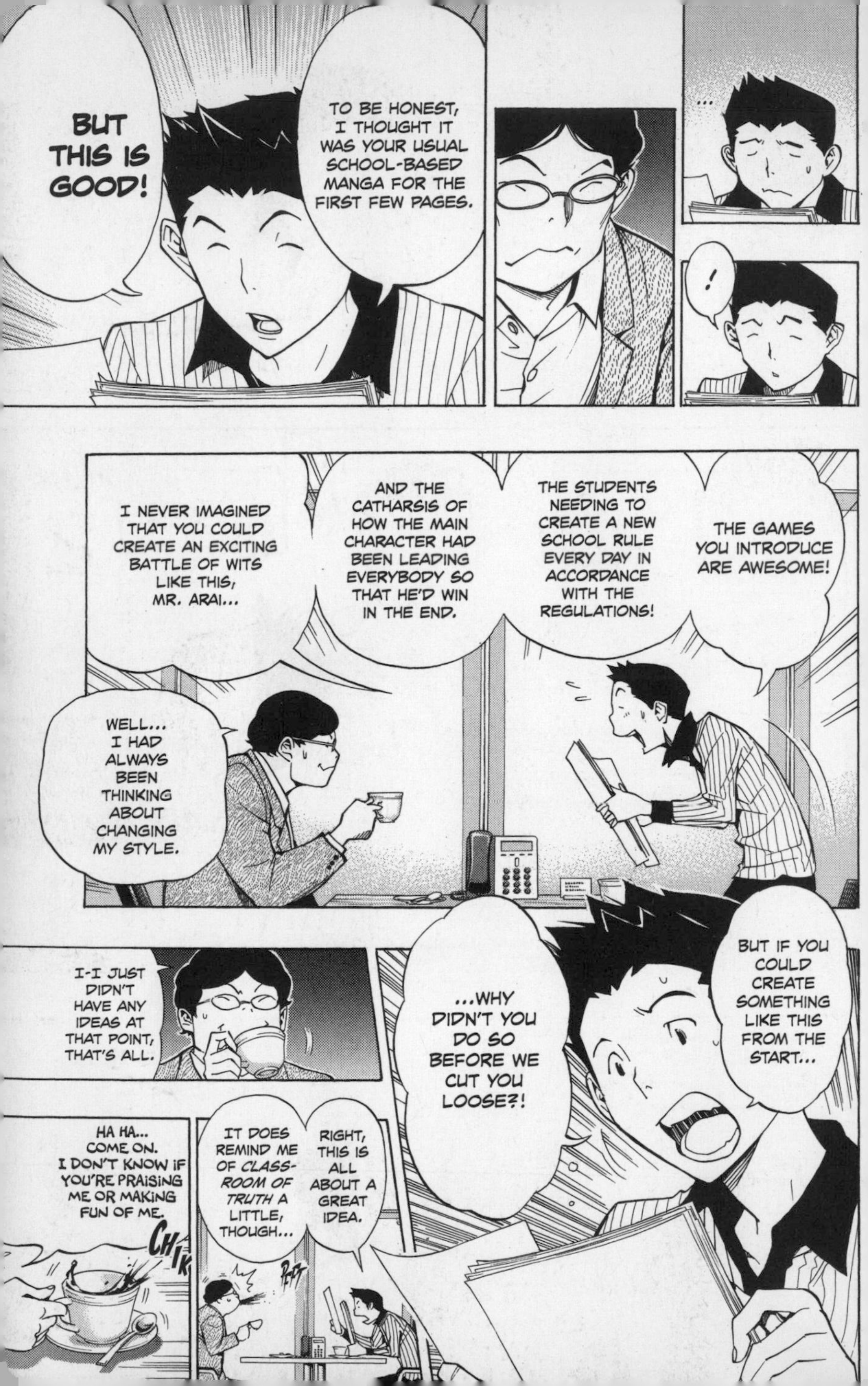
...
!
TO BE HONEST, I THOUGHT IT WAS YOUR USUAL SCHOOL-BASED MANGA FOR THE FIRST FEW PAGES.
BUT THIS IS GOOD!
THE GAMES YOU INTRODUCE ARE AWESOME!
THE STUDENTS NEEDING TO CREATE A NEW SCHOOL RULE EVERY DAY IN ACCORDANCE WITH THE REGULATIONS!
AND THE CATHARSIS OF HOW THE MAIN CHARACTER HAD BEEN LEADING EVERYBODY SO THAT HE'D WIN IN THE END.
I NEVER IMAGINED THAT YOU COULD CREATE AN EXCITING BATTLE OF WITS LIKE THIS, MR. ARAI...
WELL... I HAD ALWAYS BEEN THINKING ABOUT CHANGING MY STYLE.
BUT IF YOU COULD CREATE SOMETHING LIKE THIS FROM THE START...
...WHY DIDN'T YOU DO SO BEFORE WE CUT YOU LOOSE?!
I-I JUST DIDN'T HAVE ANY IDEAS AT THAT POINT, THAT'S ALL.
RIGHT, THIS IS ALL ABOUT A GREAT IDEA.
IT DOES REMIND ME OF *CLASSROOM OF TRUTH* A LITTLE, THOUGH...
HA HA... COME ON. I DON'T KNOW IF YOU'RE PRAISING ME OR MAKING FUN OF ME.
CHIK

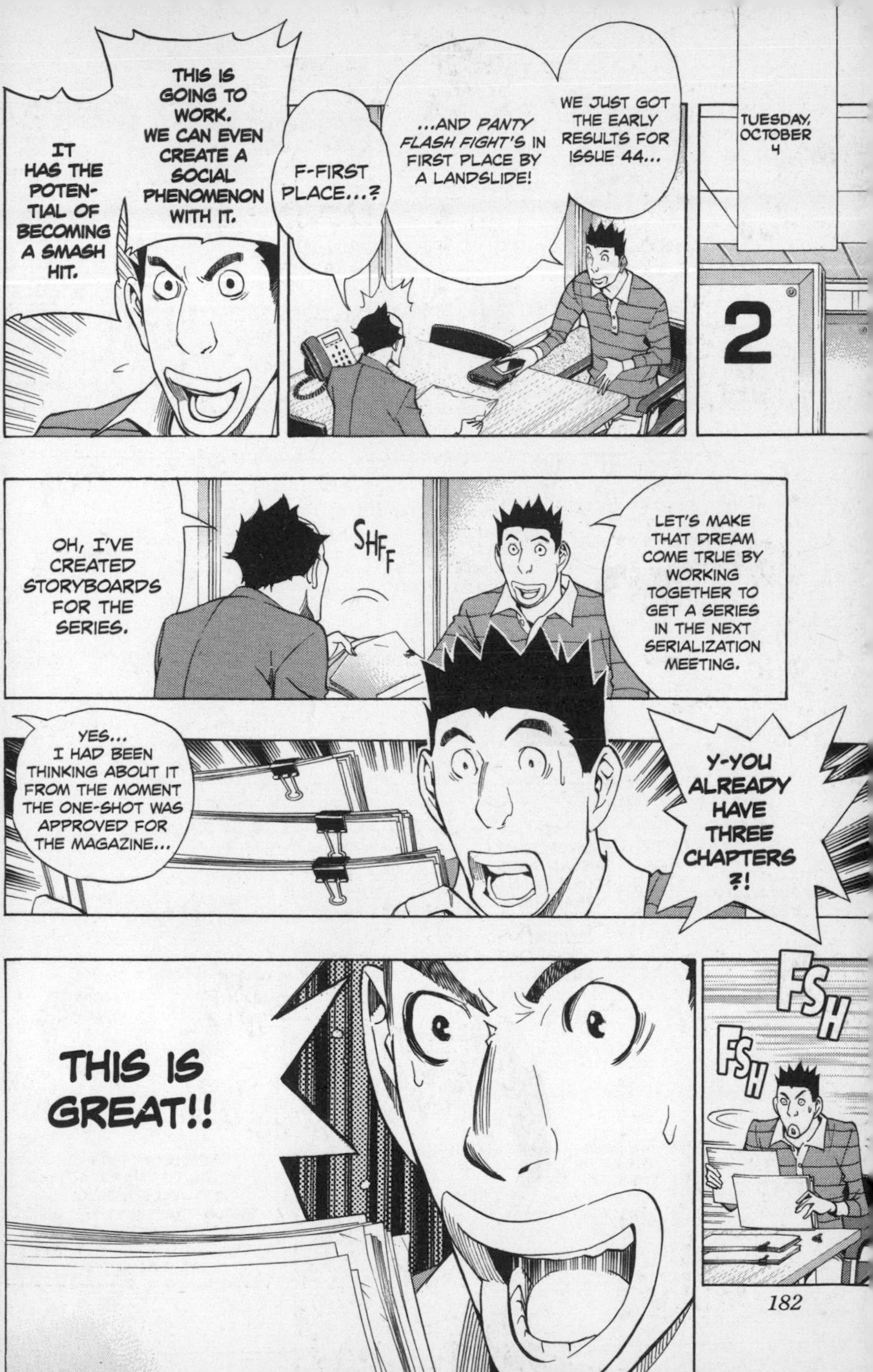
TUESDAY, OCTOBER 4
2
WE JUST GOT THE EARLY RESULTS FOR ISSUE 44...
...AND *PANTY FLASH FIGHT*'S IN FIRST PLACE BY A LANDSLIDE!
F-FIRST PLACE...?
THIS IS GOING TO WORK. WE CAN EVEN CREATE A SOCIAL PHENOMENON WITH IT.
IT HAS THE POTEN-TIAL OF BECOMING A SMASH HIT.
LET'S MAKE THAT DREAM COME TRUE BY WORKING TOGETHER TO GET A SERIES IN THE NEXT SERIALIZATION MEETING.
SHFF
OH, I'VE CREATED STORYBOARDS FOR THE SERIES.
Y-YOU ALREADY HAVE THREE CHAPTERS ?!
YES... I HAD BEEN THINKING ABOUT IT FROM THE MOMENT THE ONE-SHOT WAS APPROVED FOR THE MAGAZINE...
FSH
FSH
THIS IS GREAT!!

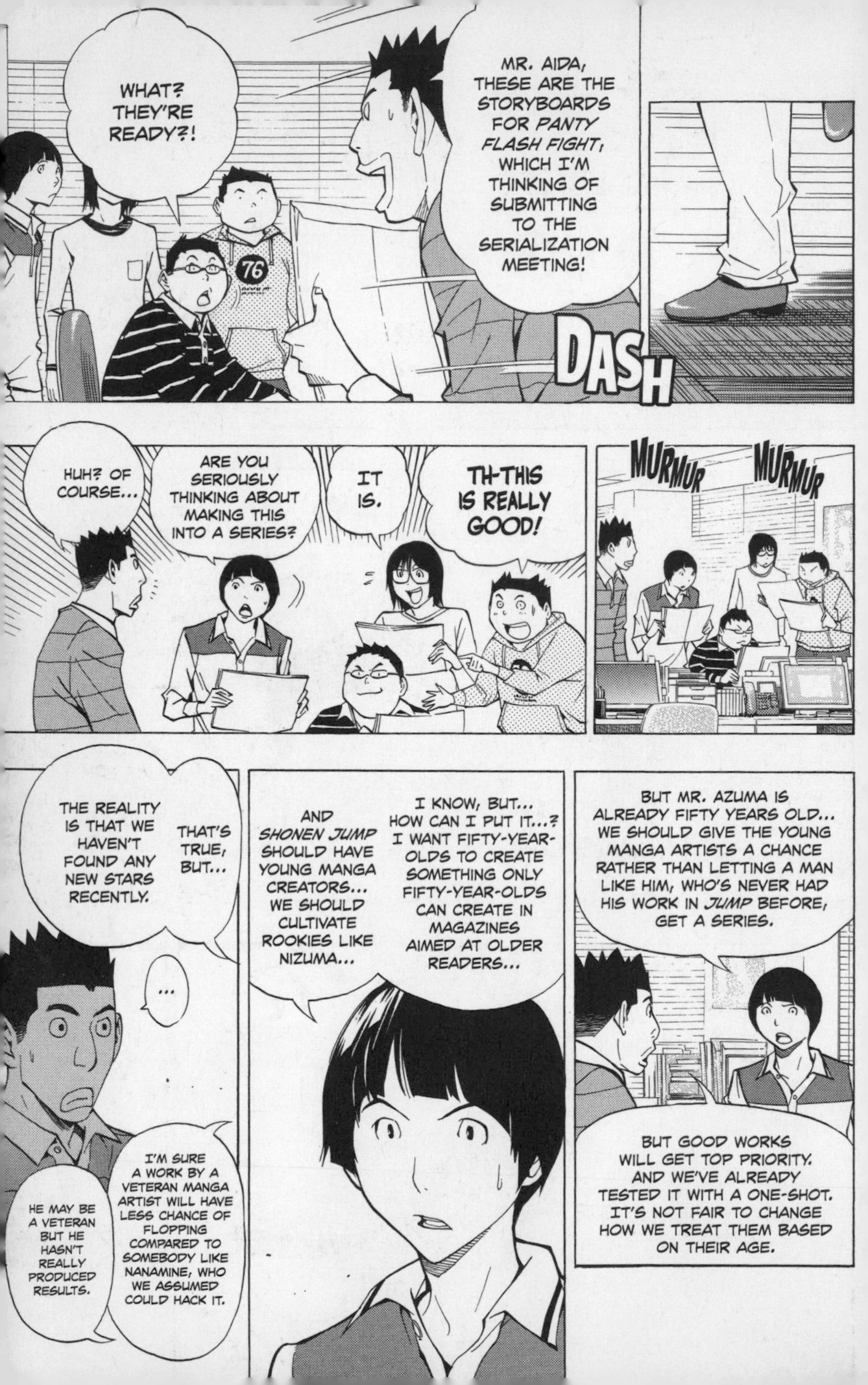
DASH
MR. AIDA, THESE ARE THE STORYBOARDS FOR *PANTY FLASH FIGHT*, WHICH I'M THINKING OF SUBMITTING TO THE SERIALIZATION MEETING!
WHAT? THEY'RE READY?!
MURMUR MURMUR
TH-THIS IS REALLY GOOD!
IT IS.
ARE YOU SERIOUSLY THINKING ABOUT MAKING THIS INTO A SERIES?
HUH? OF COURSE...
BUT MR. AZUMA IS ALREADY FIFTY YEARS OLD... WE SHOULD GIVE THE YOUNG MANGA ARTISTS A CHANCE RATHER THAN LETTING A MAN LIKE HIM, WHO'S NEVER HAD HIS WORK IN *JUMP* BEFORE, GET A SERIES.
BUT GOOD WORKS WILL GET TOP PRIORITY. AND WE'VE ALREADY TESTED IT WITH A ONE-SHOT. IT'S NOT FAIR TO CHANGE HOW WE TREAT THEM BASED ON THEIR AGE.
I KNOW, BUT... HOW CAN I PUT IT...? I WANT FIFTY-YEAR-OLDS TO CREATE SOMETHING ONLY FIFTY-YEAR-OLDS CAN CREATE IN MAGAZINES AIMED AT OLDER READERS...
AND *SHONEN JUMP* SHOULD HAVE YOUNG MANGA CREATORS... WE SHOULD CULTIVATE ROOKIES LIKE NIZUMA...
THAT'S TRUE, BUT...
THE REALITY IS THAT WE HAVEN'T FOUND ANY NEW STARS RECENTLY.
...
I'M SURE A WORK BY A VETERAN MANGA ARTIST WILL HAVE LESS CHANCE OF FLOPPING COMPARED TO SOMEBODY LIKE NANAMINE, WHO WE ASSUMED COULD HACK IT.
HE MAY BE A VETERAN BUT HE HASN'T REALLY PRODUCED RESULTS.

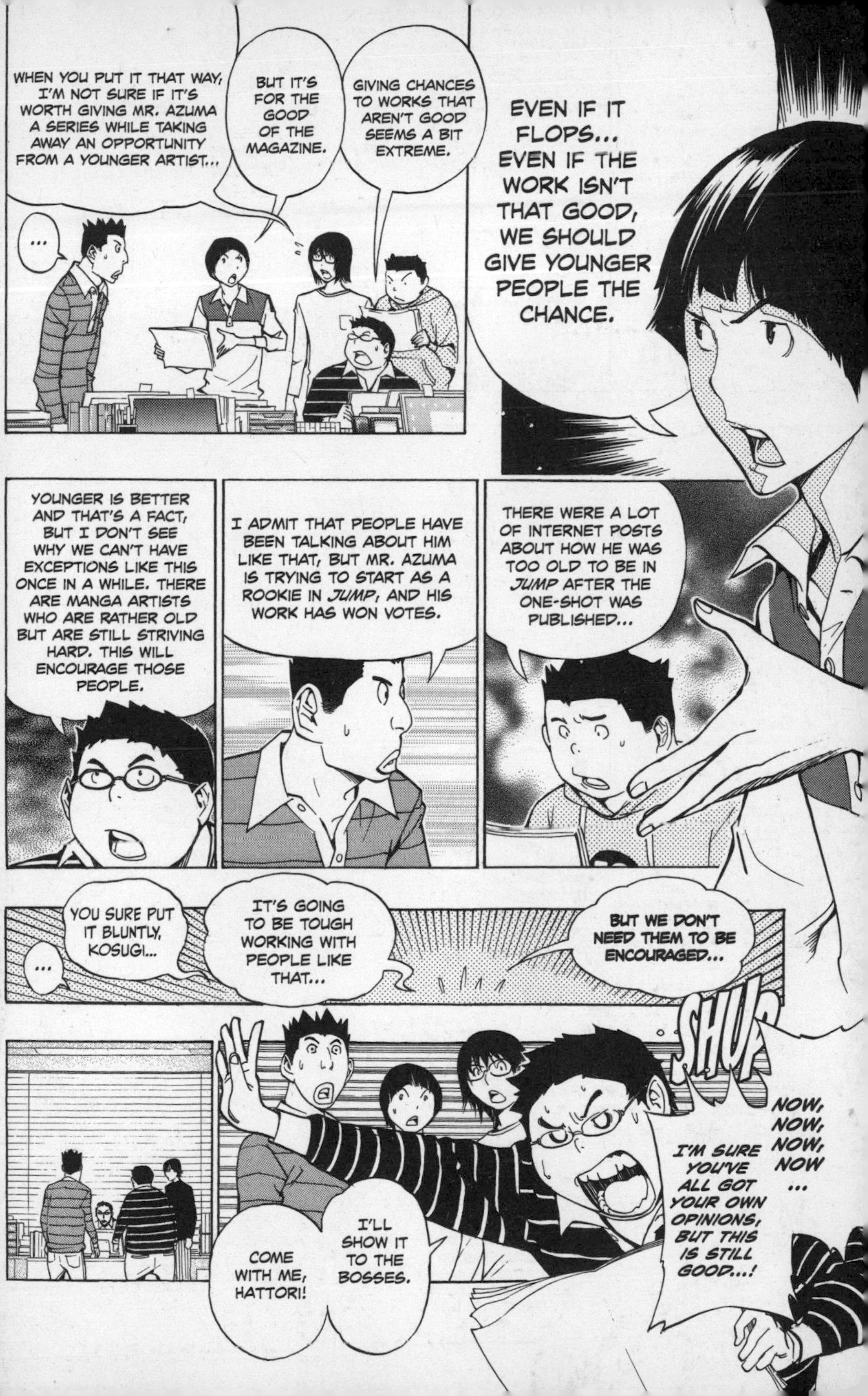
EVEN IF IT FLOPS... EVEN IF THE WORK ISN'T THAT GOOD, WE SHOULD GIVE YOUNGER PEOPLE THE CHANCE.
GIVING CHANCES TO WORKS THAT AREN'T GOOD SEEMS A BIT EXTREME.
BUT IT'S FOR THE GOOD OF THE MAGAZINE.
WHEN YOU PUT IT THAT WAY, I'M NOT SURE IF IT'S WORTH GIVING MR. AZUMA A SERIES WHILE TAKING AWAY AN OPPORTUNITY FROM A YOUNGER ARTIST...
...
THERE WERE A LOT OF INTERNET POSTS ABOUT HOW HE WAS TOO OLD TO BE IN *JUMP* AFTER THE ONE-SHOT WAS PUBLISHED...
I ADMIT THAT PEOPLE HAVE BEEN TALKING ABOUT HIM LIKE THAT, BUT MR. AZUMA IS TRYING TO START AS A ROOKIE IN *JUMP*, AND HIS WORK HAS WON VOTES.
YOUNGER IS BETTER AND THAT'S A FACT, BUT I DON'T SEE WHY WE CAN'T HAVE EXCEPTIONS LIKE THIS ONCE IN A WHILE. THERE ARE MANGA ARTISTS WHO ARE RATHER OLD BUT ARE STILL STRIVING HARD. THIS WILL ENCOURAGE THOSE PEOPLE.
BUT WE DON'T NEED THEM TO BE ENCOURAGED...
IT'S GOING TO BE TOUGH WORKING WITH PEOPLE LIKE THAT...
YOU SURE PUT IT BLUNTLY, KOSUGI...
...
SHUP
NOW, NOW, NOW, NOW...
I'M SURE YOU'VE ALL GOT YOUR OWN OPINIONS, BUT THIS IS STILL GOOD...!
I'LL SHOW IT TO THE BOSSES.
COME WITH ME, HATTORI!

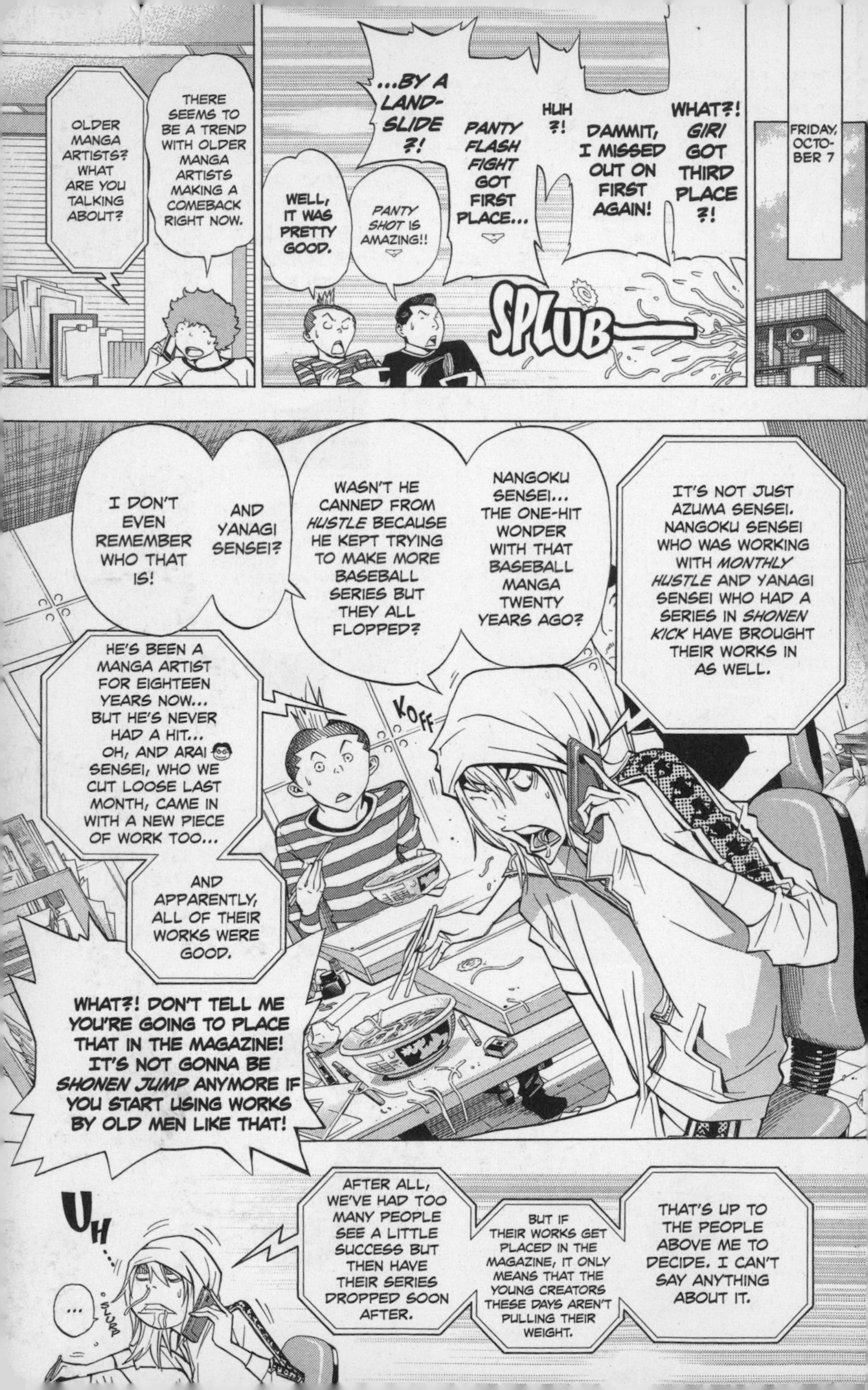
FRIDAY, OCTOBER 7
WHAT?! GIRI GOT THIRD PLACE?!
DAMMIT, I MISSED OUT ON FIRST AGAIN!
HUH?!
PANTY FLASH FIGHT GOT FIRST PLACE...
...BY A LANDSLIDE?!
PANTY SHOT IS AMAZING!!
WELL, IT WAS PRETTY GOOD.
SPLUB
THERE SEEMS TO BE A TREND WITH OLDER MANGA ARTISTS MAKING A COMEBACK RIGHT NOW.
OLDER MANGA ARTISTS? WHAT ARE YOU TALKING ABOUT?
IT'S NOT JUST AZUMA SENSEI. NANGOKU SENSEI WHO WAS WORKING WITH MONTHLY HUSTLE AND YANAGI SENSEI WHO HAD A SERIES IN SHONEN KICK HAVE BROUGHT THEIR WORKS IN AS WELL.
NANGOKU SENSEI... THE ONE-HIT WONDER WITH THAT BASEBALL MANGA TWENTY YEARS AGO?
WASN'T HE CANNED FROM HUSTLE BECAUSE HE KEPT TRYING TO MAKE MORE BASEBALL SERIES BUT THEY ALL FLOPPED?
AND YANAGI SENSEI?
I DON'T EVEN REMEMBER WHO THAT IS!
KOFF
HE'S BEEN A MANGA ARTIST FOR EIGHTEEN YEARS NOW... BUT HE'S NEVER HAD A HIT... OH, AND ARAI SENSEI, WHO WE CUT LOOSE LAST MONTH, CAME IN WITH A NEW PIECE OF WORK TOO...
AND APPARENTLY, ALL OF THEIR WORKS WERE GOOD.
WHAT?! DON'T TELL ME YOU'RE GOING TO PLACE THAT IN THE MAGAZINE! IT'S NOT GONNA BE SHONEN JUMP ANYMORE IF YOU START USING WORKS BY OLD MEN LIKE THAT!
THAT'S UP TO THE PEOPLE ABOVE ME TO DECIDE. I CAN'T SAY ANYTHING ABOUT IT.
BUT IF THEIR WORKS GET PLACED IN THE MAGAZINE, IT ONLY MEANS THAT THE YOUNG CREATORS THESE DAYS AREN'T PULLING THEIR WEIGHT.
AFTER ALL, WE'VE HAD TOO MANY PEOPLE SEE A LITTLE SUCCESS BUT THEN HAVE THEIR SERIES DROPPED SOON AFTER.
UH...
...
SLURP

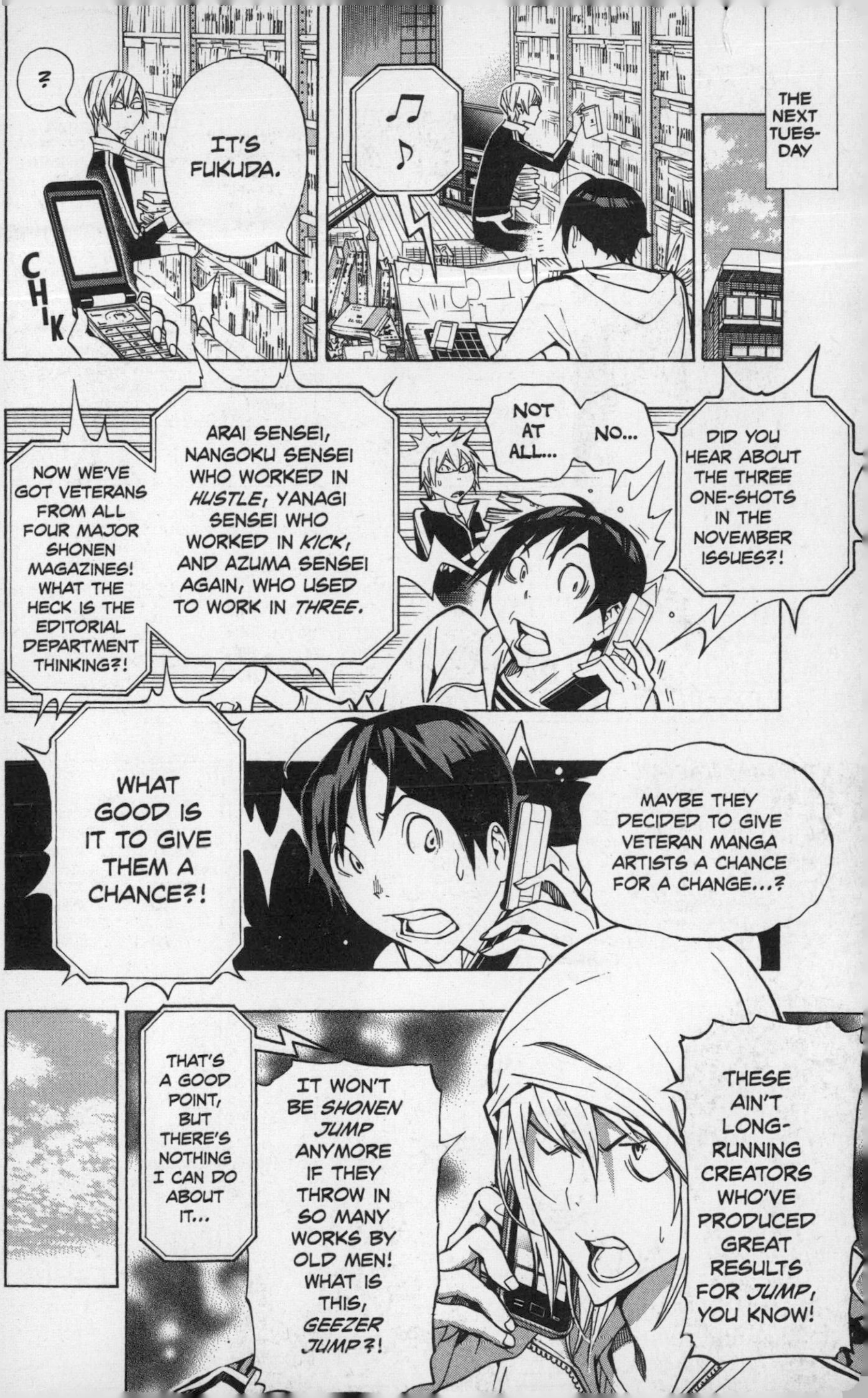
THE NEXT TUES-DAY
♫ ♪
IT'S FUKUDA.
?
CHIK
DID YOU HEAR ABOUT THE THREE ONE-SHOTS IN THE NOVEMBER ISSUES?!
NO...
NOT AT ALL...
ARAI SENSEI, NANGOKU SENSEI WHO WORKED IN *HUSTLE*, YANAGI SENSEI WHO WORKED IN *KICK*, AND AZUMA SENSEI AGAIN, WHO USED TO WORK IN *THREE*.
NOW WE'VE GOT VETERANS FROM ALL FOUR MAJOR SHONEN MAGAZINES! WHAT THE HECK IS THE EDITORIAL DEPARTMENT THINKING?!
MAYBE THEY DECIDED TO GIVE VETERAN MANGA ARTISTS A CHANCE FOR A CHANGE...?
WHAT GOOD IS IT TO GIVE THEM A CHANCE?!
THESE AIN'T LONG-RUNNING CREATORS WHO'VE PRODUCED GREAT RESULTS FOR *JUMP*, YOU KNOW!
IT WON'T BE *SHONEN JUMP* ANYMORE IF THEY THROW IN SO MANY WORKS BY OLD MEN! WHAT IS THIS, *GEEZER JUMP*?!
THAT'S A GOOD POINT, BUT THERE'S NOTHING I CAN DO ABOUT IT...

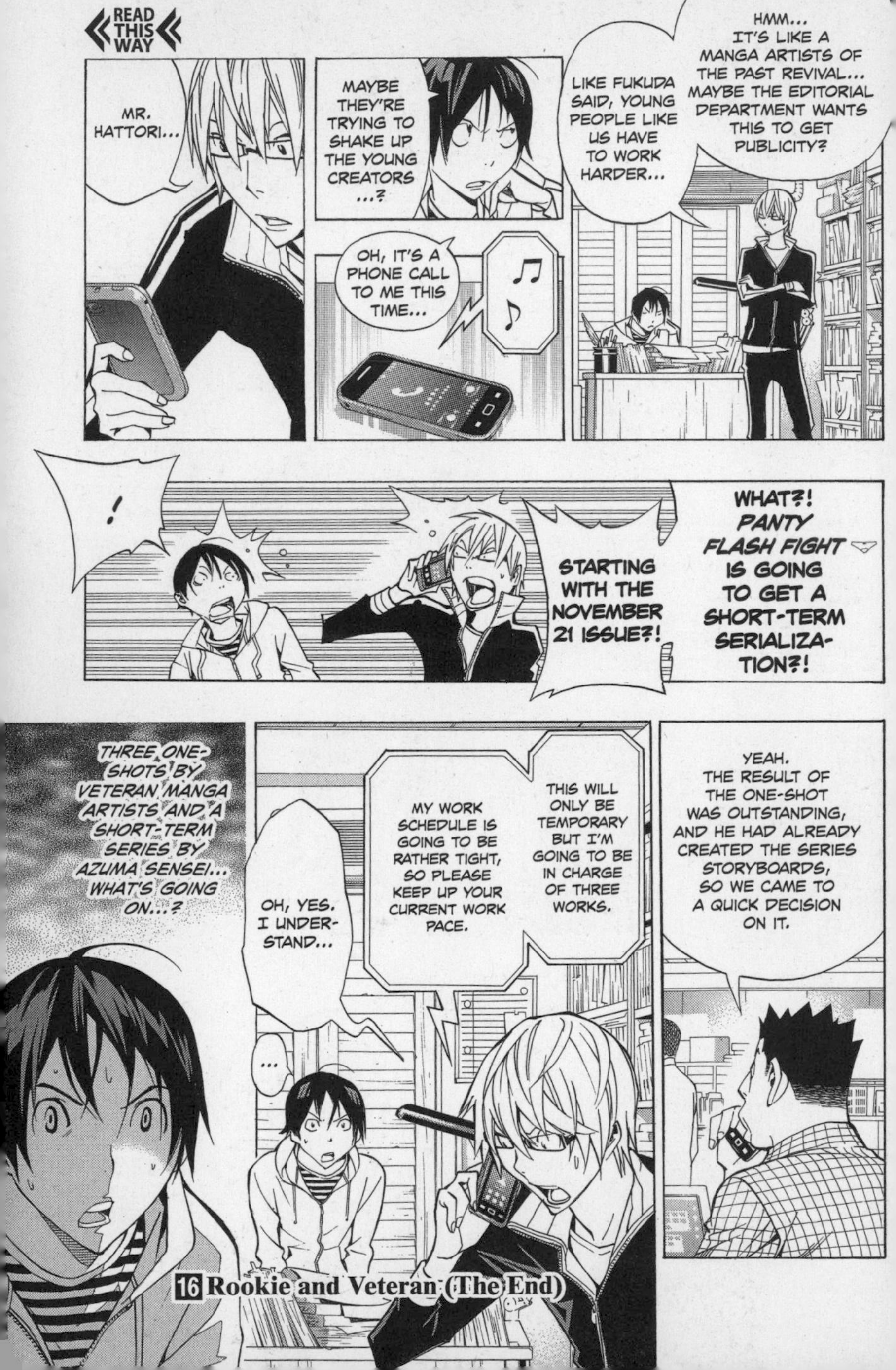
READ THIS WAY
HMM... IT'S LIKE A MANGA ARTISTS OF THE PAST REVIVAL... MAYBE THE EDITORIAL DEPARTMENT WANTS THIS TO GET PUBLICITY?
LIKE FUKUDA SAID, YOUNG PEOPLE LIKE US HAVE TO WORK HARDER...
MAYBE THEY'RE TRYING TO SHAKE UP THE YOUNG CREATORS ...?
♫ ♪
OH, IT'S A PHONE CALL TO ME THIS TIME...
MR. HATTORI...
WHAT?! PANTY FLASH FIGHT IS GOING TO GET A SHORT-TERM SERIALIZATION?!
STARTING WITH THE NOVEMBER 21 ISSUE?!
!
YEAH. THE RESULT OF THE ONE-SHOT WAS OUTSTANDING, AND HE HAD ALREADY CREATED THE SERIES STORYBOARDS, SO WE CAME TO A QUICK DECISION ON IT.
THIS WILL ONLY BE TEMPORARY BUT I'M GOING TO BE IN CHARGE OF THREE WORKS.
MY WORK SCHEDULE IS GOING TO BE RATHER TIGHT, SO PLEASE KEEP UP YOUR CURRENT WORK PACE.
OH, YES. I UNDERSTAND...
...
THREE ONE-SHOTS BY VETERAN MANGA ARTISTS AND A SHORT-TERM SERIES BY AZUMA SENSEI... WHAT'S GOING ON...?
16 Rookie and Veteran (The End)

OHBA'S STORYBOARD

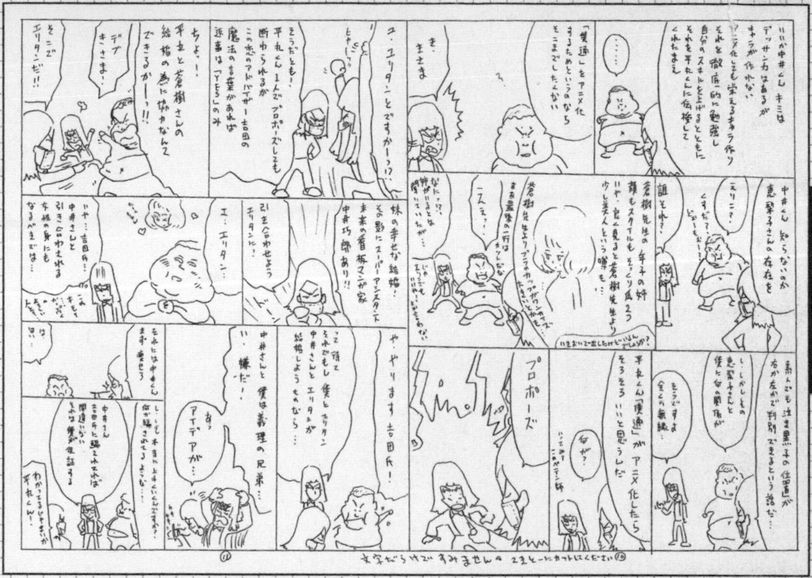

いいか中井くん キミは デッサン力はあるが キャラが作れない アニメ化とも栄えるキャラ作り それを徹底的に勉強し 自分のスキルを上げるとともに それを平丸くんに伝授してくれたまえ
……
「幸運」をアニメ化するためというのなら そこまでしたくない
中井くん 知らないのか 恵梨子さんの存在を
えりこ？
蒼樹先生の年子の妹 顔もスタイルもそっくり瓜ふたつ いや…良く見ると蒼樹先生より少し美人という噂も…
ええっ…
あくまでも泣き黒子の位置が右か左かで判別できるという話だ
し…しかしその恵梨子さんと僕たちの関係が
全くの無縁…
平丸くん「幸運」がアニメ化したら そろそろいいと思うんだ
何が？
プロポーズ
ユ…ユリタンとですか――っ!!?
そうだとも! 平丸くん1人でプロポーズしても断わられる この恋のアドバイザー吉田の魔法の言葉があれば 返事は「YES」のみ
ちょ…! 平丸と蒼樹さんの結婚の為に協力なんてできるか――っ!!
デブ きさま…
そこでエリタンだ!!
妹の幸せな結婚! その影にスーパーアシスタント 未来の看板マンガ家 中井巧朗あり!!
エ…エリタン…
引き合わせよう エリタンに!
いや… 中井さんと引き合わされる女性の身にもなるべきでは…
や…やります 吉田氏!
い…嫌だ! 中井さんと僕は義理の兄弟…
あっ アイデアが…
それには中井くん まず痩せろ

OBATA'S STORYBOARD

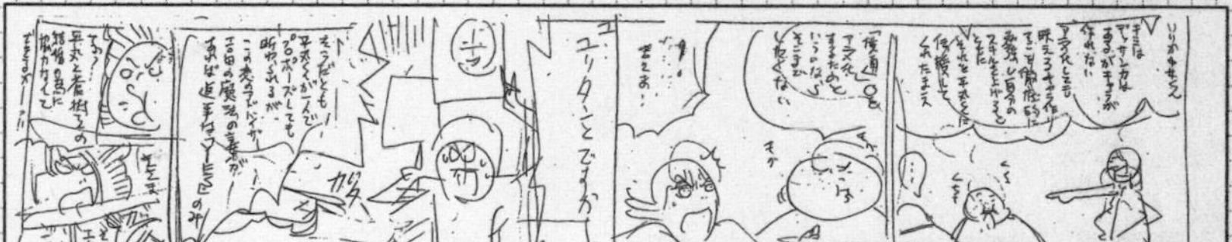

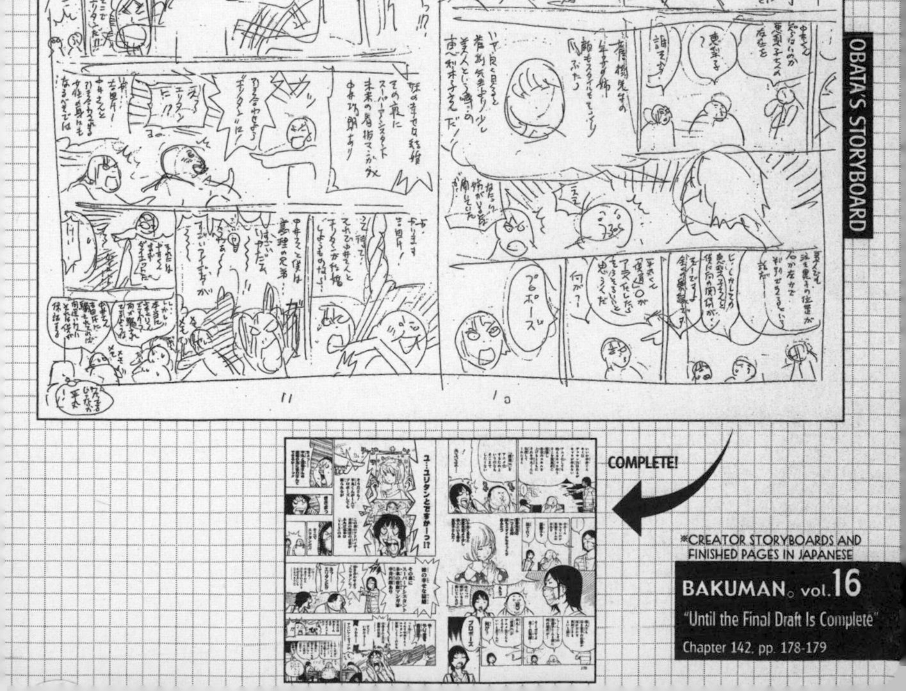

COMPLETE!

※CREATOR STORYBOARDS AND FINISHED PAGES IN JAPANESE

BAKUMAN。 vol.16

"Until the Final Draft Is Complete"

Chapter 142, pp. 178-179

BAKUMAN。

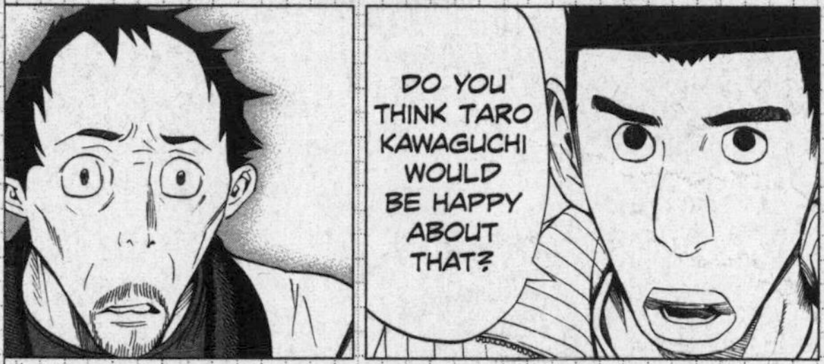
DO YOU THINK TARO KAWAGUCHI WOULD BE HAPPY ABOUT THAT?

In the NEXT VOLUME

The surge of veteran manga creators continues as their works prove to be quite popular among the readers of *Weekly Shonen Jump*. But what is behind this sudden development, and how will it affect Moritaka and Akito?

Available December 2012!

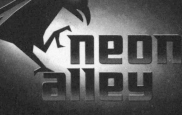

This is the
LAST PAGE.

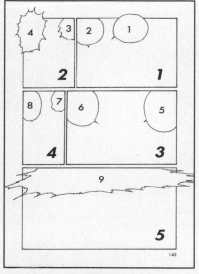

142

← Follow the action this way.

BAKUMAN₀ has been printed in the original Japanese format in order to preserve the orientation of the original artwork.

Please turn it around and begin reading from right to left. Unlike English, Japanese is read right to left, so Japanese comics are read in reverse order from the way English comics are typically read. Have fun with it!

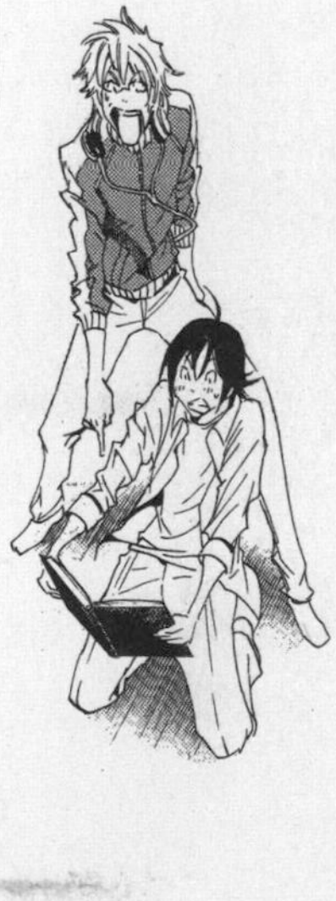